WALLACE STEVENS

WALLACE STEVENS

The Plain Sense of Things

୶

JAMES LONGENBACH

New York   Oxford
OXFORD UNIVERSITY PRESS
1991

Oxford University Press

Oxford   New York   Toronto
Delhi   Bombay   Calcutta   Madras   Karachi
Petaling Jaya   Singapore   Hong Kong   Tokyo
Nairobi   Dar es Salaam   Cape Town
Melbourne   Auckland

and associated companies in
Berlin   Ibadan

Published by Oxford University Press, Inc.,
200 Madison Avenue, New York, New York 10016

Oxford is a registered trademark of Oxford University Press

Library of Congress Cataloging-in-Publication Data
Longenbach, James.
Wallace Stevens : the plain sense of things / James Longenbach.
p. cm.   Includes index.
ISBN 0-19-506863-7; 0-19-507022-4 (pbk.)
1. Stevens, Wallace, 1879–1955—Criticism and interpretation.
2. Stevens, Wallace, 1879–1955—Political and social views.
3. Political poetry, American—History and criticism.
4. War poetry, American—History and criticism.
5. Social problems in literature.   I. Title.
PS3537.T4753Z6764   1991
811'.52—dc20   90-49690

1 3 5 7 9 8 6 4 2
Printed in the United States of America
on acid-free paper

Preface

Asked to provide a self-portrait midway through his career, Wallace Stevens replied: "I should say very briefly that I was born in Pennsylvania in 1879, studied at Harvard, am a lawyer, practiced in New York until 1916 and then came to Hartford, where I am in the insurance business." Poetry was important to Stevens, despite his reticence, but so were law and insurance. Yet when readers of Stevens take those interests into account, it is usually to wonder at his "double" life: for several critical generations, the Stevens who matters has existed in a world of words. But Stevens lived no double life. His was what he liked to call an "ordinary" life, one in which the exigencies of politics, economics, poetry, and everyday distractions coexisted—sometimes peacefully and sometimes not.

Appreciated in the context of American political and intellectual history, Stevens emerges not only as a poet aware of events taking place around him but as a poet whose work was often inspired by them. Stevens did not write poetry like a lawyer or execute surety bonds like a poet; his different activities took necessarily different shapes, and those differences kept a single life whole. Consequently, Stevens rarely asked the poet to do the work the politician might do better, even though he knew poetry could not be isolated from political concerns. (As Kenneth Burke once quipped: though all art is political, "one cannot advocate art as a cure for toothache without disclosing the superiority of dentistry.") Stevens's caution should not be confused with indifference: as both poet and lawyer, he thought long and hard about the strengths and (equally important) the limitations of literature as a historical product and force.

Stories about Stevens's politics usually describe a more or less indifferent poet who was jostled into unwelcome awareness by the social upheavals of the 1930s. In "The Irrational Element in Poetry" Stevens himself dated his fall into a political world much earlier—during the First World War—but Stevens's political awareness actually began in the final years of the nineteenth century. Although my reading of Stevens's career emphasizes his poetry's relation to the three most devastating historical events of his lifetime (the Great Depression and the two world wars), I also pay attention to the two periods in which Stevens wrote no poetry at all. Between 1900 (when he left Harvard) and 1908 (when he finally found gainful employment) Stevens was harried by the most basic economic considerations; as a reporter for the *New York Tribune,* he covered the McKinley–Bryan presidential race, confronting the nation's rise as an imperialist power. Stevens cast his vote for the Populist Bryan and, in many ways, retained for the rest of his life the uneasy combination of forward- and backward-looking ideas that characterized American Populism. During these early years, Stevens did not write poetry. But he was "silent" only if we imagine that poetry was the only thing Stevens worried about. An understanding of his poetic silence is essential to an understanding of his poetry.

In 1914 Stevens began the mature phase of his poetic career as a war poet. The result of his obsession with the First World War was not only explicit war poems like "Phases" and "Lettres d'un Soldat"; "Sunday Morning" and "The Comedian as the Letter C" were also the products of a wartime consciousness, with its attendant fantasies of death and apocalypse and its disruptions of conventional ideas of gender. After publishing *Harmonium* in 1923, Stevens again wrote no poetry for almost a decade. During these years he solidified his career as a surety lawyer. This effort, along with Stevens's essays on insurance, was in no fully meaningful way poetic—just as his poetry is in no fully meaningful way political—but it was nevertheless necessary to his poetic achievement. After this second silence, Stevens's poetry reemerged in dialogue with the economic and ideological struggles of the 1930s. These struggles were not new to Stevens the poet; Stevens the lawyer knew them well. Unlike many other American intellectuals and poets, consequently, Stevens did not retreat from political concerns when the ideals of this decade began to seem tarnished; his refusal of utopian seductions saved him from apocalyptic despair. And the great long poems of the early 1940s ("Notes toward a Supreme Fiction" and "Esthétique du Mal") were born of Stevens's continuing engagement with the realities of the Second World War.

In his old age, after he had lived through a depression and two world wars, Stevens did begin to retreat from such concerns: the Stevens of the late 1940s and early 1950s is the poet most compatible with the figure constructed by the critical tradition. During these final years of his career, Stevens offered several tempting aphorisms ("It is a world of words to the end of it"), implying that his entire corpus could be read as a self-enclosed and universal poem. The strategy was consistent with a general cold war retreat from earlier social concerns; Stevens's final drift away from a political world was politically encased. To impose those values on his work at large is to substitute the aging Stevens of the cold war for the young Stevens of the Gilded Age, the middle-aged Stevens of the First World War, and the older Stevens of the Depression and Second World War. These different Stevenses must be distinguished; his career was not static and neither was the history of which the career was a part. "The Idea of Order at Key West" articulated aesthetic concerns to which Stevens would return again and again; but the world set right in that poem included a Cuban revolution and the threat of U.S. intervention.

To show that there is an easily identifiable historical content to the poetry (a public content that has been overlooked), I stress Stevens's actual encounters with events: presidential elections, revolutions, wars, strikes, and taxes. Politics that may take more private or textual forms are also part of the story, but my approach to these matters is designed to reveal them as more than merely textual. One of Stevens's strengths as a poet (a strength for which he is too little known) was his keen awareness of the dangers of aestheticizing experience—his fear of becoming a "Secretary for Porcelain" who may blithely equate "ten thousand deaths / With a single well-tempered apricot." I have tried to remain aware of that danger as well.

In addition to historical events, ideological debates encasing the events are part of this story of Stevens's career: the fate of American liberalism, the rise of communism, the rights of women, the pressures of nationalism—and the endless debate over the relationship of literature to the political actions these debates foster. Other writers' engagement in these controversies play a part as well, and among these other voices Kenneth Burke's becomes especially important: his writing serves as a kind of descant to Stevens's. Burke and Stevens were in many ways like-minded thinkers, and they reacted to many events—and thought about the relationship of literature to those events—in similar ways. Today, Burke's work is important not only for reading Stevens but for understanding his historical moment.

In narrating this contextualizing history of Stevens's career, my ultimate focus remains on the poetry. But I have tried to remain true to the Stevens who felt that poetry was important precisely because it is part of a world that is always more than poetic. Wary as Stevens was of the danger of aestheticizing experience, he was also aware—painfully so—of its inevitability; the danger was consequently a matter of quality and degree. For Stevens at his best, these intricacies became necessities: in the poem from which I borrow my title, the plain sense of things is not easily apprehended or recorded. The condition Stevens alternately spoke of as the ordinary, the humdrum, or the commonplace was an achievement—a middle ground that was not a compromise between extremes. Ideally, it represented a position from which extremes, aesthetic and political, were clearly assessed; at its worst, it teetered on complacency. Yet that danger was often subverted because the plain sense of things is never plain for long. Stevens once lamented that he could not count himself among the "people [who] always know exactly what they think." But he suspected there might be another kind of strength in uncertainty: "The same thing keeps active in my mind and rarely becomes fixed. This is true about politics as it is about poetry."

In writing this book, my thoughts have been alternately strengthened and questioned by many friends. Milton Bates and A. Walton Litz not only read the entire manuscript; their own work made it possible for me to begin thinking about Stevens in the first place. I am also grateful for the help of Ronald Bush, Alan Filreis, Kenneth Gross, Gail McDonald, Richard Poirier, Kaja Silverman, and Jeffrey Woodward. And if all that Joanna Scott had done was read and reread my prose I could better express how much this book owes to her sensibility.

The National Endowment for the Humanities provided the fellowship during which I began my research, and I acknowledge gratefully the cooperation of the libraries at which much of my research into Stevens's unpublished work took place: the Joseph Regenstein Library at the University of Chicago, the Houghton Library at Harvard University, the McKeldrin Library at the University of Maryland, the Library of the University of Massachusetts at Amherst, the Princeton University Library, and—most of all—the Henry E. Huntington Library. I am grateful to Holly Stevens for permission to quote from material in these collections. My research assistants, Stephen Myers and John Palattella, are responsible for many details that slipped past my eyes.

Years ago, the person who first taught me the poetry of Wallace Stevens (and much else besides) asked me a question I could not answer: I offer this book to Hugh Ogden with the hope that in thinking about that question I absorbed some of his own sense of what the value of reading a poet like Stevens might be.

Rochester, N.Y.   J. L.
November 1990

Contents

I

The First Silence

1

Pecksniff and Politics

The appearance of "Sunday Morning" in the November 1915 issue of *Poetry* magazine has always seemed a remarkable feat. Stevens had published only a handful of poems in 1914 (none of them particularly memorable), and before that, he had published no poetry since leaving Harvard in the spring of 1900. His sonnets in the *Harvard Advocate* look a lot like the rest of the verse in the *Harvard Advocate*, and not even the exceptional "Ballade of the Pink Parasol" prepares us for the outburst of the earliest poems of *Harmonium*.

> Where is the maid on the road in her gig,
>   And where is the fire-side cat?
>   Never was sight more fair than that,
> Outshining, outreaching them all,
>   There in the night where lovers sat—
> But where is the pink parasol?

Here is the young poet steeped in Pater and Dowson, the poet who in 1919 would publish "Pecksniffiana," named for Dickens's Mr. Pecksniff, the architect who taught his pupils to construct castles in the air. But over a decade separates Stevens's finest undergraduate achievement from these works of early maturity. And the most important thing Stevens did during those years was to avoid writing poetry.

"Ballade of the Pink Parasol" represents only one aspect of the sensibility that produced "Sunday Morning." Stevens edited the *Advocate* during the spring term of 1900, and a few weeks before the poem appeared he published

3

the brief editorial "Political Interests." Inspired by John Jay Chapman's address "Public Opinion," delivered in the Fogg Museum Lecture Room, Stevens lamented that Harvard students had few opportunities "of becoming readily acquainted with political conditions."

[Chapman] was intent on pleading for the Independent party; but he undoubtedly came as near to a clear exposition of the state of public affairs, as any other single speaker we are likely to hear. There is no reason, however, why we should not get every side of the matter. If this is the case, then, we imagine that just as the Civil Service Reform Club presented Mr. Chapman, so the Democratic Club and the Republican Club should endeavor to present speakers to set forth their especial points of view.

It might not be too much to expect that the three clubs just mentioned should combine to form some sort of Political Union for the free discussion of political principles; for if there is one thing more desirable in our present relation to politics than another, it is that we should be informed openly and candidly just what the various parties stand for and how they are run.

Where in these sentences (about which I shall have more to say later on) are Pater, Dowson, or the old-time wig and the nights when lovers sat? Although the aesthetic side of his achievement has been overemphasized, Stevens began his career torn between an overripe *fin de siècle* desire to transcend things as they are and a rough-hewn urge to tackle the world of politics and economics head on. When he tried to bridge this gap, the quality of Stevens's verse fell below the minimum standard established by "Ballade of the Pink Parasol." His poem "Outside the Hospital" followed the editorial "Political Interests" as if to suggest a way to translate the call for political engagement into poetic terms: "See the blind and the lame at play, / There on the summer lawn." In a later issue of the *Advocate,* Stevens offered the slightly more successful "Street Songs," a cycle of four poems that included the sonnet "The Beggar." Here the porch of a cathedral is not the place to look to the transcendent but to face the world as it is: "The carvings and beauty of the throne / Where she is sitting, she doth meanly use / To win you and appeal."

These poems reveal a desire to record social conditions that could not be contained in an aesthetic nurtured by only Pater and Dowson. If the final decade of the nineteenth century was the quintessential moment of aestheticism, it was also the heyday of naturalism, and Stevens was equally moved by Norris and Crane. But they wrote prose. "Sonnets have their place," wrote Stevens in his journal, ". . . but they can also be found tremendously out of place: in real life where things are quick, unaccountable, responsive." When he directed his naturalistic impulse away from the constrictions of fourteen lines, Stevens achieved better results. He wrote a prose version of the four

"Street Songs" in "Four Characters," the second of which revealed his ambition of following Stephen Crane into a life where literature and politics were naturally compatible. The narrator of the sketch accompanies a reporter to a tenement house to investigate the death of an elderly man. An old woman answers their knock and shows them the body of her dead husband, Bigsby, lying on a broken ironing board.

> "Won't you have some tea?" she asked. "I'm just going to make some. Bigsby hated it."
> We thanked her and started to go.
> "I will light you to the stairs," she said. As she crossed the room the lamp lit up the hovel, and we saw a bed that had not been visible before. It was made of a tattered mattress with straw sticking out at the edges. It was perfectly bare, without pillow or sheet.

By the time this sketch appeared in the *Advocate*, Stevens had moved to the Lower East Side of Manhattan and was working as a reporter for the *New York Tribune*. Neither "Ballade of the Pink Parasol" nor "Outside the Hospital" would have gotten him that job, but if he had submitted "Four Characters" an editor might have been impressed by the clear expository style and the understated drama of the final tableau; it would take Hemingway years of newspaper work to cultivate that kind of flatness. Stevens's sketch is ordered precisely as it is experienced; not until the light reveals the bed do we see it ourselves, and the details (tattered straw, bare mattress, no pillow) are carefully chosen to register everything the woman does not say. There is little sense of agency in the prose; things happen, and they are observed.

That Stevens could not get this kind of social relevance into his poetry was one of the reasons he wrote almost none of it between 1900 and 1908, when he compiled his "Book of Verses" for Elsie Kachel Moll's birthday. Many years later Stevens would recall that although he experienced another period of silence in the 1920s, he had "always been intensely interested in poetry"; there was no "turning point" in his career. Instead of such a turning point, Stevens's career is marked by a tension between conflicting desires for engagement and transcendence, a tension he was not alone in feeling. Arnold offered his weary touchstone for the post-Romantic poet's dilemma in "Stanzas in Memory of the Author of 'Obermann'": "two desires toss about / The poet's feverish blood. / One drives him to the world without, / And one to solitude." And Yeats decided early on that "the mind of man has two kinds of shepherds: the poets who rouse and trouble, the poets who hush and console." Kipling and Wilde, Zola and Mallarmé, Dreiser and James: in the early years of the twentieth century these seemed the only options available to the poet. For the Pound of *Hugh Selwyn Mauberley*, the choices were Arnold Bennett (cast as "Mr. Nixon") and Ford Madox Ford ("the stylist"). The first looked only to the world without, the second only to the world within, and neither provided Pound with a means to accomplish the task that evaded him through his poem: his desire to document the effect of the Great War on twentieth-century literature and culture.

When W. H. Auden tried to renegotiate his relationship to his audience after the 1930s, he was aware that his predicament repeated that of his Romantic forebears: "Instead of the poet regarding himself as an entertainer, he becomes the prophet, 'the unacknowledged legislator of the world,' or the Dandy who sits in the café." Retreating to the world within was one option for the post-Romantic poet; equally problematic was the urge to recast the imperatives of the public world in the terms of the private. To Auden, Shelley's defense of poetry offered one precedent for the latter stance, and a similar belief in the public function of private acts allowed Whitman to trumpet a less measured credo in *Democratic Vistas*: he suggested that "two or three really original American poets" could accomplish more for his country "than all its Constitutions, legislative and judicial ties, and all its hitherto political, warlike, or materialistic experiences." Rather than breaking down the distinction between public and private worlds, this faith in the ability of private acts to perform public work ultimately reinforces the opposition; feeling marginalized in the world without, poets on the defensive marginalize the politician in the world within. In this sense, the political imperatives of the *Cantos* are the logical extension of Pound's early aestheticism. "This is [Pound's] most tenacious inheritance from the 1890's," admits Hugh Kenner, "for it entails one's life being co-extensive with one's work of art."

The terms of this opposition are themselves historically determined, and, though any division between public and private is in some sense illusory, the illusion has been powerful. Michel Foucault suggests that the great divide took place around the Enlightenment. Before that point in Western culture, there was a "reciprocal kinship between knowledge and language. The nineteenth century was to dissolve that link, and to leave behind it, in confrontation, a knowledge closed in upon itself and a pure language that had become, in nature and function, enigmatic—something that has been called since that time, *Literature*." By the nineteenth century, that is, enough evidence had accumulated to convince most people that the Garden of Eden and the Trojan Horse had never existed. Books that once had been read as reliable records of our origins needed to be redefined as something called "literature," and literature needed to be understood as something essential to our existence, even though we no longer believed in it. Literature's new status as a thing apart was emphasized as a positive value; paradoxically, its cultural importance began to depend on the strength of its disdain for culture (and the acknowledged legislators). And if language and the dailiness of things no longer marched hand in hand, then the poet needed to live in exile from the processes of history. Coming at the end of the nineteenth century, the words of Pater or Mallarmé appeared to leave scant space for politics. As Mallarmé himself put it, words are divided "into two different categories: first for vulgar or immediate, second for essential purposes." Or as Mikhail Bakhtin put it, lamenting such conditions, poetry presents in contrast to the novel "a unitary and singular Ptolemaic world outside of which nothing else exists and nothing else is needed." Instead of diagnosing a problem with poetry, that sentence rehearses the same oppositions that mark the work of Arnold or Pound.

The central works of post-Romantic literature, whether poetry or prose— "In Memoriam," *Ulysses*, "Notes toward a Supreme Fiction"—achieve their power not by avoiding the confrontation of public and private, retreating to one extreme or the other, but by dramatizing their tension and complicating their opposition. Joyce begins this task with the first two words of *Ulysses*, and the "plump" aspect of his art is as gritty and engaged as Zola's, while the "stately" is as refined and esoteric as Mallarmé's. The best readers of Joyce have realized that his book cannot be well read by focusing exclusively on either its cast of characters or the linguistic play that thwarts the text's construction of those characters at every turn. The fact that in manuscript Joyce thought of *Ulysses* having two parts (the break coming between "Wandering Rocks" and "Sirens") is especially revealing. Although he worked to wed the two halves in revision, *Ulysses* remains lodged between the exaggeratedly precise documentation of "Wandering Rocks" ("Denis Breen with his tomes, weary of having waited an hour in John Henry Menton's office, led his wife over O'Connell bridge, bound for the office of Messrs Collis and Ward") and the equally extravagant verbal music of "Sirens" ("Bronze by gold heard the hoofirons, steelyringing. Imperthnthn thnthn"). *Ulysses* also reveals that this opposition of the stately and the plump is not as simple as it might appear. "Wandering Rocks," one of the most plainly documentary episodes, is also one of the most deceptive; so objective is the presentation that there are only the barest clues (to pick one example from many) that "Mr Bloom's dental windows" refers to a Dublin dentist who happens to share the name of Joyce's protagonist. Joyce makes us wonder if his realism might not be the product of a subtler verbal music, his verbal music the only certainty in a world of solid objects that refuse to declare themselves.

If *Ulysses* and "Notes toward a Supreme Fiction" have been read more often as ingenious verbal constructions than as books that have something to say about a real world, it is because their readers have been more deeply mired in a division of public and private than the books themselves. To suggest what is lost in this way of reading, I want to juxtapose the efforts of two early critics of modernism and its politics: Edmund Wilson and Kenneth Burke. Like Yeats or Pound, Wilson believed that there were "only two alternative courses to follow" in the post-Romantic world. He explained in the conclusion to *Axel's Castle* (1931) that the modern poet could either follow Villiers de l'Isle-Adam's Axel into the entirely self-enclosed world of poetry, or follow Rimbaud on a journey through a real world that left no place for poetry at all. This sort of unshakably dualistic thinking is what leads Wilson to wonder (in the phrase he used for the opening essay of *The Triple Thinkers*) if verse is a dying technique; he leaves no room for a poet like Stevens, who often wrote a verse of high imagination but who was able to do so by understanding his place in a world of politics and economics. "Poetry is the subject of the poem" is not a dictum Stevens took for granted; settled in the world of neither Axel nor Rimbaud, it represents a hard-won understanding of both the power and (equally important) the weakness of poetry.

Wilson did come to perceive the reductiveness of his categories more fully than some of his colleagues. In "The Historical Interpretation of Literature" (1940) he surveyed the work of Marx, Engels, and Trotsky, concluding that the "insistence that the man of letters should play a political role, the disparagement of works of art in comparison with political action, were thus originally no part of Marxism." This statement has an autobiographical resonance, for that was precisely what Wilson did in *Axel's Castle*. There he could praise the Soviet Union as "a country where a central social-political realism has been able to use and inspire the artist," but a decade's experience made him skeptical. Stalin began promoting the offical doctrine of "socialist realism" in 1934, and by the end of the 1930s, his reprimands of Soviet artists had revealed to Wilson the dangers of his own distinctions between the political and the aesthetic.

When the Moscow Trials ensued in 1936, Wilson joined the writers associated with the *Partisan Review* in a more organized effort to forge a Marxist criticism independent of the party line. The *Partisan Review* had suspended publication in the turmoil surrounding the trials, and when it reappeared in December 1937, Wilson's essay "The Politics of Flaubert" revealed that the novelist who had "figured for decades as the great glorifier and practitioner of literary art at the expense of human affairs" was "primarily a social critic." Marx had come to Axel's castle. Although manifestly an analysis of Flaubert, Wilson's essay was really an allegory for the plight of the anti-Stalinist left. "We may sympathize with him today," said Wilson, because Flaubert understood most clearly that professing the correct political opinions will not necessarily save anyone: in *L'Education sentimentale* he "brought to attention a danger of which Marx was not aware. We have had the opportunity to see how even a socialism which has come to power as the result of a proletarian revolution can breed a political police of almost unprecedented ruthlessness. . . . Flaubert, who believed that the artist should rid himself of social convictions, has gauged the tendencies of a political doctrine as the greatest of doctrinaires could not." The swipe at Marx is fueled by Wilson's desire to purge his former self, and his fervor led him to equate Marxism at large with the failed dreams of the 1930s. The *Partisan Review* editors saw a kind of manifesto in "The Politics of Flaubert," and, coming at the end of the decade, the essay had many spiritual companion pieces. Philip Rahv's "Twilight of the Thirties" and James Farrell's "End of a Literary Decade" told similar tales of renunciation and recuperation.

There was another American writer who would not be driven to choose between Marx and Flaubert when the 1930s came to a close. "Whenever you find a doctrine of 'nonpolitical' esthetics affirmed with fervor," said Kenneth Burke, "look for its politics." The whole point of Burke's *Counter-Statement* (published in the same year as *Axel's Castle*) is that the dualism on which Wilson depends is unstable: "Several doctrines have come into prominence which seemed to make art questionable—and this essay aims in turn to make these doctrines questionable." For Burke, there is no such thing as a statement that is not political—though he is always careful to point out that although art is political, it is not necessarily the same thing as political action.

Counter-Statement begins with a discussion of the aestheticism of Flaubert, Pater, and de Gourmont, building to a chapter titled "The Status of Art" in which Burke shows not only that this aestheticism was a response to historical events but that it, in turn, shaped history: "No categorical distinction can possibly be made between 'effective' and 'ineffective' art. The most fanciful, 'unreal' romance may stimulate by implication the same attitudes towards our environment as a piece of withering satire attempts explicitly." Finally, Burke says that he advocates nothing "but a return to inconclusiveness"; a so-called aestheticist work of art could discourage authoritarian judgments because it distrusts the systematized and the dogmatic: "An art may be of value purely through preventing a society from becoming too assertively, too hopelessly, itself." Stevens made the same point when he stressed that poetry "represents the mind in the act of defending us against itself." And Burke would see the remark I quoted in the preface as a recipe for political health rather than a justification of aesthetic obscurity: "Some people always know exactly what they think," remarked Stevens late in his career. "I am afraid that I am not one of those people. The same thing keeps active in my mind and rarely becomes fixed. This is true about politics as it is about poetry."

Many years after he completed *Counter-Statement*, Burke recalled that in 1931 he had begun a second book that took *Axel's Castle* as its point of departure. This book never appeared, but it seems to me that much of its argument must have gone into "War, Response, and Contradiction" (1933). This essay—in which Wilson is actually mentioned only once—begins with a discussion of Malcolm Cowley's and Archibald MacLeish's debate over *The First World War*, a volume of essays that both commented on the past war and (by implication of its title) looked ahead to the war to come. Burke uses the terms of this debate only to make a more important argument about the relationship of art and politics: "Does antimilitarism produce antimilitarism, corruption corruption, quietude quietude, acceptance acceptance, individualism individualism, etc.?" Antimilitarism has been valued enough to fight for. And just as socialists may plead for unemployment insurance, which, if adequately employed, would hold off the revolution, so may the poet's retreat to Axel's castle be a revolutionary act: "Edmund Wilson has treated [such writers] somewhat unfairly, as they did not content themselves with a merely negative attitude towards the contemporary state of affairs, but went aggressively to work depicting alternative existences, other and preferable worlds."

Burke wants to show that the enemy of reform is not the retreating artist but a society which sanctions the dualism of engagement and retreat in the first place. Following Marx, Burke explains that the rise of capitalism has created a fissure between artistic experience and experience at large, resulting in two conflicting moralities—what Burke calls the "vacational" and the "vocational." The first is the realm of artistic pleasure, usually imagined as a moment, and necessarily confined to weekends. But to make such glimpses of a better world possible, we must triumph in the daily scramble of economic striving. While the "vacational" morality scorns the exigencies of the "vocational" as uncultured or base, the "vocational" sustains the possibility of culture and style. Burke suggests that it is difficult to have a vacation when one is "edged further and further into the ditch": "This contradiction led to the artistic phenomenon generally and inappropriately designated as a 'breach between art and life.'"

Joseph Brodsky has more recently said that the only things poetry and politics have in common are the letters *p* and *o*, but Burke might have said that the only difference between the opposed moralities of the "vacational" and the "vocational" is a vowel. What appears to be a breach between art and life is something far more subtle, because, as Stevens's career demonstrates, artistic vacations do not provide an escape from a world of economic necessity; rather, they are at every point facilitated by that world. Stevens discovered early on that his imaginative freedom was contingent on his economic freedom, no matter how fully his aesthetic tradition scorned the exigencies of politics and economics. To escape that world of necessity (if such a thing were possible) would paradoxically render artistic pleasures unavailable. Nevertheless, as Burke points out, the illusionary opposition of art and life exposes the artist "to the purist attacks of all rationalist criticism (of either the neo-Humanist or the neo-Marxist kind)"—and here Burke might as well be summarizing the argument of *Axel's Castle*—"which would programmatically suppress one or another aspect of this duality for critical *fiat*." Wilson's argument is a hostage to the morality he would like to attack—as much so as Arnold's or Yeats's lamentations of the artist's divided sensibility. By accepting the terms of the division, *Axel's Castle* exemplifies what Burke calls an "acquiescent" rather than a "corrective" response; and Burke could more easily turn to Joyce or Flaubert for a more insightful examination of capitalist contradictions. Even so, Burke does not believe that the "acquiescent" and the "corrective" attitudes are easily distinguished from one another: "When a wild animal grows heavier fur with the approach of winter, is it 'resisting' the demands of the season or 'acquiescing to' them?"

Stevens wore that ambiguous coat, and so did Burke himself. Both writers knew that their words made something happen, but they were simultaneously aware of the difficulty and the danger of defining that process conclusively. Unwilling to adopt Pound's prophetic voice (poetry is "the acknowledged guide and lamp of civilization") or Auden's reactionary diminution of that voice ("poetry makes nothing happen"), they occupied a middle ground that offered neither the consolation of certainty nor the support of like-minded colleagues. Like Stevens, Burke was rejected by American Marxists in the 1930s because they could not see his carefully wrought position between Axel and Rimbaud as anything but counterrevolutionary. (And unlike Stevens, who after his rejection by the *New Masses* found a home in the *Partisan Review*, Burke was not received hospitably in either camp.)

Stevens and Burke did share an important precursor. Sounding something like the Arnold of "Stanzas in Memory of the Author of 'Obermann,'" Emerson wrote in "Fate" that every human being has a "double consciousness," alternating between "his private and his public nature." Unlike Arnold, however, Emerson did not lament this uncertain condition, problematic and even painful though it sometimes was. In the second address on the Fugitive Slave Law, Emerson addressed the problem with particular eloquence: "I do not often speak to public questions;—they are odious and hurtful, and it seems like meddling or leaving your work." That sentence is not a retreat to private concerns but a recognition of the poet's troubled relationship to politics; for Emerson's address does not avoid public questions but confronts them—but with one careful equivocation always in mind: "The one thing not to be forgiven to intellectual persons is, not to know their own task." That remark distinguishes Emerson from the Whitman of *Democratic Vistas*; it marks the subtle difference between *Axel's Castle* and *Counter-Statement*. As Burke wrote the essays compiled in that book, beginning in the early 1920s with admiring essays on Pater and Flaubert and ending the decade with essays that explore the political ramifications of these writers' scorn for political action, he was negotiating his Emersonian heritage. Just as forcefully, Emerson's remark underscores the caution with which Stevens approached events of his time. Although he felt the imperatives of the First World War, the Great Depression, and the Second World War, Stevens's poems about these events took the elusive shapes of "Sunday Morning," "The Man with the Blue Guitar," and "Notes toward a Supreme Fiction."

As a young man, when he read a good deal of Emerson, Stevens noted this passage on the function of the poet in "Society and Solitude": "His products are as needful as those of the baker or the weaver. Society cannot do without cultivated men." That represents only half of Emerson and only half of Stevens, who also noted this passage in "American Civilization": "Can you convince the shoe interest, or the iron interest, or the cotton interest, by reading passages from Milton or Montesquieu?" Stevens's very life-style shows that he was just as concerned with the limitations as with the powers of poetry. He never considered that poetry could perform even the comparatively diminutive task of supporting his family, and when the *Partisan Review* asked his opinion on the far more momentous conflagration looming on the economic and political horizon of 1939, he was quick to concede that despite the uses of poetry, "a war is a military state of affairs, not a literary one." There were times in Emerson's and in Stevens's life (especially in the final years of his career) when that careful diffidence became an excuse for standing apart. But at his best, Stevens forged a middle way that was not a compromise. "Notes toward a Supreme Fiction," a poem as wildly imaginative as Joyce's *Ulysses*, ends by reminding us that the poet cannot replace the soldier or the statesman but stands beside him, each reminding the other of the necessity of his world.

Even that conclusion could not remain stable for Stevens. When John Jay Chapman spoke in the Fogg Museum Lecture Room in the last year of the nineteenth century, provoking Stevens to think about "Political Interests," the poet received one of his first powerfully Emersonian lessons. Both literary critic and political activist, the author of *Emerson and Other Essays* and *Practical Agitation*, Chapman in his very presence promised Stevens that poetry and politics could coexist peacefully inside one mind. But between that lecture and the Second World War, between his Harvard sonnets and "Notes," Stevens would have to renegotiate the relationship of his public and private worlds over and over again. Not that he spent his career jumping up and down in one place; each new historical circumstance demanded a new response. When he read Bertrand Russell's "Weekly Diary" in 1935, Stevens copied most of this sentence into his commonplace book: "A week of political excitements—Hitler's speech, the Abyssinian trouble, the increase in our air force, and so on—raise once more the perpetual question: should the philosopher concern himself with public affairs, or should he retire to a mountaintop and meditate?" At work on one of his more overtly political poems, "Owl's Clover," Stevens knew that Russell could have been speaking of poets. "Owl's Clover" is not an anomaly in Stevens's career, and neither did Stevens begin to feel the tug-of-war between poetry and politics only in the 1930s. The first phase of his education occurred in his first period of silence, from 1900 to 1908. This was also a crucial period for American cultural life, and the two struggles, one by an individual poet and the other by a nation, are inextricably bound.

2

The Literary Profession

"Come, said the world, thy youth is not all play, / Upon these hills vast palaces must rise," begins the octet of one of Stevens's early sonnets. "No cried my heart, this thing I cannot do," replies the sestet: "This is my home, this plain and water clear . . . And if you steal them from me I shall die." When this poem appeared in the New York magazine *East & West* in the spring of 1900, it was Stevens's first piece published outside the enclosed world of Harvard's student periodicals. Instinctively, he tells within the confines of the sonnet the tale of Shelley's "Alastor" or Yeats's "The Wanderings of Oisin": the doomed quest for a world beyond the call of mortality, where the wind murmurs eternally among the reeds. Unlike the protagonists of those greater poems, Stevens does not face the death of the imagination in this sonnet; he predicts it, and the poem remains poised on the fulcrum of the post-Romantic conflict between public and private, just as in 1900 Stevens himself stood poised between his student years at Harvard and a decade of often desperate economic striving.

It would be somewhat too easy, given Stevens's early sonnet and the natural way in which his later aesthetics cohere around it, to discover here the seeds of Stevens's lifelong preoccupation with what he called imagination and reality. Stevens once claimed that his "reality–imagination complex" was "entirely [his] own," and the remark seems stunning when we feel the shades of Emerson, Coleridge, and I. A. Richards pressing down. Yet there is an important sense in which Stevens's claim to originality is plainly true. By the time he codified his imagination–reality complex in the essays of *The Necessary Angel*, his argument had been bolstered by readings in aesthetics; but in his early years, the argument was made out of the stuff of experience. There is more desperation, more urgency, in the duet of the imagination and reality than the contoured melodies of *The Necessary Angel* reveal.

The presence of Emerson is crucial, but like most Americans, Stevens was taught a badly blunted version of Emerson, and he would have to supplement an easy Emersonian idealism with the hard-won skepticism that Emerson himself could rarely escape. In his senior year, Stevens entered his high school's oratory contest with a speech entitled "The Greatest Need of the Age." "There is one triumph of a republic," he said, "one attainment of Catholicism, one grand result of Democracy, which feudalism, which caste, and which monarchy, can never know—the self-made man. We cannot help but admire the man, who with indomitable and irrepressible energy breasting the wave of new conditions, grows to become the concentration of power and wealth." That makes the task sound easy. Like most intelligent adolescents, Stevens could serve up just what his adult auditors wanted without cracking a smile: a paean to self-reliance, complete with a justification of a society in which the teen-age Stevens had much less stake than his rhetoric belies. Opportunity is the greatest need of the age, he said; but a decade later, having seen how little opportunity did for him in the streets of New York, Stevens would not have written these sentences: "It is a woeful crisis to miss your opportunity. The American negroes have turned the policy of freedom into ruin, its charity into cruelty, its justice into iniquity." This speech won the oratorical prize.

After he graduated from high school, Stevens's mother gave him a complete set of Emerson, but, as all of Stevens's biographers have noted, the poet learned his first (and most blunt) version of self-reliance from his father, Garrett Stevens. The lessons probably began when Stevens was a small boy, but, as this letter of November 1898 reveals, Stevens enrolled in a correspondence course when he went off to Harvard.

Our young folks would of course all prefer to be born like English noblemen with Entailed estates, income guaranteed and in choosing a profession they would simply say—"How shall I amuse myself"—but young America understands that the question is—"*Starting with nothing, how shall I sustain myself and perhaps a wife and family— and send my boys to College and live* comfortably in my old age." Young fellows must all come to that question for unless they inherit money, marry money, find money, steal money or somebody presents it to them, they must *earn it* and earning it save it up for the time of need. How best can he earn a sufficiency! What talent does he possess which carefully nurtured will produce something which people want and therefore will pay for. This is the whole problem! and to Know Thyself!

In letter after letter Garrett Stevens preached the ministry of self-reliance to his son, reminding him that at Harvard he was "not out on a pic-nic—but really preparing for the campaign of life—where self sustenance is essential and where everything depends upon yourself." But Garrett Stevens's lessons were complicated by the fact that they were not single-minded. Like the father Henry Adams described in his *Education*, Garrett was asking his son to be simultaneously self-reliant and an image of the father. The elder Stevens began to "paddle his own canoe" at the age of seventeen when he became a schoolteacher. Three years later he took up the legal profession, and later became a successful businessman. Along the way, he published several poems and remained active in local politics; he was associate editor of the Democratic *Spirit of Berks* and was once considered a candidate for the legislature. He began to mold his son's future by naming him for a local politician, Wallace Delamater. Paddle your own canoe, he told his son, but do not consider a route that veers far from my own.

Garrett Stevens's letters hammered at one point with particular insistence: "Do not be contented with a smattering of all things—be strong in something." Stevens's problem was that he could not see where his singular strength lay. "Is literature really a profession?" he asked his journal just a few days after he had arrived in New York to find work as a newspaper reporter, and the question would resonate throughout the next decade of his life. The moment of Stevens's birth, 1879, coincided with the moment when professionalism began to transform American working habits, and by the time Stevens left Harvard the entrepreneurial spirit of his youth had been swallowed by bureaucratic capitalism. When Garrett Stevens decided to take up law in 1870, he simply apprenticed himself to the office of John S. Richards; his career was typical in that his law practice was only one facet of his professional interests. A generation later, when Stevens himself decided to follow his father into law, he had no choice but to attend law school. He also needed professional credentials. Lawyers who wanted to increase the prestige of their profession had created the American Bar Association in 1878. To practice law, Stevens had to pass an examination and earn a diploma. All his father needed to do was hang out a shingle.

The possibility of such self-reliance is predicated on the assumption of an autonomous self, and Stevens's early years witnessed the erosion of that assumption. James Gatz, born the year after Stevens, could write his recipe for self-reliance in the flyleaf of *Hopalong Cassidy* ("Study electricity, etc.; Work; Baseball and sports; Practice elocution, poise and how to attain it; Study needed inventions"), but none of that would save him from a world in which even crime had been professionalized (organized, we call it). In 1901, after a ruinous setback in business, Garrett Stevens suffered a nervous breakdown. This failure, psychological and economic, would haunt the younger Stevens until he died.

Even as a young man Stevens began to see the contradictions of self-reliance that his father (or the judges of his high school's oratorical prize) could not: "The mere prospect of having to support myself on a very slender purse has brought before my mind rather vivid views of the actual facts of existence in the world. There are astonishingly few people who live in anything like comfort; and there are thousands who live on the verge of starvation." So little had an "opportunity" done for Stevens in New York that he no longer underestimated the economic forces that thwarted individual ambition at every turn. In his destitution, Stevens now found comfort by identifying with the lower classes he once had scorned: "starting at the bottom suddenly reveals millions of fellow-men struggling at the same point, of whom one previously had only an extremely vague conception. There was a time when I walked downtown in the morning almost oblivious of the thousands and thousands of people I passed; now I look at them with extraordinary interest as companions in the same fight that I am about to join."

Given these conditions, Stevens's quest for a viable profession was difficult enough, but his problem was compounded by the fact that the literary life resisted professionalization more strongly than any other field. "Is literature really a profession?" In his college journal Stevens could foresee a "practical life of the world" as "a bustling merchant, a money-making lawyer, a soldier, a politician" but not "as a University Professor, a Retired Farmer or Citizen, a Philanthropist, a Preacher, a Poet." The choice was between poetry and politics, the world within and the world without, and Stevens dabbled in both areas with little confidence. At Harvard he had longed to become "like Keats"—"truly absorbed in the beauty and nobility of literature for itself." But that kind of single-mindedness was impossible for both Stevens and the state of literature itself. In "The Man of Letters as a Man of Business" (1893) William Dean Howells pointed out that the literary writer maintained a humiliatingly "low rank among practical people" because "literature is still an infant industry": "I wish I could make all my fellow-artists realize that economically they are the same as mechanics, farmers, day-laborers." Howells offered an ambivalent push for the professionalization of authorship, but not everyone agreed that the incorporation of the arts was a good thing. In 1918 the *Times Literary Supplement* published "Professionalism in Art," an attack on the professional that upheld the rights of the dilettante: "Decadence in art is always caused by professionalism." T. S. Eliot, a young American poet who worked even harder than Stevens to determine whether or not literature could be a profession, responded in the pages of the *Egoist*: "An attitude which might find voice in words like these is behind all of British slackness for a hundred years or more: the dislike of the specialist. . . . The opposite of the professional is not the dilettante, the elegant amateur, the dabbler who in fact only attests the existence of the specialist. The opposite of the professional, the enemy, is the man of mixed-motives." As Louis Menand has shown, Eliot could make this argument for professionalism because he was bolstered by the literary equivalent of the Bar Association—Imagism, Vorticism, and the *Egoist* itself. With Pound beside him, Eliot could conceive of literature as a profession because the field had been incorporated. As a young man Stevens had no such community, but like Eliot he assumed that "mixed motives" was the enemy and "singleness of purpose" the answer to his professional dilemma. As he prepared to leave Harvard for New York, he made this resolution: "I must try not to be a dilettante—half dream, half deed." Yet the Stevens who published "Ballade of the Pink Parasol" and "Political Interests" was just that. He could not (like his Keats) devote himself exclusively to literature.

Reading Herbert Paul's *Matthew Arnold*, Stevens marked these ominous words: "Matthew Arnold was as sociable as Browning, and as genuine a poet. But he had to work for his living, and either the Education Department or the critical faculty almost dried up the poetic vein." Such economic worries underwrote the aesthetic speculations that Stevens recorded in his journal during the summer of 1899, between his second and third years at Harvard. Like the Emerson of "Nature," Stevens was "completely satisfied that behind every physical fact there is a divine force," but his frequent musings on the nature of "facts" were informed by his growing conviction that the "mind cannot always live in a 'divine ether.'" "Facts are like flies in a room," he noted on one occasion; on another he wished "it were possible to escape from what the dreadful Galsworthy calls Facts."

Santayana, mentor of the Harvard milieu that Van Wyck Brooks (class of 1907) recalled as "Pre-Raphaelite aestheticism" and "dilettantish Catholicism," gave much attention to such matters of fact in his *Interpretations of Poetry and Religion*, published in 1900 when Stevens was editing the *Advocate*. Stevens's long-standing interest in Santayana is well known; as a young man Stevens exchanged sonnets with the philosopher, and as an adult he formed his mythology of death around him in "To an Old Philosopher in Rome." Less known is an unsigned review of *Interpretations of Poetry and Religion* that appeared in the same issue of the *Advocate* as Stevens's editorial "Political Interests." Stevens later admitted that as editor "one had to furnish much of the material himself," and the review has all the telltale signs of the early Stevens. As a reader of Kenneth Grahame, and a little "God-weary" himself, Stevens could easily have written that Santayana's work would appeal to "anyone a little God-weary, and tired of trying to compass the ultimate beings of the post-Hegelian type that want, like the little boy in Kenneth

Grahame's tale, to play at being two lions, one on either side of the road,—idea and real, perfect and imperfect, God and the universe." Stevens knew that road well, but what is most crucial about this review of Santayana is that its author ultimately finds the philosopher's vision inadequate. Santayana began his book by pointing out that the only difference between poetry and religion is that the latter pretends to intervene in life; he concluded that, like poetry, religion ought to revoke all claims to empirical truth and practical affairs: "religious doctrines would do well to withdraw their pretension to be dealing with matters of fact." The Stevens who felt facts like flies, who called for increased interest in politics among his colleagues, could not follow this extension of Santayana's aestheticism. The unsigned review politely confesses that "as an ultimate solution of the problems of existence, [*Interpretations of Poetry and Religion*] is not wholly adequate" because it does not apply itself to "the imperfect world of fact." That is precisely what Santayana wanted to avoid—but it was precisely what Stevens required. At Harvard, Stevens ultimately rejected the doctrine of "art for art's sake" because it "opposes the common run of things." Santayana, in contrast, was a professional aesthete. Financially independent, he went on to live a life virtually unimpeded by matters of fact, and Stevens was simultaneously intrigued and repulsed by this single-mindedness. (And it was not until 1948, when he wrote "Imagination as Value," that Stevens would be able to articulate his conflicted feelings about Santayana.)

John Jay Chapman, the subject of Stevens's editorial "Political Interests," provided an alternative role model. So that Harvard's aesthetes might "be informed openly and candidly just what the various parties stand for and how they are run," Stevens proposed a "Political Union" composed of the Civil Service Reform Club, the Democratic Club, and the Republican Club. Each club might follow the lead of the Reform Club, which had invited Chapman to speak on "Public Opinion." Although he "was intent on pleading for the Independent party," said Stevens, Chapman "undoubtedly came as near to a clear exposition of the state of public affairs, as any other speaker we are likely to hear." Given this admiration for Chapman (along with the need to fill up the pages of the *Advocate*), it is probable that Stevens wrote the unsigned review of Chapman's *Practical Agitation* that appeared several weeks after the editorial. The review begins by reiterating that Chapman stumps for the Independents but then points out that his ultimate goal is to reveal party politics as merely the most obvious manifestation of a world in which all actions are political.

[Chapman] believes that the country is full "of maimed human beings, of cynics and feeble good men, and outside of this no form of life except the diabolical intelligence of pure business." It is against the power of such "forms of life" that Mr. Chapman is contending. He stands for purity, to be attained by neither the Democratic nor the Republican party, but by purity itself. "If I had to make my way at the court of Queen Elizabeth," he says, "I should need more kinds of wit and more knowledge of human nature than in the New York button trade. No doubt I should be a preoccupied, cringing, and odious sort of person at a feudal festivity; but I should be a fascinating man of genius compared to John H. Painter, who, at the age of thirty, is making $15,000 a year by keeping his mouth shut and attending to business." "Practical Agitation" is an incomparable description of the battle between Mr. Chapman and John H. Painter *et al.*

The passage quoted from *Practical Agitation* pertains precisely to the problem Stevens faced as he packed up his books and moved to New York: "Almost every man who enters our society joins it as a young man in need of money. His instincts are unsullied, his intellect is fresh and strong, but he must live. How comes it that the country is full of maimed human beings, of cynics and feeble good men, and outside of this no form of life except the diabolical intelligence of pure business?" Chapman explains that this unsullied young man "goes into a law office" or "goes into a newspaper office" (Stevens's two professional alternatives) and comes out in three years with a dried-up mind due to the "intensity of self-seeking." If one could put a pressure gauge into the ironically named Painter, Chapman concludes, one could "measure the business tension in New York in 1900." Reading Santayana, Stevens saw a picture of the incomplete aesthetic years he was leaving behind. Reading and listening to Chapman, he saw a picture of the equally unsatisfactory years of politics and economics that lay before him. William James considered Chapman's *Practical Agitation* to be "the other pole of thought [from Santayana] and a style all splinters—but a gospel for our rising generation.—I hope it will have its effect." After Chapman's death, Edmund Wilson would declare that "no writer of [Chapman's] generation had dealt at once so realistically and with so much clairvoyance with the modern American world, and has in consequence so much to say to the younger generation."

Chapman probably seemed an ideal figure to Stevens; he had edited the *Advocate*, attended law school, and maintained professional interests in both literature and politics with little hint of a double life. Like William James, Chapman inherited from Emerson his sense of the ineluctable relation of our public and private lives. His explicitly political essays in *Practical Agitation* were in fact an extension of his literary work in *Emerson and Other Essays*, and he described his activism as "Emerson made coherent." Chapman's Emerson was not the tender-minded sage of Santayana's *Interpretations of Poetry and Religion* but the tough-minded instigator of Thoreauvian civil disobedience, the Emerson who wrote in "Politics" that from neither political party, "when in power, has the world any benefit to expect"; "the boundaries of personal influence," in contrast, "it is impossible to fix." That doctrine helped to make Whitman's *Democratic Vistas* possible, and Chapman likewise believed that "if a soul be taken and crushed by democracy till it utters a cry, that cry will be Emerson." Yet Chapman also saw that the doctrine of "Politics" did not represent the whole Emerson, and he understood the price he paid in rendering Emerson "coherent": Emerson presented his beliefs "in such illusive and abstract forms," said Chapman, "that by no chance and by no power could his creed be used for purposes of tyranny. Dogma cannot be extracted from it. Schools cannot be built on it." While Chapman believed that political change could be effected through the minutest of private acts, he knew that the public world of politics as it is commonly understood—the world of McKinley and Bryan, of the Republican and Democratic parties— could not be ignored. Rather than replacing the tyranny of party politics with the tyranny of the individual, Chapman explained in *Practical Agitation* that these public and private worlds are always contingent on each other: "It is hard breaking down the popular fallacy that there is such a thing as 'politics,' governed by peculiar conditions, which must be understood and respected; that the whole thing is a mystic avocation, run as a trade of high priests and low priests, and is remote from our daily lives."

Like Burke's analysis of aestheticism in *Counter-Statement*, this is an insight as important for reading Stevens as it is for understanding his historical predicament. In theory, Chapman gave Stevens the hope that his position between aesthetics and politics was not intractable; in practice, Chapman showed in his prognostic chapter "Literature" that the journalistic life could dispel the occult aura from both aesthetics and politics. He began by refuting Santayana's claim that poems are "true to feeling, untrue to fact":

Such are the convictions of the average cultivated man. His back is broken, but he lives in the two halves comfortably enough. . . . Every form of idealism appeals to him, so long as it does not ask him to budge out of his armchair. "Aha," he says, "I understand this. It takes place in the realm of the Imagination." This man does not know, and has no means of knowing, that good books are only written by men whose backs are not broken, and whose vital energy circulates through their entire system in one sweep. They have a unitary and not a duplicate philosophy.

Words, he said, can stir the fibers of other people, "and it matters little whether you label his words literature or politics." In rejecting this dualism, Chapman stood for a position that Burke would call corrective rather than acquiescent.

Honesty and intellect, truth-telling in any form, was the vehicle of change for Chapman: "The first difficulty is to see the evils clearly. . . . You must burn a disinfectant." As the anonymous reviewer of *Practical Agitation* put it in the *Advocate*, Chapman "stands for purity, to be attained by neither the Democratic nor the Republican party, but by purity itself." Forty-two years later, the poet whom this reviewer may have become would explain that "the first step toward a supreme fiction would be to get rid of all existing fictions. A thing stands out in clear air better than it does in soot." These sentences were offered as commentary on the opening canto of "Notes toward a Supreme Fiction," in which the ephebe is instructed to "become an ignorant man again / And see the sun again with an ignorant eye / And see it clearly in the idea of it." This reduction to the "first idea" was not codified until Stevens developed his specialized vocabulary in the "Notes," but the reductionist tendency filled his poetry from the start. Several years after leaving Harvard, Stevens copied this passage into his journal: "We must leave it to the aesthetic critics to explain why . . . it is easier for nearly everyone to recognize the meaning of common reality after it has passed through another's brain—why thousands of kindly people should have contemplated negro slavery day by day for years without emotion, and then have gone mad over 'Uncle Tom's Cabin.'" These sentences are taken from "Propaganda by the Play," an anonymous review of Elizabeth Robins's *Votes for Women*. The reviewer maintained that Robins's play had accomplished something never before achieved in theater: not only did it "use the drama as a means for advancing a political or social cause" (the rights of women), but it converted the stage into a political platform—without ever denying its function as a stage—by blurring the distinction between an imagined audience on stage and the actual audience in the theater. The result was not a diminishing but a heightening of the play's dramatic impact. "It is with the play that she seeks to catch their [the audience's] conscience—not with the mere similitude or mouse-trap of a play, but with the representation of the actual thing itself. People will go to an intellectually fashionable theatre who would never think of attending a meeting in Hyde Park or Trafalgar Square. They shall be made to hear what the women at such meetings have to say."

Having read Chapman, Stevens suspected that the aesthetic theory embodied in the play was more complicated than this; true, the audience heard arguments it might not otherwise hear, but whether what it saw was "the representation of the actual thing itself" was debatable. What makes such a meta-theatrical experience exciting is the tension between the artistic representation and the thing itself. When the reviewer admitted as much, pointing out that an artistic representation was more powerful than the reality of slavery itself, he threw up his hands and waited for the "aesthetic critic" to clear up the matter. Stevens obliged him: "It is because common reality is being exhibited. It is being treated objectively." The key lay in the treatment, the exhibition. Two journal entries later, Stevens offered this single sentence: "I am in the mood for suddenly disappearing." He had gotten his first glimpse of the power of beholding "nothing that is not there and the nothing that is" by becoming "nothing himself." Geoffrey Hartman once identified "The Snow Man" as a political poem because of its embodiment of the efficacy of clear seeing. With Chapman and Robins in the background, the urgency of this call for the self to empty out and behold the sheer otherness of commonplace reality becomes even clearer.

> One must have a mind of winter
> To regard the frost and the boughs
> Of the pine-trees crusted with snow.

Neither Robins nor Chapman alone made "The Snow Man" possible, of course. And, as Chapman suggested of Emerson, there is no dogma that could be extrapolated from Stevens's lines, especially when they are set in the context of poems that assert the tyranny of the self as strongly as "The Snow Man" records reality's stark imperative. Chapman did, however, answer the young Stevens's crucial question: Is literature really a profession? Chapman held up the integrity of journalism as both a literary and a political ideal, and three months after Stevens listened to him speak, he was pounding the streets of New York as a cub reporter. The year was 1900, and the nominees were William Jennings Bryan and William McKinley, Democrat and Republican, Populist and Imperialist. Covering the campaign, Stevens came face to face with political questions central to his own life. The answers determined the contours of a growing nation and poet for the following fifty years.

3

Populism and Imperialism

"In the street-life of the metropolis," wrote Horatio Alger in *Ragged Dick: Or, Street Life in New York*, "a boy needs to be on the alert, and have all his wits about him, or he will find himself wholly distanced by his more enterprising competitors for popular favor." And Stevens on the difficulties thereof: "All New York, as I have seen it, is for sale—and I think the parts I have seen are the parts that make New York what it is. It is dominated by necessity. Everything has its price—from Vice to Virtue. . . . Everybody is looking at everybody else—a foolish crowd walking on mirrors." As this journal entry suggests, Stevens was quickly disillusioned in the city. Eliot would call the condition "Unreal City" (referring specifically to the City of London, the financial district), and this reaction to the new mechanized, secularized, consumer culture was a commonplace in Stevens's youth. In his study of historical modernism, Jackson Lears concludes that for the typical American bourgeois, "authentic experience" (whether physical or spiritual) seemed a lost possibility: "There was no longer the opportunity for bodily testing provided by rural life, no longer the swift alternation of despair and exhilaration which characterized the old-style Protestant conversion. There was only the diffuse fatigue produced by a day of office work or social calls. Bourgeois existence seemed a narrow path, with no erratic emotional detours. No wonder, then, that late Victorians began to feel that they had been cut off from 'reality,' that they experienced life in all its dimensions at second hand, in books rather than action."

Stevens's own attempt to live a "sincere life" in the city of cheats and illusions led him to explore the port of Manhattan, recording in his journal

the exotic lives of foreign sailors. Later, he began his long walks in the countryside as an antidote to urban congestion, and because his vocational life
could not yet sustain its vacational pleasures, his weekend sojourns seemed
an escape from the drudgery of the work week: "the roads are strewn with
purple oak leaves, brown chestnut leaves, and the golden and scarlet leaves
of maples. I doubt if there is any keener delight in the world than, after being
penned up for a week, to get into the woods on such a day—every pound of
flesh vibrates with new strength." Stevens was beginning to understand that
only his work, as desultory as it was, could make such pleasures possible. That
the escape was illusionary was confirmed by his deeper sadness on returning
to the city, and Stevens soon realized that he would have to find his pleasures
between Monday and Friday. He stood at an impasse. Covering his territory
in Brooklyn (where the *Tribune* assigned him), he was stunned to see homeless men sleeping on the grass—images of the fate he feared for himself. Most
of all, he lamented New York's "lack of locality." It all seemed the same,
"disintegrating, dislocating & nothing is distinct, defined." In such an environment, a firm sense of selfhood was a rarity; Stevens's undergraduate worries about his profession were transformed into even more urgent worries
about basic subsistence. "Working savagely," he wrote in his journal four
years after coming to New York, "but have been so desperately poor at times
as not to be able to buy sufficient food—and sometimes not any."

When Stevens became a reporter for the *Tribune*, journalism itself was
undergoing the same struggle for professionalism that had created the American Bar Association. Most reporters found the image of the romantic adven-
turer as unacceptable as the old-style reporter who wrote for the "journals of
opinion" dominated by party politics and editorial fiat. Newspapers themselves had changed. By the 1890s, the telegraphic press service had increased
the size and circulation of city papers several times over, but it also worked
to standardize the news. The job of the "new journalism," said Joseph Pulitzer
of the *New York World*, was to recapture the arresting, readerly details that
the wire service could not carry—the authentic (if vicarious) experience that
the urban middle class craved. Stevens put this advice to work when he covered the Bosscheiter murder trial for the *Tribune*. Three of the murderers
(one of whom was actually named Death) received sentences of thirty years,
causing Stevens to remark in his journal that the "mere length of time is a
ghastly thing to contemplate. Jonah must have written the Law, where it is
so terrible as this. A Judge ought to tremble when he executes it." The article
in the *Tribune* is unsigned, but it features both a trembling judge and the same
keen eye for dramatically significant detail that Stevens evinced in "Four
Characters": "His voice trembled with emotion as he described the enormity
of the crime and the manner in which it had been committed. The courtroom

was crowded, among the spectators being the mother and the brothers of the murdered girl. Mrs. Bosscheiter sat at the end of a seat, and her skirts were brushed by the four men as they were led in and out of the courtroom."

Here was the real thing: life, death, and the "terrible avenger" of the law. But the problem with journalism was that it was all too rarely this authentic. The very ephemerality of the newspaper undermined any artistic or political aspirations that Chapman fanned in Stevens. As Stevens himself remarked in some brief notes on drawing and engraving made around 1904: "The enormous multiplication of their works by printing makes engravers only second to workers in their power over public taste." He might have said the same thing about the power of the reporter or the poet, challenged by what Walter Benjamin called the age of mechanical reproduction. Although Stevens sometimes made what he considered a good salary simply by the amount of copy he supplied to the *Tribune*, he rarely mentioned the work in his journal; the bulk of his writing paid the rent but undermined the authenticity of the writing itself. The Bosscheiter murder trial was the exception to the tedium. Stevens's other interesting assignment was to cover the funeral of Stephen Crane; but, as he confided to his journal, "the whole thing was frightful." Stevens's final words on Crane, probably the most famous journalist of the time, were a eulogy for his own career: "But he lived a brave, aspiring, hardworking life. Certainly he deserved something better than this absolutely common-place, bare, silly service I have just come from. . . . There are few hero-worshippers. Therefore, few heroes."

Chapman had promised Stevens both the professional status and the authentic experience he craved, but even if journalism could have provided them, Stevens was not patient enough to wait and see. He took the train home to discuss his future with his father: "We talked about the law which he has been urging me to take up. I hesitated—because this literary life, as it is called, is the one I always had as an ideal & I am not quite ready to give it up because it has not been all that I wanted it to be." The law offered a more firmly defined professional opportunity, but when Stevens returned to New York he took one final shot at a purely "literary life." He told his father that he planned to resign from the *Tribune* and devote himself to his own writing full-time; Garrett Stevens returned his letter torn to pieces.

That fall, after a brief stint as an assistant editor at *The World's Work* (a flashy and conservative monthly inaugurated by Walter Page, former editor of the *Atlantic*), Stevens capitulated to his father's wishes and enrolled in New York University. But the next decade of his life, spent as either law student or lawyer, was hardly different from his months at the *Tribune*. The economic difficulties continued, and the professional dilemmas remained. In the summer of 1903 Stevens took a vacation in British Columbia with W. G. Peckham, the lawyer for whom he clerked while in law school. "Well, I'm home again—busted," Stevens wrote on his return to New York. "Yet I am in such high spirits that the mere fact of having only 70 cents—no it's 40 now—to my name, doesn't worry me, that is to say not much." The worries grew steadily, since Stevens's vocational life could sustain no such vacational pleasures.

By 1909 Stevens could remark that he had lived in a score of boarding houses since his arrival in New York and had been through as many jobs. After he was admitted to the bar in June 1904, Stevens opened a practice with Lyman Ward, a friend from Harvard; many years later, after Ward's death, Stevens remarked that he "was an extremely attractive fellow, who never got anywhere . . . because he knew nothing about making money." After the partnership with Ward quickly failed, Stevens joined the firm of Philbin, Beekman, and Menken, but by September he was again out of work. He then had a stint at Eaton and Lewis and after "three months of idleness" found a temporary position with Eustis and Foster. On New Year's Eve of 1905 he made no resolution, "frightened at the way things are going, so slowly, so unprofitably, so unambitiously." The professional burden lightened in 1908 when he joined the New York branch of the American Bonding Company, and it was lifted when he became vice president of the New York office of the Equitable Surety Company in February 1914. Seven months later, "Carnet de Voyage," his first poem to be published since he left Harvard, appeared in the *Trend*.

The particular agony of Stevens's prolonged search for a profession becomes even clearer if his career is compared with Hart Crane's or William Carlos Williams's. Crane's entrepreneurial father was even stauncher than Stevens's, but Crane resisted the pressure even to attend college, sacrificing both economic stability and family loyalty to poetic ambition; his early poems dramatized the conflict of the world within and the world without with particular violence, but Crane's "imagined garden" always prevailed. Williams, in contrast, was a model of professional expediency, exhibiting none of Stevens's hesitation or Crane's daring single-mindedness. After his high-school education at the Château de Lancy near Geneva and at Horace Mann in New York City (where he studied the sciences rather than the classics), Williams bypassed the undergraduate experience and enrolled directly in the University of Pennsylvania's medical school. His *Poems* were published in 1909, and after studying pediatrics in Leipzig, he opened his private practice in 1910; the two careers would progress hand in hand until his death. With neither Crane's rebelliousness nor Williams's resolve, Stevens's protracted adolescence finds its closest parallel in the education of Henry Adams. Although Adams's American heritage was more obviously patrician, his father more professionally formidable, and his own sense of professional failure more

severe, "The Education of Wallace Stevens" is a scaled-down version of
Adams's story. After Harvard, Adams dabbled in journalism, nursed literary
ambitions half-heartedly, and then acquiesced in his search for authentic
experience by following his father's footsteps into the law. His own *Education*
described a successful life that seemed to him nothing but a string of failures.
Like Stevens, he surveyed the world around him and remained nostalgic for
a time when the groves were still sacred and the hero was acclaimed by a
society that valued hero-worship. Concerning heros, Stevens would have a
good deal more to say; in 1940 he would copy this passage from Adams's
correspondence into his commonplace book: "I need badly to find one man
in history to admire. I am in near peril of turning Christian, and rolling in
the mud in an agony of human mortification." Stevens's career is marked
throughout by a tension between forward-looking and backward-looking
ideas, and, like Adams, he remained in some ways a product of the Gilded
Age until his death.

Stevens's participation in the last presidential election of the nineteenth
century suggests how. In November 1900 Stevens concluded that his work
was "dull as dull can be." At the same time he longed to be free of his literary
ambitions ("I wish I wore no crown"), and a conversation he recorded in his
journal reveals that he had dropped back to where he began, trapped in the
illusionary space between the worlds within and without.

> I was speaking to a Tammany Hall man tonight. He had a remarkably compre-
> hensive view of things—I remember his saying—
> "Well, we are all human beings. Money is our object. Hence—"
> Politics, I suppose.
> After all, blink at it all we will, look at it from every point of view, coddle, coax,
> apologize, squirm or what one pleases we cannot deny that on the whole "money is
> our object."

Money: "We all get down to that sooner or later," Stevens added. "I won't
cross this out either." The poet wrote these sentences several days after William Jennings Bryan (the candidate for both the Democratic and Populist
parties) met William McKinley (the incumbent Republican) for the second
time and lost again. At first Stevens thought he would not vote in the election,
but after covering the campaign for the *Tribune* he took the time and money
to go "home for election day" and vote for "the Democratic ticket—Bryan."
The two confrontations between the conservative McKinley and the Populist
Bryan (in 1896 and 1900), standing at the end of the century, shaped American politics for decades; the elections were almost literally a contest between
opposing definitions of America. Bryan's vision of an isolated, agrarian United

States was inevitably displaced by McKinley's vision of an imperialist, industrial nation. It was just as inevitable, given his position as a displaced country boy in the new American city, that Stevens sided with Bryan. His position was utterly paradigmatic.

Bryan became a candidate in 1896 because of his famous "cross of gold" speech at the Democratic convention. Adopting the Populists' support of the free coinage of silver (as opposed to the eastern establishment's commitment to the gold standard), Bryan transformed an economic debate into a religious crusade: "You shall not press down upon the brow of labor this crown of thorns, you shall not crucify mankind upon a cross of gold." To Populists, free silver simply meant more money for more people; to Republicans, it meant anarchy. Bryan was championed by the Midwest as the man who would break Wall Street's hold on the American economy. (Vachel Lindsay celebrated Bryan with this wheezy yawp: "Prairie avenger, mountain lion, / Bryan, Bryan, Bryan, Bryan.") But to eastern property-owners Bryan was the "agrarian revolutionist." His sympathizers included John Altgeld, the Illinois governor who pardoned the anarchists imprisoned for the 1886 Haymarket Square bombing, and Eugene Debs, the socialist organizer of the 1894 Pullman Palace Car Company strike that literally severed the country by crippling the railroads. Theodore Roosevelt equated these three men with "the leaders of the Terror of France in mental and moral attitude." This kind of rhetoric scared off much of Bryan's natural constituency among the working classes, and McKinley's victory meant that American Populism was dead. The reform movements that had seemed so urgent in the decades following the Civil War collapsed as McKinley transformed the nation into an international presence. During his first term, the Spanish American War, the acquisition of Puerto Rico and the Philippines, and the annexation of Hawaii shifted the political focus from domestic to foreign affairs. The economy stabilized after two decades of recession. The Gold Standard Act of 1900 appeared to settle that issue, and when Bryan met McKinley for the second time that November he seemed an embarrassing anachronism. For many voters, it was still difficult to ignore the nagging feeling that the Populist underdog would live to say I told you so. In a way, Bryan (who would resign as Wilson's Secretary of State when the United States' entry into the First World War became inevitable) did.

The *Tribune* was staunchly Republican (its editor had been Harrison's vice-presidential candidate in 1892), but under its auspices Stevens covered Bryan's visit to the city on October 16, 1900: "Saw Bryan the other day," he wrote in his journal, "& heard him make 4 speeches in 3 hours." The long series of articles in the next day's *Tribune* offered a detailed account and transcription of the speeches at Madison Square Garden, the street outside the

Garden (both of which were filled to capacity due to Bryan's fame as an orator), Tammany Hall, and Cooper Union. Bryan avoided his signature domestic issues but nevertheless remained the people's candidate; his platform was
antitrust, antimilitary, and anti-imperialist. Coupling America's acquisition of
Puerto Rico and the ongoing guerrilla war in the Philippines with Britain's
contest with the Boers in South Africa, Bryan played to his nation's most
enduring self-definition myth.

They want the splendors of the empire. They want to hear the tramp of armies; they
want the glory of crowning heroes returning home, their thanks and their plaudits.
The Republicans want the drum to beat so that it can be heard around the world. . . .
I repeat, you never voted for an Imperial policy and yet if you vote the Republican
ticket this fall you vote for an imperial policy. The Republicans say that we are just
raising a scarecrow, that we are trying to frighten people. That may be, but, my friends,
we are not telling you what may be done: we tell you what has been done, for the
Porto Rican law is framed upon European ideas, not upon American principles.

This kind of thinking was enough to convince Stevens, who stood among the
young men Bryan described as victims of a domestic imperialism, "the reign
of trusts" that destroyed "the possibility of being independent." It also
enlisted the support of William James, who (though he felt that Bryan offered
only "a very mongrel kind of reform") protested in a letter to the *Boston
Transcript* that America's involvement in Cuba and the Philippines would
sacrifice "individual lives" to an imported idea of "national destiny." Like
Bryan, James saw imperialism as a fall back into "European ideas"; his pluralism, like Bryan's Populism, grew under Emerson's shadow.
    But the argument did not convince America at large. Bryan did not fully
grasp his nation's self-image, and he failed to realize that his definition of
America as a haven from Old World sinfulness would suffice only as long as
the average American did not have the power to be sinful. Bryan offered the
Edenic myth of democratic purity, but McKinley offered international status
in a fallen world of opportunity. And while Bryan criticized the Republicans
for yearning after the Old World splendors of empire, Roosevelt declared that
it was precisely at this point that the United States should imitate its European forebears: "England's rule in India and Egypt has been of great benefit
to England, for it has trained up generations of men accustomed to look at
the larger and loftier side of public life. It has been of even greater benefit to
India and Egypt. And finally, most of all, it has advanced the cause of civilization." Ironically, when McKinley was shot by an anarchist in 1901, the
Republican editors of *The World's Work* lamented that the very concept of
anarchy was an Old World idea incompatible with New World ideals: "the

assassin of President McKinley had as his provocation only a wretched 'philosophy' of foreign birth and nurture, which was directed against 'rulers,' not against any individual. . . . Even if assassination could change the government of a monarchy, it could have no effect on the government of a republic like ours." Having adopted the rhetoric of British imperialism to support American expansionism, McKinley's supporters suddenly yearned for Bryan's myth of American purity when Old World splendor was destroyed by Old World violence. This fight for control of the terms of the country's self-definition would never be won outright, since the opposing sides could not stand in clear opposition.

In one sense, it is easy to see Bryan's appeal to a displaced young American in the year 1900, but by the 1920s the world Bryan continued to fight for no longer existed. As Richard Hofstadter suggested in *The Age of Reform* (1955), this was the collective fate of American Populism: "it is often hard to tell when such a movement has passed beyond the demand for important and necessary reforms to the expression of a resentment so inclusive that it embraces not only the evils and abuses of society but the whole society itself, including some of its more liberal and humane values." In his youth, Bryan championed the labor leader Eugene Debs, who was defended in the Supreme Court by a lawyer named Clarence Darrow. As an old man, Bryan opposed Darrow in the Scopes monkey trial, his Populism having degenerated into a bloodless conservativism. He fought for Prohibition; he was accused of being sympathetic to the Klan. "Once," said H. L. Mencken, "he had one leg in the White House and the nation trembled under his roars. Now he is a tinpot pope in the coca-cola belt and brother to the forlorn pastors who belabor half-wits in galvanized iron tabernacles behind the railroad yards."

It is worth pointing out that Hofstadter's stern critique of American Populism has been challenged by historians who see the movement not as reactionary but as a kind of home-grown American Marxism. In my reading, Hofstadter's account of the movement already contains the terms of this critique: Populism was marked not so much by a movement from left to right, from reform to reaction, as by an uneasy alliance of these opposing ideologies. And though Bryan presents an exaggerated example of the fate of American Populism, his fate highlights the peculiar combination of reaction and reform that can be found throughout American modernism. As it is exemplified in either Stevens or Eliot, literary modernism is often historically antimodern, open to all manner of experimentation but doubled over with nostalgia for a world that no longer exists. That the author of *The Waste Land* would declare himself "classicist in literature, royalist in politics, and anglo-catholic in religion" does not puzzle us today. By 1933 Eliot was nearly as strung out as Bryan, and before a room full of southern Agrarians (who had composed the political left in Eliot's youth) he could mention the undesirability of "any large number of free-thinking Jews" as if he were uttering one of common sense's most obvious clichés. Similarly, the cub reporter who voted for Bryan's anticorporate, anti-imperialist America had been the student who could blame African-Americans for squandering their "opportunity" and would become the insurance executive who, when Mussolini invaded Ethiopia, remarked that the "Italians have as much right to take Ethiopia from the coons as the coons had to take it from the boa-constrictors." When the United States's entry into the Second World War was debated a few years later, Stevens remarked in a *Partisan Review* questionnaire that it should not be considered unless the nation "does so with the idea of dominating the world that comes out of it." In feeling this way, Stevens was not alone, even in the *Partisan Review* circle. Soon after this questionnaire was circulated, the editorial board split violently, and Dwight Macdonald left the magazine, leaving its editorial policy in the charge of Rahv and Phillips, who supported the Allied cause: "Now we have reached the stage," wrote Rahv, "where the war will either be won by the combined might of the Anglo-American imperialism and Stalin's Red Army, or else it won't be won at all."

Given their development in the American political mainstream, Stevens's contradictory views were not idiosyncratic. The uneasy Populist alliance of ideologies culled from the political right and left lived on long after Bryan died; in offering a critical account of Populism in the 1940s and 1950s, Hofstadter was also responding to the wave of neo-populism that had surfaced in the 1930s and was exacerbated by the surge of nationalism during the Second World War. Similarly, Stevens's later political views are clarified when we see them as part of his Populist heritage. In "Canonica," a sequence of twelve poems that Stevens would reprint as the opening movement of *Parts of a World* (1942), "The Latest Freed Man" extols the joy of "having just / Escaped from the truth." The poem's call for a rejection "of the old descriptions of the world" underscores once again the political dimension of "The Snow Man."

> To be without a description of to be,
> For a moment on rising, at the edge of the bed, to be,
> To have the ant of the self changed to an ox
> With its organic boomings, to be changed
> From a doctor into an ox, before standing up,
> To know that the change and that the ox-like struggle
> Come from the strength that is the strength of the sun,
> Whether it comes directly or from the sun.
> It was how he was free. It was how his freedom came.

This paean to the wonder of change depends, as Stevens phrases it in "Extracts from Addresses to the Academy of Fine Ideas," on "that difference between the and an"—the freedom that comes when we understand "the" truth to be a plurality of possibilities, one choice among many. "Where was it one first heard of the truth?" asks the man on the dump: "The the." And wedged between "The Latest Freed Man" and "The Man on the Dump" in "Canonica" is "On the Road Home," which offers this advice: "There is no such thing as the truth."

Juxtaposed with this benevolent pluralism in "Canonica" is a contradictory impulse: on the one hand, Stevens wants to leave room for every individual, but, on the other hand, he cannot help thinking that some individuals should lead the majority of others. David Bromwich has explained this tension by naming the opposed tendencies in Stevens's thought as "James" and "Nietzsche," but we might come even closer to the intricate shape of Stevens's politics if we see that the tension is contained within the American tradition we could identify with James or Bryan. Jamesian pragmatism, the philosophical tradition in which Stevens's poetry so comfortably fits, offers the freedom and space for every possible "the," but it does not offer a collective or social vision that keeps the latest freed man from becoming the hero who dictates the terms of freedom to others. (Charles Sanders Peirce objected to James's version of pragmatism specifically because it could not offer a rationale for a community.) The central thrust of "Canonica" might be summed up in the great line from "The Poems of Our Climate"—"The imperfect is our paradise"—yet beside the poems extolling the freedom available in a jagged world of disunified particularities are poems that hint at the darker side of this social vision. "The Idiom of the Hero" complements "The Latest Freed Man" in its call for a world of open possibility, but here that freedom is most crucial for "The great men" who "will not be blended" with the workers' chaos. Even as it clears the space for every "the," Stevens's "Canonica" asserts the priority of one "the" over another.

Stevens's hero poems could sometimes evoke the response that Auden had to the hero-worship evident in his own *Orators* (1932): he described his earlier self as "someone talented but near the border of sanity, who might well, in a year or two, become a Nazi." That characterization of Stevens would be strong, however, since his work differs from Auden's in that it finally offers no dogma or program. As Chapman suggested of Emerson, the creed is so elusive that it is not easily appropriated by the forces of tyranny. Or as Eliot suggested in a particularly lucid moment, fascism "suggests Authority and Tradition, certainly, but Authority and Tradition . . . do not necessarily suggest Signor Mussolini." It may not simply be one of history's terrible ironies that Mussolini admired William James; but the dictator could do so only by reducing James's irresolute individualism to a program, for James also offers the terms in which the potential threat of the hero is diagnosed. As the guerrilla war in the Philippines progressed, an enraged James imagined President McKinley's "bouffe-proclamation" to the inhabitants of those islands: "We are here for your own good; therefore unconditionally surrender to our tender mercies, or we'll blow you into kingdom come." In a similar mood, Stevens revealed the lunacy of such a statement in "Owl's Clover" (1936). The third part of that almost maddeningly dialectical poem, "The Greenest Continent" is both a rewriting of the "Anecdote of the Jar" and a response to Mussolini's invasion of Ethiopia. In this anecdote of imperialism, the work of art is placed on a foreign hill, but it cannot take dominion over bird or bush.

> If the statue rose,
> If once the statue were to rise, if it stood,
> Thinly, among the elephantine palms,
> Sleekly the serpent would draw himself across.
> The horses are part of a northern sky
> Too starkly pallid for the jaguar's light.

"The black will still / Be free to sing," concluded Stevens rather too easily, "if only a sorrowful song." All but the most dogmatic of Stevens's poems on the hero are palatable as poetry because Stevens usually remembered (as Kenneth Burke suggests) that although poetry may be political, it is not the same thing as political action. The crucial value that Stevens and James share, following Emerson, is the one that made Stevens extol the virtue of not maintaining fixed thoughts about the nature of poetry or politics. To put it another way, if poetry is a kind of money, Stevens's poems are off the gold standard, and they do not ask us to accept unconditionally or unproblematically the world they represent. Cornel West's characterization of James's political position could stand for Stevens as well: "James is a man of neither the left nor the right. He certainly does not 'transcend' politics, but, like Emerson, he fits uncomfortably with any political party or movement. He is a libertarian, with circumscribed democratic sentiments, an international outlook, and deep moral sensitivity. This perspective is one of political impotence, yet it buttresses moral integrity and promotes the exercise of individual conscience."

In October 1907, when he had been without work for several months, Stevens copied down these sentences from an essay on Sully-Prudhomme, the Parnassian poet who had died the previous month: "Art for art's sake is an aristocratic concept. . . . [The artist] draws into himself, encloses himself in his pride and individualism. He disdains the crowd and the literary genres it admires, like the theater: He places himself above it." Stevens had long since faced the fact that he was no Parnassian; his own poems would have to be compatible with a life of bourgeois striving. This judgment of art-for-art's-sake is one of the antecedents behind "Tea at the Palaz of Hoon," in which the aristocratic Hoon descends in purple, enclosing "himself in pride and individualism."

> Out of my mind the golden ointment rained,
> And my ears made the blowing hymns they heard.
> I was myself the compass of that sea:
>
> I was the world in which I walked, and what I saw
> Or heard or felt came not but from myself;
> And there I found myself more truly and more strange.

There were surely times when Stevens found this aristocratic state of mind attractive, but he knew that it was a pose incompatible with the life of a newspaper reporter or junior lawyer. "The Snow Man" is the alternative vision to the aristocratic Hoon, and together these companion poems of 1921 have often seemed to condense the aesthetic dialectic of Stevens's entire career: discovering and imposing, the poet as finder and the poet as maker, the world within and the world without. If "The Snow Man" looks forward to the reduction to the first idea in "Notes toward a Supreme Fiction," "Tea at the Palaz of Hoon" forecasts the apotheosis of the self that is the climax of Stevens's masterpiece: "I have not but I am and as I am, I am." With John Jay Chapman and Sully-Prudhomme in the background, it becomes clear that the terms of this dialectic are not only aesthetic, that the terms of both economic necessity and moral imperative are part of Stevens's endlessly elaborating poem. In "Effects of Analogy" (1948) he described the dialectic this way: "The poet is constantly concerned with two theories." While the first leads poets to employ the imagination to overpower reality, the second leads them to "press away from mysticism toward that ultimate good sense which we term civilization." *Civilization* was one word Stevens used for that good sense; other words were *normal, ordinary, medium,* and *humdrum*—words that made the poet's mission seem part of everyday life without even exalting the everyday as the "civilized."

In "The Glass of Water," a poem that stands in the center of the "Canonica" sequence, Stevens offered another version of this dialectic. To realize that "the glass would melt in heat" or "freeze in cold" merely reveals that "this object is merely a state, / One of many, between two poles." This wisdom is summed up as the "metaphysical," and Stevens opposes its terms to another point of view: the ordinary, the eye of fat Jocundus (the name Stevens gave to "medium man" in the final lines of "Owl's Clover").

> But, fat Jocundus, worrying
> About what stands here in the centre, not the glass,

> But in the centre of our lives, this time, this day,
> It is a state, this spring among the politicians
> Playing cards. In a village of the indigenes,
> One would have still to discover. Among the dogs and dung,
> One would continue to contend with one's ideas.

Here Stevens is unwilling as ever to fix his argument in one certain place. But even while he confesses that the mind can never be rid of metaphysical questions, those questions are always encased in the village of dogs and dung, the ordinary world that we call civilization.

Stevens came to this realization before he published any poems he ultimately chose to preserve. After eight years of silence in New York City, he began to write poems again in 1908 when he compiled the "Book of Verses" for Elsie Kachel Moll; the following year he wrote "The Little June Book," another birthday present for his future wife. Elsie Moll was the muse of these poems, but from the beginning, she and poetry were rivals for the poet's attention. Stevens would not have—could not have—written the poems if he had not found the beginning of his professional security in his position with the American Bonding Company, his metaphysics spoken by his fat Jocundus. During his first years in New York, Stevens tried unsuccessfully to find his aesthetic satisfaction by escaping to the country on the weekends, but by the time he had achieved some professional security as well as some aesthetic satisfaction, he had also realized just how close the words *vocation* and *vacation* necessarily are. He sent Elsie Moll a newspaper clipping that described an ancient text by Kuo Hsi, "The Noble Features of the Forest and the Stream": "This is not the time," said the sage, "for us to abandon the busy worldly life for one of seclusion in the mountains. . . . Though impatient to enjoy a life amidst the luxuries of nature, most people are debarred from indulging in such pleasures." Kuo Hsi advised that we must learn to find those pleasures within a worldly life we cannot simply escape: "To meet this want, artists have endeavored to represent landscapes so that people may be able to behold the grandeur of nature without stepping out of their houses." In such houses, freedom grew from a confrontation with necessity, not a denial. The "Book of Verses" ended with this poem.

> What have I to do with Arras
>   Or its wasted star?
> Are my two hands not strong enough,
>   Just as they are?
>
> Because men met with rugged spears,
>   Upon the Lombard plain,

> Must I go forth to them, or else
> Have served in vain?
>
> And does the nightingale, long lost
> In vanished Shalott's dew,
> Sing songs more welcome, dear, than those
> I sing to you?

When he left Harvard, Stevens vowed that he would become neither half-dream nor half-deed, and in the early sonnet with which I began this discussion of his first period of silence, he equated the call of the world outside the self with death. That poem, to borrow Kenneth Burke's words, was "acquiescent" to social conditions that nurtured the illusionary opposition of the public and private worlds. In this poem from the "Book of Verses," nearly a decade later, the alternatives are the same—the death of the active self on the Lombard plain or the death of the retreating self in the castle of Shalott—but now a third term complicates the dualism: the possibility of a life that may look occasionally to either extreme but need not succumb to either. The discarded alternatives come from literature, but the new place in between, the place of Stevens's poetry, was found by the work of two hands "just as they are." The lesson is maudlin, but for Stevens it was an important victory—especially if we hear in Stevens's poem an echo of the beginning of *Walden*, where Thoreau describes how he built his house and earned his living "by the labor of my hands only": writing is not a diversion from such labor but part of the daily economy of house-building. Looking back to Thoreau and looking forward to Stevens's mature work, the final poem of the "Book of Verses" is "corrective" rather than "acquiescent." Stevens became a poet when he realized that "mixed motives" were not necessarily the enemy of professionalism, when he learned to appreciate the halfway house described by Kuo Hsi. He became a poet by living in the suburbs of the mind.

Stevens once said, "I have no life except in poetry." But he knew that was a lie: "No doubt that would be true if my whole life was free for poetry." Stevens saw quite clearly that every happiness, social or aesthetic, has its cost. Had he wanted to, Stevens could have led a life that was "free" for poetry—but he was much more canny than poets who need to imagine that they do so, and he understood that even if it were possible, a life free from economic concerns would not be any form of life as we know it. "I am far from being a genius," wrote Stevens in 1911, "and must rely on hard and faithful work." Stevens began to write poetry again when his economic future was secure. His private world of imagination was nurtured by a public struggle, and only with the support of the claims man did the poet end his silence. But Stevens's earliest poems speak with a curtly diminished voice. They are the product of a circumscribed ambition, important only because of the greater poems that follow them. Greater challenges would provoke those poems. And if the appearance of "Sunday Morning" six years after "The Little June Book" still seems an inexplicable feat, it is because we have sought the poem's provenance in Stevens's stylistic development alone and not in his economic and political life as well. A steady job helped to make the "Book of Verses" and "The Little June Book" possible; the Great War helped to shake Stevens into the state of mind that produced "Sunday Morning."

II

Thinking About War

4

The Great War and
Post-Romantic Ambition

"Well a book of poems is a damned serious affair," counseled Stevens in a letter William Carlos Williams printed in the prologue to *Kora in Hell* (1918). Ostensibly responding to Williams's earlier volume *Al Que Quieri!*, Stevens really described the tentative progress of his own work: "to fidget with points of view leads always to new beginnings and incessant new beginnings lead to sterility." Stevens would delay his own book of poems until 1923. And he began the decade of active publishing that led to *Harmonium* with the same measured consideration with which he settled into a profession. Five years after "The Little June Book" was written, Stevens went public with "Carnet de Voyage" and "Two Poems" (1914). But six of these poems were culled from the two collections written as birthday presents for Elsie Moll, and Stevens probably offered the sequence to the *Trend* as a favor to its editor, Pitts Sanborn, an old Harvard friend. Among the best of the new poems was "From a Junk," which ends with these lines.

> It glistens in the flapping wind,
> Burns there and glistens, wide and wide,
> Under the five-horned stars of night,
> In wind and wave . . . It is the moon.

As every student of Stevens's development has noticed, early poems like this one seem (depending on the date of composition) either to anticipate or to be influenced by the Imagist movement. Pound wrote a startlingly similar poem, "Fish and the Shadow," which plays on the same confusion of substance and illusion: "The salmon-trout drifts in the stream, / The soul of the salmon-trout floats over the stream / Like a little wafer of light." And Yeats offered the same image ("Although you hide in the ebb and flow / Of the pale tide when the moon has set") in an early poem called "The Fish." Both Stevens and Pound knew Yeats's proto-Imagist work in *The Wind Among the Reeds*, but something more intricate than Yeats's powerful influence on Stevens's generation is at work here. The impulse that led Stevens to write poems like "From a Junk" is the same impulse that made him keep silent for almost a decade and then advise Williams that a book of poems is a damned serious affair: diffidence, hesitancy, caution. Stevens appears to have Imagist tendencies—as does Yeats or Rossetti—not because Imagism was so powerful a movement but because the "diminished" aesthetic it embodies was a common response to the pressure of the achievement of the high Romantics.

Like many other post-Enlightenment poets, Stevens felt that the loss of the pantheon diminished possibilities for poetry. Although he resisted an easy nostalgia for lost worlds, Stevens confessed in "Esthétique du Mal" (1944) that the "death of Satan was a tragedy / For the imagination." By the time he wrote these lines, Stevens was secure in his belief that this tragedy for the imagination was also "the imagination's new beginning"; we "require / Another chant" to replace the phantoms in which we no longer believe. But Stevens's early letters and journals record a young poet's yearning for the spirit of romance: "I wish that groves still *were* sacred—or, at least, that something was. . . . I grow tired of the want of faith—the instinct of faith." Most Victorian or modern poets felt this longing equally acutely, but William Morris expressed a common insecurity when he began *The Earthly Paradise* not by lamenting the loss of a transcendental world but by accepting his inability to say anything about it. For Morris, the function of the post-Romantic poet was severely diminished: "Of Heaven or Hell I have no power to sing, / I cannot ease the burden of your fears, / Or make quick-coming death a little thing." A recognition of the limited and possibly solipsistic nature of human knowledge kept poets like Morris and Rossetti humble; with no firm belief in a transcendental order outside the self, they confined their poetry to the small world of which they could be relatively certain. In their relationship to the high Romantics, then, Pound's Imagist poems or Stevens's early lyrics may be aligned with the poems of Rossetti, Hardy, the Rhymers, and even the Georgians.

When Stevens opened his journal in the year 1900, he gave this passage from Keats's "Dear Reynolds" a page to itself: "But my flag is not unfurl'd / On the Admiral-staff, and to philosophise / I dare not yet." More diffident even than the young Keats, Stevens cultivated a poetry of diminished particulars. Poetic speculation on the "vast and broad effects" of freedom, beauty, or power was not for him: "This feeling of having exhausted the subject is in turn succeeded by the true and lasting source of country pleasure: the growth of small, specific observation." Even as he began to write poetry again in 1908, Stevens asked Elsie Moll if she did not agree "that if we could get the Michael Angeloes out of our heads—Shakespeare, Titian, Goethe—all the phenomenal men, we should find a multitude of lesser things (lesser but a *multitude*) to occupy us?" Small thoughts, little things, specific observation: this is the credo of a poet staking a claim for the tiny world he can master, a world even tinier than Keats's. "Carnet de Voyage" begins with a poem that sings of the wonder of the "odor from a star," "Sweet exhalations, void / Of our despised decay." But just as Shelley's high-minded skylark fell to the earth and died for Hardy, this ethereal longing will not suffice for Stevens, and the remainder of the sequence examines our earthly decay with a judiciously limited eye.

> Here the grass grows,
> And the wind blows.
> And in the stream,
> Small fishes gleam,
> Blood-red and hue
> Of shadowy blue.

If these lines sound to some ears like H.D. and to others like Arthur Symons, it is because these poets stand in a relation to the Romantics that is similar to Stevens's. That relation was doubly intractable for a poet not only post-Romantic but American. A diminished aesthetic was especially attractive to American artists because it sanctioned the thinness of American culture as a positive value. As Henry James put it, explaining why American painters chose to live abroad, "a furnished country is still more to his purpose." For those artists who chose to stay at home, a diminished aesthetic offered the means to transform the unfurnished rooms into an artistic ideal. The danger of this rationalization is that the wonder of the ordinary might decay into what Stevens called "the malady of the quotidian" in "The Man Whose Pharynx was Bad." In poems like "Gubbinal" and "Banal Sojourn" a diminished aesthetic becomes a prison: "For who can care at the wigs despoiling the Satan ear?" asks Stevens in a poetry that only allows him to say flatly, "Two wooden tubs of blue hydrangeas stand at the foot of the stone steps. / The sky is a blue gum streaked with rose. The trees are black." One desires so much more than that. Stevens asked the appropriate question straight out in "The American Sublime."

> How does one stand
> To behold the sublime,
> To confront the mockers,
> The mickey mockers
> And plated pairs?

For Pound, who came from a half-savage country, out of date, and moved to sparsely furnished rooms in Kensington, an aesthetic that denied the possibility of the sublime was a troublesome limitation from the start, and even as he presented "In a Station of the Metro" as the ideal Imagist poem in "Vorticism" (1914) he appended a nervous footnote: "I am often asked whether there can be a long imagiste or vorticist poem." The question still resonates. How did Pound get from "In a Station of the Metro" to the first cantos in four years? How did Stevens get from "Carnet de Voyage" to "Sunday Morning" in just one? The extraordinary leap in ambition and accomplishment that occurred between these two poems, standing only one year apart, is as great as the fourteen-year leap from the Harvard sonnets to "Carnet de Voyage."

My solution to this mystery takes us out of the realm of purely literary investigation, for it has to do with the event that erupted in Europe the month before Pound published his essay on Vorticism. When the First World War began on August 4, 1914, it presented a generation of judiciously limited lyric poets with an epic subject. The advice of T. E. Hulme, who said that modern poetry "no longer deals with heroic action" but with "momentary phases in the poet's mind," now seemed irrelevant. Pound might have rephrased his question this way: How do I take on the necessary task of understanding mass death and massive political struggle, and how do I do so in the face of the Romantic poets who confronted similar issues raised by the French Revolution in their long poems? That the years from 1922 to 1925 saw the publication of *The Waste Land, Spring and All, Harmonium, Observations,* and *A Draft of XVI Cantos* is no accident but the product of a postwar historical imperative.

Although most readings of Stevens's development focus on the Great Depression as the event that forced the poet to take notice of social conditions, Stevens himself tells a different story in "The Irrational Element in Poetry" (1936). There he dates the awakening fifteen years earlier—at the Great War.

The pressure of the contemporaneous from the time of the beginning of the World War to the present time has been constant and extreme. No one can have lived apart in a happy oblivion. For a long time before the war nothing was more common. In those days the sea was full of yachts and the yachts were full of millionaires. It was a time when only maniacs had disturbing things to say. The period was like a stage-setting that since then has been taken down and trucked away. It had been taken down by the end of the war, even though it took ten years of struggle with the consequences of the peace to bring about a realization of that fact. People said that if the war continued it would end civilization, just as they say now that another such war will end civilization. It is one thing to talk about the end of civilization and another to feel that the thing is not merely possible but measurably probable.

To emphasize his sense of the war as a turning point in modern history, Stevens indulges in a myopic nostalgia for the prewar period (we have seen that his own prewar years were spent in anything but "happy oblivion"); nevertheless, he reveals in this paragraph a subtly informed sense of the illusions of 1920s prosperity and the long-range effects of the Treaty of Versailles. Equally sophisticated is his diagnosis of the illusions of the apocalyptic rhetoric that both the First World War and the war already looming on the horizon of 1936 encouraged. Stevens knew that talk of "the end of civilization" could paradoxically cheer people up, relieving them of the work of forestalling the end; consequently, he worked to understand both the war and the Depression as events in the continuing process of history. And at the same time that "The Irrational Element in Poetry" offers a reading of that historical continuity, it also offers an important interpretation of the continuities of Stevens's own career. In contrast to the accepted understanding of the shape of his career, "The Irrational Element in Poetry" shows that Stevens himself considered the wartime poems of *Harmonium* to be as much the product of social conflict as *Ideas of Order* or *The Man with the Blue Guitar*, the volumes of the 1930s. As early as 1923 Stevens would make explicit in "Academic Discourse at Havana" his interest in exploring "the function of the poet" in a time when "Politic man ordained / Imagination as the fateful sin."

For Stevens, that time began when the First World War made aestheticism seem more ridiculous than ever before. His understanding of the war's place in modern culture is close to that of Kenneth Burke in *Counter-Statement*: "Disciples of Art for Art's Sake might advocate art as a refuge, a solace for the grimness about them, but the spirit of social mockery could no longer fit the scene. One can mock death, but one cannot mock men in danger of death." This statement describes Burke's own development, for it was the First World War that shook him out of his early aestheticism and made him explore the social implications of art; *Counter-Statement*, beginning with essays on Pater and de Gourmont and moving on to Burke's later essay "The Status of Art," is a kind of autobiography. As the passage in "The Irrational

Element" suggests, the war similarly knocked Stevens out of the comfortably diminished aestheticism that allowed him to compose "The Little June Book" and "Carnet de Voyage." The latter sequence was Stevens's first adult publication, but "Phases," written in response to *Poetry* magazine's announcement of a prize for the best poem "based on the present European situation," was his first collection of new poetry. Stevens began his adult career as a war poet.

Stevens did not win the war-poem prize, but to a world more comfortable with the familiar beauties of "From a Junk," "Phases" seemed to be unforgivably stern stuff. One anonymous reviewer asked: "if anyone could suggest to me a magazine that had worse poems through its whole existence than this individual War Poem Number had, I would like to see the magazine. Moreover, we read enough about the war in the newspaper, why should we also have ranting poems thrust into our faces, which are untruthful, and nauseating to read. Here are two excellent examples." The first example was from "Phases."

> There's a little square in Paris,
> Waiting until we pass.
> They sit idly there,
> They sip the glass.

With these lines Stevens announced his dissatisfaction with a diminished aesthetic. The private, little, domestic world of "Carnet de Voyage" is left behind as the poet marches off to greater challenges. "Carnet de Voyage" had begun by idealizing a world "void / Of our despised decay," but "Phases" begins by declaring that there once was such a "heaven, / Full of Raphael's costumes," but now we have no choice but to look to earth, "Stiff as stone," where "A dead hand tapped the drum." In a sense, the aesthetic is still diminished, in that the emphasis remains on earthly particulars rather than spiritual goals; but now the physical world is recognized as the ultimate value in itself—not as a mild substitute for a world we no longer have ambition or power enough to conjure up. Stevens is beginning to make major poetry out of a diminished world, a subtle but crucial adjustment of his aesthetic that separates "Sunday Morning" from the *fin de siècle* or postwar hedonism of the *Rubáiyát* or *The Sun Also Rises*. If "Sunday Morning" was the first fruit of Stevens's lifelong ambition to write the great poems of the earth, then the war propelled the shift in attitude that made the poems possible. Stevens surely learned from William James's *Pragmatism* that "the earth of things, long thrown into shadow by the glories of the upper ether, must resume its rights"; and Emily Dickinson would have taught him that "Death sets a

Thing significant / The Eye had hurried by." But as Stevens explained in "From the Journal of Crispin" (an early version of the poem that became "The Comedian as the Letter C"), the war and its attendant consciousness of death gave these lessons their power: "poems are transmutations of plain shops, / By aid of starlight, distance, wind, war, death."

Unlike Stevens and Burke, other American writers often retreated into a more aggressive aestheticism during the war, especially in the years before the United States declared war on Germany in 1917. Among Stevens's circle of New York friends, Donald Evans was the most influential and charismatic. His *Sonnets from the Patagonian* (1914) epitomized the last-ditch aestheticist tone of the group (Glen MacLeod has named them the "Patagonians"), but Stevens could never devote himself completely to this esoteric enclave. When Evans reissued *Sonnets from the Patagonian* during the war, he offered this prefatory letter: "If we could purge ourselves of our fear of Germany we should capture Berlin. Could I enlist a Battalion of Irreproachables, whose uniforms should be walking suit, top hat and pumps and their only weapon an ebony walking stick and sail tomorrow, we should march down Unter den Linden in a month, provided wrapped in our kerchiefs we carried the Gospel of Beauty, and a nonchalance in the knot of our cravats." Rather than over-throwing his aestheticism for an equally exaggerated warmongering, Evans fought the war with the power of art itself.

Stevens was particularly sensitive to that illusion. And between 1914 and 1917 his inner life was fueled by a series of attempts to comprehend a war he could not experience directly. "Phases" appeared two months after Germany crossed the Belgian border and Britain issued its ultimatum. Although the anonymous reviewer found Stevens's war poems to be unacceptably gritty and historical, Stevens himself felt that he needed to acquire a more intimate knowledge of the war. In February 1915 Germany declared a war zone around the British Isles, warning that even neutral ships would be attacked; on May 7, a German submarine torpedoed the *Lusitania*, killing 128 American citizens. In the months that followed, as President Wilson crafted his responses, the possibility of an American declaration of war seemed imminent. During the summer of 1915, Stevens read the London *Times* in order to follow the events of the war more closely. At the beginning of each month, the *Times* published a summary of the war's progress, which, after reading it himself, Stevens would send to his wife, who was spending the summer at a resort in Woodstock, New York; during the *Lusitania* crisis, he also sent his copies of *The New Republic*, along with a subscription to the *New York Tribune*. The "Roll of Honor" for the June 1 *Times* listed 80 officers and over 1600 soldiers, their names divided into various categories: missing, killed, accidentally killed, died of wounds, died of gas poisoning, wounded, wounded and suffering from gas poisoning. Such statistics offered an accounting of the public side of the war, but Stevens required a more intimate knowledge of the fighting. In the summer of 1917, when he joined his wife in Woodstock, he read Eugène Lemercier's *Lettres d'un soldat*, the letters of a young French painter who was killed in 1915. Like the accounts of the fighting that Ezra Pound received from Henri Gaudier-Brzeska and T. E. Hulme, these letters offered Stevens some of the materia poetica he required, and that summer he wrote his own "Lettres d'un Soldat," a sequence of poems based on Lemercier's experience.

Stevens never saw Lemercier's France, but after 1914 France came to Stevens's New York and brought the war with it. Refugees from the Parisian art scene retreated to American shores, and from the likes of Marcel Duchamp and Francis Picabia, Stevens received a more immediate sense of the wages of war. The American painter and organizer of the 1913 Armory Show, Walter Pach, was also driven home by the fighting, and through him Stevens became directly involved in an expatriate effort to rebuild what the war had destroyed, to make some corner of a foreign town forever Paris. In February 1918 Pach published "Universality in Art" in *The Modern School*, a lament for lost culture that sounds the same alarm Pound was ringing in London: "One cannot think without a shudder of the artists of great talent still in the trenches. Derain, Braque, de la Fresnaye, and Guillaume Apollinaire among painters and poets of creative power have been severely wounded, but have returned to the field eager to continue the work they look on as the most important at present. . . . 'I am sorry for the man who has not seen this war,' writes Jean Le Roy, the poet."

I am sorry for the man who has not seen this war: Stevens felt himself such a man, and he worked to comprehend Jean Le Roy's experience. In October 1918 Carl Zigrosser, editor of *The Modern School*, organized a special issue "as a tribute to Paris." Along with drawings by Odilon Redon, Aristide Maillol, and André Derain, the issue included the essay on "Paris in Wartime" by the art critic Élie Faure, a tribute to Jean Le Roy (who had just died in combat) by Walter Pach, and Le Roy's own "Moment of Light"—illustrated by Redon and translated by Wallace Stevens. "With Jean Le Roy," wrote Pach, ". . . we come to one of the most grievous individual losses that France, or indeed the world has suffered in the war." Pach admired the poem for its expression of "that rising above the tyranny of things, that right of place in the mind which is indeed the mark of Le Roy's generation." Stevens was also known to lament the tyranny of things, but even as he preserved the dead soldier's vision in translation, the poem's final address to "my fellows" spoke an irony that overshadowed the mind's victory over things:

And are you not surprised to be the base
on which the eternal poising turns?
To know that, without you, the scale of lives
would sink upon death's pitty under-place?
And are you not surprised to be the very poles?

By the time Stevens translated these lines, he had already undermined such idealism in his own war poems, and he confessed to Zigrosser that he could not admire Le Roy's poem as much as Walter Pach did. Neither art nor vision saved Jean Le Roy from death, and Eugène Lemercier suffered the same fate, despite a similar scorn for the tyranny of things. The experience of the soldier taught Stevens two things: that death would invade the palaz of Hoon as it infiltrated Prospero's castle in "The Masque of the Red Death"; and that the effort to avert such an inevitable end is worth preserving. In "Lettres d'un Soldat" Stevens became ambitious enough to heed both imperatives.

Still, the posthumous voice of Le Roy, saying "I am sorry for the man who has not seen this war," confirmed Stevens's insecurities, and before he wrote these poems he sought firsthand experience of a soldier's life. After the sinking of the *Lusitania,* Wilson had declared that "there is such a thing as a man being too proud to fight," but events conspired to make that statement appear beside the point. Early in 1916 Germany reinstated submarine warfare, and in March an unarmed French vessel was sunk, causing Wilson to issue an ultimatum to the kaiser. At the same time, the United States was faced with the possibility of war with a politically volatile Mexico: to undermine the Mexican government, a revolutionary faction killed eighteen Americans at Santa Isabel and then raided Columbus, New Mexico, where seventeen Americans were killed. Wilson sent 12,000 troops into Mexico, and, though no war was declared, the signs of military development were everywhere. Stevens was traveling on an extended business trip. "The Mexican mess attracts great attention here," he wrote to his wife from the Minnesota Club in St. Paul. "Every morning there are squads of recruits drilling in the square which this club faces. I see them as I walk through on my way to the office. This is [a] capital place for young men and the recruits are husky fellows. I hope to see them in camp at Fort Snelling, but I have so much work to do that there is little time to spare." These drilling troops gave Stevens a new kind of contact with the war effort, unmediated by the printed page. Despite the workload, he found the time to visit Fort Snelling, an army post near Minneapolis, and a few months later he watched the troops drilling in Canada: "Toronto is full of soldiers. They wear uniforms that make boot-blacks look like wild-cats or bullocks or something savage, although, after all, they can't be such tremendous warriors. I hope they are better men than the Germans, at all events." As he idealized these soldiers, Stevens saw in their lives the urgency and authenticity his own seemed to lack, and visits to army camps became a standard part of his business schedule. A soldier seemed to represent the man that Stevens—as a poet of little things—feared he was not, and his need to confirm his masculinity by identifying with these men even overwhelmed the residual racism of his youth. When he watched African-American soldiers drilling in Johnson City, Tennessee, this was his response: "I want to cry and yell and jump ten feet in the air; and so far as I have been able to observe, it makes no difference whether the men are black or white. The noise when the train pulled out was intoxicating."

A year later, while Stevens was on a business trip in Wisconsin, the war hit closer to home, forcing him to recognize more clearly that it was the imminent threat of death that made these sights so exciting. Catharine Stevens, the poet's youngest sister, had been working with the Red Cross in France when she died suddenly of meningitis. "I am completely done up by the news of Catharine's death," Stevens wrote his wife. ". . . How horrible it is to think of the poor child fatally ill in a military hospital in an out-of-the-way place in a foreign country, probably perfectly aware of her helplessness and isolation!" Stevens had not seen his sister for years, and the only way he could grieve was to lose himself in the nation's wartime sorrow. He was involved in a particularly difficult and protracted case for the Hartford, and when the courts closed for Memorial Day, he took a long, solitary walk along the shore of Lake Michigan: "The lake was so calm that there was scarcely a sound of water to be heard. The air was clean and soft and warm." Only later in the day was Stevens able to vent his sorrow. Joining the crowds along the streets of Milwaukee, he watched the Memorial Day parade march past: "in my present state of mind on account of Catharine," he told his wife, the parade "affected me deeply. There was a group of women, war-mothers, each of whom carried a gold-star flag, which it was impossible to continue to look at." A few months later Stevens acquired a copy of the *Harvard College Class of 1901 War Records* so that he might discover the fates of old friends. And when Catharine Stevens's effects were shipped home, her journal revealed the horrors that awaited soldiers drilling in the camps of Minnesota, Tennessee, and Toronto.

Never as long as I live will I forget that ride along the Menin road. It was raining to be sure, and the mud was feet thick—our car was splashing along at a great clip. To the right, to the left of us, ahead of us and behind of us was nothing but shell-gutted fields—these holes now filled with water. By the side of the road, lying just where he fell I suppose, was the grave of some brave soldier—a bare white cross marked his grave. As we went on passing high piles of ammunition at either side of the road, and passing here and there a tank, we came to the dug-outs. It was here we got out of the machine, and too full for utterance we each wended our own particular way over this Flander's field. How gruesome it was. I kept wondering why I went on, and yet just ahead of me was another white cross. This time with an American helmet tied to it. I just had to go to it to see if I could read the name. As I came upon it I discovered that the mere bones and uniform were just scantly covered with earth, and the skull, hands and feet were plainly discernible, but no name could I see. As I turned from that I nearly fell over a boot out of which projected a long white bone—. Oh, how horrible— all about me lay these signs of human sacrifice—a skull, or a vertebra, and all about me as far as I could see was just so. Nothing to break the skyline except the charred tree trunks and a bit of barbed wire.

This was an experience Stevens did not share, despite his effort to know the war intimately. He was preoccupied with the soldier's experience and worked hard to understand it; his two sequences of war poems are only the obvious fruit of that effort. But a wartime anxiety—a civilian male's curiously displaced and unanchored anxiety—fills the poems of *Harmonium* at large.

Without downplaying the widespread effect of the war on either American culture or Stevens's development, however, it is important to recognize that like all historical turning points, this one was not sharply defined. Jackson Lears's careful description of the war's general effect also applies to Stevens's career in particular: "the twentieth century's 'revolution in manners and morals'" was "not an overnight result of post–World War I disillusionment but the outcome of gradual, almost imperceptible fits and starts of cultural change stretching back into the late nineteenth century." The American myth of the war as apocalypse and of the 1920s as the decade of the postwar "lost generation" dies hard—even though its illusions were apparent from the start. In the eyes of Stevens's friend Robert McAlmon, T. S. Eliot's reputation suffered a severe blow when he realized that much of his poetry "had been written before the war. . . . I knew his 'spirit' had not been created by war events." McAlmon's problem was that the sexual anxieties of "Prufrock" and *The Waste Land* now seemed to be a personal rather than a cultural affliction; historicizing such an anxiety as an inevitable wartime experience saved Eliot from the charge of having "unmanly" fears.

In many ways, the First World War and the fantasies it provoked were the perfect antidotes to what Ann Douglas has analyzed as the "feminization" of American culture that took place in the later years of the nineteenth century. But the urge for a life of action, manly and militant, predated the war. As Frank Lentricchia has demonstrated, the young Stevens often felt himself mired in a "feminine" conception of poetry. In this mood, he spurned poets of little things, longing for the great "man-poets" of the premodern past:

"Poetry and Manhood: Those who say poetry is now the peculiar province of women say so because ideas about poetry are effeminate." As Pound turned to the troubadours as a model for manly poetry, Stevens looked to Bliss Carman and Richard Hovey. Their *Songs from Vagabondia* (1894) extolled the bonds between men that "outlast art / And a woman's love"—men who "like Vikings" await the "grim, ungarlanded carouse." Stevens was still writing poems in the flyleaf of *Songs from Vagabondia* in 1907. Two years later, he offered this fantasy of war in a letter to Elsie Moll: "The trenches are dug, the guns are brought up, the regiments manouevre, the walls tumble. It is all visionary." During the First World War, when Stevens took time out from his business trips to watch drilling soldiers, he was attempting to assuage a longing that had tugged at him for years. But by the time he wrote the poems of *Harmonium*, the war had overshadowed the fantasies, and Stevens could no longer imagine comfortably a scene of wartime destruction. He had watched drilling soldiers, he had read the newspapers, but even his sister had confronted death and destruction he would never know.

Virginia Woolf remarked in *To the Lighthouse* that the war revived people's interest in poetry, and it is true that the war made poetry respectable by offering the large-scale role of "war poet" to sonnet-scribblers like Rupert Brooke. In the terms I have used to describe Stevens's post-Romantic predicament, the war shook poets out of a diminished aesthetic once and for all. Like Pound, poets may have felt dissatisfied with the aesthetic before the war; like Stevens, they may have toyed with the idea of a masculine, militaristic poetry: but for those who felt the real pressure of the Great War, new ambitions were kindled—and prewar fantasies of militarism (however much they prepared for war poetry) were revealed as grossly inadequate to historical reality. The poems of Bliss Carman, despite their pretensions, had no room for Catharine Stevens's journals, and neither did "Carnet de Voyage." The poems of *Harmonium* were part of an effort to make sense of a world that to Stevens seemed more threatening than ever before.

5

Writing War Poetry

Even as the war aroused Pound's ambitions and he began planning the *Cantos,* he lamented in "1915: February" that the war "will make me no sagas." The question was not only whether this modern war would support epic heroism but whether the modern war poet could adapt his lyric sensibility to an epic subject. Although he did not feel the conflict of love poetry and war poetry, lyric and epic, so acutely as Pound did, Stevens's "Phases" reveals a similar hostility toward poets who would turn the Great War into fodder for poetry.

> The crisp, sonorous epics
> Mongered after every scene.
> Sluggards must be quickened! Screen,
>
> No more, the shape of false Confusion.
> Bare his breast and draw the flood
> Of all his Babylonian blood.

"Phases" is a poem at war with itself, for at the same time that Stevens disparages the "sonorous epics" he locates his poem in an epic tradition. Throughout, the sequence reveals what in "Le Monocle de mon Oncle" he would call "an ancient aspect touching a new mind." Two parts of "Phases" offer simple versions of what Eliot would do more successfully in "Sweeney Among the Nightingales" a few years later: first, the modern soldier's lot is not "Like Agamemnon's story. / Only, an eyeball in the mud"; later, a fallen soldier feels "the pride / Of Agamemnon / When he died." Aside from these allusions, Stevens's epic ambitions are revealed more subtly and importantly when "Phases" is compared with Du Bellay's "Sonnet from the Book of Regrets," which Stevens translated in 1909. Du Bellay based his poem on the fifth book of the *Odyssey*, when Odysseus is waylaid on Calypso's island, longing to see the hearth-smoke rising above his home: "When shall I see once more, alas, the smokey haze / Rise from the chimneys of my little town." Five years after he translated these lines, Stevens appropriated Du Bellay's Homeric image in "Belgian Farm, October, 1914," the finest poem in "Phases": "The vaguest line of smoke, (a year ago), / Wavered in evening air, above the roof." But Stevens is unable to offer his soldier even Odysseus's small consolation. In "Phases" the hearth-smoke does not survive Germany's invasion of Belgium in August 1914, and Stevens equates the smoke with the shadowy arm of "some Old Man of the chimney" who no longer watches over the earth.

> Now, soldiers, hear me: mark this very breeze,
> That blows about in such a hopeless way,
> Mumbling and musing like the most forlorn.
> It is that Old Man, lost among the trees.

"Phases" reveals its epic dimension in its longing for the *nostos*, the homecoming, but for Stevens the postwar world will never be the same. In the tenth section of "Phases," the one poem of the sequence that most recalls the gaudiness of "Carnet de Voyage," he explains that "Peace means long, delicious valleys, / In the mode of Claude Lorraine." But even in the lushness of peacetime we remain pilgrims, far from home; although these lines look forward to "all things, as before," the opening line of the eleventh and final section of "Phases" revises that easy conclusion by pointing out that even after war ends, "war has no haunt except the heart." The very verse of "Phases" embodies this lesson: before the war, Stevens was able to write the lovely music of "Carnet de Voyage," and he is able to invoke it for a moment in the tenth section of "Phases"; but the sequence of war poems begins and ends in a world deaf to such inconsequential songs.

Given these tentative movements toward a poetry that encompasses a public world, why then did Stevens simultaneously need to condemn the "sonorous epics"? Like Pound, Stevens was talking to himself as he chastised other poets, and his conflicting attitudes reveal a more personal question: How does one write a poem that encompasses a public world, the epic, without surrendering completely the inner world of the self, the lyric voice? John Jay Chapman had offered some advice concerning this problem, and "The Snow Man" dramatizes the self's necessary surrender to reality's imperative. But even if such abnegation were utterly possible, asks Stevens, could a work of art (*qua* work of art) participate in politics and still remain a work of art? As Richard Poirier has pointed out, this characteristically American effort to "write off" the self is paradoxical, since it is precipitated by an act of will that affirms selfhood; the effort to arrive at the "thing itself" is equally paradoxical, since "the very idea of the 'thing itself' is a great poetic invention." Stevens illustrates this lesson in "Nuances on a Theme by Williams" when, elaborating Williams's call for the ancient star to "shine alone in the sunrise," he undermines the call with the vigor of his own language: "Shine alone, shine nakedly, shine like bronze, / that reflects neither my face nor any inner part / of my being." Or as Stevens would put it many years later in "The Plain Sense of Things," "the absence of the imagination had / Itself to be imagined." In less esoterically developed ways, Stevens became aware of these issues by trying to overthrow his diminished aesthetic and address the war. "Phases" dramatized his ambivalent desire for an ambitious poetry of soldiers and civilians (hence Stevens's interest in the *nostos*, when soldiers and civilians meet). Concerned about the status of the poet's self, he focused instead on the soldier's selfhood, revealing that this "public" man confronts the same dichotomies as the "private" poet.

The second poem in the sequence offers a view of the poet's private world seen through the eyes of passing soldiers: "They sit idly there, / They sip the glass." Soon this inner world, untouched by historical events, is transformed into a common, public place when compared with the even more insulated inner world of the soldier on the battlefield. Paradoxically, in the fourth poem of "Phases" it is the public call of the military bugle that gives soldiers "wings that bore / To where our comfort was"—a world even more private than the artist's cafe.

> Arabesques of candle beams,
> Winding
> Through our heavy dreams.

In "Phases" the master of this internalized world of imaginative fullness is not the poet but the soldier; in the ninth poem, the common run of life "never came / Near" the soldiers' "mysteries of flame." And the inevitable conclusion of the sequence is, again, that "war has no haunt except the heart." Unlike Stevens's Harvard sonnets, "Phases" complicates the opposition of public and private worlds and ultimately criticizes the terms of their opposition. Having begun "Phases" by establishing a duality between public and private, epic and lyric, Stevens ends by asserting that to understand war we need to "peer inward, with the spirit's lamp, / Look deep."

That was one way to retain the poet's selfhood while writing political poetry—like Donald Evans, the poet could assert that the political world is contained within an even more private place. Yet one more nagging question remained: this strategy, far from making public events available to poets, could be nothing more than the poet's self-serving vindication of his lack of knowledge of political events; indeed, war may have no haunt but the heart, but Stevens had no direct experience of war, as much as the experience of the soldier fascinated him from afar. In "Phases" Stevens tries to recapture Whitman's confidence, expressed best in "Adieu to a Soldier," that the poet and the soldier "shared" the "rude campaigning" in a time "all fill'd / With war and war's expression." Such an affirmative commitment to "weightier battles" eluded Stevens, and, given his situation, for good reasons. "Who indeed knows how best to think about victims?" asks the political philosopher Judith Shklar, writing on the difficulty of appropriating public disasters as images for personal pain. A poet like Sylvia Plath does just that to jarring effect. But the young Stevens, even as he pushed beyond the limits of "Carnet de Voyage," wondered if he had the poetic (or human) capacity to match his ambition. "I am sorry for the man who has not seen this war," said the posthumous voice of Jean Le Roy, confirming Stevens's own insecurities. And as much as Stevens felt a Whitmanian imperative to give expression to those weightier battles, he also felt the injunction Emerson appended to such a demand: "The one thing not to be forgiven to intellectual persons is, not to know their own task." More important for Stevens's career than the success of his ambition to address the world outside the self were the difficulties he encountered trying to do so. His lifelong musings on the intricacies of epistemology were given their first rigorous test by the war, a phenomenon that stubbornly resisted any kind of internalization.

Consider in this light a representative early poem, "Lunar Paraphrase," written in 1917 but collected in the second edition of *Harmonium*.

The moon is the mother of pathos and pity.

When, at the wearier end of November,
Her old light moves along the branches,
Feebly, slowly, depending upon them;
When the body of Jesus hangs in a pallor,
Humanly near, and the figure of Mary,
Touched on by hoar-frost, shrinks in a shelter
Made by the leaves, that have rotted and fallen;
When over the houses, a golden illusion
Brings back an earlier season of quiet
And quieting dreams in the sleepers in darkness—

The moon is the mother of pathos and pity.

Here are all the hallmarks of *Harmonium*, especially visible in what is one of the less remarkable poems of the volume: the latent but ever-present threat of death, and the inability of Christian belief to account for it; the reduction of the gods themselves to beings "humanly near"; the imagination's moonlight transforming the "wearier end" of bare reality; a temporal reversal in which a belated world, "rotted and fallen," is saved by an older light that paradoxically restores an even "earlier season of quiet." Since "Lunar Paraphrase" so stresses the transformation of historical reality (the paraphrase of historical particulars by the universalizing moonlight), it would be difficult to locate the poem itself historically were it not for the fact that "Lunar Paraphrase" began its life as a war poem. Although it was not published until 1931, the poem was originally the seventh section of "Lettres d'un Soldat"; when Harriet Monroe and Stevens sifted through this sequence, they cut this poem. The historical circumstances surrounding the gestation of "Lunar Paraphrase" reinforce the retrospective comment Stevens made about *Harmonium* in a 1935 letter to Ronald Lane Latimer: "I wonder whether, if you were to suggest any particular poem, I could not find an actual background for you. I have been going to Florida for twenty years, and all of the Florida poems have actual backgrounds. The real world seen by imaginative man may very well seem like an imaginative construction."

The "actual background" for "Lunar Paraphrase" came from a letter the young French painter Eugène Lemercier wrote to his mother from the trenches early in the war.

Yesterday a terrific wind tore to pieces a veil of clouds which were hanging low and they got caught on the top of the hills. Perhaps the background of my H. picture may give you a feeble idea of what I saw. But how much more majestic and full of life was the emotion I felt when I saw the reality. These hills and valleys pass by turns from shadow to light, sometimes coming out very clearly and then again appearing somewhat veiled, depending on how much or how little the mist uncovers them. High up in the sky are big, blue holes fringed with light.

Such were some of the beauties of yesterday. What can I tell thee of the preceding evenings when the moon reflected on the roads the embroidery made by the bare branches of the trees, the pathetic outlines of the calvaries, and the shadows of houses which we know to be only heaps of ruins but which the obscurity of the night presents as if peace had built them up again?

It is easy to understand why Stevens found Lemercier's meditations attractive: the sense of "reality" emerging from the clouds coupled with the suggestion that the actual landscape might be visualized from a painting; the revealing power of sunlight contrasted with the intricate deceptions of moonlight; and—most important for reading "Lunar Paraphrase"—the sense that these imaginative transformations are motivated by historical urgency, that a lunar paraphrase of the world is not frivolous but a desperate illusion that fades away to reveal landscapes ruined by war, houses emptied by death. At large, the poems of *Harmonium* teeter on the edge of this wartime vision of loss.

Stevens composed "Lettres d'un Soldat" during the summer of 1917, just after the United States entered the war, increasing its citizens' interest and stake in the fighting. As every reader of "Lettres" has noticed, Lemercier's letters gave Stevens what "Phases" had lacked: a firmer sense of the "true subject" of the war. The letters do provide a striking portrayal of a soldier's life in the trenches; but more important for Stevens, as the passage that inspired "Lunar Paraphrase" suggests, the letters dwell not only on the brute reality of the war but on the difficulty of representing it. Consequently, they gave Stevens a way to extend the meditation on the relationship of the private self and the public reality that he had begun in "Phases."

Early in his letters Lemercier voices the doubt that had haunted Stevens throughout "Phases": "You do not know the lesson taught by him who falls. I do." Unlike Stevens, Lemercier experienced the war firsthand; yet like Stevens, he felt that the reality of the war surpassed any conceivable product of the private imagination. Soon after he arrived at the front, Lemercier read an essay by Maurice Barrès that expressed his feelings "exactly": Barrès counseled poets to "abandon your song, even if it be in the midst of a strophe and however exactly it reflects your soul. Even say a hasty good-bye to your heart of yesterday, for when you come back from the Rhine, you will have mounted so high and on such strong wings that you will surpass all your dreams." Lemercier himself felt the irrelevance of the private, imaginative world when he told his mother that at night he finds himself "back in my *Arabian Nights* days," building "all sorts of castles" and furnishing "them with recollections of the past." But upon awakening, he was greeted by a world that "surpasses all our fancies of the night before." Lemercier's letters contributed to Stevens's imagining of the war not only by offering accounts of the fighting but by confirming Stevens's own doubts about the power of imagination.

Like "Phases," Lemercier's letters also question this opposition of public reality and private imagination. The fact that Lemercier only understood his feelings by reading Barrès's essay complicates the issue, and a few months later he confessed that he reread the article and found it "out of tune with the spirit of the moment." Shortly before his death, Lemercier realized that what he thought of as the brutally "other" world of the war was in fact available to him because of (not in spite of) the power of the self: "What I had kept about me of my own individuality was a certain visual perceptiveness

that caused me to register the setting of things that dramatized itself 'artisti-
cally' as in any stage-management." Lemercier had mounted E. H. Gom-
brich's hobby horse, recognizing that his descriptions of experienced reality
were mediated by previous representations. His painter's eye described the
landscape around him as that of Corot, Bruegel, and Dürer, and at one particularly revealing point he wrote that he had "lived in a picture of my
beloved primitives." Throughout, his letters vacillate between a faith that love
and beauty triumph "over every kind of violence" and a confrontation with
unalterable reality: "From time to time the pickaxe strikes some poor dead
body which the war thus torments, even in his humble grave." Not coinci-
dentally, Stevens used both these passages as the starting point for poems in
his own "Lettres d'un Soldat."

What is most striking about Stevens's war poems, however, is that they
tilt the scales in this balance, favoring the brute otherness of historical reality
far more than Lemercier does. The danger Stevens wanted to avoid, as he
would disclose in "Extracts from Addresses to the Academy of Fine Ideas"
(1940), is the easy aestheticization or internalization of experience; he did not
want to be the "Secretary for Porcelain" who "equates ten thousand deaths"
with "a single well-tempered apricot." Stevens's "Lettres d'un Soldat" begins,
consequently, by reversing the conclusion of "Phases": "No introspective
chaos," insists Stevens, once again wary of his own admonition to "peer
inward" to find war's haunt. As the sequence progresses, Stevens uses as epi-
graphs Lemercier's more confident assertions of the power of imagination to
overcome the sheer brutality of experience—but the poems that follow turn
ironically on Lemercier's letters. When Lemercier wrote, "Never before has
the majesty of night brought me so much consolation as in the midst of these
trials. Sparkling Venus is my friend," Stevens responded in the second poem
of "Lettres" that "multiform beauty" was merely "sinking in night wind, /
Quick to be gone." The third poem quotes an even more confident Lemercier
("What you must accustom yourself to is to recognize love and beauty triumphant over every kind of violence") and responds with a grotesque street
scene in which a man who literally bears the burden of violence tries to force
his way through a crowd of blind men.

> Am I to pick my way
> Through these crickets?—
> I, that have a head
> In the bag
> Slung over my shoulder?
> I have secrets

>   That prick
>   Like a heart full of pins.

Overturning Lemercier, the poem reads like a parody of the second poem in "Phases": now the civilians in the café are literally blind, content that beauty triumphs over violence, while the soldier is locked in a much more deeply private world, trapped by the secret knowledge of death he carries on his back. The blind men are like Donald Evans, who suggested that the war could be won by an army of aesthetes if their cravats were tied stylishly enough—or the young Jean Le Roy, who too quickly praised the mind's power to overcome the tyranny of things.

When Lemercier confessed that he had "a firm hope and a real confidence in eternal justice, whatever may be the surprise that this eternal justice sometimes causes in us because of our preconceived human idea of what it should be," Stevens suggested in the sixth part of "Lettres d'un Soldat" ("The Surprises of the Superhuman") that "somehow the brave dicta of its kings / Make more awry our faulty human things." And in "Negation," ninth in the sequence, he offered a more caustic rebuke of Lemercier's belief that "we must confide in an impersonal justice which is independent of all human influence, and have faith in useful and harmonious destiny notwithstanding the horrible form which it seems to assume at the present moment."

>   Hi! The creator too is blind,
>   Struggling toward his harmonious whole,
>   Rejecting intermediate parts,
>   Horrors and falsities and wrongs.

Once again Stevens declares his distance from the Secretaries for Porcelain who believe a world at war can be cured by words alone. While in the third poem of "Lettres" Stevens presented the blind men who shun the burden of death, here the creator (original or artistic) is also blind to the horror of brief lives. As Margaret Peterson has pointed out, this poem almost sounds like a précis of William James's attacks on idealistic monism, but if we want to idealize the poem itself a little less, we can see it as another expression of a poet's troubled diffidence in the face of unalterable reality. The war called for epics, but Stevens was unwilling to write a poem so ambitious that it disregarded the world's particulars. Yet "Negation" itself is not a diffident poem; its turn on Lemercier (or idealism in general) is stern. The poem looks forward to the great anthology pieces of *Harmonium*, where Stevens would paradoxically make major statements by defending the prudence of a diminished aesthetic. And like "Lunar Paraphrase," both "The Surprises of the Superhuman" and

"Negation" were added to *Harmonium* in 1931, and they fit comfortably in that context: there, like many other poems, they look like deft expressions of Jamesian pragmatism and do not betray their birth as war poems. That Stevens could so easily fit these war poems into *Harmonium* should alert us to the historical engagement of the volume at large.

In the spring of 1918, on the same business trip during which he marveled at the soldiers in Chattanooga and Johnson City, Stevens stopped in Washington, D.C. There, as he remembered in a 1944 letter to Hi Simons, he strolled around the terraces of the Capitol; "unreal enough at the right moment," the marble terraces, at that particular moment apparently irrelevant to a national war, became for Stevens "completely unreal" and "more or less somnambulistic." From this experience grew the poem "Anecdote of Canna," in which "X," Stevens told Simons, stood for Woodrow Wilson.

> Huge are the canna in the dreams of
> X, the mighty thought, the mighty man.
> They fill the terrace of his capitol.
>
> His thought sleeps not. Yet thought that wakes
> In sleep may never meet another thought
> Or thing. . . . Now day-break comes . . .
>
> X promenades the dewy stones,
> Observes the canna with a clinging eye,
> Observes and then continues to observe.

An elaboration of the argument of the war poems "The Surprises of the Superhuman" and "Negation," these lines undermine the authority not of spiritual but of political omnipotence. The canna are huge because they are filtered through the thoughts of the "mighty man"; the capitol itself is "his" because it exists only in his dream of the world; and his thoughts ramble unchallenged because in this private world, one thought meets only itself, not "another thought / Or thing."

By the spring of 1918, Stevens's view of the president's detachment was a commonplace. From the beginning of the war, Wilson was the aristocratic man of principle; in 1914 Americans accepted his message that it was "a war with which we have nothing to do." But after the *Lusitania* was sunk, Wilson's declaration that America was "too proud to fight" sounded thin. In 1916, when Wilson finally dispatched troops to Mexico, Stevens himself responded this way: "That's a sad business down there. It seems to me that the president ought never to have sent the army into Mexico, or, if he did, he ought to have declared war simultaneously. He has an unfortunate ease in getting into messes. A good fright would do him good. . . . He is too much a politician." Even when asking Congress to declare war on Germany, Wilson remained the idealist, calling young men to fight "for a universal dominion by such a concert of free peoples as shall bring peace and safety to all nations and make the world itself at last free." Stevens agreed with John Maynard Keynes, who pictured Wilson at Versailles as a "blind and deaf Don Quixote."

Writing these poems of unchecked idealism, Stevens did not believe that human beings could achieve an utterly unmediated perception of their world. Lemercier was able to describe his experience so fruitfully because his inner eye lingered on the canvases of Dürer and Bruegel; but the same impulse taken too far allowed him to indulge in the idealistic excesses Stevens mocked in "Negation." In the final poem of "Lettres d'un Soldat" Stevens worked from a letter in which Lemercier witnesses the breakdown of all his own talk about the power of ethereal beauty to overcome earthly horror: "From time to time the pickaxe strikes some poor dead body which war thus torments, even in his humble grave." Stevens's poem begins by rejecting old metaphors for death as "symbols of sentiment" that have no power over such a brutally materialistic confrontation with mortality: "Death was a reaper with sickle and stone. . . . Or Death was a rider beating his horse." Then he instructs the "Men of the line" to "take this new phrase / Of the truth of Death." The soldiers know the phrase, but the poet will not utter it; whatever it is, the new metaphor will be punctured by the same pickaxe that strikes the dead. Stevens knew that speaking in metaphor is inevitable, but he also recognized (like Frost) that the most important thing about metaphors is that they break down. "War is a realist," said Emerson, "shatters everything flimsy & shifty, sets aside all false issues, & breaks through all that is not as real as itself." Stevens knew that statement mattered because of his experience of war—and because of his lack of it.

Many of the poems of *Harmonium* may be placed on a continuum whose extremes are marked by the naive idealism of "Negation" and the untransformable reality of the soldier's corpse—or, to put it in more familiar terms, the Palaz of Hoon and the Snow Man. "The Bird With the Coppery, Keen Claws" (1921) offers Stevens's sharpest condemnation of an unbreakable metaphor. This "parakeet of parakeets" (which would be recast as "The Rabbit as King of the Ghosts" in the 1930s) is Stevens's final caricature of the soldier who felt that beauty triumphed over death, the poet who thought Germany could be conquered by a couturier, the president who waged a war using the spirit of American idealism for ammunition: he is blind, the perfected specimen of his species (in this case a parakeet, more commonly found in cages than forests—only the "rudiments" of the tropics are around him); he is motionless, dry, still (in both senses of the word), and sublimely self-referential, "His tip a drop of water full of storms"; most important, he is pure intellect, applying self-begotten laws upon a world he cannot see.

> But though the turbulent tinges undulate
> As his pure intellect applies its laws,
> He moves not on his coppery, keen claws.
>
> He munches a dry shell while he exerts
> His will, yet never ceases, perfect cock,
> To flare, in the sun-pallor of his rock.

If we remember that this parakeet of parakeets is caged and that his laws, however nobly pronounced, are not likely to have much effect on the world that moves on with or without him, then the poem loses much of its force. But Stevens witnessed the effects of such detachment in the political struggles of his time. More than twenty years after he wrote "The Bird With the Coppery, Keen Claws," Stevens read Nicola Chiaromonte's essay "Croce and Italian Liberalism" in the June 1944 issue of *Politics* (founded by Dwight Macdonald after he left the *Partisan Review*, objecting to Philip Rahv's support for the Allied forces in the Second World War). In these sentences, copied into his commonplace book, Stevens saw an analysis of the dangers of the detached intellect that he had dramatized in poems written during the First World War: "a small minority . . . was living, . . . rearing intellectual structures . . . without any real connection with and without any real care for the life, the toil, the feelings and the mentality of the enormous majority of their fellow men; actually, without any real care for each other. And there, in that compact and dumb ignorance, were the roots of their frightful unreality."

An awareness of the frightful unreality that may arise from a poetry that tries to be political is what kept Stevens's ambitions circumscribed. In contrast to Stevens, Chiaromonte's words help to describe Pound, who would begin to insist during the First World War that "all values ultimately come from our judicial sentences." If the First World War gave a major subject to Stevens as it did to Pound, forcing him out of the diminished aesthetic of "Carnet de Voyage" to take on more pressing questions concerning the relationship of poetic imagination and political reality, Stevens's new-found ambitions did not obscure the inherent limitations of his craft. The potential trouble with overturning a diminished aesthetic is that the mundane particulars which that aesthetic embraces will be lost in a vision of epic proportion. In "Reinforcements," an uncollected poem of 1918, Marianne Moore was adamant that the war effort "is not to / Be exalted into epic grandeur." Because she felt that to emphasize the war's grandeur was to become implicated in its horrors, she resisted the call of epic ambition: "The words of the Greeks / Ring in our ears, but they are vain in comparison with a sight like this." Poems focused on the minute, the domestic (and on the vast worlds contained within those tiny spaces) were Moore's political response to the First World War.

As much as the war kindled grand ambition in modern poets, it also made Stevens even more painfully aware of the measure of little things; it made him preserve part of the diffidence he admired in the young Keats. Part of the task of writing war poetry was to remain painfully aware of the limits of his experience of war. In "Meditation" (1917) Stevens asked, "What is it that I think of, truly?"

> The lines of blackberry bushes,
> The design of leaves—
> Neither sky nor earth
> Express themselves before me . . .
> Bossuet did not preach at the funerals
> Of puppets.

These lines nearly constitute a manifesto, for in rejecting an ambitious poetry of sky and earth, the poem does not condescend to the utterly transient and particular beauty of the veined leaves of blackberry bushes. Stevens read Jacques-Bénigne Bossuet's *Lettres spirituelles* as early as 1903, and Bossuet's famous funeral orations revealed the grandeur of the merely mortal. Stevens painted a puppet's life in "Gray Room," a poem originally paired with "Meditation," but he knew that the merest sign of death ("The leaf that has fallen from the branches of the forsythia") would make even a puppet's heart beat furiously. In all its Keatsian opulence, "Sunday Morning" tells this story on a grander scale. Yet as I have suggested, it was not Bossuet or Keats alone who made Stevens write this mythology of modern death. Stevens was troubled by the willing death of thousands, and his poem grew from voices like Lemercier's, saying that "the death of the soldier is almost a natural thing."

6

The Fellowship of
Men that Perish

Paradoxically, one way to witness the war's presence in Stevens's early poems of the earth is to notice how much of the argument of "Sunday Morning" or "Peter Quince at the Clavier" is latent in Stevens's prewar letters and journals. It would seem natural that Stevens would have penned "Sunday Morning" immediately after this meditation of May 2, 1909.

To-day I have been roaming about town. In the morning I walked down-town—stopping once to watch three flocks of pigeons circling in the sky. I dropped into St. John's chapel an hour before the service and sat in the last pew and looked around. It happens that last night at the Library I read a life of Jesus and I was interested to see what symbols of that life appeared in the chapel. I think there were none at all excepting the gold cross on the altar. When you compare that poverty with the wealth of symbols, of remembrances, that were created and revered in times past, you appreciate the change that has come over the church.... I do not wonder that the church is so largely a relic. Its vitality depended on its association with Palestine, so to speak.

One would like to know whose life of Jesus Stevens was reading (Pound was reading Renan's at about the same time) so that his own thoughts could be anchored more firmly in theological modernism; his redefinition of Jesus' immortality in "Sunday Morning" would appear to have grown from his response to Strauss or Harnack or Renan: "People doubt the existence of Jesus—at least, they doubt incidents of his life, such as, say, the Ascension into Heaven after his death. But I do not understand that they deny God." Even more striking than the way this early meditation anticipates the sub-

65

stance of "Sunday Morning" is the way its opening sentence forecasts the poem's final Keatsian tableau: "three flocks of pigeons circling in the sky." It seems that by 1909 Stevens had most of his intellectual equipment in place, and though it is tempting to see his early prose as the springboard for the poetry, I think we need to ask why "Sunday Morning" did not come into the world in 1909—especially when we recall that the poems of "The Little June Book" recognize a fallen world of death only as something to be transcended.

In "Our Attitude Towards Death" (1915) Freud predicted that the war would sweep away civilized people's conventional treatment of death: "Death will no longer be denied; we are forced to believe in him. People really are dying, and now not one by one, but many at a time, often ten thousand in a single day. Nor is it any longer an accident. To be sure, it still seems a matter of chance whether a particular bullet hits this man or that; but the survivor may easily be hit by another bullet; and the accumulation puts an end to the impression of accident." As Freud surmised, the unprecedented slaughter of the First World War put an end to what Ann Douglas has more recently called the nineteenth century's "domestication of death." To take only one example from many, Elizabeth Stuart Phelps's best-selling novels, *The Gates Ajar* (1868) and its sequels of the 1880s, strongly denied that death was a foreign (and therefore to be feared) state of being. The protagonist of *Beyond the Gates*, one of the sequels, finds in heaven "much of the familiar furniture of a modest home"; her long-dead father has been waiting for her there and, upon greeting her, says how good it is to have "somebody to come home to." Stevens himself suggested the anxiety concealed behind this cozy vision of the afterlife when he remarked in "Three Academic Pieces" (1947), "what a ghastly situation it would be if the world of the dead was actually different from the world of the living."

Of course Stevens was no stranger to death before the First World War, but judging from his letters and journals, in which his father's death in 1911 is not mentioned, this loss seemed to elicit little grief. A year later, the death of his mother caused him to return to his journal—the pages he had originally titled "The Book of Doubts and Fears." These entries, lovely for the way Stevens avoids a direct emotional response in favor of quiet observation of his mother's house, end with the comment, "After all, 'gentle, delicate Death,' comes all the more gently in a familiar place warm with the affectionateness of pleasant memories." Seen in the larger sweep of his life, however, Stevens's earliest response to death begins to feel less lovely than creepy for its detachment—evidence of the implacable coldness that Stevens recognized in himself even as a boy of twelve. In sharp contrast to his journal entries on his mother's death stands this 1918 letter to Harriet Monroe.

I've had the blooming horrors, following my gossip about death, at your house. I have not known just what to do. I had hoped to set things right, personally; but find that I am not likely to see you in Chicago for some little time. Accordingly, so that you may not think I am unconscious of the thing, nor indifferent, I write this to let you know that I have been sincerely regretful and hope that you and your family will forgive me. The subject absorbs me, but that is no excuse: there are too many people in the world, vitally involved, to whom it is infinitely more than a thing to think of. One forgets this. I wish with all my heart that it had never occurred, even carelessly.

What happened to Stevens between 1912 and 1918 was what Freud predicted in "Our Attitude Towards Death." The journal entries of 1912 offer a portrait of an utterly domesticated death; Stevens's mother approached "her end . . . with the just expectation of re-union afterwards; and if there be a God, such as she believes in, the justness of her expectation will not be denied." Yet in 1918, for no personal reason, Stevens found himself absorbed in the subject of death. Judging by the uncharacteristic fervor of his letter to Monroe, it was not only his obsession but the fact that he had revealed it that gave him the blooming horrors. Stevens even recognized that his obsession was anchored to no direct contact with death, yet this self-consciousness only increased his anxiety. As Freud suggested, the great unknown reality of death could no longer be domesticated or denied, and the war unearthed a medieval horror of mortality. T. S. Eliot voiced a similar wartime anxiety when he confessed that the protracted suffering of his personal life seemed paltry when compared with the news in the daily paper: "Everyone's individual lives are so swallowed up in the one great tragedy, that one almost ceases to have personal experiences or emotions, and such as one has seem so unimportant!—where before it would have seemed interesting even to tell about a lunch of bread and cheese. It's only very dull people who feel they have 'more in their lives' now—other people have too much."

Like Stevens, Eliot became much obsessed by death during these years, and for both poets, their distance from the war was as important as their knowledge of it: that lack of a "vital involvement" with death made the longing for a soldier's active life more urgent and the pressure of death's penumbra more acute. "I am sorry for the man who has not seen this war," said Walter Pach's soldier; "You do not know the lesson taught by him who falls," said Eugène Lemercier. When Stevens opened his copy of the *Harvard College Class of 1901 War Records*, it told him that 337 of his Harvard colleagues had contributed to the war effort, but, more importantly, it told him that Wallace Stevens had done nothing. Even Lyman Ward, with whom Stevens had attempted to establish a law practice, had a brief entry in the book: "Applied for voluntary induction as a private into the Motor Transport Corps.

The application was granted, and I was admitted to the service on October 21, 1918, at Camp Johnston Florida, being ultimately commissioned 2d Lieutenant. . . . Before entering the service of the Motor Transport Corps I had organized and placed on a secure basis the Four Minute Men movement, and was its first chairman. After this task had been completed I became a member of the Legal Advisory Board. All of this work took many months of time to the exclusion of my profession." Many years later, after Ward's death, Stevens would remember him as a fine person who had no talent for making money; but Ward, unlike Stevens, had been willing to sacrifice his profession for a larger cause. And Catharine Stevens had been willing to sacrifice her life.

Like the nameless soldiers Stevens admired, Lyman Ward and Catharine Stevens were involved in the war as the poet was not, but the insurance man found his distanced anxieties mirrored in a business associate who visited Hartford in August 1914, just a week after the war began. Stevens reported that Heber Stryker "has been ill—no: nervous, sleepless, full of the war, and wanted to forget it." The cure for this anxiety was found in a Sunday afternoon walk through a Hartford cemetery. "On Sunday evening," Stevens told his wife, "we sat at the edge of their meadow until one o'clock in moonlight and dew." The antidote for an abstract and unanchored fear of death lay in a confrontation with the natural evidence of mortality. One wonders if they watched the undulation of a flock of pigeons, descending to darkness.

Faced with poems like "The Emperor of Ice-Cream," "Cortège for Rosenbloom," "Thirteen Ways of Looking at a Blackbird," or "Sunday Morning" itself, readers have often noticed that death infects the lovely world of *Harmonium*, that a consciousness of mortality keeps that world alive. But death does not enter *Harmonium* the way its shadow pierces the glass coach in the eleventh section of "Thirteen Ways of Looking at a Blackbird." For Stevens, such an invasion occurs only when we foolishly attempt to survive in something like a glass coach—the glassy essence of the mind—whose equipage itself reminds us of what we attempt to avert. Rather, death exists in the whole of *Harmonium* more as it does in "The Emperor of Ice-Cream": as an unavoidable aspect of being.

> If her horny feet protrude, they come
> To show how cold she is, and dumb.
> Let the lamp affix its beam.
> The only emperor is the emperor of ice-cream.

In his well-known essay "Wallace Stevens' Ice Cream," Richard Ellmann says that the point of this poem is the deliberate acceptance of death with life; but it seems to me that such acceptance is not easily won for Stevens.

During 1916 and 1917 Stevens wrote three plays, each of which simplifies the more esoteric matters of *Harmonium*. "Three Travelers Watch a Sunrise" centers on death: the primary stage prop is a corpse, around which the three Chinese travelers sit and offer their consolatory wisdom. The corpse does not, as in the final section of "Lettres d'un Soldat," force its unalterable material presence on these quiet observers; rather, they are able to explain it away by equating the corpse with a porcelain water bottle that may be "one thing to me / And one thing to another," just as "sunrise is multiplied . . . By the eyes that open on it." This is not the deliberate acceptance of death but the bland ignorance of its horror: the three travelers are all the Secretaries for Porcelain whom Stevens would name in "Extracts." The corpse was a young man who hanged himself in front of his lover, Anna. Although she dressed in Hoon's purple and wore gold earrings, "he wanted nothing. / He hanged himself in front of me." Stevens's sympathy lies not with the travelers, who sit for hours without even noticing the corpse; rather, it lies with Anna, who sits quietly through the night staring at the dead body of her lover—she "felt the evil." While the third traveler believes "There is a seclusion of porcelain / That humanity never invades," the second concludes that because of its seclusion, the court from which they came had knowledge of neither love nor wisdom.

> When the court knew beauty only,
> And in seclusion,
> It had neither love nor wisdom.
> These came through poverty
> And wretchedness,
> Through suffering and pity.
>   [*He pauses.*]
> It is the invasion of humanity
> That counts.

Poverty, wretchedness, suffering, pity. If the only emperor of *Harmonium* is the emperor of ice cream, he rules in consort with the corpse of the woman whose horny feet protrude when we attempt to cover her with her own embroidery. *Harmonium* is the second book of doubts and fears that Stevens wrote. Freud said in his essay that the new awareness of mortality aroused by the war would make life more "interesting again; it has regained its full significance." Or as Stevens explained in lines from "From the Journal of Crispin" I quoted earlier, "poems are transmutations of plain shops, / By aid of starlight, distance, wind, war, death."

Of all the poems of *Harmonium*, Harold Bloom has called "The Death of a Soldier" the first "emergence of the poet's most characteristic voice."

Life contracts and death is expected,
As in a season of autumn.
The soldier falls.

He does not become a three-days personage,
Imposing his separation,
Calling for pomp.

Death is absolute and without memorial,
As in a season of autumn,
When the wind stops,

When the wind stops and, over the heavens,
The clouds go, nevertheless,
In their direction.

Here indeed is an early manifestation of Stevens the reductionist. As a poem about death, these lines call for no pity; they call for no metaphor and little meaning. The dead soldier does not partake of the grandeur of Jesus' rebirth; the death calls for no pomp, in either the rituals of culture or the gaudiness of language. Even the one rather weak metaphor offered for the death ("As in a season of autumn") is protracted into meaninglessness when it is repeated in the third tercet, not to enlarge the single death by locating it in a natural cycle, but to reveal that this seasonal decline is indifferent to human sorrow. In "The Need of Being Versed in Country Things" Frost says that one would need to work hard "not to believe the phoebes wept" at the charred remains of a house; but Frost also shows those birds rejoicing "in the nest they kept," humanizing the birds who have no human values. More stringent still, Stevens offers even less consolation, causing Bloom to remark that "the human in us demands more of a poem, for us, and where *pathos* is so excluded a death-in-life comes which is more than that of the poem's shaper, speaker, reader than it could have been of the fictive soldier before he fell."

Stevens's poem is this stern because he is writing not about the death of his mother, say, but the death of the soldier—and not an unambiguously "fictive" soldier but Eugène Lemercier. Although "The Death of a Soldier" nestles comfortably among the other fictive musings of *Harmonium*, it is, like "Negation" or "Lunar Paraphrase," a poem that began its life as part of "Lettres d'un Soldat." And its utter bareness derives from the fact that Stevens was writing not about natural death (the death of a loved one that, however terrible, can be accepted in its inevitability) but about a new kind of unnatural death, the daily death of thousands of soldiers on French battlefields. In "Extracts from Addresses to the Academy of Fine Ideas" Stevens would codify this opposition between good and evil death, between the mass death of war and the individual death of a loved one.

It is death
That is ten thousand deaths and evil death.
Be tranquil in your wounds. It is good death
That puts an end to evil death and dies.

I have already spoken of the thirteenth and final poem in "Lettres" and of its rejection of all previous metaphors in the face of the unalterable presence of death, a pickaxe striking a soldier's buried corpse. Eleventh in the sequence, "The Death of a Soldier" shows Stevens resisting new metaphors. He used as its epigraph the final sentence from this passage in Lemercier's letters: "how harmonious death is in the ground, and how much more genial it is to see the body returning to mother earth than to see it the victim of the human paltriness of our conventional funeral ceremonies. But yesterday I would have felt that those poor abandoned dead were wronged, yet now, after attending a few hours ago, the formal burial of an officer, I am convinced that nature has a more tender pity for her children than has man. Yes, indeed, the death of a soldier is almost a natural thing." Since it looks forward to the rejection of the conventional pomp of funerals in "Cortège for Rosenbloom" and "The Emperor of Ice-Cream," this passage probably seemed honest to Stevens. But he could not agree that nature has "more tender pity" for the dead: Lemercier says that the death of the soldier is almost a natural thing, and Stevens's poem, with its manipulation of the seasonal metaphor, opens up the trouble latent in the *almost*.

Lemercier's mood was not always that of what Stevens called the "vague idealist." Beginning with the sensibility of Jean Le Roy's "Moment of Light" or the travelers of Stevens's own play, Lemercier progresses in his letters from a sorrow easily consoled by faith in a Christian afterlife to a recognition of the utter materiality of death that even nature cannot dignify. Stevens's sequence of poems follows the same trajectory, and the stark vision of "The Death of the Soldier" is closer to the following passage from Lemercier's letters than to the one Stevens chose for his epigraph: "nature is indifferent to all that we are doing. The dead will not stop the coming of spring." Given his growing skepticism, it is not surprising that Lemercier sat in the trenches reading what Stevens had absorbed in 1909: nineteenth-century challenges to the ahistoricity of Christian doctrine. Somehow Lemercier obtained an issue of the *Revue des deux mondes* from 1886, where he found Renan's essay "The Origins of the Bible." A fashionably skeptical Lemercier told his mother that the Scriptures owe their "beautiful and poetic philosophy" to "their affiliation with the old philosophies": "You get the impression that all religions, as they succeed one another, hand down the same stock of symbols, to which our ever young and poetic humanity gives new life each time."

These letters occupy the same moment in intellectual history as "Sunday Morning," but even if Stevens first read Lemercier when the letters appeared in the August 1915 issue of the *Revue de Paris*, these meditations on nature, death, and divinity could not have found their way into Stevens's poem; "Sunday Morning" was complete by June. Juxtaposing these texts nevertheless exposes the historicity of "Sunday Morning" itself and emphasizes that for Stevens, as for Lemercier, a wartime consciousness of death gave the higher criticism's challenge to Christianity an urgency that demanded a response as never before: If death is no longer explained by the consolation of an afterlife, how do the survivors of mass death carry on? The answer Stevens offered to this question in "Sunday Morning" is suggested by a letter from the front that Walter Pach quoted in "Universality in Art": "This life has an irresistable attraction for any man who has once tasted it; everything back of the fighting line seems to you mean and miserable; the nearness of death gives a powerful savor to life and makes you enjoy every aspect of it." The wisdom of "Sunday Morning," in other words, is as close to a soldier's fate as Stevens could get.

Although "The Death of the Soldier" was written two years after "Sunday Morning," there are (as Robert Buttel first noticed) important continuities between "Sunday Morning" and "Phases," the 1914 sequence of war poems—the only poems, barring a few minor pieces, that stand between "Sunday Morning" and "The Little June Book." Recall that "Phases" begins by declaring that "There was [a] heaven" before the war; in antique language that both mocks and eulogizes the heaven that has been lost, the fourth stanza of "Sunday Morning" takes this postwar condition for granted.

> There is not any haunt of prophecy,
> Nor any old chimera of the grave,
> Neither the golden underground, nor isle
> Melodious, where spirits gat them home,
> Nor visionary south, nor cloudy palm
> Remote on heaven's hill, that has endured
> As April's green endures; or will endure
> Like her remembrance of awakened birds,
> Or her desire for June and evening, tipped
> By the consummation of the swallow's wings.

By contrasting the permanence of April's green with the ephemerality of any absolute mythology of death, Christian or pagan, however, Stevens begs the question raised by both Lemercier and "The Death of a Soldier": Do we fall for an even thinner prophecy when we accept nature's apparent benevolence as consolation for our human demise? The second section of "Phases" approached that question with its portrait of the café-dwellers attempting to remain aloof from the soldier's knowledge of death; for them, "The season grieves. / It was silver once, / And green with leaves." The opening stanza of "Sunday Morning" is marked by the same tension between an uneasy enclave (like the unsullied court described in "Three Travelers Watch a Sunrise") and an impending invasion of suffering and wretchedness. But in the later poem the stakes are raised: instead of café-dwellers, we have the even more private and tenuous (since not communal) world of the peignoir; and instead of soldiers marching to their death, we have a visionary "procession of the dead."

> She dreams a little, and she feels the dark
> Encroachment of that old catastrophe,
> As a calm darkens among water-lights.
> The pungent oranges and bright, green wings
> Seem things in some procession of the dead,
> Winding across wide water, without sound.
> The day is like wide water, without sound,
> Stilled for the passing of her dreaming feet
> Over the seas, to silent Palestine,
> Dominion of the blood and sepulchre.

Here April's green does not endure for long, since nature's bounty is not merely eclipsed by encroaching death: that bounty (the oranges and bright green wings) becomes the harbinger of death itself. The second stanza asks why the cloistered woman may not find comfort in "pungent fruit and bright, green wings, or else / In any balm or beauty of the earth," and the answer has already been given. That is why in the third stanza the vision of Jove, who (unlike Jesus) "had his inhuman birth"—"No mother suckled him"—is so attractive. Although he entered the natural world, "moved among us," he did not see the mirror of his own mortality in ripening fruit.

In "Phases" a time of peace is imagined as just what will not suffice in "Sunday Morning": nature's fecundity—"delicious valleys," "Rivers of jade, / In serpentines, / About the heavy grain." That world of peace is insufficient because illusionary, and in the sixth stanza of "Sunday Morning" Stevens discards a vision of eternal ripeness for the same reason.

> Is there no change of death in paradise?
> Does ripe fruit never fall? Or do the boughs
> Hang always heavy in that perfect sky,
> Unchanging, yet so like our perishing earth,

> With rivers like our own that seek for seas
> They never find, the same receding shores
> That never touch with inarticulate pang?

In "Phases" these images of eternal peace ("all things, as before") pale beside the beauty of wartime mortality: "Death's nobility again / Beautified the simplest men" in a way that the eternity of all things as before could not. As Walter Pach's soldier put it, "the nearness of death gives a powerful savor to life." Or as Freud remarked, the wartime consciousness of death made life regain "its full significance." The Stevens of "Sunday Morning" said it better, and said it twice: "Death is the mother of beauty." This is his response to both the antique vision of April's green and the last-ditch effort to find paradise in a nature glazed to unchanging, if peaceful, perfection. As final as this statement is, however, "Sunday Morning" does not end with it. After the repetition of the phrase in stanzas V and VI, stanza VII offers a vision of the men who understand the price incurred in this lesson, men who "know well the heavenly fellowship / Of men that perish."

This vision of masculine camaraderie, excluding the solitary woman, seems (like Stevens's prewar military fantasies) to be an example of what Nancy Huston has called the "Samson Complex," a sexual dynamic that operates at all times but is thrown into high relief in a time of war: "Contact with women is perceived as debilitating, enervating and ultimately destructive of virility, whereas battles can apparently indefinitely recuperate the strength of males." Reading stanza VII in the context of the whole of "Sunday Morning," however, it becomes more difficult to tell exactly where Stevens's sympathies lie. By the time he wrote "Sunday Morning," as we have seen, Stevens had come to realize that his own experience was very different from that wartime fellowship of men that perish: he envied that experience, but he feared it more. Trying to convince his friend Kenneth Burke to join him in the American Ambulance Service, Malcolm Cowley said that the war was "the great common experience of the young manhood of today." Burke did not participate, and neither did Stevens. More than any other part of "Sunday Morning," the seventh stanza marks the poem as the product of this wartime anxiety: like the woman, Stevens is excluded from this fellowship—he feels extraordinary anxiety about the war's new threat of undomesticated death, but he cannot trust his feelings because he was not "vitally involved" in that terror as soldiers were.

> Supple and turbulent, a ring of men
> Shall chant in orgy on a summer morn
> Their boisterous devotion to the sun,

> Not as a god, but as a god might be,
> Naked among them, like a savage source.
> Their chant shall be a chant of paradise,
> Out of their blood, returning to the sky.

Imagined in the world of 1915, this is not so much hedonism as desperation, an expression not only of Stevens's desire but of his worst nightmare, the hyperbolic chant of mortal men for whom the beauty of the earth is not consolation enough. Kenneth Burke could write that he knew "nothing of a life without a war"—without following Cowley to the trenches. He told his friend that there was a peculiar value in "the ruthless denial of action": it "fosters that feeling of incompleteness in us which makes us turn to art"; but at the same time, "people who don't do things are invariably thrown into a state of agitation which is not healthy, but is productive." "Sunday Morning" is a product of such denial, and it records the anxiety such denial produces.

"Sunday Morning" does not end here because not everyone, certainly not Stevens himself or the woman of the poem, may participate in its ritual, in the experience of young manhood shared by Cowley, Lemercier, and Walter Pach's soldier. Consequently, the poem returns to the less desperate consolation of death as "the mother of beauty," something known not only by the fellowship of men that perish but by young women who "sit and gaze / Upon the grass" and boys who "pile new plums and pears / On disregarded plate." The final stanza of "Sunday Morning" suggests that even Jesus himself was no "three-days personage," but the final tableau does not strand us with that potentially disheartening realization by offering a vision of the hushed, indifferent nature of "The Death of the Soldier" or the seductive but finally stingy ripeness of April's green; instead, we are given an image of natural decline in which we are allowed to join and see ourselves—a sky, as stanza III has it, that is friendly precisely because it is "A part of labor and a part of pain."

> Deer walk upon our mountains, and the quail
> Whistle about us their spontaneous cries;
> Sweet berries ripen in the wilderness;
> And, in the isolation of the sky,
> At evening, casual flocks of pigeons make
> Ambiguous undulations as they sink,
> Downward to darkness, on extended wings.

To use the terms Stevens developed in "Extracts From Addresses to the Academy of Fine Ideas" during the Second World War, this is a good death taking the place of evil. Even Lemercier—a willing victim of evil death, a member of the "fellowship / Of men that perish" who saw that "nature is indifferent" to death—could be comforted (if not placated) by the same vision. In one of his last letters, he described to his mother "the wild ducks which turned their wings northwards. They formed various patterns as they flocked together in the heavens and then disappeared on the horizon like a long floating ribbon." He might have been paraphrasing the last lines of "Sunday Morning" when he said that the migrating birds were like "a dove from Noah's ark; not that I dissimulate the dangers which remain, but these ambassadors of the air brought me a more visible assurance of the universal calm which prevails in the midst of our human frenzy." Finally, nature's indifference is not a threat but the most reliable source of consolation for soldier and civilian alike.

Stevens may have discovered that lesson when he and Heber Stryker sat in the meadow beside a suburban cemetery until after midnight, assuaging the abstract fear of death with the natural evidence of death. But if I had to hypothesize the moment at which "Sunday Morning" came to be, I would choose April 4, 1915. This particular Sunday was an Easter Sunday, the first Easter since the war had begun. The following year, Stevens would wonder "why a man who wants to roll around on the grass should be asked to dress as magnificently as possible and listen to a choir." But in April 1915, neither of those alternatives was possible. The *Tribune* reported that church attendance hit a record high on Good Friday, and, due to the war, the Easter crowds were predicted to be even larger. Billy Sunday's service was expected to draw thousands to Paterson, New Jersey. (William Carlos Williams recorded one of the evangelist's speeches: "Come to Jesus! . Someone help / that old woman up the steps.") But the crowds did not appear. Neither did April's green. In the very early hours of that Sunday morning, almost two feet of snow fell on New York City, as if from nowhere, the greatest blizzard of the year. Few people could travel anywhere. Among those who did, over seventy died in accidents on land and sea. And the following day, the editors of the *Tribune* offered thoughts that no doubt occurred to men and women cogitating on the fate of Sunday morning everywhere: "A sunny Easter, resplendent with gay apparel, an Easter which ushered in spring as a thing of joy, would have been an incongruity in such a year. Better the bleak dirge of wind and snow and rain. For here in New York, notwithstanding our peace and security, we can share the dread of Will Irwin's English companion, who supposed 'that the spring was never before so unwelcome in this world. Before the wheat is ripe a million fine, tall fellows will be underground.' No wonder Nature protests at the celebration of such a season."

Stevens once said that he had "avoided the subject of death with very few exceptions." Reading his thoughts about death in "Sunday Morning" through its historical moment, I may have ignored what is perhaps most obvious about the poem. No matter how we approach it, suggests A. Walton Litz, "Sunday Morning" remains "somewhat aloof, probably because it is the only truly great 'traditional' poem that Stevens wrote." To take only the most obvious instance of this debt, the final tableau of "Sunday Morning" is clearly a rewriting of the ode "To Autumn." And as Milton Bates has quite properly demonstrated, the poem owes a larger debt to all manner of aesthetes who cogitated on the conjunctions of death and beauty. If Stevens is giving us Keatsian or Paterian wisdom in these lines, then, how can they be claimed as the poet's response to the world as he found it in 1915?

This question returns us to the problem of post-Romantic ambition. We have seen that Stevens began his career as a self-consciously limited poet, one who lived by Keats's reminder that "to philosophise / I dare not yet." But a letter of 1909 reveals that Stevens had begun to chafe at these limitations. He was reading Paul Elmer More's Shelburne Essays, admiring the critic's "tendency to consider all things philosophically": "that, of course, gives his views both scope and permanence." Scope and permanence: Stevens now wanted to philosophize himself, offering "principles of moral conduct that should guide us in every-day life—as distinct, say, from the peculiar life of Sundays." Stevens mulled over the philosophical program of "Sunday Morning" for years, but his poetry remained diminished. Reading an essay on Lafcadio Hearn in the second series of Shelburne Essays, Stevens offered a paraphrase of More's philosophy: "It is considered that music, stirring something within us, stirs the Memory. I do not mean our personal Memory—the memory of our twenty years and more—but our inherited Memory, . . . in which we resume the whole past life of the world, all the emotions, passions, experiences of the millions and millions of men and women now dead."

These sentences once again seem an uncanny preview of the mind that would produce "Sunday Morning" and "Peter Quince at the Clavier" six years later. Seated at the clavier, the bumbling carpenter invokes a spiritual music that not only reaches to the woman in the room but conjures up "the strain / Waked in the elders by Susanna." Stevens began "philosophizing" in this poem, but the verse of "Peter Quince" itself embodies his hesitation. Parts I through III are cast in contrasting forms, but the melodies are delicate and the language is more imagistic than philosophical. Only in the final section does Stevens open all the stops to make a statement of scope and permanence.

> Beauty is momentary in the mind—
> The fitful tracing of a portal;
> But in the flesh it is immortal.
> The body dies; the body's beauty lives.

These lines are the rehearsal for the music (and the philosophy) of "Sunday Morning," but "Peter Quince," in its combination of verse forms, reveals the struggle to make that music as the opulent pentameters of "Sunday Morning" do not. The great singing lines of "Sunday Morning," which do sound like a mighty act of ventriloquism, could consequently be seen as Stevens's substitution of the Keats of the Hyperion poems and the odes for the Keats of "Dear Reynolds." Yet as Frank Lentricchia has proposed, "the literary historicity of 'Sunday Morning' is no autonomous alternative to its economic materiality," and the key to the literary mystery of the provenance of "Sunday Morning" is not exclusively literary. If the music of this poem does seem to come out of nowhere, without precedent in Stevens's career, it is because the philosophy he had nurtured for years could no longer go unspoken or be constrained in a diminished verse. While in "Phases" Stevens struggled with a need for an epic scope to take on the events of his time, in "Sunday Morning" he turned to the great sonorous voice of the tradition as the only music vast enough to accomplish the task that finally eluded him in the war poems. In the fifth stanza of "Sunday Morning" Stevens turns on the "topos of the fallen leaves" common to Homer, Virgil, Milton, and Shelley. Tracing these echoes, Eleanor Cook has noticed that throughout the tradition, the topos is associated with the losses of warfare; but she concludes that Stevens's poem "is not situated in a time of war." "Sunday Morning" employs the topos precisely because it is situated in a time of war: the world of 1915 made the music of the leaves meaningful. The First World War turned Stevens into a major poet, one who could take on the major voices of Shelley and Keats instead of heeding the latter's injunction against precocious philosophizing.

As the little poem "Meditation" suggested, the result of this watershed in Stevens's career was his effort to make an ambitious poetry out of a diminished world. In "Sunday Morning" he does not leave the world of Keatsian particulars behind, but they are treated completely differently than in the apparently Imagist poem "From a Junk." If death is the mother of beauty, then earthly things are not images of "our despised decay," as they are in "Carnet de Voyage," but the fruit of a philosophy that will guide us outside the peculiar life of Sundays. As Helen Vendler has suggested, the natural objects offered in the final lines of "Sunday Morning" are allegorical instances of the philosophy offered in the opening lines of that stanza: the deer walk in "solitude," the quail are "unsponsored," and the pigeons undulate "in an old chaos" that leads to "inescapable" demise. Unlike Vendler, though, I am not so troubled by the presence of ideas in Stevens's verse, since it seems to me that the commingling of objects and ideas enacted in the close of "Sunday Morning" is throughout the whole of *Harmonium* Stevens's answer to the horror of death. Without this allegorizing of the world's bounty, nature would always appear as stoic and severe as the impenetrable autumn in "The Death of the Soldier," and all human beings would die the inconsolable death of the battlefield. As "On the Manner of Addressing Clouds" has it, the world must be magnified "if in that drifting waste / You are to be accompanied by more / Than mute bare splendors of the sun and moon."

Given the complete success of "Sunday Morning" it seems natural that in his next major effort Stevens's ambition would rise even higher. As "Sunday Morning" took on Keats and Whitman, "For an Old Woman in a Wig" took on Shelley and Dante, but here the challenge of terza rima proved greater than the challenge of the great English line, and the poem was left unfinished. Yet "For an Old Woman in a Wig" extends the lessons of "Sunday Morning" by suggesting that an afterlife in heaven or hell is barren when contrasted to "those old landscapes, endlessly regiven, / Whence hell, and heaven itself, were both begotten." Here the spirits of the dead are drawn by "conscious yearning" back to earth, their mission to wander "the green-planed hills" seeking "maids with aprons lifted up to carry / Red-purples home." As in "Sunday Morning" the pressure of death makes flowers and plums more lovely, and "For an Old Woman in a Wig" is an even more explicit attempt to sing a grand song of diminished things. The final lines of the fragment explain what the final stanza of "Sunday Morning" demonstrates by its structure: that although we must look to the poetry of the earth, not the false grandeur of some world beyond, we must seek the revelation in the commonplace and not settle for a simple naturalism.

> *O pitiful lovers of Earth, why are you keeping*
> *Such count of beauty in the ways you wander?*
> *Why are you so insistent on the sweeping*
>
> *Poetry of sky and sea? Are you, then, fonder*
> *Of the circumference of earth's impounding,*
> *Than of some sphere on which the mind might blunder,*
>
> *If you, with irrepressible will, abounding*
> *In . . .   wish for revelation,*
> *Sought out the unknown new in your surrounding?*

To find the unknown new in the mundane is Stevens's way of surviving in the shadow of death. And although this ambitious lesson proved too much for him in "For an Old Woman in a Wig," it is sustained in a score of less expansive but more finely finished poems in *Harmonium*. One sees it in the narrative of "The Paltry Nude Starts on a Spring Voyage" (which looks forward to "The American Sublime") or tucked away in "The Apostrophe to Vincentine," a deceptively casual poem in which the "Monotonous earth" becomes "Illimitable spheres" when the poet sees the lovely Vincentine walking the earth "In a group / Of human others." In "A High-Toned Old Christian Woman" Stevens explains that his method of redeeming mortal human beings is similar "in principle" to the old woman's; while she begins with a "moral law" and from it builds "haunted heaven," he begins with the physical world to build his "hullabaloo among the spheres" and "project a masque / Beyond the planets."

Yeats said explicitly in the first version of *A Vision* (1925) that he was charting the heavens to replace a worldview that "German bombs" had destroyed: "why should we complain, things move by mathematical necessity, all changes can be dated by gyre and cone." In his own way, Stevens was doing the same thing—forging a new mythology of modern death that could stand up to the challenge of the war as the nineteenth century's domesticated vision of the afterlife could not. Yet Stevens was careful not to do exactly what Yeats did in his postwar work—create a new totalizing mythology in place of an older one. Stevens came close to doing that in "To the One of Fictive Music" (1922), when he asked his muse, "give back to us what once you gave: / The imagination that we spurned and crave." In manuscript these final lines read, "Unreal, give back to us what once we gave: / The imagination that we spurned and crave." Here the source of rejuvenation is not imagined as something other than the self: *we* give what *we* once gave. Of course, this muse of otherness is nothing but a fictive thing; but the final version of the poem so hypostatizes her that she stands as something discernibly alien to the self, a creation given substance as creator. Here Stevens approaches the lure of the "ultimate Plato"—the danger he diagnosed so well in "Anecdote of Canna" or "The Bird With the Coppery, Keen Claws." Having dispensed with a mythology that the higher criticism and the war worked together to dispel, the new pantheon threatens to take over.

Although he strongly warned against such exaggerated ambition in poems like "Anecdote of Canna," Stevens spent most of his career looking for a positive articulation of the properly limited power of human imagination. In this context, the relatively unnoticed "Stars at Tallapoosa" (1922) becomes an important poem. Unlike "To the One of Fictive Music," this poem forces the self to take responsibility for its own creations, and it reminds us that however comforting the sympathetic nature of "Sunday Morning" may be, behind it lies the stark battlefield of "The Death of the Soldier." The town of Tallapoosa lies on the Tallapoosa River in Georgia, and Stevens's poem probably grew from a visit he made there during the same trip that took him to Washington and gave him "Anecdote of Canna." The Tallapoosa is not

Wordsworth's river Wye and certainly not Whitman's ocean endlessly rocking, but "Stars at Tallapoosa" begins with a turn against "Out of the Cradle
Endlessly Rocking," insisting that the lines (forming either constellations or
poems) originate in the human intelligence.

> The lines are straight and swift between the stars.
> The night is not the cradle that they cry,
> The criers, undulating the deep-oceaned phrase.
> The lines are much too dark and much too sharp.

These lines are already "much too sharp" because we have come too close to
the solipsism of "The Bird With the Coppery, Keen Claws": at Tallapoosa
the mind is "an eye that studies its black lid," closed to the world without.
To extricate himself from this dead end, the poet must become the "secretive
hunter," not following the lines of the mind's eye but (with verbs that emphasize acts of penetration) "Wading the sea-lines, moist and ever-mingling, /
Mounting the earth-lines, long and lax, lethargic." Yet this is not the world
of pure experience, unsullied by the mind's abstracting power, since none of
these things ("the melon-flower nor dew nor web of either") is "like" any
other thing except "in yourself is like": the mind takes in these objects and
makes the connections, draws the lines. The word that the ocean whispered
to Whitman was *death* (the same word Wordsworth heard in the valley of the
Wye), and it was for Stevens the final word of "Lettres d'un Soldat," the
unutterable phrase. At Tallapoosa, the poet steadies himself against nature's
word not by retreating into the rarefied world of the self but by turning out-
ward—not in order to oversee the earth and sky but to mediate between them,
conscious of the limitations of the mind. Finally, the lines of order we see in
nature are not too dark and sharp but "brilliant" and "bright-edged" and
moving: "Making recoveries of young nakedness / And the lost vehemence
the midnights hold."

Harold Bloom shows some discomfort with this trial run of "The Idea of
Order at Key West" because he is unwilling to accept Stevens's reduction of
his supremely expansive conception of the self; for Bloom, "Stars at Tallapoosa" leaves us with only lines "too dark and much too sharp" because it
insists that imagination be circumscribed. But a reading of Stevens's poems
against the historical world in which they were written leads us to see that
they sometimes find themselves more truly in a tradition that tempers the
purely transcendental strain that Bloom so admires: as Robert Frost put it in
"On Emerson," explaining what Emerson taught him, "there is such a thing
as getting too transcended. There are limits." Throughout, Stevens's poems
of art and idealism run amok reveal that peculiarly American combination of

attraction to and repulsion from what William James called "big ideas"; the poems' speakers inhabit the same ambiguous place occupied by the narrator of *The Blithedale Romance* or any number of tales by Henry James. Unlike Eliot, who pushes his idealists to a moment of horrific discovery, Stevens attempts to forge a sensibility that will prevent such blindness from reaching that moment of attenuated grief. A poem like "The Bird With the Coppery, Keen Claws" uncovers the dangers of idealism, and a poem like "Stars at Tallapoosa" shows not exactly the opposite—not a rejection of the mind's power, since such an absolute was not possible for Stevens—but a representation of what Stevens called "the mind in the act of defending us against itself." For Stevens, big ideas fall down in the face of big events that the ideas, the metaphors, cannot encompass. By giving historical weight to Emerson's dictum that "no picture of life can have any veracity that does not admit the odious facts," the Great War made Stevens write bigger poems about the virtues of thinking small.

Beginning with the explicit war poems of "Phases" and "Lettres d'un Soldat" I have isolated the two themes on which the later poems of *Harmonium* play variations: the shadow of unnatural death and the blindness of unchecked imagination. Growing out of Stevens's responses to the war, these variations begin to make *Harmonium* seem more similiar to the displaced war poetry of *The Waste Land* and *A Draft of XVI Cantos*, other works of postwar and post-Romantic ambition. But as the comparison with Yeats's *A Vision* already suggested, there is a crucial difference between *Harmonium* and these works, which, as they were initially received in the 1920s, appeared self-consciously "postwar": they mirrored their readers' grief in fantasies of cultural apocalypse that obscured their authors. *Harmonium* and its postwar poem of apocalypse, "The Comedian as the Letter C," suffered no such fate. The question we must ask of these poems by Stevens, Eliot, or Pound is the question Geoffrey Hartman suggests we ask of all Romantic poems of apocalypse: "Does the artist become his own iconoclast and, like Descartes, methodically question his world to achieve an authentic cogito? Or is the zero point a cataclysm like the Black Death, Protestantism, the French Revolution, the German 'Kahlschlag'? Does our creative despair come from the fullness of the past, or is each man sufficiently subversive to himself? Can we even tell whether it comes from within or without?" That Stevens was aware of this very question prevented him from writing a poem that presented the war as the modern apocalypse—even though he sometimes felt that it was. Because his musings on death were almost always tempered (explicitly so in "Stars at Tallapoosa") by his distrust of the self's power to grant its own machinations the status of fate, Stevens's poem of apocalypse did not take the shape of *The Waste Land* but of "The Comedian as the Letter C."

7

Postwar Comedian

Just before he left Harvard to join the newspaper business, Stevens published "Hawkins of Cold Cape," a story about "Sly" Hawkins, editor of the Cold Cape *Traveller*. The tale begins with Hawkins's realization that "there was little or no money in the provincial newspaper business." Barker, Hawkins's equally frustrated reporter, hears that John Havers of North Point has seen a meteor, and he writes an article for the paper that begins like this.

As is well known to most of those who do us the honor of reading the *Traveller*, Man is but mortal. Mountains crumble to dust, patches of beautiful meadow turn into deserts; the very sea at whose feet we sit becomes dry and leaves in its place a frightful chasm. And even this chasm disappears. Where are the icebergs that have come from the North? where are the clouds that have frequently covered the sky? Gone—all gone! Why, then, should not earth go, too? We regret to inform our readers that something of the kind is likely to happen within a short time. Only last night John Havers of North Point saw a great ball of fire surrounded with immense flames pass through the sky and go down beyond the horizon. It has not been heard of since; but it was coming directly toward the earth and by next Tuesday's issue of the *Traveller* something more definite may be expected in regard to it.

Barker ended his apocalyptic fantasy here, but Hawkins understood the retail potential of doom, and he continued the article, bolstering its claims with more reputable accounts of the catastrophe ("The metropolitan journals are at the present hour given up entirely to the great event"), along with allusions to historical precedent ("As is well-known the time which observers

83

from the day of Copernicus to that of the latest authority have settled upon as that of the end of earth will be at hand Wednesday of next week") and the opinions of more cultured Europeans ("All government has been practically discontinued in France and Italy; and as for Austria which has no sea-front it is said that the reservoirs of the various cities are scenes of bloody contest"). The next day an "extra" to the *Traveller* further legitimized the story with "a scientific post-script," and on Sunday the Reverend Mr. Freeman offered "passages of the Bible" that confirmed the "mournful tragedy." After the appointed day passed without incident, the citizens of Cold Cape were greeted by the news that Hawkins, who had spent the previous week purchasing their doomed chickens and cows at reduced prices, had discontinued the *Traveller* and begun wholesaling dairy produce.

Stevens learned at an early age not only that doom sells; he knew the best marketing techniques. Set side by side with the twentieth century's best-selling apocalypse, *The Waste Land*, "Hawkins of Cold Cape" offers a catalogue of Eliot's most successful strategies: more reputable accounts of the catastrophe ("Cf. Hermann Hesse, *Blick ins Chaos*"), allusions to historical precedent ("You who were with me in the ships at Mylae!"), the opinions of more cultured Europeans ("London Bridge is falling down"), and the authority of Scripture ("He who was living is now dead"). As professionally prudent as Hawkins, Eliot gave up doomsaying for a more nourishing enterprise just as *The Waste Land* was published and, from the pages of the *Criterion*, led a generation out of the cultural impasse he had dramatized for them. Of course, Eliot did much more and much less than that (given what we now know of the role of Eliot's personal experience in the composition of *The Waste Land*), but in order to understand the place of Stevens's work in the 1920s, it is important to see how Eliot's poem captured the apocalyptic imagination of his time.

As Frank Kermode demonstrated in *The Sense of an Ending*, every generation offers a new image of apocalypse that paradoxically rejects even as it depends on the old. The immediate predecessor of Eliot's vision of modern culture as a wasteland was the fatalism that captured the imagination of both American and European intellectuals between the panic of 1893 and the Russian Revolution. When Stevens moved to New York City, he confronted the changes wrought in American culture by the rise of immigration, labor organizations, and various leftist groups. By 1909 his complaints about New York were tempered by his growing feelings of camaraderie with the city's poor, but older New Yorkers thought that the end of life as they knew it was imminent. With the same letter in which he told Elsie Moll that the 1909 "Little June Book" was completed ("You've no idea how hard it is to write these little verses"), Stevens included a letter clipped from the New York

Evening Post. Its anonymous author (who might as well have been named Sly Hawkins) described a trip to "revisit old St. Mark's, a famous American church": "reaching Astor Place, once well known as part of America and New York, I sighted my church in the distance. Wending my way along, I passed many people—hundreds, but not an American face, and not a word of English. At Third Avenue, I was startled by seeing a very small group huddled around the American flag, held proudly aloft. This group was surrounded by a wild-eyed foreign mob. I realized it all in a moment: this was the last stand of America—of Manhattan against the foreign invasion. It was the glorious End." This letter offers only one example of prewar apocalyptic rhetoric plucked from a wide political spectrum: predicting the coming debacle was the response to a rapidly changing American culture from both the left and the Boston aristocracy. Barrett Wendell, one of Stevens's teachers at Harvard, proclaimed that American democracy must perish in "the morass of such catastrophe [as] we have never known." Tom Watson, the Populist leader, proclaimed that given the social conditions of the time, "revolution is as inevitable as the laws of the universe." Unlike Marxists, these American cataclysmists felt that the crisis would come because tradition was rejected—not because the end was the inevitable result of old-fashioned ways. Eastern aristocrats and Populist farmers, political enemies, were uneasily united by their idealization of a golden age.

As the United States built an empire under McKinley's guidance, comparisons with the fate of imperial Rome became inevitable, and predictions of a great world war were already common two decades before the war finally came. In the wake of the Russo-Japanese War, Russia or Japan, rather than Germany, was usually seen as the threat. Joyce lampooned that prediction in the Eumaeus episode of *Ulysses*, written after the First World War but turned back upon the Dublin of 1904: "But a day of reckoning, he stated *crescendo* with no uncertain voice, thoroughly monopolizing all the conversation, was in store for mighty England. . . . There would be a fall and the greatest fall in history. The Germans and the Japs were going to have their little lookin, he affirmed." The First World War was so quickly hailed as Armageddon not simply because its battles were truly horrific; as Joyce recognized, the rhetoric of apocalypse had been heard for several decades, and the war surpassed the fantasies. Studying American versions of the sensibility Joyce dramatized, Christopher Lasch suggests that "the war was more than a historical event, it was a collective fantasy," the "fulfillment of a dark and unacknowledged wish." As these events were transformed into the apocalypse, prewar fantasies of conflagration were quickly forgotten; here was *the* end, and it superseded all prior claims for historical ultimacy, coloring assessments of both modern politics and literature. When Eliot described *Ulysses* in terms that the book itself undermines (the "immense panorama of futility and anarchy which is contemporary history"), it seemed that everyone knew what he was talking about.

In 1936 Stephen Spender published a study of modern literature in which he offered this generalization about Eliot, Yeats, Pound, Lawrence, and James: "All these writers seem to me, faced by the destructive element; that is, by the experience of an all-pervading Present, which is a world without belief. This situation is accurately described by I. A. Richards, who finds in *The Waste Land* the expression of the predicament of a generation." Spender's book is titled *The Destructive Element*, a phrase taken from a novel to which he merely alludes in the passage I have just quoted: "In the destructive element immerse," wrote Conrad in *Lord Jim*. For Spender, the "destructive element" is not simply a metaphor but a phrase that names a historical condition experienced by typically modern authors. Yet Spender's use of the phrase conceals a genealogy that leads backward through Richards and Eliot to nineteenth-century cataclysmists; he did not borrow the phrase directly from Conrad. Richards, one of the first critics to treat Eliot's poetry seriously, wrote in a 1925 essay, "A Background for Contemporary Poetry" (incorporated into *Science and Poetry* the following year), that modern life is distinguished by a "sense of desolation, of uncertainty, of futility, of the baselessness of aspirations, of the vanity of endeavor, and a thirst for a life-giving water which seems suddenly to have failed." To this sentence Richards added a now famous footnote describing Eliot's "considerable services for this generation. He has given a perfect emotive description of a state of mind which is probably inevitable for a while to all those who most matter. . . . 'In the destructive element immerse. That is the way.'" For Richards, Eliot's achievement was to have written a poem that expressed the plight of a whole generation. Even though Richards describes his historical predicament by drawing his metaphors of desiccation and destruction from *The Waste Land* and *Lord Jim*, he says that this wasteland state of mind preceded the poem, and that it was Eliot's triumph to have named it. The title of *The Waste Land* was not mere metaphor to Richards but mimetic truth, and Spender, following Richards, took secondhand metaphors as even surer realities. Edmund Wilson transformed the wasteland metaphor into historical truth in much the same way. In *Axel's Castle* he first notes that "the Waste Land of the poem is a symbol borrowed from the myth of the Holy Grail"; but then he disregards its figural status and claims that the wasteland *is* "our post-War world of shattered institutions, strained nerves and bankrupt ideals, [where] life no longer seems serious or coherent."

Although the author of *The Waste Land* was as successful an appropriator of apocalyptic rhetoric as Hawkins of Cold Cape, he was far more aware of the pitfalls and illusions of this practice than his interpreters. Late in his life Eliot often insisted that he never intended anything so grand as a dramatization of a generation's dilemma; *The Waste Land* was a poem of "rhythmical grumbling." But Eliot also recognized that the metaphors in which he grumbled helped to invite a world-historical interpretation. In a 1930 essay on Tourneur, he provided an analysis of *The Revenger's Tragedy* that is clearly a misplaced commentary on *The Waste Land*: "We are apt to expect of youth only a fragmentary view of life; we incline to see youth as exaggerating the importance of its narrow experience and imagining the world as did Chicken Licken. But occasionally the intensity of the vision of its own ecstasies or horrors, combined with a mastery of word or rhythm, may give to a juvenile work a universality which is beyond the author's knowledge of life to give and to which mature men and women can respond." Eliot knew that his wasteland was not so much the embodiment of modern experience as a young man's interpretation of his narrow range of experience. Yet Eliot still became the Chicken Licken for a generation: although *The Waste Land* is haunted by this realization that the crisis is psychological rather than cultural, the poem represents that crisis in metaphors that transfer the responsibility for a disintegrating world from the self to a world that victimizes the self.

That was precisely what Hart Crane tried to point out when he responded to *The Waste Land* in an early draft of "Atlantis," the poem that in its final form would end *The Bridge* (1930).

> And midway on that structure I would stand
> One moment, not as diver, but with arms
> That open to project a disk's resilience
> Winding the sun and planets in its face.

Eliot's poem ends with a bridge falling down, but Crane asserts that the bridge (understood in both its actual and metaphorical senses) exists because the poet sees it: the fragments of the universe cohere in the self, and the failure of those fragments to coagulate is a failure of the self. By pointing this out, Crane replaces one apocalypse with another, and the new age is inaugurated by an unveiling of a new self rather than the unveiling of a new world.

This was a common way of responding to *The Waste Land* in the apocalyptic climate of the 1920s. Since a new revelation, a new apocalypse, can undo a previous one, Williams (like Crane) strained to the heights of another apocalypse when he set out to undermine *The Waste Land* in *Spring and All* (1923); but in the midst of his vision of the old world's destruction, Williams confesses, "If I could say what is in my mind in Sanskrit or even Latin I would do so." While this reference to Eliot's mastery of dead languages legitimizes

Williams's own insecurity, it also emphasizes the self-undermining excess of this apocalyptic response to Eliot's apocalypse. Williams ends his extended hyperbolic passage by admitting that all the destruction has been for nought: having destroyed all traditions of Sanskrit and Latin, "EVOLUTION HAS REPEATED ITSELF FROM THE BEGINNING," reestablishing the very same restrictions on the modern imagination. Like Crane, however, Williams still wants to dramatize the birth of a new world, whatever his sense of the illusions of apocalyptic rhetoric. "Someone has written a poem," he says at the climax of the prose fantasy that opens *Spring and All*, and the poem that follows the prose is "By the road to the contagious hospital." In "the / waste of the broad, muddy fields" the sprouting weeds enter "the new world naked." This tiny change in a tiny world hardly seems apocalyptic, yet in the prose that follows these lines, Williams infuses the poem's description of natural change with catastrophic consequences. It is the real thing this time, not a repetition of the past but the unveiling of a new beginning that actually rewrites postwar history, sinking Woodrow Wilson's ship on the way to Versailles: "A terrific confusion has taken place. No man knows whither to turn. There is nothing! Emptiness stares us once more in the face. Whither? To what end? . . . It is HOPE long asleep, aroused once more. Wilson has taken an army of advisers and sailed for England. The ship has sunk. But the men are all good swimmers." For Williams as for Crane, this new world is made by the powers of the imagination, and all manner of cultural and political consequences may erupt because "someone has written a poem." Instead of undoing the apocalyptic vision of *The Waste Land*, these poems invert its terms.

Inasmuch as Stevens is interested in change, he also anticipates the unveiling of a new age; there is an apocalyptic urge in his work that is epitomized by a sentence in his late essay "Two or Three Ideas": "To see the gods dispelled in mid-air and dissolve like clouds is one of the great human experiences." Yet in answering an apocalyptic vision like Eliot's, he does not follow Williams or Crane into a contrary fantasy. If *The Waste Land* tries to make civilization do the work that is properly the self's, *Spring and All* tries to make the cultural apocalypse the exclusive work of the imagination—and each poem is haunted by the possibility of the other. In "The Comedian as the Letter C," the long poem that occupies the same cultural moment as *The Waste Land* and *Spring and All*, Stevens is aware of both of these dangers. His vision is comic and social, set deeply at odds to the apocalyptic climate into which the poem was born.

When Hi Simons published the first major reading of "The Comedian as the Letter C" in 1940, he could promote the importance of the poem only by saying that it was Stevens's *Waste Land* in both structure and sensibility: "It discloses the sources of the skepticism and fatalism that run through all his later work." Stevens himself canonized this interpretation, when, in a rare moment of authorial benevolence, he wrote to Simons to praise the essay. Comedy has always taken a back seat to the more rugged values of skepticism and fatalism, and Stevens was no doubt pleased by the high seriousness with which Simons approached his work. After all, Stevens had recently written in a "Tribute to T. S. Eliot" in the *Harvard Advocate* that Eliot's "prodigious reputation is a great difficulty," and Simons offered Stevens poetic legitimacy in Eliotic terms. But at what cost? The early success of Eliot's poem depended on the discovery of a generation's malady in its metaphors, and Stevens's long poem, despite Simons's effort, not only cannot sustain such an effort but undermines it. Which is not to say that this "sustained nightmare of unexpected diction," as Frank Kermode has so aptly called it, is not a poem of high seriousness as well as verbal high jinks. Given Eliot's own comments in his Tourneur essay on the provenance and reception of *The Waste Land*, it appears that *The Waste Land* could be read more fruitfully in terms provided by "The Comedian as the Letter C" or "Hawkins of Cold Cape."

"I should guess that in all its excesses it is meant as a kind of reply to *The Waste Land*." That was Roy Harvey Pearce's verdict on "The Comedian" in 1961, as Eliot's hegemony was waning and Stevens's reputation was on the rise. Stevens's "spring, / A time abhorrent to the nihilist" does seem a taut response to the cruelest month; and Stevens's description of his poem as "anti-mythological" does appear to answer the "mythical method" Eliot described in "*Ulysses*, Order, and Myth." But more than these parallels (or Crispin's thunder, nightingale, cathedral, or sea-masks), this passage from "A Nice Shady Home," the penultimate canto of "The Comedian," reads like Stevens's most sustained rebuttal to Eliot.

> Was he to company vastest things defunct
> With a blubber of tom-toms harrowing the sky?
> Scrawl a tragedian's testament? Prolong
> His active force in an inactive dirge,
> Which, let the tall musicians call and call,
> Should merely call him dead? Pronounce amen
> Through choirs infolded to the outmost clouds?
> Because he built a cabin who once planned
> Loquacious columns by the ructive sea?
> Because he turned to salad-beds again?
> Jovial Crispin, in calamitous crape?
> Should he lay by the personal and make
> Of his own fate an instance of all fate?

Crispin, Stevens's introspective voyager, contemplates an apocalyptic vision ("a blubber of tom-toms harrowing the sky"), a "tragedian's testament" complete with dirge and amen, because he has failed to fulfill his grander expectations. But this essentially comic Crispin knows, especially in his diminished state, that such "calamitous crape" will not suit him. Like the Eliot who likened himself to Chicken Licken, Stevens's Crispin realizes that his narrow range of experience has little to do with a generation's dilemma: "Should he lay by the personal and make / Of his own fate an instance of all fate?" Of course not. When Stevens read *The Waste Land* in the *Dial*, this was his response: "Eliot's poem is, of course, the rage. As poetry it is surely negligible. What it may be in other respects is a large subject on which one could talk for a month. If it is the supreme cry of despair it is Eliot's and not his generation's."

Stevens was confident enough to make this statement because he had a Parisian informant. Robert McAlmon told him that he had seen *The Waste Land* before its publication, "but never in finished form": "Eliot is devitalized; bad health; not much audacity; but he's a good workman, and almost authentic in his perceptions, perhaps, but a vapour of 'mood' clings to him and his work a little. That's not quite desirable. I prefer vicious belly aching to despondent knowingness; but that's a matter of the type of civilization we're forced to live in the middle of, and the type of resistance one sets up against its forces, that incline one to neuroticism and morbidity." When he saw *The Waste Land* himself, Stevens agreed with McAlmon up to a point; while McAlmon was already reading the poem as the expression of a cultural impasse, Stevens was more resolute in seeing the despair as "Eliot's and not his generation's."

But Stevens was echoing his own Crispin in his response to Eliot's poem—*echoing* him, because even though "The Comedian as the Letter C" was first published in 1923, Stevens actually completed it before he read *The Waste Land*. He began the early version of the poem, "From the Journal of Crispin," late in 1921 after seeing an announcement of the Blindman Prize of the Poetry Society of North Carolina. Neither the canto that I quoted above, "A Nice Shady Home," nor the final canto, "And Daughters with Curls," is part of this version of the poem; Stevens added them at the same time that he trimmed down the existing cantos to form "The Comedian" during the summer of 1922. By September, the poem was completed, and none of its lines could possibly have been written in response to *The Waste Land*. My point in establishing this chronology, however, is to reveal the more important ways in which Stevens's work does offer a kind of carnivalization of the common understanding of Eliot's work (especially that of Spender,

Williams, or Crane). The apocalyptic sensibility apparently embodied in *The Waste Land* was, as I have shown, a cultural commodity long before 1922 (McAlmon read the poem in those terms instantly, despite his knowledge of Eliot's personal life), and Stevens had formulated a cogent critique of that sensibility in "Hawkins of Cold Cape."

As the poem's more recent readers have noted, "The Comedian as the Letter C" is a poem of imaginative voyaging in the tradition of Shelley's "Alastor" and Yeats's "The Wanderings of Oisin." Yet the map that Hi Simons first drew for the voyage remains useful in its broadest turns: as Crispin moves from Bordeaux to Yucatán to the Carolinas, he progresses from a "romantic subjectivism" through a "realism almost without positive content," an "exotic realism," a local-color "objectivism," and a more "disciplined realism," finally, to marriage and the begetting of children (rather than poems). In other words, although the poem follows a pattern common in Romantic poetry, it also dramatizes Stevens's own fluctuations between the aesthetics of Hoon and of the Snow Man, and within the stylized meanderings of "The Comedian" we can trace the evolution of *Harmonium* itself. And it is consequently inevitable that the poem finds its center in the problem of post-Romantic ambition, the problem Stevens faced as he overthrew his diminished aesthetic, attempting to answer the epic challenge of war without hailing the new apocalypse.

Crispin, a "skinny sailor peering in a sea-glass," begins his poetic career as the "lutanist of fleas," a cataloguer of the small, the insignificant. On his first voyage at sea, he is consequently "washed away by magnitude"; the world's expansiveness is too much for his diminished aesthetic. But Crispin does not even attempt to encompass the sea's vast mythology, becoming instead a more severe realist, a chastened "auditor of insects" rather than of the mighty ebb and flow. In Yucatán, his first stop, he confronts a world more lush, more grand, yet he merely commits his "couplet yearly to the spring," and only when he hears the Mayan thunder is his ambition aroused. Although Crispin would now like to make this "note / Of Vulcan"—this "thing that makes him envious in phrase"—his own, he (like Stevens facing the war) has neither the poetic nor the human capacity to take on the challenge.

> his vicissitudes have much enlarged
> His apprehension, made him intricate
> In moody rucks, and difficult and strange
> In all desires, his destitution's mark.
> Qua interludo: Crispin, if he could,

Would chant assuaging Virgil and recite
In the oratory of his breast, the rhymes
That drop down Ariosto's benison.

The last four lines of this passage appear only in "From the Journal of Crispin"; though Stevens cut them from the final version of his poem, they offer the most succinct account of both his persona's and his own predicament (and more especially his own, since Stevens deleted the more personal lines of "From the Journal of Crispin" in order to increase the distance between himself and his persona in "The Comedian"). Although faced by an epic subject, his apprehension "much enlarged," Stevens was, like Crispin, unwilling to make of his own fate an instance of all fate, to become his culture's Virgil or Eliot. "The Comedian" was the closest Stevens came to writing his epic, but, as in "Phases," the poem's mock-epic irony is at war with his desire to make a major statement, and it paradoxically tells a story of epic ambition renounced. Although in the earlier version of the poem Crispin chastises the Mexican sonneteers because their modest lines cannot possibly embody the great "Andean breath"—"A more condign / Contraption must appear"—Crispin soon comes to understand that he himself can muster no such contraption, and he moves on from the Andes to the Carolinas to confine himself to "lesser things," a "searcher for the fecund minimum." It is at this point in "From the Journal of Crispin" that Stevens's persona realizes (in lines later deleted) that "Imagination soon exhausts itself / In artifice," and he focuses more intently on the world's vulgar particularities, all those things made valuable "By aid of starlight, distance, wind, war, death"—the wartime lesson of "Sunday Morning."

As these lines make more clear, the introspective voyager of "The Comedian as the Letter C" goes in search not only of aesthetic but of social ideals. The poem is written in response to a postwar world, and its self-conscious renunciation of a cultural apocalypse is a position achieved through a close look at attitudes common in the early 1920s. In the poem's fourth canto, Crispin comes to see that his celebration of "rankest trivia," carried to its extreme, is just as dangerously ambitious and potentially deceiving as the imagination's vaporous flights. So Crispin abandons his aesthetic questing altogether and gives himself over to his biological progeny—a song, as lines in "From the Journal of Crispin" explain, that "Crispin formulates but cannot sing": "This late discoverer / Discovers for himself what idler men / And less ambitious sires have dawdled with." Had Crispin been less ambitious from the start, he would have discovered his fecund silence sooner.

"From the Journal of Crispin" leaves Crispin at this point, but it is just this condition, elaborated in the final two cantos Stevens added to his poem in the summer of 1922, that has so bothered the poem's readers: in a stunning reversal of the conventional wisdom of sexual and artistic economies, Crispin subverts his poetic energy into his children, four daughters with curls. Harold Bloom finds this conclusion so demoralizing that he can only wonder "if Stevens is attempting to write badly." Yet "The Comedian as the Letter C" appears to be the product of a defeated imagination only if we judge it according to the exclusively aesthetic terms that the poem itself overthrows. Better than anyone else, Bloom has shown how "The Comedian" offers the last gasp of the Romantic quest-poem tradition epitomized by Shelley's "Alastor," a story of a poet who "can tolerate neither nature nor other selves and who voyages until he dies, a victim of his own visionary intensity." But is Crispin really a victim of his own visionary intensity? Sensing the poem's relationship to "Alastor" and "The Wanderings of Oisin," readers have desired the apocalypse with which those poems conclude. But "The Comedian" is not precisely that kind of poem. In rejecting the cultural apocalypse apparently portrayed in *The Waste Land*, it does not offer the alternatives of *The Bridge* or *Spring and All*; Stevens's poem refuses to end with the apocalypse of the self, a new world revealed by a new vision. Bloom ultimately disregards the most important part of his reading of "The Comedian" when he forgets that the poem is not a simple imitation but a self-conscious parody of Shelley's and Yeats's voyaging. We have seen that in the final poem of the 1908 "Book of Verses" Stevens had reached the position Kenneth Burke called corrective rather than acquiescent; in contrast to his Harvard sonnets, which tell the story of "Alastor" in miniature, this poem opened up a space between the death of the active self and the death of the utterly isolated self. "The Comedian as the Letter C" is the mature version of this poem, and instead of the mutually exclusive alternatives of public action and visionary retreat, it shows Crispin sailing into an extraordinary mildness, to a place where continuities are affirmed. Crispin's self-conscious rejection of all manner of apocalyptic rhetoric is no sign of Stevens's failure of imagination.

To put it in positive terms, Crispin's fate is a sign of the success of Stevens's historical vision, for it was in Crispin's ordinary world that Stevens wrote all his best poems. The final canto of "The Comedian" offers Crispin's "return to social nature." And here is the turning point of the poem's comedy: rejecting both the apocalypse of the isolated self and the apocalypse of a culture's demise, "The Comedian as the Letter C" affirms historical continuity, a social and comic vision chosen over the tragedian's lonely fate. If Stevens gives us Crispin "Concluding fadedly," it is because he is more interested in the poem's moral victory than in what appears to some as its aesthetic failure, and he is unwilling to write a poem that writes off social nature in a self-serving vision of the end. "The Comedian as the Letter C" concludes with what finally lurks at the center of either *The Waste Land* or *Spring and All* when the intricate desires and deceptions of its rhetorical strategies are swept away: one poet's narrow range of experience. As the poem's final lines have it, Crispin may be the hero of his own life, his final pronouncement "muted, mused, and perfectly revolved"; or he may be the windy protagonist of a voyage to nowhere, "a profitless / Philosopher." But either way it does not matter, since Crispin's tale "comes, benignly"—not grandly, not with universal consequence—"to its end." The rest of the world moves on.

Perhaps Crispin's fate would not seem troubling to many of Stevens's readers if it did not seem to mirror Stevens's own life. Published in 1923, "The Comedian" stands near the brink of Stevens's second decade of silence; in 1924 he had his own daughter with curls, in 1932 his nice shady home in the suburbs, and the poems would not return in full force until 1934. But to understand both Stevens's "Comedian" and his silence, I think we need to see more clearly that poetry was not necessarily the highest value in Stevens's world. He also valued Crispin's "social nature"—or what he would come to call the "ordinary" or the "humdrum"—and he would not neglect his responsibilities for his poetic ambition. To say this is not to transform Stevens from poet to sociologist or politician but to get a little closer to what he was: a man who made his living as an insurance executive, enjoyed his bourgeois life-style, kept a responsible watch over the fortune of his family, felt the suburbanite's concern about local, national, and international issues (especially as they affected his and his family's fortune), and, when these important concerns either provoked him in the right way or left him the time and energy, wrote wonderful poems. Stevens was always amused by Marcel Duchamp, who lived by the "old-fashioned" idea of the "artistic type."

As much as they do resemble each other, Wallace Stevens is not exactly Crispin, for despite another decade's silence, Stevens was able to continue to write poetry without neglecting the other responsibilities of his "social nature." And he did not capitulate to his second silence immediately upon the completion of "The Comedian as the Letter C," the capstone to *Harmonium*. Between 1922 and 1924 Stevens wrote some of his very best poems: "The Emperor of Ice-Cream" and "To the One of Fictive Music" are not products of an exhausted imagination. Those years also gave Stevens "Stars at Tallapoosa," which looks forward to the poems of order he would write in the 1930s and, like "The Comedian as the Letter C," tries to isolate a careful middle ground where the imperatives of poetry and history can coexist.

Like "Stars at Tallapoosa," in fact, most of the poems from this coda to the first phase of Stevens' career elaborate the antiapocalyptic lessons of "The Comedian." "The babble of generations magnifies / A mot into a dictum," wrote Stevens in "The Woman Who Blamed Life on a Spaniard" (published in 1932 but probably written in 1924), as if versifying his judgment of Eliot's personal wasteland. "Discourse in a Cantina at Havana" (first published in 1923 and later titled "Academic Discourse at Havana") offers a more detailed analysis of this kind of sensibility. Some of the details of "Academic Discourse" grew from Stevens's visit to Havana in February 1923, but since Stevens remembered that the poem was cut down from a "considerably longer" form, he may have conceived it first as a canto for "The Comedian as the Letter C." There are telling verbal continuities between the two poems. At the end of the first canto of "The Comedian" we are told that Crispin's voyage would have taken him from "Bordeaux to Yucatan, Havana next, / And then to Carolina," but Crispin skips the Cuban interlude and sails directly from Yucatán to Carolina. "Academic Discourse" provides the missing leg of the narrative. The poem begins by recapitulating some of the details from the first two segments of Crispin's voyage—the voice of "elemental fate" that had echoed in the Andean thunder, the nightingale to whom the "Maya sonneteers" had "made their pleas," and the great sea creatures Crispin had encountered on the sea voyage between Bordeaux and Yucatán:

> Canaries in the morning, orchestras
> In the afternoon, balloons at night. That is
> A difference, at least, from nightingales,
> Jehovah and the great sea-worm. The air
> Is not so elemental nor the earth
> So near.

These lines begin to sketch the Cuban narrative that would have been part of "The Comedian"; and the rather more disjunctive "Academic Discourse" reads like a collection of passages culled from that narrative.

After the grandeur of the earthy wilderness in Mexico, the city of Havana seems laden with "a grand decadence" that "settles down like cold": "Life is an old casino in a park," begins the second part of "Academic Discourse," "The bills of the swans are flat upon the ground." This transparently weak metaphor ("Life is") hints that Stevens is extending his investigation of what Nietzsche called "anthropomorphic error": the reification of the personal into an image of all fate—the temptation Crispin avoided. As if to parody the easy comparisons of present decadence and past grandeur that mar some of Eliot's shorter poems, Stevens explains in part III that before these swans laid down their bills, the casino of life was full of the "centuries of excellence to be." But even then, the swans were really as indifferent to human achievement as the French landscape was to the fallen comrades of Eugène Lemercier; "The toil / Of thought" made the swan's erect carriage seem to usher in the promising future, just as their sleepy lethargy now seems redolent of the present decadence. These birds are the wild swans of Yeats's Coole, but the autumnal minds that watch them drift have all of Yeats's nostalgia with none of his awareness of the mind's contribution to their meaning. If the "indolent progressions of the swans" once "Made earth come right" in Havana, it did so only as "a peanut parody / For peanut people." And the danger of this pint-size illusion is that as the "Gruff drums" of change began to beat, they did not "alarm the populace." When the drums were finally heard, the change they heralded could seem nothing but catastrophic.

With the recognition that life in the old casino is an all-too-easy projection of life in the mind, the remainder of part III offers a series of alternative bird views. In a last-gasp season of imaginative fullness, the swans regain their mythic resonance, and the "clearest woman" is capped with "apt weed," the "thickest man" mounted on "thickest stallion-back"; but these exaggerated transformations cannot sustain themselves. Like Crispin approaching Carolina, Stevens leaves these grander visions for the details of a smaller world: "Grandmother and her basketful of pears / Must be the crux for our compendia." Recognizing that our compendia of thought necessarily exceed the empirical cruxes from which they grow, part III ends by suggesting a point of view (remembering both the burgher at the vast Pacific and the pilgrim in the valley of the Tallapoosa) that guards against the danger of apocalyptic myopia.

> The burgher's breast,
> And not a delicate ether star-impaled,
> Must be the place for prodigy, unless
> Prodigious things are tricks. The world is not
> The bauble of the sleepless nor a word
> That should import a universal pith
> To Cuba.

Since the world is not the dictum of human dreaming, since our words do not join easily with universals, we must be careful not to let our metaphors run wild. The "decadence" of Havana has its stark reality, but it does not necessarily herald a world-historical collapse, a disintegration of all past mythologies: that illusion is imported to the island. In "Academic Discourse" Stevens suggests that when "too great rhapsody" is annulled by a world that resists the rhapsody, then the very particulars of that world "Will drop like sweetness in the empty nights" and console as no apocalyptic vision could. As in "Sunday Morning," the earth's bounty remains our ultimate consolation, but only when our grand illusions are dispelled does that consolation become clear.

Yet Stevens's skepticism in the face of apocalyptic rhetoric introduces another danger: in resisting the reductions of exaggerated apocalypse, we might succumb to the opposite blindness should the real catastrophe occur, dismissing it as illusory. What if this bleak metropolis really does augur a collapse of everything we have known?

> This may be benediction, sepulcher,
> And epitaph. It may, however, be
> An incantation that the moon defines
> By mere example opulently clear.
> And the old casino likewise may define
> An infinite incantation of our selves.

In these last lines of the poem, Stevens allows for both possibilities: these words may be an epitaph, and the decadence of Havana may be a true sign of the apocalypse; or Havana may be the "infinite incantation" of the selves who disguise their finitude by granting it universal import. Before he comes to this final point of mediation, however, Stevens asks one more difficult question. Given that the health of both our selves and our cities depends on such measured foresight, what is "the function of the poet," the imaginative man, the one who offers all those ominously seductive metaphors for the significance of perished swans? In avoiding "ornatest prophecy," should he confine himself to "mere sound" and nothing more?

> As part of nature he is part of us.
> His rarities are ours: may they be fit
> And reconcile us to our selves in those
> True reconcilings, dark, pacific words.

In lines that look back to "Stars at Tallapoosa" and forward to "The Idea of Order at Key West," Stevens suggests that it is the poet himself who, by articulating our experience, not only offers us the metaphors by which we live, but (more importantly) articulates the moments at which they break down: the poet has the power to make the personal "an instance of all fate"—to magnify "a mot into a dictum"—but the poet also has the power to expose those illusions as ill-considered metaphors. The poet's words themselves "may be benediction, sepulcher / And epitaph" or may be an "infinite incantation of our selves"; by their very doubleness, the words help keep us alert to the ways in which our private and public spheres impinge on each other, preventing the terms of one sphere from obscuring the other.

Kenneth Burke remarks in *Counter-Statement* that it is remarkable that "the doctrines of art's ineffectualness have flourished in a period noted for its intense utilization of art." Yet what seems remarkable is only logical when we understand the use of even the most ingrown and convoluted eloquence.

Irony, novelty, experimentalism, vacillation, the cult of conflict—are not these men trying to make us at home in indecision, are they not trying to humanize the state of doubt? . . . Perhaps there is an evasion, a shirking of responsibility, in becoming certain too quickly. . . . Since the body is dogmatic, a generator of belief, society might well be benefited by the corrective of a disintegrating art, which converts each simplicity into a complexity, which ruins the possibility of ready hierarchies, which concerns itself with the problematical, the experimental, and thus by implication works corrosively upon those expansionistic certainties preparing the way for our social cataclysms. An art may be of value purely through preventing a society from becoming too assertively, too hopelessly, itself.

That makes the power of art seem rather certain and dogmatic itself, but Burke characteristically adds that if action could "be destroyed by such an art, this art would be disastrous. But art can at best serve to make action more labored." It may prevent us from transforming a mot into a dictum, a certainty into a catastrophe. For Stevens too, such are the uses of poetry in a time when "Politic man ordained / Imagination as the fateful sin."

Stevens first published those lines of "Discourse in a Cantina at Havana" in 1923. When the lines appeared in the middle of *Ideas of Order*, where they now rest in the *Collected Poems*, they seemed utterly the product of the Stevens who worked hard in the 1930s to renegotiate his understanding of the place of poetry in a politicized society. That he did not write those lines during the Depression but in 1922 to 1923, the wasteland years, forces us to remember something about both the shape of Stevens's career and the continuities of American culture. If "Academic Discourse" began, as I think it did, as part of the project of "The Comedian as the Letter C," then it even more specifically reveals that a deep concern with the place of poetry was from the start an essential part of Stevens's introspective voyage. As a deleted episode of "The Comedian," "Academic Discourse" reveals that when Crispin stopped at Havana, en route from Mexico to the Carolinas, he believed that "the sustenance of the wilderness / Does not sustain us in the metropoles." At the end of this fragmented narrative, Crispin would have come to understand that such "grand decadence" may have a positive beauty of its own when seen clearly enough. And that is precisely what Crispin does believe when he arrives in the Carolinas in "The Comedian"—the lessons of "Academic Discourse" remain intact in Crispin's tale. In the longest passage Stevens deleted from "From the Journal of Crispin," Crispin learns to appreciate the loveliness of what used to strike him as urban decline. "Academic Discourse" begins with Crispin's dissatisfaction with the "metropoles," but here, "Crispin is happy in this metropole."

> A short way off the city starts to climb,
> At first in alleys which the lilacs line,
> Abruptly, then, to the cobbled merchant streets,
> The shops of chandlers, tailors, bakers, cooks,
> The Coca Cola-bars, the barber-poles,
> The Strand and Harold Lloyd, the lawyers' row,
> The Citizens' Bank, two tea rooms, and a church.
> Crispin is happy in this metropole.

It would seem that Stevens cut these lines (leaving the more general comment that Crispin "gripped more closely the essential prose" of this world) because their force depended on their contrast with the deleted Cuban canto of the poem. Here the decadence of Havana is indeed revealed to have been an incantation of the self, and as the passage continues, there follow the crucial lines about poems being nothing more than "plain shops" transformed into loveliness by the power of war and death. Then, even more crucially, Stevens wonders what the limits of such metaphorical transformations might be.

> At just what point
> Do barber-poles become burlesque or cease
> To be? Are bakers what the poets will,
> Supernal artisans or muffin men,
> Or do they have, on poets' minds, more influence
> Than poets know?

As in "Academic Discourse," the poet's function is once again not simply to make our metaphors but to test their breaking points. In "The Irrational Element in Poetry" (1936) Stevens would use the phrase "the pressure of reality" to discuss this issue: the poet cannot escape but resists this pressure, and the poems are the product of the struggle. The extravagant language of the completed "Comedian" offers greater resistance than the sober pronouncements of "Academic Discourse" (and Stevens probably deleted the academic discourse because, though it articulated the philosophical underpinnings of "The Comedian," it did not rhyme with that poem's more raucous music). Although the tone of "Politic man ordained / Imagination as the fateful sin" stands at odds with "Exchequering from piebald fiscs unkeyed," that political imperative supports both poems' explorations of the apocalyptic state of mind. And the final lesson of "Academic Discourse" may be, as Burke suggests, that given the limited range of poetry's power, the extravagant music of "The Comedian" enacts a more challenging lesson than the balder statements of "Academic Discourse."

"Academic Discourse at Havana" is even one of the more explicitly political poems of *Ideas of Order*, and, given its measured assessment of a catastrophic sensibility, how ironic it is that when Stanley Burnshaw reviewed this volume he looked back on *Harmonium* and complained: "It is the kind of verse that people concerned with the murderous world collapse can hardly swallow today except in tiny doses." The obfuscation of such rhetoric was precisely what Stevens was trying to expose: as a metaphor for the state of culture, "murderous world collapse" requires some more rigorous testing. Burnshaw's statement implies that there once was a time when poets could legitimately ignore such responsibilities, a prelapsarian age swept away by the present collapse. Many readers in the 1930s were unsympathetic to Stevens not so much because his politics did not lean far enough to the left but because he did not offer a catastrophic vision of doom and gloom. Consequently, the openly conservative Eliot would fare much better with the left. Only when he capitulated to an obvious phrase like "a slime of men in crowds" did it occur to some readers that he lived a life outside the palaz of Hoon. Lines like that one emerged in Stevens's work of the 1930s because, like most first-generation modernists, Stevens was provoked to reconsider the relationship of literature to politics during that decade. But Stevens understood "politic man's" challenge to the imagination before the battles of the 1930s forced him into a more obvious defense of poetry.

The challenge had been clear for some time. Reviewing Max Eastman's poems in the *Liberator* in 1918, Floyd Dell complained that it was "more *interesting* to talk truth than to create beauty" in the age of the Great War and the Russian Revolution. "How can one be an artist in a time when the morning paper may tell of another Bolshevik revolution somewhere?" This particular condemnation of imagination as the fateful sin was quite drastic, since Eastman was no aesthete but an editor of the *Masses*—the journal whose glamour the editors of the *New Masses* (in which Burnshaw reviewed *Ideas of Order*) tried to resurrect. (The *Liberator* replaced the *Masses* in 1918 when the latter was banned, and Eastman, Dell, John Reed, and several others were brought to trial for conspiring to obstruct enlistment in the armed forces; Dell was angry at Eastman, in part, for having renounced his opposition to the war.) Stevens did not need Burnshaw to shake him into awareness of this literary climate. In 1921, when he had not heard from his friend John Rodker for some time, Stevens suggested to the novelist Ferdinand Reyher that "Rodker has been gobbled up by the Bolsheviki or some other anti-literary coterie." Responding from Berlin, Reyher informed Stevens that "furthermore and forever, your proper channels of complaint will lead you to the Bolshevik bureau in London and from thence to headquarters in Moscow."

That remark came shortly after the most widespread Red Scare the United States has ever seen. Spearheaded by Attorney General A. Mitchell Palmer, the scare began in November 1919, when 250 members of the Union of Russian Workers were arrested in a dozen cities, and it peaked one night the following January, when more than 4000 alleged Communists were arrested in 33 cities, coast to coast. These raids, with their wholesale denial of civil liberties, attest to the power and visibility that American Socialist and Communist parties had achieved by 1920; but the raids drastically reduced that power, and Warren Harding came to the White House proclaiming, "too much has been said about Bolshevism in America." One remnant of a radical past festered throughout the 1920s. Nicola Sacco and Bartolomeo Vanzetti were arrested in the Palmer Raids, and their execution, delayed for seven years, awakened many American intellectuals to the struggles the following decade would bring.

Even so, as William Phillips would recognize in "Three Generations" (1934), the fact that there existed an organized radical movement before the stock-market crash of 1929 was something of which even younger radicals of the 1930s needed to be reminded. As Stevens surveyed his own career, he understood how the continuity of that political challenge had affected his own work. Responding to Hi Simons's reading of "The Comedian," he stressed that the poem's comic vision, stemming from the postwar period, applied equally well to the apocalyptic rhetoric of the 1930s. In his effort to make Stevens look like Eliot, Simons had stressed "The Comedian" as the source of the "skepticism and fatalism" he found throughout Stevens's work, and the poet disagreed. While Stevens admitted that the cycle from romanticism through realism to fatalism was probably inevitable, he cautioned Simons that the cycle never stopped turning—either in his own poetry or in the culture of the present day, the end of the 1930s: "At the moment, the world in general is passing from the fatalism stage to an indifferent stage: a stage in which the primary sense is a sense of helplessness. But, as the world is a good deal more vigorous than most of the individuals in it, what the world looks forward to is a new romanticism." Stevens saw continuity in Crispin's return to social nature, not an end. And it was precisely this point that Stevens stressed in explaining his second decade of silence to Simons. After the eight years of sustained poetic activity that produced *Harmonium*, Stevens felt that he was listing dangerously away from ordinary experience: "I began to feel," he told Simons, "that I was on the edge: that I wanted to get to the center: that I was isolated, and that I wanted to share the common life. . . .

People say that I live in a world of my own: that sort of thing. Instead of seeking therefore for a 'relentless contact', I have been interested in what might be described as an attempt to achieve the normal, the central. So stated, this puts the thing out of all proportion in respect to its relation to the context of life." Stevens's second silence appears to be a sharp break in his career only if we imagine that poetry was the only thing of which Stevens's career consisted. During the Second World War, when Stevens compiled a selection of poems ranging from "Earthy Anecdote" to "Asides on the Oboe," he saw the selection as an emblem of his career's continuity—and he explained that the continuity lay in the poems' relation to social nature: "The period during which they were written, the last twenty years, has been terribly alive, and these poems have been at least related to that life."

III

The Second Silence

8

Surety and Fidelity Claims

The election of 1920, said the Republican vice-presidential candidate Calvin
Coolidge, marked "the end of a period which has seemed to substitute words
for things." A few years later, after Warren Harding had died and Coolidge
assumed the presidency, William Carlos Williams forwarded a postcard from
Ezra Pound in Rapallo to Stevens in Hartford. Pound wanted poems, but
Stevens was deeply mired in the dailiness of things. "I'm as busy as the proud
Mussolini himself," he told Williams, presumably responding to the plug for
Italian politics that accompanied Pound's request for poetry. "I rise at daybreak, shave, etc.; at six I start to exercise; at seven I massage and bathe; at
eight I dabble with a therapeutic breakfast; from eighty-thirty to nine-thirty
I walk down-town, work all day [and] go to bed at nine. How should I write
poetry, think it, feel it?" From 1916, when he moved to Hartford, until his
death in 1955, Stevens adhered to such a routine. Williams called these
remarks "undecipherable," and Pound, who organized his life so that nothing
would stand in the way of his ambition to be a great Romantic poet, must
have found them bizarre. "Can you tell me why you work so hard to earn a
living?" asked Williams two decades later, when Stevens refused to retire.
What did that man do all day? Stevens himself answered the question best in
"Surety and Fidelity Claims," written for the *Eastern Underwriter* in 1938.

People suppose, since there is so much human interest in selling Fuller brushes
or sorting postcards in a post office, that the same thing must be true of handling
fidelity and surety claims. After all, over a period of time, you spend an immense
amount of money, millions.

But, actually, you never see a dollar. You sign a lot of drafts. You see surprisingly few people. You do the greater part of your work either in your own office or in lawyers' offices. You don't even see the country; you see law offices and hotel rooms. You try to do your traveling at night and often do it night after night. You wind up by knowing every county court house in the United States. . . .

The major activity of a fidelity and surety claim department lies, of course, in paying claims. This involves much more than merely drawing drafts. It involves making sure that there has been a loss; that the company is liable for it; that you are discharging the liability by the payment, and that you are protecting whatever is available by way of salvage. There is nothing cut and dried about any of these things; you adapt yourself to each case.

Varieties of insurance coverage proliferated during the first years of the twentieth century, and when Stevens entered the field bonding companies were relatively new. The first American company to undertake corporate suretyship did so in 1878, the year before Stevens's birth, and yet of all forms of insurance, suretyship is undoubtedly the oldest. Proverbs 11:15 warns against it ("He who gives surety for a stranger will smart for it, but he who hates suretyship is secure"), and the most famous surety case of all time opens *The Merchant of Venice*, when Antonio guarantees the repayment of 3000 ducats borrowed by his friend Bassanio. About 100 years after Shakespeare's death, the first effort to organize a company to insure the fidelity of employees was made in London's Devil Tavern. The *London Daily Post* carried the announcement: "This society will insure to all masters and mistresses whatever loss they shall sustain by theft from any servant that is ticketed and registered in this society."

Fidelity bonds (such as a bank might acquire for its tellers) guarantee the honesty of employees; surety bonds guarantee the satisfactory performance of a contracted obligation (such as the construction of a building). Within these two broad categories, there now exist hundreds of varieties of bonds, but in theory, all of them involve three parties: the principal, the surety, and the obligee. The principal secures the bond in order to guarantee his obligation— to repay a loan, appear at a trial, execute a will, lay a highway—to the obligee. The surety issues the bond to the principal and must assume the obligation if the principal is unable to do so. Yet the surety usually assumes no risk— and for this reason suretyship is often not considered a form of insurance at all. Not only does the surety undertake a thorough investigation of the principal before issuing the bond, but it often requires an indemnity agreement that holds the principal responsible for any funds the surety may have to advance on the principal's behalf. Stevens once remarked that being in bond claims "is like being in Oriental languages at a University," stressing the distance that lay between him and his colleagues in casualty or fire.

Stevens's work was even more specialized because he dealt almost exclusively in surety bonds. And after 1921 he no longer saw law offices, hotel rooms, and county courts; an assistant was hired to do the traveling, nearly all the court cases were farmed out to local attorneys, and Stevens oversaw the operations from Hartford. "A man in the home office tends to conduct his business on the basis of the papers that come before him," said Stevens in "Surety and Fidelity Claims." "After twenty-five years or more of that sort of thing, he finds it difficult sometimes to distinguish himself from the papers he handles and comes almost to believe that he and his papers constitute a single creature, consisting principally of hands and eyes: lots of hands and lots of eyes."

Stevens emphasized the plurality of bodily parts composing this singular creature because he found that settling claims is a little like playing bridge: the rules of the game never change, but no two tricks are alike. Should the principal fail to meet his obligation, the surety does not cover the loss as a matter of course but investigates the principal and obligee to ensure that the terms of the contract have otherwise been upheld. The first step is to determine the precise nature of the loss. Stevens explained that in cases of embezzlement that step is more complicated if the crook is a public official; public officials never keep records. The common bookkeeper, however, usually keeps scrupulous accounts. "It may seem morbid of an embezzler to keep a memorandum, yet many of them do. It may be mere neatness. Public officials seem to be a little less fastidious. They collect taxes without making records." The second step is to determine if the surety is indeed liable for the loss. To illustrate this stage of the investigation, Stevens's hypotheticals become somewhat more complicated: "A manufacturer of cement sues you for $80,000 on a bond which ordinarily would protect him. His right to sue you is based on a statute which limits the time for suit. It is too late and besides the manufacturer has taken $65,000 from payments made to him by the contractor out of the proceeds of the job covered by your bond and has applied the money (as he is free to do) to a balance due on a job not bonded by you. You contest the suit and defeat the claim."

There is usually more than one way to win the case. The claim of the cement manufacturer who mixed his moneys is clearly defeatable. Other aspects of claim handling, especially those in which it is not clear if paying the claim would in fact discharge the surety's liability, begin to sound like Kantian moral dilemmas. In a discussion of his own poetry, Stevens differentiated between mere obscurity and a functional ambiguity, and he seems to have felt that in surety claims, as in poems, the clearest possible definition of things essentially ambiguous actually enhances the possibility that those things will mean one thing to one person and one thing to another.

Stevens might have titled this hypothetical claim "Anecdote of the Electrician":

You have a bond guaranteeing that an electrician will pay his bills. The bond is for $1,000. His books show that he owes $3,000 and, if his books are incorrect, he may owe twice as much. You are threatened by suits; how are you to proceed?

And this one "Two Versions of the Same Death":

A family is killed by fumes from a gas stove in a cabin in a tourist camp. If the husband died first, his estate goes to A, B and C; if the wife died first, the husband's estate goes to X, Y and Z. The estate amounts to $50,000. You are on the bond of the administrator of the husband's estate. The $50,000 consisted of cash on deposit in a bank which failed several years after you gave your bond. A, B and C will settle for $10,000, but X, Y and Z want $50,000. What had you better do?

And, finally, "The Widow Who Wanted More Money than That":

You are on a very large bond for a woman as executrix of her husband's estate. She has not accounted and you are unable to form any idea respecting her ability to account. What is more, she does not reside in the jurisdiction of the court, and you are not at all sure even that she exists. She was represented by lawyers who are willing to tell you what they know if you will first pay them the fee which she has failed to pay. They want, say, $25,000. You do not know whether what they will tell you will clear you or will disclose a liability for some hundreds of thousands of dollars. Shall you pay the $25,000?

Stevens answered none of these questions, almost as if to suggest, as he once told R. P. Blackmur, that "nothing has made me unhappier than the fact that I have in the past on one or two occasions explained." Hypothetical situations are the meat and potatoes of the lawyer's intellectual diet, and it seems proper that a poet with a lawyer's training would consistently return to the intricacies of "as if." As a lawyer in surety work, Stevens's job was to construct viable solutions to these essentially ambiguous puzzles—to reduce those intricacies and make the fictions pay off. The facts might mean one thing to one person and one thing to another, but Stevens needed to make his version of the story unassailable. Another lawyer at the Hartford recalled how Stevens was a stickler for the facts: "This is where it becomes arcane. This is where underwriters and claims people alike have to be very sharp-eyed and understand all the details of exactly what the contract was, who said what to whom, what defenses are available. All of the facts have to be dug out and disclosed. And where you're talking about the construction of a dam, a highway or a coliseum roof that collapses, an awful lot of expertise has to come into play. This is where [Stevens] had his expertise and demanded it of those he was directing." In other words, Stevens had to be a lot like his own Crispin: a searcher for the fecund minimum, for lesser things, for the essential prose, a celebrant of rank trivia, a marvelous sophomore, a lutanist of fleas, the Socrates of snails. "Poetry and surety claims aren't as unlikely a combination as they may seem," Stevens once remarked. "There is nothing perfunctory about them, for each case is different."

That statement does not deny the fact that poems and surety claims are an unlikely combination, whatever their superficial similarities. To give Stevens's hypothetical claims titles reminiscent of his poems (as I just did) is to recognize that his scenarios are self-consciously and artfully contrived. As a comparison with any lengthy manual on the subject reveals, the business of surety claims is a dull and intricate affair; and as Stevens himself admitted in the opening sentences of "Surety and Fidelity Claims," sorting postcards might be more interesting. When he declined Pound's request for poems, Stevens sent greetings for a Happy New Year to Williams, adding "—in fact just about one single, really happy day would be enough for a claims man." That sounds like the Stevens who, when his daughter considered dropping out of college to find a job that mattered, said, "None of the great things in life have anything to do with making your living." Given the circumstances of that remark, it is not to be taken at face value. At other times, the poet who kept puzzling over surety claims long after the mandatory age of retirement was more sanguine about his work: "It gives a man character as a poet to have daily contact with a job. I doubt whether I've lost a thing by leading an exceedingly regular and disciplined life."

Both those statements imply a tension between the work of poetry and of surety claims, but one might ask how it is possible *not* to devote the principal amount of time to making a living, whether one is a claims man, a poet, or a member of any other profession. "As a writer faces the point of honor that concerns him as a writer," wrote Stevens to Blackmur in 1946, "he must apparently choose between starvation and that form of publishing (or being published) in which it is possible to make money. His problem is how to support himself while engaged in the most honorable capacity. There is only one answer. He must support himself in some other way." No poet really makes his living as a poet. Stevens worked hard both at poetry and at surety claims. Frost worked with equal fervor both at poetry and at transforming himself into what Stevens called, without admonition, "an institution." On one of his many trips to Florida, Stevens found that Frost was spending the winter there too, and the poets discussed their ways of earning a living. Frost was then receiving $6000 a year from Amherst College. He was also making $3000 or

$4000 a year in royalties as well as over $15,000 a year from readings and lectures. The year was 1935, the middle of the Depression, and Frost was pulling in an annual $25,000 compared with the $20,000 Stevens was then making at the Hartford. Both salaries were extraordinary for the time. "There is not the slightest possibility of making one's way as a poet without doing the sort of thing that Frost has done," Stevens told Blackmur. "My own total receipts from poetry are not worth calculating." But Stevens also saw that the sort of thing that Frost did was closer to the work of surety bonds than the work of poetry. When the *Partisan Review*'s editors suggested that teaching and editorial work were a poet's "crutches," Stevens responded: "Most people avail themselves of crutches of one sort or another; lawyers promote business enterprises; doctors marry rich women and buy and sell securities."

Does any poet devote himself full time to the occupation of being a poet? Probably not, though the answer may depend on how one words the poet's job description. Stevens gave contradictory answers to inquiries about his work because the questions made him testy: why didn't people ask the same questions of lawyers and doctors? The common idealization of the poet's life did not interest Stevens, and neither did the attempt to undermine it, since the pleasure of revealing the bard as a businessman depends on the strength of the original stereotype. In 1942 Harvey Breit contacted Williams, offering to do a story about great poets who held full-time jobs. Williams liked the idea and asked Stevens to offer himself up as another specimen. Breit wanted to confound the popular wisdom that one "can't reconcile a man of sound logic . . . with the exploration of the imagination," but Stevens wanted to confound the confounder: "After all, what is there odd about being a lawyer and being or doing something else at the same time? . . . If Bacon was Shakespeare, then, since Bacon was Lord Chief Justice, what better instance could you want?"

Stevens pointed out to Breit that both Archibald MacLeish and Edgar Lee Masters were lawyers. There were other examples. After Charles Ives graduated from Yale with a bachelor's degree in music, he went to work for the Mutual Life Insurance Company. Later, at the Raymond Insurance Agency, he met Julian Myrick, and in a few years the newly formed Ives and Myrick Agency was the largest life-insurance concern in New York. In addition to his music, Ives wrote *The Amount to Carry—Measuring the Prospect* (1912), still a standard text in the field. Franz Kafka worked the single shift, 8:00 A.M. to 2:00 P.M., at the Workmen's Accident Insurance Institute for the Kingdom of Bohemia—but, unlike Ives, he lamented his "horrible double life, from which madness probably offers the only way out." The poet Clarence Stedman entered banking soon after he published his first volume, and in 1865 opened a brokerage firm that he ran for most of his life. Poems accumulated with capital, and his office used a telegraphic code in which *Keats* meant "cancel order to buy" and *Shelley* meant "select and sell at discretion."

Stevens indulged in no such foolishness (however delightful, it does not signal any meaningful conjunction of money and poetry), and consequently his work paradoxically seemed to some readers to be divorced from serious experience. Near the end of the 1920s, Edmund Wilson complained that poets had nothing to write about except poetry as poetry: "Does it really constitute a career for a man to do nothing but write lyric poetry?" While Stevens invoked a mythical intermingling of Bacon and Shakespeare, Wilson offered the poets of Johnson's *Lives* as productive role models, since almost all of them were clergymen or ambassadors or statesmen. Although he conceded that in twentieth-century America, the high degree of specialization required by most professions made such Renaissance men scarce, he concluded that "a young poet in America should not be advised at the outset to give up all for the Muse." Neither would Wilson advise a poet to become a magazine editor or to work for a publisher. His ideal poet sounds like a description of Wallace Stevens: "The poet would do better to study a profession, to become a banker or a public official or even to go in for the movies. What is wrong with the younger American poets is that they have no stake in society."

One can imagine Stevens the claims man taking heart at these remarks. Yet they were written by the same critic who called Stevens's work "impervious to life." Responding to Wilson's essay in the *New Republic*, John Crowe Ransom contested Wilson's claim that most American poetry had no roots in contemporary reality: "Poetry is automatically and inevitably contemporary, and in reflecting the most actual and important experiences of the poet reflects indubitable contemporary data. Sometimes its comments upon these data are direct, and sometimes they are by way of indirection; and the latter case is not the less significant, though it is the more difficult for the critical analysis." That explains why Wilson, who called for poets to lead the exemplary life of a Wallace Stevens, found no apparent relation to contemporary life in Stevens's own poetry: the question Wilson raised was crucial but more complicated than he was willing to admit. To assume that the poetry Stevens wrote should reveal direct evidence of his daily life in a world of surety bonds (and that such evidence should make his poetry different from any other poetry) is to assume that there may exist a life which is not subject to such economic concerns. Where do those poets whose work is not marked by such a reality live their lives? As Ransom suggested to Wilson, all poetry bears the marks of its author's experience in one way or another; and it is not logical to assume that the poetry of a claims man will be closer to the concerns of daily life—especially since being in surety bonds is like being in Oriental languages at a university: not even his colleagues down the hall knew what Stevens was talking about.

What is special about Stevens is not that he was a lawyer, or that he periodically fell silent, but that those periods of poetic silence caused him remarkably little anxiety as a poet. A handful of poems like "The Sun This March" (1930) record Stevens's dismay over his silence; and near the end of his life, he could admit that his friend Henry Church, an independently wealthy expatriate, had enjoyed the kind of life "which was truly a much larger experience than that of the hard-pressed business-man." We will see that these kinds of feelings were most acute for Stevens in the early 1930s, when the Depression threatened to topple the economic achievements for which the hard-pressed businessman forsook his poetry: at that point in his life he had to wonder if he was in any sense a "success." But by and large, Stevens worked hard (as his comments to Harvey Breit suggest) to accept a life of economic necessity without mythologizing it or lamenting it. The fact that Stevens ended his poetic silence in the 1930s after his economic success was insured suggests something crucial about his sensibility. In contrast to the 1930s, when social conditions made poetry seem largely beside the point, the 1920s were probably the most mythologized and productive literary decade in American history, and, as a poet, Stevens sat it out. If, like Arnold Schoenberg, Stevens had been silent during the violent years of the First World War instead of the 1920s, or if, like George Oppen, he had abandoned poetry in the 1930s, then his silence would make more obvious sense. Oppen stopped publishing in 1934, organized workers, moved to Mexico, and worked as a tool and die maker. Schoenberg's last composition appeared at the beginning of the war, and nothing would be heard from him until 1923—but then he unveiled the "Method of Composing with Twelve Tones Which are Related Only with One Another." Stevens did not stop publishing because of an ideological commitment or because he needed time to alter the course of Western music. Nor did his silence carry the ontological weight of Wittgenstein's or Beckett's meditations on the empty page. Most of the time, Stevens could accept his poetic silences as quietly as he entertained the dispersion of the self in poems like "The Snow Man." Neither silence caused Stevens much anxiety *as a poet*: but just as his first silence was filled with the anxiety of a newspaper reporter and junior lawyer, the second silence was filled with the anxiety of a claims man. Seen in the light of the economic considerations that dictated them, these were not "silences" at all. To say, as Stevens sometimes did, that surety bonds and poetry bear some similarities is disingenuous in that Stevens never expected the latter to bring in any income.

On a good day, money may be a kind of poetry, but poetry is not a kind
of money. Which is not to say that poetry is not bound up with capitalist
fetishism and desire; Picasso could pay for an expensive meal by scribbling
something on a napkin. But Stevens never could. One would be mistaken to
think of Stevens's life as double, the economic man distinct from the poetic,
since economic concerns shaped his poetic production at every turn. At the
same time, one would be mistaken to think that poetry and surety bonds
served him the same purpose. Seen as anecdotes on pieces of paper, poetry
and surety bonds may begin to look similarly ambiguous, as do poems and
parking tickets and lists scribbled on blackboards; as Stevens remarked, a
claims man and his papers become indistinguishable after a time. But in anything we think of as the real world, in a world where words lead to actions,
these similarities are mostly irrelevant. Stevens's most considered remarks on
this subject came at the end of "Surety and Fidelity Claims," where he admitted that when the claims man and his papers begin to constitute a single
creature it is merely a phase: "Fortunately, this singular creature yields to
more mature types: fortunately, because a business alive and expanding in
other respects must be alive and expanding equally in respect to claims. The
truth is that the most conspicuous element from the point of view of human
interest in the handling of claims is the claim man himself." While Wilson
suggests that poets would improve their poetry by holding down a job outside
the ivory tower, Stevens points out that the home office can be just as limiting,
just as much a barrier to fresh thoughts and creative living. Imagine this statement by the claims man rewritten by the poet, and I think we have the best
explanation of Stevens's silences and their necessity: "A man in the home
office tends to conduct his business on the basis of the papers that come
before him," or, to rewrite Steven's advice,

a poet in the ivory tower tends to further his art on the basis of the poems that come
before him. After twenty-five years or more of that sort of thing, he finds it difficult
sometimes to distinguish himself from the poems he writes and comes almost to believe
that he and his poems constitute a single creature, consisting principally of hands and
eyes: lots of hands and lots of eyes. Fortunately, this singular creature yields to more
mature types: fortunately, because an art alive and expanding in other respects must
be alive and expanding in respect to the poems themselves. The truth is that the most
conspicuous element from the point of view of human interest in the writing of poetry
is the poet himself.

For Stevens, the tensions of a double life began when he confused aspects
of a single life (such as bonds and poems) that operate on different terms.

The problem did not lie in the fact that he was a lawyer and a poet but in the possibility that the interests of the lawyer or of the poet might expand to take over his life in all its aspects. Speaking of his reluctance to paraphrase his poetry, Stevens remarked: "It is very difficult for me to change things from one category to another, and, as a matter of fact, I dislike to do so." Poetry and insurance were different categories for Stevens, and he kept them separate most of the time. That separation does not divide a life between its vocations and vacations but marks one of the necessary differences that keep a single life whole. A claims man who is also a poet brings different expectations to those different aspects of his life in the same way as would a poet who is also a parent: the values of one sphere will not necessarily suffice for another, even though the spheres may overlap. The claims man (or the poet) who devotes himself so exclusively to his work that he becomes his papers is not a human being but a monster—lots of hands and eyes. He is the bird with the coppery keen claws, he is Valéry's M. Teste, who addressed his wife as "Being" or "Thing" when he happened to notice her. Valéry stopped writing poetry for twenty years in order to explore more deeply the rarefied intricacies of self-consciousness; poems offered too strong a link to the real world. Stevens stopped writing for the opposite reason—not to become a poet more pure but because a pure poet was what he feared he could become.

The poem in Stevens's oeuvre that most fully resembles the work of the ingrown monster of "Surety and Fidelity Claims" is "Sea Surface Full of Clouds," perhaps the last thing he wrote before closing shop. Often considered the purest of Stevens's poems, bearing no "relation" to society (in Wilson's terms), "Sea Surface" is really his best approximation in poetry of what a claims man's work is like on a bad day. If surety claims at all resemble poems because they offer a refreshing variety within a framework of similarity, then "Sea Surface" is a bridge game in which all tricks are the same, or (more to the point) a poem in which all iambic pentameter lines are identical: "In that November off Tehuantepec" begins each of the five movements of the poem. The movements play variations on the sun's rise on the ship's deck, which may make one "think of rosy chocolate / And gilt umbrellas" or "chop-house chocolate / And sham umbrellas" or "porcelain chocolate / And pied umbrellas" or "musky chocolate / And frail umbrellas." The water's green may be, in turn, paradisiacal, sham-like, uncertain, or too-fluent. The machine of ocean may be perplexed, tense, tranced, or dry. Those two parties, variously denoted, may stand to each other in the relation of giving suavity, capping summer-seeming, holding piano-polished, or suggesting malice. This is a poem written by a claims man, late one night, filling in the standard forms with different names, and having trouble isolating any life beyond this sheet of paper.

Know All Men by These Presents.

That . . . . of . . . . as Principal and . . . . of . . . .
as Surety are held and firmly bound unto . . . . of . . . . in the penal
sum of . . . . Dollars to the payment whereof to the said . . . . they bind
their heirs, executors, administrators, successors and assigns.

Whereas the said . . . . has been employed by the said . . . . as
. . . . ,

Now, therefore, the condition of the foregoing obligation is that if the said
. . . . shall well and truly perform the duty of . . . . then this bond
shall be null and void, otherwise it shall be in full force and effect.

Signed, sealed and dated this . . . . day of . . . . . . 19 . . .

With a self-consciousness that is difficult to measure, "Sea Surface Full
of Clouds" is more or less calculatedly monotonous. The poem commemorates the sea voyage during which Stevens's daughter was conceived, and the
force of the poem's final lines, invoking that event, depends on their contrast
with the increasingly tedious repetitions that precede them: "Then the sea /
And heaven rolled as one and from the two / Came fresh transfigurings of
freshest blue." Just what kind of transfiguration Stevens had in mind is not
clear. Each movement of "Sea Surface" pushes for some kind of unveiling,
especially the fourth, where the too-fluent green suggests malice in the dry
machine of ocean. But each movement is checked by stasis, and the poem's
structural repetitions overcome the wish for difference. To use the terms of
"Surety and Fidelity Claims," "Sea Surface Full of Clouds" reveals a mind
made of papers, a mind too immature to see a world alive and expanding beyond
the page. As Stevens said in "The Noble Rider," speaking out of his own fears,
"The imagination loses vitality as it ceases to adhere to what is real."

To continue with the terms of "Surety and Fidelity Claims," Stevens
wrote a more mature poem than "Sea Surface" on Valentine's Day in 1925.
These occasional verses are perhaps the only poetic effort Stevens mustered
during the second silence.

> Though Valentine brings love
> And Spring brings beauty
> They do not make me rise
> To my poetic duty
>
> But Elsie and Holly do
> And do it daily—
> Much more than Valentine or Spring
> And very much more gaily.

If "Sea Surface Full of Clouds" is as close as Stevens could come to the work of surety bonds, then these lines are as far away from that work as he could get. To say so seems willfully paradoxical, since "Sea Surface" is one of Stevens's most esoteric poems, while this Valentine's Day verse is among his most occasional. But "Sea Surface" comes close to surety bonds precisely because it is so self-enclosed; it is to poetry what suretyship is to insurance—like the department of Oriental languages at the university. In contrast, the Valentine's Day poem (though much closer to the daily life that surety bonds engage) stands utterly apart from the discourse of suretyship. As a poem about "poetic duty," it is itself paradoxical since Stevens wrote almost no other poetry in the later 1920s. The poem suggests that Stevens fulfilled his duty to his family by rising at daybreak, shaving, exercising, eating his therapeutic breakfast, walking to work, and putting in his full day at the Hartford. Such actions became his "poetic duty" when they helped him out of the aesthetic cul-de-sac epitomized by "Sea Surface Full of Clouds."

Stevens once advised a young poet that he "should be more in contact with the real things of life. . . . You have to think about what you read, but you have to think about your life and the things around you." That wisdom seems less hackneyed when one realizes, reading "Surety and Fidelity Claims," that Stevens would offer the same lesson to a young insurance agent. Several years after his second silence came to an end, Stevens offered a similar nugget of advice to Ronald Latimer, who was contemplating the end of his career in publishing. In utter seriousness, Stevens suggested that Latimer might be refreshed by getting down to a career in business for "say, the next twenty-five years." (Stevens's stomach for sheer drudgery is never to be underestimated.) Then he compared Latimer's desire to give up publishing with his own poetic silences.

A good many years ago, when I really was a poet in the sense that I was all imagination, and so on, I deliberately gave up writing poetry because, much as I loved it, there were too many other things I wanted not to make an effort to have them. I wanted to do everything that one wants to do at that age: live in a village in France, in a hut in Morocco, or in a piano box at Key West. But I didn't like the idea of being bedeviled all the time about money and I didn't for a moment like the idea of poverty, so I went to work like anybody else and kept at it for a good many years.

This letter is commonly read as Stevens's explanation of his midcareer silence. The claims man who wrote "Sea Surface Full of Clouds" in 1924, the year that Stevens turned forty-four, does seem like a poet given over completely to the imagination. But it seems to me that in his letter to Latimer,

Stevens describes not his second silence but his first. Could he really have been thinking of himself at forty-four, married and about to become a father, when he remembered yearning to live in a piano box? The period when Stevens was "all imagination" was not the *Harmonium* years, when he worked full time at the Hartford, but his Harvard years, the time he would recall in "Imagination as Value" as "the years of imaginative life" in contrast to his "later economic and political years." Stevens left Harvard wanting to do all those romantic things but knowing that such experiences require money, and by the time he had achieved financial security, he no longer desired the experiences. "Independence to do as you please," quipped Stevens, "is my idea of being out of a job." In the 1920s he had no interest in such freedom. And the voice counseling Latimer in the 1930s echos the father who admonished his son not to squander his years at Harvard: "Our young folks would of course all prefer to be born like English noblemen with Entailed estates, income guaranteed and in choosing a profession they would simply say— 'How shall I amuse myself'—but young America understands that the question is—*Starting with nothing, how shall I sustain myself and perhaps a wife and family—and send my boys to College and live* comfortably in my old age.'"

That Stevens's letter to Latimer has often been read as an explanation of the second silence is not entirely surprising, however; aside from the desire for life in a Moroccan hut or French village, the letter describes the dynamics of both silences, which were induced for the same reasons and resolved in the same terms. Stevens stopped writing poetry in 1900 and devoted himself full time to answering his father's question, and only in 1908, after he had found his first dependable source of income with the American Bonding Company, did the poems begin to return. Full economic security and professional status came in 1914, when Stevens was hired as a vice president at the New York office of the Equitable Surety Company of St. Louis, and "Carnet de Voyage" followed soon after—his first publication since he had left Harvard. Ten years later, when his daughter was born, Stevens again decided to give up poetry and devote himself to pecuniary interests. By 1929, his salary had reached a level nearly five times what it had been when Stevens wrote "Sunday Morning," and he began to think of poetry again. It was a self-conscious decision, as it had been in 1908, and a few poems did appear. *Harmonium* was reprinted in 1931. But in the following year, two events conspired to perpetuate the silence. Not only did Stevens purchase his home on Westerly Terrace for $20,000 cash, but after three years of receiving no raise at all he was forced to take a 10 percent salary reduction. "Generally speaking," he told a colleague, "there seems to be a feeling in Hartford that things are going to grow better rather than worse. There are no intimations of any further reductions in salary." Stevens remained cautious. "I am no longer a poet," he had told his wife in 1907, just a few months before he began to write again, and near the end of his second silence he was equally convinced that his poetic career was over for good: "Nothing short of a coup d'état would make it possible for me to write poetry now." After two more years of watching his paychecks stand still, 1934 suddenly brought a 27 percent salary increase, along with the vice presidency of the entire corporation (he had been appointed vice president of a particular office in 1914). Stevens told the same colleague, "I was so up in the air for a few days, as a result of being a vice president . . . that it was hard for me to do anything except to drop notes to people telling them how tickled I was by their congratulations." The other thing Stevens was able to do was write poetry. "The Idea of Order at Key West" appeared with nearly a dozen other poems that year. A second decade of poetic silence had been as important for that masterpiece as the first had been for "Sunday Morning."

Although Stevens's dissatisfaction with the detached aesthetic of "Sea Surface" contributed to his waning interest in poetry, the dynamics of his two silences were more precisely economic than aesthetic. To write poems, Stevens needed to be "the master of the situation": that was the phrase he used to describe his satisfaction with owning a house (which he could not yet afford to furnish). By 1908 he had achieved sufficient economic security to allow him the freedom to write, but by 1924 Stevens felt insecure about his future. He always remembered the years he had spent in New York, "working savagely; but . . . so desperately poor at times as not to be able to buy sufficient food—and sometimes not any." That was a decade he would never allow himself to repeat. Even more powerful was the memory of the fate of his father, who suffered a nervous breakdown after a business failed. That too was an event that threatened to repeat itself: Stevens must have mulled it over every time his doctor disqualified him for life insurance, every time he set aside money for his wife and child's future, banking against his father's shadow, and every time he sent money to his brother, Garrett, Jr., who broke down and succumbed to that shadow during the Depression.

Stevens was not just secure, however, he was rich: in the year of the stock-market crash he was making ten times the national average income. Yet for all his affluence, Stevens was not able to enjoy everything his money could have bought. Just as he needed to achieve a certain level of economic security before he allowed himself the pleasure of poetry, so did Stevens parcel out his daily pleasures, denying himself the very things he desired most of all— the grown-up versions of the desire to live in a Moroccan hut or a piano box at Key West. Stevens wanted to know that he could afford to fulfill his dreams, but he shrank from actually making them come true. This is where most consequential tension of Stevens's life may be found—not in the career that seems "double" to people who conceive of the imaginative life as inimical to a life of economic striving. Dana Goia, himself a successful businessman and poet, has made the point succinctly: "What was most odd about Stevens was not his occupation, but rather that he never visited Paris or Rome, since most company vice-presidents do that."

9

ᜰ

Paris and the Florida
Land Boom

Stevens cultivated his isolation in the 1920s. During the First World War, he
had benefited from an expatriate movement that carried artists to New York
rather than Paris. But by 1916, when he moved from Manhattan to Hartford,
Stevens's artistic life became distanced from the currents of international
modernism, and by 1922 he no longer cared to preserve the attachments he
once enjoyed. Tired of the "art crowd," Stevens packed up his collection of
exhibition catalogues (which he considered a complete survey of what had
been shown in New York for the previous ten years) and gave them to the
Wadsworth Atheneum. Settled in Hartford, Stevens wanted to believe that
he could ignore Paris as easily as he unburdened himself of his catalogues,
and he did his best to dismiss both New York and Paris as equally provincial
alternatives.

Alice Corbin Henderson (Harriet Monroe's assistant at *Poetry* magazine)
had moved to Sante Fe for health reasons, and Stevens told her about the
annual exhibition of the Society for Independent Artists in New York: "it has
grown almost fashionable and attracts large crowds. . . . Besides, of course,
there isn't a damned bit of independence about it. You must do as the independents do or be a laughing-stock. . . . It is well to live in Hartford or Santa
Fe and not be bothered by any public even the public of a small group of
friends." Stevens's effort to equate Santa Fe and Hartford was a gesture meant
to cheer the ailing Henderson; as a justification of his increasing isolation, the
logic weakens and his letter seems tellingly defensive. At the same time that
he wrote these letters to Henderson, Robert McAlmon was writing to Stevens
from Paris about the hidden terrors of places like Hartford, Connecticut: "I

know the god awful isolation that America inflicts upon its intelligent and semi-intelligent souls." The point of McAlmon's remarks on Williams's fate in Rutherford could not have been lost on Stevens in Hartford: "He simply should not permit life to keep him a doctor in a small town—but one can't advise. I can't." It was probably McAlmon who persuaded Pound to ask Stevens for a poem in 1927 (Pound was editing *Exile*, in which McAlmon appeared), but even the mastermind of the Great English Vortex could not arouse the suburban muse.

Almost all of Stevens's friends lived abroad during the 1920s—even Williams; expatriation was the natural complement to an equally common disdain for American consumer culture. "Feeling like aliens in the commercial world," said Malcolm Cowley, "they sailed for Europe as soon as they had money enough to pay for their steamer tickets." But, of course, if they could afford the passage, they were not aliens in the commercial world: the postwar success of the American economy made their extended vacations possible, and living off a favorable exchange rate became a profession in itself. (Near the end of his life, Stevens confessed that he did not mind "too much" that he spent each day "working at the office" so that someone else "may sit at the Cafe X at Aix or go to lectures at the Sorbonne.") By conceiving of an extended European vacation as an escape from the consumer culture, expatriate writers were leading the double life Stevens was not. But Stevens was trapped by a culture that made scorn for the American business world a prerequisite for foreign pleasures; Stevens could not muster the scorn without turning against himself. And he could not nurture a businessman's contempt for expatriates without slighting himself as well; most people who stayed behind to keep the wheels of the economy spinning did not publish poetry in the leading avant-garde magazines of the day. There was a natural conjunction of economics and artistry, vocations and vacations in Stevens's career; but, given that conjunction, Stevens had a peculiar need to deny himself the vacations he could have afforded. Cultural forces made the expatriate lifestyle self-contradictory for him, but Stevens's particular psychic economy forced him to take his pleasures at a calculated distance. Stevens also made this confession late in his career: "I wanted all my life to go to Paris." No financial constraints prevented him from sitting in a café in Aix or attending lectures at the Sorbonne.

"I dislike niggling, and like letting myself go," said Stevens apropos of "The Emperor of Ice-Cream." "This poem is an instance of letting myself go." Stevens did like letting himself go, but he liked niggling too. In fact, he could not abide extravagance without sacrifice, and sometimes he liked niggling most of all. When Stevens bought his home in 1932, he explained to a business associate that it was the best thing he had ever done: "it prevents me from throwing my money away on anything." When the same associate bought his own home two years later, Stevens was still grinding the same axe: "It was probably wise of you to buy the sort of house you appear to have bought, because having it will prevent you from doing something extravagant. . . . For my part, I never really lived until I had a home, and my own room, say, with a package of books from Paris or London. But then there is always the anxiety that follows overindulgence." The romance of a package from Paris or London was not lost on Stevens, but the indulgence—the letting go—of actually visiting those places remained out of the question. For compensation, Stevens maintained an almost prurient interest in his friends' Parisian adventures. He made a particular effort to keep the novelist Ferdinand Reyher informed of his other friends' travel plans, and he also kept Alice Henderson up to date on the expatriate scene: "I have had nothing recent from Alfred Kreyemborg. He separated from Loeb, spent the winter in Rapallo, where Gordon Craig and Max Beerbohm are spending their old age, and will be back here, I daresay, shortly." These letters amount to little more than catalogues of names and places; when Stevens boasts that he has "a good deal of correspondence with people abroad and receive[s] quite a number of magazines from London and Paris," one begins to feel that his purpose is not so much to keep his friends informed but to impress them with his knowledge of a world he also dismissed. Stevens needed to have it both ways. Real independence was to be found in the isolation of Hartford, he assured Henderson (by way of assuring himself), but real extravagance was nowhere but Paris: "John Rodker is trying to interest me in buying a Wyndham Lewis, writes about his latest manner as being something amazing and refers me to the reproductions in the last number of the *Tyro*. Fancy the swank of Wyndham Lewis."

More than a painting by Lewis, Stevens fancied his personal drama of the letting go and the niggling. Ultimately, he kept in touch with his expatriate friends not so much as fellow artists but as fellow connoisseurs. This is the opportunity of a lifetime, he told Reyher after the novelist had arrived in England. Stevens meant that it was an economic opportunity, for he was asking Reyher if he would consider purchasing some odds and ends and shipping them to Hartford, as John Rodker had been doing. Unwilling to make the trip himself, Stevens sent Reyher a shopping list that by its extravagant bulk reveals the intensity of Stevens's need for the substitutions for travel that money could buy. The list wanders over five single-spaced typed pages—Sicilian honey from a particular shop in Piccadilly, apples from the Tyrol (but not plum pudding), a list of the publications of the British Museum, the manual on Japanese prints from the Victoria and Albert, catalogues from current exhibitions of Spanish paintings and South American artifacts, Italian prints (preferably old ones, which are cheaper than new ones), etchings by Augustus John, woodcuts by Camille Pissarro's son Lucien, Herbert Giles's "Strange Stories from a Chinese Studio" (unless it is printed on rice paper and bound in silk), and anything relating to life in Venice in the eighteenth century.

Stevens would have saved money and time by crossing the Atlantic and doing the shopping himself. But that was not the point. The Pennsylvania Dutch boy who grew up to become an insurance executive could rationalize the expense but could not face the pleasure of acquiring the experience head-on: Stevens collected souvenirs from trips he never took. But in this case, a box from Rehyer never arrived, and a few months later Stevens received what must have been a rather cool postcard from the novelist: a contrite Stevens wrote back suggesting that Reyher was sensible not to sweat over the shopping list.

In part, Stevens was relieved to have Reyher's postcard because he did not really want his list of desires fulfilled. Most of his pleasure was in the listing and the waiting. He told Reyher that the shopping would have been an extravagance, cautioning that he could not afford to be extravagant just then because the income tax was due. Stevens was expecting no refund, for in the early 1920s the income tax was a novelty. In 1913 Congress enacted a personal income tax of 1 percent on income over $3,000 (or in Stevens's case, over $4,000, since he was married) along with a surtax on incomes over $20,000. Sharp increases followed during the war. In 1918 the rates were made progressive, with taxes ranging from 1 to 6 percent and surtaxes from 1 to 65 percent. To people of Stevens's generation, the tax seemed like a penalty their parents did not have to pay. But Stevens also derived a vicarious pleasure from the tax, for it gave him a socially respectable explanation for his personal need to curtail his extravagance and prolong his shopping lists. In 1935, when he had asked Harriet Monroe's sister to do some shopping for him, Stevens then requested that she wait "because I have an income tax to pay this week." And in the 1920s, when Reyher finally did find several of the books Stevens had asked for, Stevens shot back a letter accusing his buyer of unwarranted extravagance—didn't Reyher realize that the income tax was payable in March?

Of all Stevens's friends, Robert McAlmon understood the economy of Stevens's desires best. He did not send Stevens things; he responded to the shopping lists with longer shopping lists. This letter surely satisfied Stevens as much or more than a package of honey and books.

I bravely steered past the tiny carved wooden animals, a cat nursing two kittens, a goat with two kids, a pig, a peacock, some tough looking pirates in highly colored garments; some ivory flowers; and necklaces—what could Stevens do with an ivory flower or a necklace.... And I steered by some spanish gold jewelry—and a magnificent snail with its long body bravely bearing a gold snail coach. You can't have it. Cost too much. Might make you pay duty. I don't trust the delivery service. Besides I don't know whether your interest in the simple, cute, childish, toylike oddity, would quite agree with my own. But I recognize that emotionally you aren't any more sophisticated than I am, for all our ironic whimsy, and grand display of cerebration and intellect.

McAlmon and Stevens would not meet until 1927, but they came to know each other through Williams in the early 1920s, and once McAlmon settled in Paris, Stevens lived out his dream of extravagance through McAlmon's personal life in the same way that he visited Paris by mail-order. Through Williams, McAlmon did meet H.D., and through H.D. he met Bryher (Winifred Ellerman). The story of their marriage is well known. Bryher wanted a husband to placate her aristocratic father, and in exchange for the occasional family appearance, the husband would receive a generous allowance. Stevens reported the scuttlebutt to Reyher on two occasions (as if the expatriate novelist would know less of the situation than the isolated Stevens), taking a slightly condescending amusement in McAlmon's marriage. But McAlmon's actions revealed not only great extravagance but great canniness. His new fortune backed up Contact Editions, which published Hemingway, Williams, Stein, and McAlmon's own collection of stories, *A Hasty Bunch* (so named by James Joyce). McAlmon became Joyce's closest confidant in Paris; Joyce frequently sought his opinion and said that McAlmon's own stories reminded him "in a way of *Dubliners*—not in treatment or the characters—rather the mental predisposition." And perhaps even more flattering than this praise from Joyce and Pound was the swank of Wyndham Lewis's attack on McAlmon along with Joyce and Stein in *Time and Western Man*.

Learning of these connections, Stevens was stunned by McAlmon's swift penetration of the Parisian inner circle; he told Reyher that the young man's evolution was one of the most extraordinary things going on in the world today. Although Stevens had tried to tell Alice Henderson that life in New York or Paris was equally stultifying as life in Hartford, he knew it was not so. McAlmon had parlayed youthful extravagance (and a hefty income) into a prominent literary career, and though there is honest glee in Stevens's account of his achievements, there is an undercurrent of jealousy too. McAlmon had set out to live in a hut in Morocco or a piano box at Key West, and he had succeeded.

When William Carlos Williams went to Paris in 1924, McAlmon sent Stevens a progress report on the suburban doctor's artistic health: "Am here with W.C. Williams en route to Riviera. He goes on to Italy & Vienna. I stay there and work. Are you coming over here?" By that time the question was moot, and after returning to Rutherford, Williams asked Stevens how he managed to fill his days. "The baby has kept us both incredibly busy," Stevens replied. "True she is not under my jurisdiction and has been as well-behaved as a south-wind yet the fact remains that she dominates the house and that her requirements have to a large extent become our own." That excuse mystified Williams, who had delivered hundreds of those blasphemously pink creatures into the world, while managing to write poems and travel abroad. "But oh la-la," Stevens continued, "my job is not now with poets from Paris. It is to keep the fire-place burning and the music-box churning and the wheels of the baby's chariot turning and that sort of thing. Perhaps if I am fortunate, I shall be able to drop down into Florida for a few weeks bye and bye."

What made trips to Florida permissible (to use the insurance agent's word) as trips to Paris were not? Stevens had ridiculed the "independence" of the Society for Independent Artists ("You must do as the independents do or be a laughing-stock"), and Williams mocked Stevens's southern excursions in exactly the same way. In "This Florida: 1924" Stevens appears as "Hibiscus," and Florida is nothing but "cottages in a row / all radioed and showerbathed."

> it's a kind of borrowed
> pleasure after all (as at the movies)
> to see them
>
> tearing off to escape it
> this winter.

Florida sunshine was one stimulus for the great exodus to that state in the 1920s, but so was land speculation. Once a playground for the wealthy, Florida was opened to the middle class by the automobile, and real-estate developers were quick to exploit their burgeoning prosperity. Here was the consumer culture at its American best: a real-estate agent in Coral Gables hired William Jennings Bryan—he of the cross of gold and the monkey trial—to sit under a beach umbrella and employ his renounced oratorical skills to extol the beauty of the Florida landscape. Swamps became lagoons, land was sold and resold at prices far exceeding any value it could retain, and the speculative frenzy that rose and as quickly fell was an ominous forerunner of the stock-market trouble to come. Stevens invested only his imagination in Florida, and for him the returns were substantial. His relationship with McAlmon and his mail-order gormandizing offered some compensation for the extravagant voyages he denied himself; but trips to Florida became the most fulfilling consolation of all.

If independence was Stevens's idea of being out of a job, here was an independence that was specifically job related. Most of Stevens's trips to Florida, especially early on, were business trips, and as he tended his vocation in Atlanta and Miami, he could allow himself the few extra miles for a vacation in Key West—that was permissible. And, unlike the Left Bank, Florida was not "literary," at least until Frost and Hemingway appeared on the scene. "Since my return," wrote Stevens to Reyher after his first visit to Key West with Arthur Powell, "I have not cared much for literature." Powell was a lawyer and judge in Atlanta who was to become one of Stevens's closest friends. During almost every winter from 1922 to 1940, Powell, Stevens, and a selected few would meet at the Long Key Fishing Camp, an exclusive sportsman's resort in the Florida Keys. Stevens described his first visit to Reyher, attempting to match his expatriate friends' tales of the carefree life in Paris.

Now, that trip to Florida would have unstrung a brass monkey. I went down there with half a dozen other people from Atlanta. I was the only damned Yankee in the bunch. I was christened a charter member of the Long Key Fishing Club of Atlanta. The christening occupied about three days, and required just two cases of Scotch. When I traveled home, I was not able to tell whether I was travelling on a sound or a smell. As I remember it, it was very much like a cloud full of Cuban señoritas, coconut palms, and waiters carrying ice water.

That was how Stevens wanted Florida to appear to an American in Paris. For his wife in Hartford, he regained his Pennsylvania Dutch sobriety, emphasizing that the same trip was more business than pleasure, and the pleasure simply unavoidable.

The attorneys in Miami drew up the contract yesterday. Powell came down here and I spent the day in Key West arriving here shortly after nine o'clock. The contract arrived this morning, but instead of taking tonight's train for the North I am going to wait until tomorrow night's which should get me home on Friday night or Saturday morning. Powell is with a party of friends here on a fishing trip. They are going out in boats tomorrow and I am going with them. This is one of the choicest places I have ever been to. . . . The place is a paradise—midsummer weather, the sky brilliantly clear and intensely blue, the sea blue and green beyond what you have ever seen. What a fool I should be not to come down here when I can give the results already achieved in return and still have a little fun out of it.

Stevens needed to justify this extravagance to a woman who had little taste for the pleasures of travel herself, but even more he needed to satisfy his own ambivalent conscience. All the Florida poems of *Harmonium* turn on his double image of Florida as both an earthly paradise and a dangerous illusion; in a poem that momentarily broke the second silence in 1929, "Annual Gaiety," Stevens returned to that fine-honed theme.

> In the morning in the blue snow
> The catholic sun, its majesty,
> Pinks and pinks the ice-hard melanchole.
>
> Wherefore those prayers to the moon?
> Or is it that alligators lie
> Along the edges of your eye
> Basking in desert Florida?
>
> Père Guzz, in heaven, thumb your lyre
> And chant the January fire
> And joy of snow and snow.

Stevens's attitude toward southern pleasures depended on his particular mood, but here he finds all the extravagance he needs by staying close to his northern home. As in his overseas shopping, moderation and denial gave Stevens more pleasure than fulfillment. But Florida could also figure in Stevens's personal economy as a world of just denial—especially when compared not with the wintry isolation of Hartford but with the utter extravagance of literary Paris: "I pride myself on being a member of the Long Key Fishing Club of Atlanta and of the Brown Derby Club of East Hartford, and I take damned little stock in conversation on philosophy, aesthetics, poetry, art, or blondes." As Milton Bates has shown, the manly burgher was a role Stevens enjoyed playing for the literary world, but in the next sentence in this letter to Reyher he tips the mask: "Of course, I hanker for all those things as a fly hankers for fly paper." That was precisely the pleasure bound up in denying himself such extravagance. And the next sentence completes the cycle: "But experience has taught me that fly paper is one devil of a thing to get mixed up in." Stevens would not allow himself any pleasure that might endanger his economic security or even tempt him to change his life. For that reason, trips to Paris were not permissible: he desired that pleasure too urgently. Yet Stevens was able to parlay strategic denial into a life of satisfaction, since even the longing and the nostalgia gave him pleasure. Had he thrown over his career for an expatriate's life-style (even for a short time, as Williams had done), he would have gleaned no pleasure at all.

After writing "Annual Gaiety" in 1929 and "The Sun This March" the following year, Stevens lapsed back into silence. More than either of these poems, his essay "Cattle *Kings* of Florida" (1930) reveals the elaborate system of checks and balances of Stevens's economy of pleasure. Stevens knew Florida and he knew cattle, since as a claims man he had first specialized in the insuring of cattle being sent to market. The tales of the lost world of Florida's cattlemen entranced him in 1930, just as the exotic port of New York had entranced him in 1900 and as drilling soldiers had entranced him in 1915— and for many of the same reasons. Here was authentic experience somehow lost to him, work that was both productive and pleasant. Seen from the aftermath of the crash of 1929, here too was a world where money was abundant and cast in gold. Over 1300 banks closed in 1930, and another 2300 would fold in the following year. But in Stevens's Florida, no one bothered with banks that could close their doors, dissolving money that had hardly seemed to exist in the first place. In "Cattle *Kings* of Florida" money is gold and work is the stuff of romance: "Saddle bags filled with gold left lying on the front porch or even in the stable! Coffee cans or kitchen pots filled to the brim with the yellow Spanish coins and left unguarded on kitchen shelves of isolated ranch homes!" Stevens knew that world was gone for good. "The old careless days of half a century ago with their easy money will probably never return," he wrote in the first year in which he received no salary increase. Still, even as he watched the Depression congeal around him, Stevens did not let this nostalgia for the past overwhelm his present day world: "but the manner in which the Florida cattle industry is adapting itself to the new conditions indicates that it will be a big business there for a long time to come."

Stevens could not have mustered that optimism in 1900. "Cattle *Kings* of Florida" reveals why he could begin to do so in 1930, for even though the remainder of the article offers several romantic stories of Florida ranchers, the stories are really allegories for the life of niggling and denial that Wallace Stevens chose for himself. He probably learned the tale of T. L. Wilson from Arthur Powell, who often delighted Stevens with his stories of the South. Without much "book learning," Wilson set out to become a cattle king, and by the age of eighteen he had acquired a large herd. But soon he needed new challenges. After a long stormy night of herding the stampeding cattle, he decided it was time to change his career. He rode to Fort Myers and offered to sell the cattle to his uncle, explaining that "he was going to take the money and study law." Unlike Stevens's father, who pushed him to give up the extravagant literary life for law school, Wilson's uncle "didn't think much of his nephew's decision," but he agreed to buy the herd, directing Wilson to help himself to the saddlebags of gold coins lying unguarded on the porch.

Mr. Wilson counted out the nearly two thousand dollars that his cattle came to and left for home. And he stated that there was probably a thousand dollars more still in the bags left on the porch for the night.

The youth never regretted his change of profession from a financial viewpoint at least. He went direct from the range to Washington and Lee University at Lexington, and was said to have been one of the two men ever to complete the law course there in one year, and that without even a complete grammar school education. He was admitted to the bar before he was 21 by a special act of the Florida legislature, and from that time on his success justified his choice of a career.

His success justified his choice of a career. Having given up the extravagant life of a cattle rancher, Wilson the lawyer eventually became a member of the war finance board appointed by Woodrow Wilson—a fate as good as gold. Having given up a life as a professional poet and denied himself the cafés in Aix and the lectures at the Sorbonne, Stevens also became a lawyer, and I wonder if in 1930—when he watched his salary drop and thought he would never write another poem—Stevens knew in his heart that his success had justified his choice of a career. He wanted to believe that it did, and we have seen that it eventually would, especially after Stevens was named vice president and began furiously writing poems again. In 1932, when his salary had dipped even lower and the poems seemed gone for good, Stevens began keeping his commonplace book, *Sur Plusieurs Beaux Sujects*, and the first entry was this: "Les carrières réussies sort celles qui réalisent dans l'homme les rêves de l'enfant" [Successful careers are those that realize in the man the dreams of the child]. Toward the end of his second silence, if Stevens was unsure that his economic success was great enough to have justified his denial of a life devoted to poetry, he was surely unable to say that his career embodied his dreams. The third entry in *Sur Plusieurs Beaux Sujects* reads, "Success as the result of industry is a peasant ideal." In that statement one feels Stevens's disdain for such success, but Stevens also knew that the ideal was his own.

Stevens's need to feel economically successful, to feel himself "master of the situation" before he could allow himself the extravagance of poetry kept him out of step with the expatriate generation; the same trait allowed him to reclaim his poetry only after the economic extravagance of the 1920s had dissipated. One of the clearest indications of the impulse behind this renewed interest in poetry may be found in a long passage Stevens entered into *Sur Plusieurs Beaux Sujects* in 1932. It begins with a quotation from Christopher Wren ("Nunc me jubet Fortuna expeditius philosophari" [Now Fortune decrees that I should more readily philosophize]), a remark made when the architect lost his "appointment as Surveyor-General." Stevens then explains that he found the quotation in an essay by Walter Leaf: "The paper seems to have been written after a considerable reverse in business and illustrates Leaf's 'seriousness and sincerity.'" Stevens copied down a long passage from Leaf's paper—in which (like Wren) Leaf turns from professional setback to philosophy—and the words hint at the dark side of Stevens's obsession with professional success. At the beginning of his career, shortly after his father's catastrophic business failure, John Jay Chapman provided Stevens with a model for youthful aspiration, and at this mid-point in his career, Walter Leaf—who achieved considerable success in insurance, banking, and classical scholarship—served a similar function. When his own father died, Leaf was forced to leave Cambridge and take over the family business, which he soon converted into a limited liability company. In 1891 he was named a director of the London and Westminster Bank, and after the First World War he was elected president of the International Chamber of Commerce. He published a book on banking for the Home University Library in 1926, but his first book was a prose translation of the *Iliad* (1882), undertaken in collaboration with Andrew Lang and Ernest James Myers. Leaf then produced a two-volume edition of the *Iliad* with extensive commentary and later published *Troy, a Study in Homeric Geography*, the first of several volumes of Homeric scholarship. (Like Victor Bérard, whose work was central to the development of Joyce's *Ulysses*, Leaf mapped ancient trade routes, arguing that the origins of the Trojan War were commercial.) These accomplishments were enticing enough to Stevens, but Leaf's eloquence in the face of failure attracted him even more. Leaf faced his public losses by turning inward; yet much more than the health of the self depended on that turn: "It is undeniably a good thing that [the individual] should try, if he can, to reduce this [inner] chaos to order—in the first place, of course, for his own sake." And in the second place, for the sake of the culture at large, for (as Leaf writes in the passage Stevens recorded in his commonplace book), the "progress of the world" depends upon that individual will to order.

Those are mighty claims, but Stevens's attention to them brings into focus one of the guiding principles of his poems from "Stars at Talapoosa" through "The Idea of Order at Key West" to "Notes toward a Supreme Fiction." In "A Fading of the Sun" (1933), the first poem of the 1930s to refer openly to the Depression, Stevens followed Leaf's advice. By the time Stevens published these lines, the personal income of most Americans had dropped by more than 50 percent; 25 percent of the population was unemployed; Roosevelt had been in office for nine months.

> Who can think of the sun costuming clouds
> When all people are shaken
> Or of night endazzled, proud,
> When people awaken
> And cry and cry for help?

Given these conditions, the "warm antiquity of self" grows cold, and the pleasures once enjoyed (tea, bread, and wine) grow stale. But if people will only look "within themselves," they will see that "The tea, / The wine is good. The bread, / The meat is sweet."

"A Fading of the Sun" concludes too easily; a great deal of public power inheres in the private act of introspection. The poem is written by someone who desperately needed to feel successful, someone who had to overcome the fear of necessity and the threat of poverty, someone who actually required the title of vice president before he could allow himself the pleasure of writing poetry; the poem is also written by someone deeply uncomfortable with the success he achieved, someone who needed to deny himself whatever he desired most of all, someone who found the true subject of poetry in a recognition of the power of necessity and the threat of poverty. Stevens could write only out of a condition of success, but "A Fading of the Sun," his poem of success, does not ring true. Although he would never extricate himself from this dilemma completely, Stevens would find it more and more difficult to offer this poem's easy consolation as the 1930s progressed. In "How to Live. What to Do," a poem he considered a companion to "A Fading of the Sun," he would dramatize once more the private self's victory over public adversity; but in discussing both poems with Latimer, he confessed that they sounded "like a lot of fiddle-dee-dee." Throughout the 1930s, Stevens's poems would continue their vacillation between the Snow Man and Hoon, between the world within and the world without, but in the central poems he would build on the mediating position of "Stars at Talapoosa," aware at once of the ideas of order and the fiddle-dee-dee that the self is capable of producing. The Emersonian ideal proposed by "The Idea of Order at Key West" is not so very different from that of "Stars at Talapoosa," but the historical circumstances that propagated the poem were strenuous enough to make Stevens reformulate his ideal from scratch. "Writing again after a discontinuance," said Stevens in 1933, "seems to take one back to the beginning rather than to the point of discontinuance."

Even Stevens's most perceptive readers still feel that the poet remained aloof from social and political conditions until he published *Ideas of Order* (1935), eliciting Stanley Burnshaw's review. But Stevens had been struggling with those conditions ever since he was an undergraduate, capable of writing poems like "Ballade of the Pink Parasol" but wanting to write poems like "Outside the Hospital." The poetry of *Ideas of Order* does differ from that of *Harmonium* in that it more often and more openly thematizes the struggles which the entire body of poetry embodies; nevertheless, if Stevens appears to awaken to political turmoil in the 1930s, it is because the challenge of the American left focused more clearly the terms of an ongoing struggle. In his belated response to "Mr. Burnshaw and the Statue" (and to the mythologization of Stevens's dialogue with Marxism in general), Stanley Burnshaw appealed to Stevens's readers to understand the context of his review: "to think that the Marxist critics were an undifferentiated right-thinking Left-minded phalanx is to create a monster that simply did not exist." To understand Stevens's work in the 1930s, we must begin with the social and political conditions that shaped not only Burnshaw's review but the poems of *Ideas of Order*.

IV

Poetry and
Social Change

10

Lefts and Lefts

In the *Partisan Review*, May 1935, three months before *Ideas of Order* was published by the Alcestis Press: "Wallace Stevens is remembered by *Harmonium*; he is no longer a living poet." That was the judgment of Edwin Rolfe in a comment on the state of American poetry, and anyone who had not picked up the first issue of *Alcestis* would have agreed. Even if Rolfe had read the poems Stevens published there—"The Idea of Order at Key West" along with seven others—he would hardly have considered them the work of a poet "alive" in any meaningful sense. Rolfe illustrated his poetic ideal with a few lines from his own "Homage to Karl Marx."

> His dialectic enervates the doomed,
> inspired the mass to courage: not for long
> can our foes delay our unfolding destiny.

There is little room here for what Stevens once called the gaudiness of poetry. At the end of the 1930s, the editors of the *Partisan Review*, William Phillips and Philip Rahv, summed up the decade's literary imperative this way: "The mood of the thirties required objectivity, realism, and an interest in the social manifestations of individual life." Such prescriptions marginalized not only Stevens but poetry itself. Not even Edwin Rolfe could compete with the social resonances of the proletarian novel, and, to many ears, Stevens might have been speaking for all poets when he confessed in "Sailing After Lunch" (1935) that he was "A most inappropriate man / In a most unpropitious place."

This feeling was not new to Stevens. Poets had bristled under the charge of irrelevance at least since Shelley responded to Peacock, and the social and political conditions of the 1930s recharged the terms of an old debate. "Is literature really a profession?" That was the question Stevens asked when he left Harvard for the newspaper business, and his personal answer to the question was no. Literature would not support his family; it would not be Wallace Stevens's profession. But any post-Romantic poet chafing at the charge of irrelevance is trapped in a highly professionalized conception of poetry. "Every profession is a secret society," said Virgil Thomson in *The State of Music* (1939), perhaps the wisest account of the arts' social function that the 1930s produced. The first requirement of a profession is that it specialize, and Thomson understood that poets had been forced to specialize so narrowly that poetry appeared to have no function at all: "What subjects, then, are available to the poet today?" That question was rarely asked of musicians, whose society was so secret that nobody expected them to have something to say to the world outside; for poets, however, the prospects looked bleak. A poet like Homer or even Dryden could write about political events or mathematical logic and still write "poetry." But after novelists made narrative their métier and poets began specializing in the imagination, the poetic profession appeared marginal by definition. Stevens made that point when he remarked that it "was a great loss to poetry when people began to think that the professional poet was an outlaw or an exile." In this sense, it is all too easy for literature to be a profession. Seen in the larger context of the post-Romantic poet's social predicament, the Depression's challenge to poetry was not radically different from the challenge of the First World War, when poets who had overspecialized in a severely diminished conception of poetry were confronted with an epic subject. Yet "war poet" is still part of a poet's description in a way that "Depression poet" never was, and unlike the Great War, the Great Depression put poets on the dole.

Of course poets were not alone, since by 1932, 25 percent of the American population was out of work. By the time of Roosevelt's inauguration in March 1933, the national income had been cut in half; nearly a million farmers had capitulated to creditors, and the nation's monetary system was teetering on the brink of collapse. To both professional economists and common citizens, drastic action seemed the only solution to what was now being called a "depression" rather than a "crisis" that would naturally be followed by a "recovery." Malcolm Cowley told Kenneth Burke that "only a man of superhuman ability" could jump-start the economy. That feeling was not Cowley's alone, and for many Americans, Roosevelt fit the heroic measure. The first "Hundred Days" of his administration witnessed the most widespread series of reforms in the nation's history: the gold standard was abandoned, unemployment relief organized, bank deposits guaranteed, Wall Street regulated, and enormous sums of money set aside for the construction of public works or the financing of private homes and farms. American businessmen were often outraged, and even old-time Wilsonian Democrats thought that Roosevelt had gone too far. But for young people like Burke and Cowley, the reforms were not superhuman enough. In the United States, the Communist Party had for all practical purposes died with the Palmer Raids of 1919–1920, even though the party was not legalized until 1923. But in the election of 1932, the party suddenly received the kind of support it had not known since Eugene Debs ran for president in 1912. In September 1932, Cowley joined Granville Hicks, Sidney Hook, Edmund Wilson, and forty-nine other artists and intellectuals in signing a letter supporting the Communist Party's presidential candidate, William Z. Foster.

Two years later, Wallace Stevens was asked (in a questionnaire circulated by Geoffrey Grigson's *New Verse*) the question posed to every artist and intellectual in the 1930s: "Do you take your stand with any political or politico-economic party or creed?" Stevens's answer was a weary, "I am afraid that I don't." That was a carefully constructed answer to a particular question. Stevens had all manner of political opinions, but he did not subscribe to any particular creed. As Burke put it when Cowley questioned his unwillingness to call himself what he seemed to Cowley to be (a communist), "I am not a joiner of societies, I am a literary man." That was not a popular stance, and, like Stevens, Burke would pay for it. Communism and fascism seemed to be the only alternatives, and a position between the two that was not merely a compromise seemed inconceivable. Consequently, to doctrinaire Marxists like Rolfe, poetry that did not stake out a position was simply dead.

Writing in the pages of the far from doctrinaire *Partisan Review*, Rolfe was expressing a minority opinion. Rahv and Phillips made the keen observation that critics who charged poetry with irrelevance were not making a statement about the nature of poetry but about ideological conflict: "It is only in times like the present, when opposing philosophies battle for power and art is compelled to choose between several public viewpoints, that the presence of social thought in poetry is questioned." To understand the place of Wallace Stevens's poetry in the 1930s, it is essential to uncover those battles and see that the literary and political left was far from homogeneous. After Stanley Burnshaw's review of *Ideas of Order* appeared in the *New Masses*, Stevens told Latimer, "I hope I am headed left, but there are lefts and lefts, and certainly I am not headed for the ghastly left of MASSES." There were indeed lefts and lefts that stood as far apart from each other as Stevens and Burnshaw, but Stevens may not have realized how much more ghastly his confrontation with the left might have been: Burnshaw was no Edwin Rolfe.

In responding to Rolfe's proclamation on the death of poetry, none other than Stanley Burnshaw pointed out that a revolutionary poetry such as Rolfe's own "Homage to Karl Marx" was far from dead; it was simply awful: "as a matter of fact there is a great deal [of revolutionary verse] being written—and most of it by the very poets whose failings in form permit them to turn out poem after poem most of them sagging with weary passages, tottering under the weight of lines which any self-criticism execrates at once."

As Burnshaw himself recognized, there were certain aspects of the left that Stevens welcomed, and there were certain factions of the left that embraced Stevens (especially after the inauguration of the Popular Front in 1935). The fragmentation of the American left became obvious in 1936 with the opening of the Moscow Trials and the more prominent rise of the anti-Stalinist and Trotskyist left; but the left was divided against itself from the beginning of the decade. As Alan Wald has demonstrated in a recent account of the political fortunes of American intellectuals, the Moscow Trials and the Nazi-Soviet Pact caused only the most obvious and dramatic conflicts within the left: "For the later members of the *Partisan Review* group, literary conflicts and a refusal to relinquish modernism exacerbated their increasing distrust of the Communists prior to the public break with the party." For other radical groups, "the Stalinized Marxism of the Communist Party—its dogmatism and dread of criticism, its sectarianism in practice, its authoritarianism—was from the very beginning of their collaboration incompatible with their burning intellectual vivacity." Despite these tensions, however, Rahv and Phillips recognized in "Problems and Perspectives in Revolutionary Literature" (1934) that "the illusion has been allowed to spread that revolutionary writers constitute one happy family." To the American Communist Party, almost any disagreement with party policy was tantamount to apostasy; absolute unity was considered the first prerequisite to revolutionary power. For Lionel Trilling or Max Eastman (and later on, for Rahv and Phillips), the vilified Trotsky became an attractive alternative to Stalin precisely because he maintained that "a Marxist who . . . does not draw his conclusions to the end betrays Marxism. To pretend to ignore the different Communist factions, so as not to become involved and compromise oneself, signifies . . . covering oneself with the abstraction of the revolution, as with a shield, from the blows and bruises of the real revolutionary process."

Given the tension-ridden heterogeneity of the left, no writer of any stature came through the decade unscathed, and most were treated more harshly than Stevens; his run-in with the *New Masses* was not an isolated or unusual incident. In 1936 the relatively even-tempered *Partisan Review* called for "Sanctions Against Williams" after the poet proclaimed that "the American tradition is completely opposed to Marxism." Especially harsh was the reception given to Kenneth Burke's "Revolutionary Symbolism in America" at the First American Writers' Congress (1935). Burke must have known what he was up against, since even his close friend Malcolm Cowley found *Counter-Statement* (1931) insufficiently concerned with how art is "organically related with its social background"; always one step ahead, Burke told Cowley, "I was trying to show . . . that even art which is, by the Marxian-psychoanalytic hybrid of thinking, called retreatist or 'escape,' can have a function of this sort." Burke extended this argument in his speech at the Writers' Congress, suggesting that "the writer's best contribution to the revolutionary cause is *implicit*"; while some art may focus explicitly on the worker's plight, most poets serve a political cause by remaining "alive to all the aspects of contemporary effort and thought." While the *New Masses* had criticized Dos Passos and Edmund Wilson as "vacillating intellectuals" who "by the very nature" of their work were "not directly engaged in the day to day struggle to forge proletarian unity," Burke maintained that any intellectual had a necessarily problematic relationship with the working class. So did workers themselves, for that matter: "there are few people who really want to work," said Burke, and for that reason he felt that the "symbol" of the "people" ought to be substituted for that of the "worker." Burke explained that as a symbolic category, the people would not elicit our sympathies but our ambitions—and the ambitions not only of the lower classes but of the middle classes as well: "I am suggesting fundamentally that one cannot extend the doctrine of revolutionary thought among the lower middle classes without using middle-class values. . . . The symbol of 'the people' . . . contains the *ideal*, the ultimate *classless* future which the revolution would bring about."

Burke's recollection of the response to these responsible and even optimistic remarks deserves to be quoted at length.

The point was this: As regards the question of the workers, the proletariat, I had admitted that I was a petit bourgeois, and could speak only as petit bourgeois. But Joe Freeman gets up, throbbing like a locomotive, and shouts, "We have a snob among us!" I was a snob in conceding that I was a petit bourgeois and would have to speak like one. Then Mike Gold followed, and put the steamroller on me. Then a German émigré, Friedrich Wolf, attacked my proposal to address the "people" rather than the "workers." He pointed out the similarity between this usage and Hitler's harangues to the *Volk*. And so on, and so on—until I was slain, slaughtered. . . . I remember, when leaving the hall, I was walking behind two girls. One said to the other, as though discussing a criminal, "Yet he *seemed* so honest!"

Burke's two most vicious assailants, Joseph Freeman and Michael Gold, were both founding editors of the *New Masses*. Burke's discussion of the inherent ambiguities of propaganda (in the widest sense of the word) opened him to attacks from critics whose aesthetics allowed only the most straightforward realism: if Burke could not identify with the workers, then he had to be a fascist; if a poet did not portray the workers' dilemma, then his art was devoid of social content.

When Freeman and Gold organized the *New Masses* in 1926, they wanted writers to be what Burke conceded they could never be: undivided members of the working class. Most representative of their magazine's point of view was Granville Hicks's "The Crisis in American Criticism" (1933). Hicks, who became an editor of the *New Masses* soon after this essay was published, maintained that since the primary function of art is to "lead the proletarian reader to recognize his role in the class struggle," the writer must insist on the "centrality of subject matter" that reveals "the effects of class struggle"; the reader must "feel that he is participating in the lives described"; and the writer himself "should be, or should try to make himself, a member of the proletariat." Hicks believed that these qualities were a standard by which not only the proletarian novel but all literature should be measured—but he had to concede, as if to admit the sheer dogmatism of his position, that "no novel as yet written perfectly conforms to our demands."

Phillips and Rahv set out to combat that dogmatism in the *Partisan Review*. The magazine was originally proposed in 1934 as a companion to the *New Masses*, a forum for discussing of literary and cultural matters, which would leave space in the *New Masses* for more detailed discussions of political issues. But in their opening editorial statement, Phillips and Rahv made their perspective clear: "We shall resist every attempt to cripple our literature by narrow-minded, sectarian theories and practices." Tensions between the *New Masses* and the *Partisan Review* erupted immediately (not just in 1937, when the *Partisan Review* formally distanced itself from the Communist Party). Admiration for the verbal extravagance of the modernist achievements of the 1920s marked one clear separation between the editors of the two magazines. Although Rahv and Phillips cautioned against the adoption of the "sensibility of writers like Joyce and Eliot without a clear sense of the revolutionary purposes to which these influences should be bent," they spent more energy condemning the revolutionary sensibility that was not tempered by a taste for modernism. Kenneth Burke was too much of a renegade to belong (or to be invited) to any particular group, but the position of Phillips and Rahv ultimately came close to the Emersonian subtleties of *Counter-Statement*. In an essay on criticism that stood side by side with Edwin Rolfe's remarks on poetry, Phillips and Rahv took up the question, "Well, does this poem make me want to go out and do something about it?" and in their answer stressed not only that poetry is always involved in politics but that there is always

something more than politics involved in poetry: "In asking such a question
. . . the reader assumes that poetry can undertake all the tasks of political
education. At most a poem usually helps to crystalize latent urges to action
stimulated by a variety of other influences. . . . If the poem's effect is isolated
from these other factors, a burden it cannot bear is placed upon literature."
It was this recognition of the limitations as well as the strengths of poetry
that led Burke to remark that while no poetry is uninvolved in politics, no
poem will offer a cure for toothache.

Such an argument should leave room in the canon for "The Comedian
as the Letter C" as well as *Ulysses*, but only pages away from Phillips and
Rahv's remarks on criticism, Edwin Rolfe was declaring the death of Wallace
Stevens and more. Six months later, Stanley Burnshaw (who responded to
Rolfe in terms amenable to Phillips and Rahv) would review *Ideas of Order*
in the *New Masses*—where Rolfe's judgment would have found comfortable
company. As his response to Rolfe suggests, Burnshaw was one of the most
sensitive critics Stevens could have hoped for in the *New Masses*. He was not
assigned the review; Burnshaw admired the poet of *Harmonium* and was
excited enough by the appearance of a long-delayed second volume that he
instigated the review himself. (For enthusiasms like that, Burnshaw was
known as the "aesthete" among the *New Masses* editors.) Far from dismissing
Ideas of Order (as Geoffrey Grigson did in *New Verse*), Burnshaw perceived
Stevens as a poet who stood precariously in the "middle ground," a poet who
leaned variously to the right and left and who might benefit from a push in
the left direction. Stevens saw himself in much the same way ("I hope I am
headed left"), but while he found Burnshaw's remarks "extraordinarily stimulating," Stevens was understandably skeptical of the *New Masses* at large:
"*Masses* is just one more wailing place and the whole left now-a-days is a mob
of wailers. . . . These people go about it in such a way that nobody listens to
them except themselves." Stevens did not really maintain that opinion of the
whole left; he also considered the *Partisan Review* to be "the most intelligent
thing that I know of," even in contrast to the "rather violently one-sided"
Nation and *New Republic*.

Under the watch of Gold or Hicks, the *New Masses* was nothing if not
one-sided, but Burnshaw's work for the journal was part of a change in direction that in 1935 was shaping the future of both the *New Masses* and the
Communist Party at large. The First American Writers' Congress (at which
Burke was excoriated) convened in April 1935, and its most substantial
accomplishment was the creation of the League of American Writers, a group
that (as Burke explained without admonition) had "been formed to consoli-
date in one organization the efforts of those who, whatever their positive
divergences, can at least unite on the basis of negatives, as enemies of fascism

and war." The damage done by the party's inability to join other forces against Hitler was becoming clearer, and this new effort to unite the various factions of the left became official party policy a few months later. In August 1935 the Seventh Congress of the Communist International in Moscow formally adopted the "People's Front" against fascism, and party members were encouraged to reach out even to left-leaning New Dealers. Ironically, the very proposition for which Burke was labeled a fascist (the substitution of the people for the workers as the party's unifying symbol) had become the keynote of the party's stepped-up war on fascism itself.

Between the Writers' Congress in New York and the Seventh International in Moscow, Burnshaw published "'Middle-Ground' Writers," one of the more reasonable essays ever to appear in the *New Masses*. Anticipating the Popular Front strategy that would soon become party policy, Burnshaw explained that while the politically uncommitted "middle ground" had been thought of as "incipient fascism," the *New Masses* now realized that it could "afford to drive away no one who can be turned into a friend of the revolutionary movement": "potential allies can be found within the ranks of the waverers—confused writers who believe themselves to be standing in a supposed middle ground between capitalism and revolution." The job of the Marxist critic, said Burnshaw, is not to "excoriate" these waverers but to "analyze" their work so that they might find a way out of their "condition of creative crisis." Although Burnshaw still believed that there was in fact no such thing as a middle ground between communism and fascism, he ended his essay with a recognition of the value of the kind of ideological independence that Burke championed more forcefully: "So long as he is true to himself as a writer he is *potentially anti-fascist to the degree to which he is a maker of literature.*"

Burnshaw's review of *Ideas of Order*, "Turmoil in the Middle Ground," was published in October 1935, just after the Seventh International. Following the precepts of his proto–Popular Front essay, he presented Stevens (along with Haniel Long, whose *Pittsburgh Memoranda* he also reviewed) as a potential ally as well as a potential enemy: "Acutely conscious members of a class menaced by clashes between capital and labor, these writers are in the throes of struggle for philosophical adjustment. And their words have intense value and meaning to the sectors within their class whose confusion they articulate. Their books have deep importance for us as well." Although Burnshaw saw *Harmonium* as the book of an unsullied paradise, indulging in the decade's apocalyptic cant to say so, he saw more clearly that in *Ideas of Order* Stevens was not lounging in the ivory tower: to Burnshaw, that book revealed "a considered record of agitated attitudes toward the present social order" that was shaped by a "troubled, searching mind." His harshest criticism of

Stevens was that he seemed like "a man who, having lost his footing, now scrambles to stand up and keep his balance"; but that sentence was a paraphrase of Stevens's own admission of waywardness in "Sailing After Lunch," the opening poem in the Alcestis edition of *Ideas of Order*.

> My old boat goes round on a crutch
> And doesn't get under way.
> It's the time of the year
> And the time of the day.

What finally bothered Burnshaw was not that Stevens's verse was uninvolved with the social order or that it clearly represented the political right (since Burnshaw saw that it did neither of these things) but that the verse was *ambiguous*. To a degree, Burnshaw accepted the ambiguity as indigenous to poetry; "uncertainties are unavoidable," he said, because the very texture of Stevens's thought "is made of speculations, questionings, contradictions." But in examining a line from "The Comedian as the Letter C" Burnshaw's frustration with a poetry that exchanged political clarity for verbal extravagance began to show: "Realists have been bitter at the inanity of Pope's 'whatever is is right,' but Stevens plunges ahead to the final insolence: 'For realists, what is is what should be.' And yet it is hard to know if such a line is not Stevens posing in self-mockery. One can rarely speak surely of Stevens' ideas." A less generous critic at the *New Masses* might have banished Stevens outright for that line, not permitting the possibility of irony. Burnshaw felt certain that a challenging remark from "Botanist on Alp (No. 1)" was ironic ("Marx has ruined Nature, / For the moment"); as a Marxist himself, Burnshaw was willing to give Stevens the benefit of the doubt. But finally, when his frustration won over his generosity, Burnshaw quoted this passage from "Like Decorations in a Nigger Cemetery," merely observing that here Stevens "pours out in strange confusion his ideas of order."

> If ever the search for a tranquil belief should end,
> The future might stop emerging out of the past,
> Out of what is full of us; yet the search
> And the future emerging out of us seem to be one.

The point Burnshaw ultimately missed here is that Stevens was attempting to present confusion and ambiguity as positive artistic and political values: the search for a tranquil belief must never end if we are to remain open to the imperatives of a world anything but tranquil. Writing for the *New Masses*, even Burnshaw ultimately wanted the poet to declare his allegiances, but like

Burke, Stevens distrusted certainty and the dogmatism certainty can breed. "On the one hand," he said to a business associate in 1938, "people believe that a writer must be sincere, serious, Baptist, Methodist, Communist; on the other hand, people believe that a writer is a thinker, an artist, and that he observes and hears and feels. I am one of the latter group." For Stevens, the greatest danger was to settle into a tranquil belief, and he did not want his ideas of order to become too clear or codified. As Burnshaw himself maintained in "'Middle-Ground' Writers," a writer is *potentially anti-fascist* as "long as he is true to himself." Or as Burke said in a passage in *Counter-Statement* that I have already juxtaposed with "The Comedian as the Letter C," "perhaps there is an evasion, a shirking of responsibility, in becoming certain too quickly. . . . Since the body is dogmatic, a generator of belief, society might well be benefited by the corrective of a disintegrating art, which converts each simplicity into a complexity, which ruins the possibility of ready hierarchies."

Stevens made straightforward comments about his political preferences only rarely, and, as I suggested in Chapter 3, there is a disturbing current of single-mindedness in his endlessly ambiguous poetry. Burnshaw sensed it when he wondered if Stevens made a "political reference" in the final lines of "Decorations": "Union of the weakest develops strength / Not wisdom." Burnshaw was wary enough in the face of Stevens's ambiguity not to condemn this sentiment outright, but with the context of Stevens's later work now in place, we can see more clearly that these lines are one of the first indications of Stevens's Nietzschean romance with heroes. This is the same Stevens who once expressed his sympathy for Mussolini and often expressed his antipathy for Roosevelt and the New Deal. This is also the same Stevens who voted for William Jennings Bryan. While examining Stevens's politics in the 1930s, I think the most important thing to remember is that Stevens's values were shaped in the world of Bryan and McKinley, a world that already seemed like ancient history from the vantage point of the Depression. Stevens cast his first vote for the Democratic and Populist parties, and, like many old-style Democrats in the 1930s, he no longer recognized the party as his own and changed his affiliation but not his politics. Near the end of his life, Stevens remarked that the Democrats had "gone incredible lengths in introducing their conception of things into American life and practice; and just to think of things as they were twenty-five years ago makes one feel like William Cullen Bryant's great, great grandfather." Fifty-three years earlier, Stevens had voted for William Jennings Bryan; even then, the world Bryan represented was fading fast.

In the 1930s, Stevens was no longer a young man, and while it is crucial to remember his resistance to certain aspects of the left, it is equally important to recall how seriously he engaged its challenge. Stevens recoiled at Hi Simons's suggestion (in the 1940 essay on "The Comedian") that the poet was "on the right": "I believe in any number of things that so-called social revolutionists believe in, but I don't believe in calling myself a revolutionist simply because I believe in doing everything practically possible to improve the condition of the workers, and because I believe in education as the source of freedom and power, and because I regret that we have not experimented a little more extensively in public ownership of public utilities." Even as Stevens made that comment, he felt compelled to add that this was "rather a ridiculous thing for me to be talking about." If he did not want to be pegged on the right, he did not want to be pegged on the left either. Like Burke, Stevens felt that as a middle-class poet and businessman he would necessarily remain somewhat distanced from labor struggles, no matter how completely he tried to understand the worker's plight. Just as he recognized the crucial differences between the poet and the businessman in his own life, he recognized the differences between poetry and political action—intertwined as those things may be. Faced with the First World War, Stevens had been reluctant to make major statements about a world he did not know well, even though its violence penetrated his dreams. For similar reasons, his direct comments about politics in the 1930s always seemed somewhat "ridiculous" to him, important as the Depression and the rise of the left were. Stevens felt insecure about his own statements precisely because he thought the issues were important.

The most straightforward statements he made about his politics came in an exchange of letters with Latimer following Burnshaw's review; but even here Stevens appears anxious as soon as he commits those statements to writing. In an immediate response to the review, Stevens wrote that he hoped he was headed left, and several months later, while completing "Mr. Burnshaw and the Statue," he was more specific about the route he was following.

The last question is whether I feel that there is an essential conflict between Marxism and the sentiment of the marvellous. I think we all feel that there is conflict between the rise of a lower class, with all its realities, and the indulgences of an upper class. This, however, is one of the very things which I at least have in mind in MR. BURNSHAW. My conclusion is that, while there is a conflict, it is not an essential conflict. The conflict is temporary. The only possible order of life is one in which all order is incessantly changing. Marxism may or may not destroy the existing sentiment of the marvellous; if it does, it will create another. It was a very common fear that Socialism would dirty the world; it is an equally common fear that Communism will do the same thing. I think that this is all nonsense. Of course, that would be the immediate effect, as any upheaval results in disorder.

So that there may be no doubt about it, let me say that I believe in what Mr. Filene calls "up-to-date capitalism". I don't believe in Communism; I do believe in up-to-date capitalism. It is an extraordinary experience for myself to deal with a thing like Communism; it is like dealing with the Democratic platform, or with the provisions of the Frazier-Lemke bill. Nevertheless, one has to live and think in the actual world, and no other will do, and that is why MR. BURNSHAW, etc. has taken a good deal of time.

A FADING OF THE SUN is a variation of this theme; possibly MOZART 1935 also is. But I think that the last poem expresses something that I have very much at heart, and that is: the status of the poet in a disturbed society, or, for that matter, in any society.

Before offering his own point of view here, Stevens first explains that he does not see the rise of the Marxist left as a catastrophic change—in either positive or negative terms. Other programs preceded it, and others will follow: "The only possible order of life," says Stevens, reiterating the point of his "ideas" of order, "is one in which all order is incessantly changing." That precept is what makes Stevens reluctant to specify his own beliefs, as if writing them down could prevent them from changing. As the letter goes on, he nevertheless does so, explaining that although he is not a communist he does believe in Edward Filene's conception of up-to-date capitalism. Filene, a Boston businessman, supported Roosevelt and the New Deal, believing that the nation's wealth could be radically redistributed even in a capitalist economy: "Why shouldn't the American people take half my money from me? I took all of it from them." That seemed fair even to a tax-time grumbler like Stevens, but even as he makes his allegiance clear to Latimer, he recoils again. While the world of communism and the Frazier-Lemke bill (a piece of New Deal legislation providing for the refinancing of farm mortgages) seemed alien to him, Stevens recognizes that he has no choice but to live in the "actual world."

The struggle to live in that world seemed to Stevens the theme of both "A Fading of the Sun" (1933) and "Mozart 1935," but those two poems approach that struggle in subtly different ways. While the first poem advocates retreating into the comfortable world of the self, the second questions the very possibility of such a retreat or such a world. "Mozart 1935" vacillates between a call for the poet to "Play the present" and to retreat to "That lucid souvenir of the past, / The divertimento"; but ultimately Stevens stakes out his middle ground with the help of the "Ode to the West Wind," diminishing Shelley's invocation of the spirit to a call for music made from human pain.

> Be thou, be thou
> The voice of angry fear,
> The voice of this besieging pain.

> Be thou that wintry sound
> As of the great wind howling,
> By which sorrow is released.

All that Stevens will allow here (as he put it in other poems of the 1930s) is a "slight transcendence"—"a voice beyond us yet ourselves." In the terms of his letter to Latimer, the poem searches for a mediation between a Marxist imperative to sing the present and a poet's desire to sing the sentiment of the marvelous.

Stanley Burnshaw's review did not suddenly awaken Stevens to that conflict. The conflict motivated the poems of *Ideas of Order* from the start, and it is not coincidental that the poems in the volume calling for mediation, inconclusiveness, and change seem to provide an answer to ideological single-mindedness. The questions raised by Marxist aesthetics were not simply applied to Stevens's poems in 1935; what Helen Vendler has called Stevens's poetry of "qualified assertions" developed in response to those questions, and, in a very real way, the poems already contained the answers to the questions Burnshaw asked. The review in the *New Masses* was Stevens's *second* important encounter with Marxism in the 1930s. The first came in 1931, and it shaped a decade of his achievement.

11

~•~

Ideas of Ambiguity

Troubled with his reading of "The Emperor of Ice-Cream," R. P. Blackmur took a moment away from his job at a Cambridge bookshop to write to Stevens for advice on his now classic essay, "Examples of Wallace Stevens" (1931). Stevens read the pages in question and was struck by this sentence: "By associating ambiguities found in nature in a poem we reach a clarity, a kind of transfiguration even, whereby we learn *what* the ambiguity was." In a decade's time, that would become a kind of New Critical dogma, but in 1931 Blackmur was speaking Stevens's private language, and the poet told him so: "One of the essentials of poetry is ambiguity. I don't feel that I have touched the thing until I touch it in ambiguous form.... Ambiguity does not mean obfuscation. The clearest possible definition of things essentially ambiguous leaves ambiguity." This response elated the young bookstore clerk, who wrote back, "I hadn't thought anyone, beyond a mere personal friend of mine, and vaguely myself, had ever considered ambiguity as the *explicit* virtue of poetry." Blackmur told Stevens of his excitement over Empson's recently published *Seven Types of Ambiguity*, and then he asked a question that brought their mutual interest in ambiguity closer to home.

Has it ever occurred to you that in this country Kenneth Burke is writing (in his treatises on rhetoric and eloquence) another face to the coin of ambiguity? It is precisely that consequence of his notions, I think, which made possible Granville Hicks' lame review of *Counter-Statement* in the N. R. [*New Republic*] recently. Hicks couldn't understand how Burke could profitably expect people to differ about fundamentals. Hicks failed to distinguish the fundamentals of the arts from the fundamentals of philosophy or what he calls philosophy. That is the natural failing of the "atmosphere of science impregnated mind:" what we were all brought up on. It makes the twin notions of eloquence and ambiguity as precise instruments seem *nothing but* paradox.

As this letter suggests, my juxtapositions of Burke and Stevens have not been utterly fortuitous. Blackmur sensed their affinities when each writer had published only one book, and it seems to me that Stevens must have read *Counter-Statement* after receiving this letter if he had not read it before. He probably saw the confrontation between Burke and Hicks as well, since he was a regular reader of the *New Republic*. Hicks's review—and Burke's response to it—revealed what was at stake when the value of ambiguity or disagreement is asserted in the realm of art or politics.

Hicks complained that Burke was interested only in eloquence and not in politics, that he valued a convoluted art of retreat rather than a directly communicative art engaged with contemporary chaos. As Blackmur sensed, this complaint ignores the essential thrust of *Counter-Statement*, which was (as Burke explained in his response to Hicks, quoting from his own book) to show how "a system of aesthetics subsumes a system of politics." "Far from confining myself to the choice which Mr. Hicks would force upon me," Burke continued, "I had thought that my approach enabled me to avoid precisely such academic choices." These remarks did not convince Hicks, who responded to Burke's objections by reiterating his belief that Burke was concerned exclusively with "technique." Challenged to outline another method of judging the relationship of politics and art, Hicks could do no better than trot out the ghost of Matthew Arnold: "The critic approaches a piece of literature as an interpretation of life." And in his influential *New Masses* essay, "The Crisis in American Criticism," Hicks would insist again that "Burke's theory is really one more attempt to separate literature from life."

What troubled Hicks about Burke was what troubled Burnshaw about Stevens: ambiguity. Unwilling to say that any piece of language could speak univocally for any particular point of view, Burke summed up *Counter-Statement* as "a return to inconclusiveness." As Blackmur told Stevens, Hicks could see inconclusiveness or ambiguity as nothing but paradox—something that breaks down the communicative power of language and renders art irrelevant. But inasmuch as "art remains an 'inefficient' business" in the world of political struggle, Burke felt that its very strength was its being "primarily a process of disintegration, of making propaganda difficult, of fostering intellectual distrust." Hicks wanted to make propaganda easier, so he denied the political efficacy of ambiguity. Burke's point was that, pressed for its politics, art conceived as intrinsically ambiguous "would observe the principle of democratic distrust (government through conflict of selfish interests) over against Fascist hopefulness (centralization of *benevolent* authority)."

Burke's thoughts became crucial for Blackmur's development as well as Stevens's. Blackmur's essay "A Critic's Job of Work" (1935) echoes *Counter-Statement* in its cautious assessment of the dangers of certainty: "Thought is a beacon not a life-raft, and to confuse the functions is tragic. The tragic character of thought . . . is that it takes a rigid mold too soon." Later New Critical writing would descend into a dogmatism of its own, rejecting (at least in principle) any discussion of the bearing of the world beyond the text of a poem. Almost none of that dogmatism appears, however, in Blackmur's struggles to formulate his own principles in the early 1930s. In a consideration of Blackmur as "the greatest of native American critics produced in the first half of the twentieth century," Edward Said points out that Blackmur was never seduced by "the antinomian stabilities" that might be deduced from a category like "ambiguity"; for Blackmur, "criticism is best seen as a provisional act," and Said consequently finds him "the least doctrinal, the least serviceable (in the base sense of the word) of the New Critics." Like Burke's, Blackmur's work grew in response to a vulgar Marxist challenge, and unlike a later, doctrinaire New Critic, he was not offering a conservative alternative to that challenge but trying to present a more sophisticated account of how language is involved with the world outside the text. Blackmur maintained in "A Critic's Job of Work" that nothing "could be more exciting, nothing more vital, than a book by Granville Hicks whose major theme hung on an honest, dramatic view of the class struggle—and there is indeed such a literature now emerging." But he accused Hicks of being "concerned with the separable content of literature, with what may be said without consideration of its specific setting and apparatus in a form." Because of his unwillingness to see how language necessarily complicated that drama, Hicks wrote only "a casuist's polemic" in which certain novels (and no poems) are included by the sole criterion of their subject matter.

Whatever the political position in question, Stevens feared the political ramifications of certainty as much as Blackmur or Burke did: that distrust of dogmatism runs like a refrain throughout his prose of the 1930s. Against the typical "poet of ideas," Stevens proposed the poet who constantly "changes, and I hope, constantly grows." Contrasting the haphazard life of Crispin with the world of "The Idea of Order at Key West," where "life has ceased to be a matter of chance," Stevens immediately recoiled at the implicit dogmatism of the contrast: "But then, I never thought that it was a fixed philosophic proposition that life was a mass of irrelevancies any more than I now think that it is a fixed philosophic proposition that every man introduces his own order as part of a general order." Asked by Latimer to supply a preface to his own poetry, Stevens resisted, reiterating that "there is nothing more tiresome than the doctrinal positiveness that one so often finds." But even as he resisted such fixity, Stevens also recognized that his faith in the power of ambiguity and change might be a "romantic evasion" of political responsibilities: "I dare say that the orderly relations of society as a whole have a poetic value, but the idea sounds like something for a choral society, or for Racine. It is hard to say what so vast an amplification would bring about. For my own part, I take such things for granted. Of course, this is merely one more romantic evasion in place of the thinking it out in which one ought to indulge." To that objection Burke would have responded that poems are not the best place for such thinking, and given poetry's circumscribed power, what it does best is complicate and question our beliefs. "If you can't tell the difference between yourself and a trained economist," said Williams to an increasingly dogmatic Pound in 1935, "if you don't know your function as a poet, incidentally dealing with a messy situation re. money, then go sell your papers on some other corner."

As aware of his limitations as a poet as Pound was unaware, Stevens offered a decidedly unfashionable description of his work as "pure poetry" on the jacket for the 1936 edition of *Ideas of Order*: "We think of changes occurring today as economic changes, involving political and social changes. Such changes raise questions of political and social order. While it is inevitable that a poet should be concerned with such questions, this book, although it reflects them, is primarily concerned with ideas of order of a different nature. . . . The book is essentially a book of pure poetry. I believe that, in any society, the poet should be the exponent of the imagination of that society." That statement would color many of the reviews *Ideas* received, but it is crucial to understand the precise way in which Stevens understood poetry to be "pure." As A. Walton Litz has demonstrated, Stevens owed his understanding of pure poetry less to Mallarmé than to Croce, for whom the Mallarméan concept of the term, which "excludes, or pretends to exclude, from poetry all the meaning of words," is paradoxically an "impure" conception of pure poetry: for Croce, the truly pure poem dwelt in a middle ground between the extremes of reference and music, between the life of the world and the life of the text. Consequently, although poetry always participates in economic and political change, its effect in that world is curtailed. "Poetry," wrote Croce in a passage Stevens marked in *The Defence of Poetry* (1933), "far from gaining by being expanded over the whole world, loses its proper and distinctive character, and therewith its proper strength and efficacy." Croce continued: "If we call to mind the conception of poetry in its strict character, circumscribed within its proper limits, it must not only decline all those particular functions to which it has been invoked or bent against its nature, but also it must lose the supreme place of honor assigned to it by Shelley, when he called it the fountain of all forms of civil life. . . . In short, we must only look upon it as one among other paths leading to a single goal. Other paths lead there too: the paths of thought, of philosophy, of religion, of conscience, of political action." A similar sense of "proper limits" was what led Rahv and Phillips to say we place an unfair burden on literature when we expect it to perform political actions directly. And when Stevens said in the jacket copy to *Ideas* that poetry by its nature approaches questions of social order in poetic terms, he was not isolating poetry from political action but being careful to discriminate between the two. Stevens's poems of order were (as he would put it in the jacket statement) "confronting the elimination of established ideas" and exploring the uses of ambiguity—not (as later New Critics or some deconstructionists would have it) as the purely literary function of a text, but (as Burke would have it) as a characteristic of the site where texts lead—or may not lead—to actions.

Stevens wrote the jacket copy after he had written both *Ideas of Order* and "Owl's Clover"; it should be read as a concluding statement about the body of work and not as the foundation on which the poems stand. In the ideas of order Stevens was writing into his poems in 1934 and 1935, he left the power of the ideas tenuous and their duration brief. "Table Talk" asserts the randomness of all our orders ("One likes what one happens to like"), and "The Pleasures of Merely Circulating" presents a vista of order so vast that it seems anything but orderly: "The garden flew round with the angel, / The angel flew round with the clouds." That "things go round and again go round," Stevens admits, has "rather a classical sound," but that orderly music should not lull us into complacency or blind us to a world where things are not so orderly. In "A Room on a Garden" he is more explicit, asserting that "order is the end / Of everything." With a long tradition of literary gardens behind him, Stevens rejects "the law of hoes and rakes," welcoming an order that is not imposed but "perceived in windy quakes / And squalls." As for Marianne Moore, truth for Stevens is no formal thing, no Apollo Belvedere; against such stasis Stevens reiterates the necessity of permitting chance and variance into our all too orderly worlds: the gardener might "espy" the truth in the "lilies' stately-statued calm," but he might conduct his search more fruitfully "in this fret / Of lilies rusted, rotting, wet / With rain."

In other poems, the ideas of order Stevens interrogates are presented in more culturally specific terms. "Gray Stones and Gray Pigeons" exposes the poverty of religious authority that does not change; the church is gray, the light fixed, and the pigeons "never fly / Except when the bishop passes by."

In "Winter Bells" the church's chimes are silent, its power simply that of regulation and propriety: "How good life is, on the basis of propriety, / To be followed by a platter of capon!" More interesting than these poems, however, are others that complicate a sense of the emptiness of old ideas of order with a sense of the difficulty of creating new ones—or with a recognition of how a new order, open to disorder though it may be, is nevertheless infected by the old. In "Lions in Sweden" Stevens abjures the quest for "sovereigns of the soul" yet recognizes that the soul rejecting those absolute values (whether, as Stevens's language implies, monetary, political, or purely theoretical in nature) is itself composed of those values and "hankers after sovereign images." In "Polo Ponies Practicing" Stevens points out that the mere reiteration of a cry against an established order (such as we get in "Gray Stones" and "Winter Bells") may become stultifying itself: "The constant cry against an old order, / An order constantly old, / Is itself old and stale." When it becomes divorced from action, even the impulse to rebel against authority becomes an orthodoxy. Similarly, in "Hieroglyphica," a minor poem that looks forward to "Parochial Theme," the opening poem of *Parts of a World*, Stevens satirizes the poet's detached and ineffectual calls for change.

> Let wise men piece the world together with wisdom
> Or poets with holy magic.
> Hey-di-ho.

"Piece the world together, boys," Stevens would say in "Parochial Theme," "but not with your hands," reiterating his distrust of poets whose "halloo, halloo, halloo" (their "descant of a self") drowns out the voices of "those whom the statues torture and keep down" even as those halloos offer a freshening of life.

When Moore read *Ideas of Order* she immediately recognized that the volume was a "progression on certain individual poems of previous years." As many subsequent readers of Stevens have noticed as well, it is possible to map many of these later poems on the continuum marked in *Harmonium* by the imaginative fullness of "Tea at the Palaz of Hoon" and the stark barrenness of "The Snow Man"; the poems of *Ideas of Order* make the political dimension of that continuum clearer. I pointed out in Chapter 3 that the Parnassian poet Sully-Prudhomme stands behind Stevens's vision of the solipsistic Hoon, and that Stevens realized early on that such an aristocratic stance was not for him, despite its attractions. In the 1930s, faced with the demand to "play the present" in flat and colorless tones, that stance occasionally became more seductive to Stevens; around 1934 he copied this passage from George Chapman's dedicatory epistle to Ovid's *Banquet of Sense* into his commonplace book: "The profane multitude I hate, and only consecrate my strange Poems to these searching spirits, whom learning hath made noble, and nobility sacred. . . . [That plainness should be the special ornament of Poesy], were the plain way to barbarism." We have seen how that attitude manifested itself in poems like "A Fading of the Sun" and "How to Live. What to Do," but we have also seen how quickly that aristocratic stance is dissipated in the face of an aggressively barren world. In his introduction to Williams's *Collected Poems* (1934), Stevens remarked that life in the ivory tower "would be intolerable except for the fact that one has, from the top, such an exceptional view of the public dump and the advertising signs of Snider's Catsup, Ivory Soap and Chevrolet Cars." More stringent was the banishing of Hoon and the destruction of his palaz that Stevens insisted on in "Sad Strains of a Gay Waltz" (1935).

> And then
> There's that mountain-minded Hoon,
> For whom desire was never that of the waltz,
>
> Who found all form and order in solitude,
> For whom the shapes were never the figures of men.
> Now, for him, his forms have vanished.
>
> There is order in neither sea nor sun.
> The shapes have lost their glistening.
> There are these sudden mobs of men.

Stevens's Hoon would like to piece his world together—but not with his hands; his detached ideas of order have no consequence. Like "Mozart 1935," "Sad Strains of a Gay Waltz" explains that the old music played in the old way will no longer suffice, no matter how much we mourn its passing. Stevens calls for a new "skeptical music" that will "unite these figures of men," insisting that this music not be fixed but "be motion" itself, pliant enough to accommodate a radically changing world.

Throughout *Ideas of Order* the world of Hoon is rejected not simply for the Snow Man's world but for a collective or social vision that protects us from the Snow Man's utterly inhuman existence—"these figures of men." Stevens will insist in "Evening Without Angels" that "Bare night is best. Bare earth is best. Bare, bare"; but in other poems like "Autumn Refrain" he will insist that we require something more than that. The old music once again will not suffice for the protagonist of "Anglais Mort à Florence," and though he remembers "the time when he stood alone," he can now stand only "by

God's help and the police." Stevens's original title for this poem was "God and the Police": explicating the lines from which the title came, Stevens told Simons, "If men have nothing external to them on which to rely, then, in the event of a collapse of their own spirit, they must naturally turn to the spirit of others. I don't mean conventions: police." Recognizing that one must use one's hands to piece the world together, that actions as well as ideas are necessary, Stevens wanted to stress that he was talking about the social institutions of the actual world. Yet in other poems, these institutions, whether God or the police, become stale and oppressive authorities. That is why the protagonist of "Anglais" must remember the time when he appeared to stand alone: so that he will not accept God or the police uncritically or come to think of his dependence on them as inevitable and unalterable. Even as the poems of *Ideas* reject that mountain-minded Hoon for a more communal vision, they do not forget that the rejection may become one more of the mind's illusions.

Stevens draws a fine line in *Ideas of Order* between order and disorder, and he fears the stultifying suppressions of the former as he fears the anarchic energies of the latter. In the major poems of the volume, he tries to describe the tenuous place of what he would come to call "sensible ecstasy," a place where ambiguities hover unresolved and the mind offers only tentative or self-canceling ways of ordering its world—a place where Granville Hicks would not permit Kenneth Burke to dwell. Stevens visited that place in "Stars at Tallapoosa," the poem in *Harmonium* that most anticipates "The Idea of Order at Key West," itself the poem in *Ideas* that delineates that place most clearly. Both poems show us "the mind in the act of defending us against itself," or what Stevens liked to think of as "*littérature contre la littérature*"; but the two poems were written in radically different historical circumstances. If "Sunday Morning" consoled Stevens by reminding him that "death is the mother of beauty," the lesson mattered because it carried the historical weight of a particular place and time, a world at war. The lesson of "The Idea of Order at Key West" may seem universal as well, but to understand why its idea of ambiguity was indeed a thing of consequence, I would like to consider what the historical circumstances of its gestation might have been.

"The Idea of Order" was first published in October 1934 in a group of eight poems that also included "Lions in Sweden" and "Evening Without Angels." Stevens had been named vice president the previous February, and during that month he had attended the premiere of Virgil Thomson's and Gertrude Stein's *Four Saints in Three Acts* at the Wadsworth Atheneum in Hartford. With its music of studied simplicity, its maddeningly repetitive text,

cellophane stage set, and all-black cast, the opera seemed "delicate and joyous
. . . all round" to Stevens, "an elaborate bit of perversity." Less enjoyable was
the audience of Hoon-like aesthetes: "There were, however, numerous asses
of the first water in the audience. New York sent a train load of people of
this sort to Hartford: people who walked round with cigarette holders a foot
long, and so on. After all, if there is any place under the sun that needs
debunking, it is the place where people of this sort come to and go to." As
his "Polo Ponies Practicing" would suggest, Stevens felt that while the production of the opera flouted convention in every way, the audience simply
repeated a conventional set of radical gestures. The gestures seemed especially irrelevant in Hartford in 1934, where (as Stevens had explained a few
months before), "because of the depression, there are so many burglars about
that, instead of living in a neighborhood that is poorly lighted, the neighborhood is in reality brilliantly lighted."

Stevens attended the opera on February 8, received his promotion on February 15, and a few days later left for one of his annual business and pleasure
trips to Key West. That place, which in Stevens's private mythology was an
enclave both antiliterary and economically extravagant, might have seemed
the perfect antidote to both the depressed conditions of Hartford and the
pretensions of the New York aesthetes. But it was neither. During previous
visits to Florida, Stevens had seen crowds of men out of work who roamed
the streets and slept on the porches. When he returned in February 1934,
there was not much order at Key West, and then due not only to the Depression. Across the water, a revolution was taking place in Cuba. Stevens
described the American military presence to his wife.

Owing to the disturbed conditions in Cuba there have been warships in port here
for a good many months. At the moment, the *Wyoming* is lying at anchor out near the
Casa Marina. The men from this great vessel and from others that are in the basin at
the Navy Yard come on shore in large numbers and from about four o'clock until all
hours of the night they are walking up and down the streets. In Florida they have
prohibition under the state laws. The result is that these men flock to ice-cream shops
and drug-stores and in general look like a lot of holiday-makers without any definite
ideas of how to amuse themselves. Key West is extremely old-fashioned and primitive.
The movie theatres are little bits of things. Well, last night it seemed as if the whole
navy stood in the streets under our windows laughing and talking.

The trouble with Cuba dated back to McKinley and the Spanish American War, after which the island had become a protectorate of the United
States. In 1902 Cuba became a sovereign state, but the Platt Amendment to
its constitution guaranteed the United States the right to intervene in its
affairs. Those affairs were almost constantly troubled, and U.S. forces inter-

vened several times, often at the instigation of revolutionary factions who needed leverage against the current regime. In September 1933, when the Cuban economy was on the verge of complete collapse, Fulgencio Batista led a takeover by the army, and the American ambassador called for U.S. troops to intervene. Roosevelt refused to do so, but twenty-nine warships were sent to Cuban waters, making the American threat clear. As Stevens looked out over the water beside the Casa Marina at Key West, those were the ships he saw.

In the letter to his wife, Stevens does not express much interest in Cuban political disorder; though he speaks of "the disturbed conditions in Cuba" he is more obviously concerned about the disorder created by the sailors sent to stabilize those conditions: Stevens was kept awake at night. But the measured periods of "The Idea of Order at Key West" (written when Stevens returned to Hartford) bespeak a serious consideration for what the words *order* and *disorder* might account for. Even if Stevens knew almost nothing about the disturbance in Cuba, it seems to me that the evidence of political disorder that he witnessed—the battleship *Wyoming* and its crew—are part of the world set right in the poem. To grant this historical weight to so sublime an utterance is to invoke the ghost of Granville Hicks, however, and to find a political reading of "The Idea of Order" convincing, I think we need to recall Kenneth Burke's rejoinder to his critic: ambiguity and inconclusiveness do not undermine a text's political content but mark the uneasy space where that content may be found.

At the same time that I am suggesting that the "disturbed conditions in Cuba" played a part in the poem's gestation, consequently, I also want to examine other possible points of origin. Around March 1934, after returning from Florida, Stevens copied this sentence from Richard Storr's *The Divine Origins of Christianity Indicated by Its History Effects* (1884) into his commonplace book: "The philosopher could not love the indefinite and impersonal principle of order pervading the universe, any more than he could love atmospheres or oceans." To which Stevens responded, "For myself, the indefinite, the impersonal, atmospheres and oceans and, above all, the principle of order are precisely what I love; and I don't see why, for a philosopher, they should not be the ultimate inamorata. The premise to Storrs is that the universe is explicable only in terms of humanity." That is the response of the same Stevens who as a young poet wished that the groves were still sacred, or that something was. He hankered after the sublime, yet at the same time that "The Idea of Order at Key West" tries to provide an indefinite and impersonal principle of order, it also reveals the inadequacy and inaccessibility of the sublime: the poem remains haunted by the disorder Stevens witnessed in the streets and waters of Key West.

In the poem's opening lines, Stevens offers an endlessly deferred and contingent sense of the relationship between literature and experience—or, more
specifically, between the self, voice, poetry, and the otherness of the real
world.

> She sang beyond the genius of the sea.
> The water never formed to mind or voice,
> Like a body wholly body, fluttering
> Its empty sleeves; and yet its mimic motion
> Made constant cry, caused constantly a cry,
> That was not ours although we understood,
> Inhuman, of the veritable ocean.
>
> The sea was not a mask. No more was she.
> The song and water were not medleyed sound
> Even if what she sang was what she heard,
> Since what she sang was uttered word by word.
> It may be that in all her phrases stirred
> The grinding water and the gasping wind;
> But it was she and not the sea we heard.

In a discussion of Stevens's musical metaphors, John Hollander has usefully
described the tradition against which these opening lines of the poem turn:
"Drawing upon two conventions of literary pastoral—the echoing of poetic
song by nature and the catalogue of pleasant sounds in the *locus amoenus* (the
wind in the trees, the eloquence of moving water, bird song, etc.)—the figure
undergoes a romantic transformation, becoming the basis in all but a few
English poets for a new authentication of human music as an instance of
something transcendent." Stevens is one of those few poets, since while he
feels that there is a powerful force at work in the beachcomber's song, he is
unwilling to locate the source of the power. A human music is all we hear,
yet, unlike Storrs, Stevens resists the idea that the song's effect is explicable
in exclusively human terms. The woman sings beyond the genius of the sea
with a voice that seems inhuman at the same time that it is nothing but
human, a song uttered word by word. Both the singer and the sea are nothing
but themselves, not masks, but even after all these terms are sorted out the
question still remains: "Whose spirit is this?"

In response to the question, Stevens articulates the kinds of ambiguities
described by Blackmur: "By associating ambiguities found in nature in a poem
we reach a clarity, a kind of transfiguration even, whereby we learn *what* the
ambiguity was." In "The Idea of Order" there is no certain answer to the
question "Whose spirit is this?" because a certain answer does not exist:

the poem asks us to understand a world in which ideas of order are necessarily provisional and continuously changing. The poem enacts that ambiguity on a syntactical level, throwing its own answers into question, and even the clearest explanation of the woman's song does not remain clear for long.

> It was her voice that made
> The sky acutest at its vanishing.
> She measured to the hour its solitude.
> She was the single artificer of the world
> In which she sang. And when she sang, the sea,
> Whatever self it had, became the self
> That was her song, for she was the maker. Then we,
> As we beheld her striding there alone,
> Knew that there never was a world for her
> Except the one she sang and, singing, made.

These lines echo the language of Hoon's solitary chant, asserting the nearly solipsistic nature of the maker's vision and the autotelic nature of the poem she makes. The poem itself cannot end here, though, because Stevens knows that these lines provide too easy an answer to the original question ("Whose spirit is this?")—that Hoon's solipsistic world never lasts for long, that the universe is explicable not only in terms of humanity. Many of the lesser poems about ideas of order confound any certainty about precisely where those ideas emanate. In "Re-statement of Romance" (1935) Stevens asserted that the "night knows nothing of the chants of night. / It is what it is as I am what I am." The human and inhuman worlds are as strongly delineated here as in "The Idea of Order at Key West," but in "Re-statement of Romance" Stevens also explains that such an impasse does not exist between two human beings: "we two may interchange / Each in the other what each has to give." Or as he put it in one of the "Adagia": "Poetry is not the same thing as the imagination taken alone. Nothing is itself taken alone. Things are because of interrelations or interactions." The inexplicable magic of "The Idea of Order" exists not in the private world of the solitary singer but in the fact that other human beings hear the song and feel its power over their minds. The poem's final question is unanswerable.

> Ramon Fernandez, tell me, if you know,
> Why, when the singing ended and we turned
> Toward the town, tell why the glassy lights,
> The lights in the fishing boats at anchor there,
> As the night descended, tilting in the air,
> Mastered the night and portioned out the sea,

Fixing emblazoned zones and fiery poles,
Arranging, deepening, enchanting night.

These lines turn from a solipsistic vision to a world shared by many people, and at the same time might be understood to hint most provocatively at
the state of Key West as Stevens found it in February 1934. In his letter to
his wife, Stevens does not remark on fishing boats in the harbor but battleships. And while there is of course no sharp evidence that Stevens was thinking of those ships when he wrote "The Idea of Order," consider what happens to a reading of the poem when those historical conditions are kept in
mind: Stevens's rage to "master" the night sky and "portion" out the sea
encompassed a desire to transform battleships into fishing boats, suggesting
not revolution but life in its essential mundanity—not "disturbed conditions"
but the daily life of Key West as Stevens usually knew it. Harold Bloom has
said that "The Idea of Order at Key West" affirms "a transcendental poetic
spirit yet cannot locate it," and the weight of the poem's inability—or unwillingness—to mark locations increases when we consider the historical location
of the poem itself.

In an important reading of "Tintern Abbey," Marjorie Levinson notes a
similar anxiety about locations. When Wordsworth visited it, the abbey was
a refuge for homeless beggars and the wretchedly poor; the landscape around
it was scarred by the early excesses of the industrial revolution. Little of that
historical evidence appears in Wordsworth's poem, and there is less evidence
still that Wordsworth had these social conditions in mind when he wrote
"Tintern Abbey"—or as much evidence as there is for Stevens's thinking of
"the disturbed conditions in Cuba" as he wrote "The Idea of Order." Nevertheless, Levinson concludes that "what we witness in this poem is a conversion of public to private property, history to poetry." But if "Tintern
Abbey" is indeed a poem, what else could it do? While suggesting a historical
content for "The Idea of Order at Key West," I do not want to insist that
poems must represent history in direct or uncomplicated ways. The danger
in Levinson's reading of Wordsworth is the danger Blackmur saw in Hicks—
that the critic is "concerned with the separable content of literature, with
what may be said without consideration of its specific setting and apparatus
in a form." And if the conversion of "history" into "poetry" is one danger for
a poet, another is (to use the words as casually as Levinson does) the conversion of poetry into history: witness the naive realist work of Edwin Rolfe.
With an aesthetic capable of representing historical conditions more directly,
William Carlos Williams might have visited Key West and written a poem
describing the battleship *Wyoming*. But when Rahv and Phillips surveyed

Williams's more socially conscious poetry in the 1930s, they concluded that he "merely added the proletariat to his store of American objects." That did not make Williams's poetry "more" historical; the poems registered their historicity in a different way. With an innate Emersonian diffidence reinforced by Burke and Croce, Stevens approached a disordered world and answered it as a poet—more precisely, as a poet who always felt somewhat insecure commenting on political situations he knew less well than he knew poetry. But Stevens also distrusted the poetry he knew, and "The Idea of Order" does not affirm the sublime power of "Tintern Abbey" ("something far more deeply interfused") precisely because its author was skeptical of the ideas of order such power may appear to provide. Someone named Ramon Fernandez, Stevens felt, was not skeptical enough.

Stevens always insisted that "Ramon Fernandez" was "not intended to be anyone at all," and, in a sense, like the "Mr. Burnshaw" of "Mr. Burnshaw and the Statue," he is a caricature. Yet most of Stevens's readers will know that Fernandez was a critic familiar to Stevens from the pages of the *Nouvelle revue française*, the *Partisan Review*, and the *Criterion* (where he was translated by T. S. Eliot). Fernandez's criticism became increasingly politically engaged in the 1930s, especially after the violent riots and the general strike he witnessed in Paris in the wake of the Stavisky Affair. (The mastermind of illicit financial deals in which the French government was implicated, Stavisky was found dead—apparently by his own hand, though his suicide seemed to most French citizens to have been far too convenient.) After the riots, Fernandez published an open letter to Gide in the *Nouvelle revue française*, asserting that while he had not opposed the fascist cause before the riots, he was now converted to the struggle of the proletariat. The letter provoked a number of letters in response, some of them challenging Fernandez, others simply canceling subscriptions to the *Nouvelle revue française*.

That this controversy lay behind Stevens's use of Fernandez's name in "The Idea of Order" would have seemed apparent to anyone who read Stevens's poem in *Alcestis* along with the concurrent issue of the *Partisan Review*, which contained a translation of Fernandez's "I Came Near Being a Fascist." There Fernandez confessed that he had "a professional fondness for theorizing, which tends to make one highly susceptible to original 'solutions.'" It was just that susceptibility that bothered Stevens and made him challenge Fernandez to answer a question to which he knew there was no certain answer. Stevens's interest in the ambiguity of ideas did not mean that he took ideas lightly; on the contrary, he lamented what he thought of as "the Lightness with which ideas are asserted, held, abandoned" in "the world today." Nor did Stevens mean to equate ambiguity with the intentional obscuring of an ambiguous world; he condemned the poet "who wrote with the idea of being deliberately obscure" as "an imposter." With his public announcements of political commitments and conversions, Fernandez was the opposite of Stevens, who recoiled at the idea of associating himself with any group or program that offered "solutions." Fernandez, suggests Stevens in "The Idea of Order," might have been certain about the source and effect of the singer's song, but the only thing Stevens was sure of was that in his certainty, Fernandez would have been wrong.

In an essay criticizing the New Humanism (with which Fernandez was associated early in the 1930s), Blackmur protested that their ideas of order were too rigidly conceived; for Blackmur, the "true business" of what might be called humanism would be to "feel the experience upon which the intellect works as ambiguous, present only provisionally"; in the face of such a constantly shifting world, the ordering intellect must restore "its proper sense of strength and weakness in necessity, that in setting up its orders and formulas of order, it is coping with disorder. It should remember that an order is not invalidated by disorder; and that if an order is to become imaginative it must be so conceived as to accommodate disorder." Stevens believed that we cannot live without ideas of order, but like Blackmur he understood that he could not talk about order without raising the specter of disorder, and that any idea of order that did not leave space for its own dissolution could not be tolerated. In this sense, responding to Fernandez's dogmatism, Stevens might have titled his poem "The Idea of Disorder at Key West." As he would put it in "Mr. Burnshaw and the Statue," "even disorder may, / So seen, have an order of its own." In the terms of Kenneth Burke that both Blackmur and Stevens admired, these poems of order do not offer "the seasoned stocks and bonds of set beliefs," but "a questioning art, still cluttered with the merest conveniences of thinking, a highly fluctuant thing often turning against itself and its own best discoveries."

That may be, admittedly, a generous or at least an optimistic reading of Stevens's aesthetic. With a political background set behind it, "The Idea of Order" emerges as a poem that retreats from political revolution and chastises Fernandez for committing himself to change. And since I have already examined Stevens's affinity with certain aspects of the New Critics' interest in ambiguity, it is chastening to remember how that interest was sometimes enlisted in a program of self-conscious conservatism; in his final years following the Second World War, Stevens himself would find the house of ambiguity a rather more comfortable than tenuous place in which to dwell. More recently, the deconstructive critics' interest in a text's radical ambiguity has been condemned for similar reasons. Barbara Johnson has summed up the case for the opposition: "Nothing could be more convincing than the idea

that political radicality requires decisiveness, not indecision; haste, not hesitation. . . . The privileging of ambiguity would always appear to be an avoid-
ance of action." Johnson poses these questions in order to answer them, however equivo-
cally; and even Frank Lentricchia, one of the critics of undecidability to
whom Johnson responds, defends Kenneth Burke's particular interest in
ambiguity by suggesting that because he engages "in ideological struggle on
the discursive level," the "fluidity, or undecidability, of the symbol is not . . .
the sign of its social and political elusiveness but the ground of its historicity
and of its flexible but also specific political significance and force." These
arguments might answer the charges that might be brought against Stevens's
ideas of ambiguity, but it is perhaps more important to remember that Stevens
brought the charges Johnson rehearses against himself—and found them difficult to answer. Stevens was sure that order and disorder were necessarily
intimate with one another; but he worried that his sense of order—by its very
rhetorical power—disguised its provisionality. This concern made Stevens
reconsider "The Idea of Order at Key West" almost as soon as he finished it.
That Stevens appears to rewrite this poem throughout the poems of "Owl's
Clover" and "The Man with the Blue Guitar" is not a sign that he took its
answers for granted; it is evidence that he felt its answers were provisional,
requiring revision over time. That concern accounts in turn for some of the
waywardness of the poems of "Owl's Clover," coming on the heels of the
mastery of "The Idea of Order at Key West." These poems represent Stevens's effort to reformulate an idea of order that (in Blackmur's terms)
"accommodates disorder," stretching itself "constantly to the point where it
can envisage the disorder which its order merely names."

"You know," Stevens told Latimer soon after *Ideas of Order* was published,
"the truth is I had hardly interested myself in [order] (perhaps as another
version of pastoral) when I came across some such phrase as this: 'man's passionate disorder', and I have since been very much interested in disorder."
Two references are conflated here. In the terms of Empson's second book,
Some Versions of Pastoral (1935), Stevens sees that his own ideas of order
might depend on a comparison of "the social arrangement to Nature," making the arrangement appear inevitable and unchanging—despite his insistent
calls for change. Empson maintained that even revolutionary proletarian literature "is usually Covert Pastoral": the point is not that such conventions
should not be used, he said, but that what the Communist Party had recently
named "socialist realism" is never as simple or single-minded as it appears.
Flying in the face of the hermeneutic certainties of such an aesthetic, the
entire point of "The Idea of Order at Key West" is to expose the dangers of

single-minded dogmatism. Still, however tentatively he presented them, Stevens knew that his ideas of order could be read as one more version of pastoral; if the charge could be brought against the proletarian novel, it could certainly be brought against "The Idea of Order"—especially since this ode to the idea of ambiguity could be said to obscure an imperialist response to revolution. Consequently, at the same time that Empson's work intrigued him, Stevens became fascinated with what Anne Treneer called "passionate disorder" in *Charles M. Doughty: A Study of his Prose and Verse* (1935). Stevens may not have read the entire book, but he copied this passage from a *Times Literary Supplement* review into his commonplace book, sensing that, like Doughty, he was a poet who sometimes "insisted on creating a world for himself in his poetry . . . with most of the troublesome humanity left out":

Miss Treneer . . . in her final summing up . . . puts it . . . :—
"Could he have presented the passionate disorder in the hearts of men as he presents the passionate heat at the core of the earth he would also have been a great tragic poet. As it is, there is something in Doughty, call it moral fibre, or a sense of rectitude, or of noble reserve, which limited his field when treating of what is human in poetry".
     To use Keats's antithesis, Doughty as poet belonged to the "egotistical sublime" and "the men of character". That is no defect in itself. . . . He belonged to the "egotistical sublime" because he insisted on creating a world for himself in his poetry . . . with most of the troublesome humanity left out.

     Extrapolating from Treneer's analysis of the lack of "passionate disorder" in Doughty's verse, the *TLS* reviewer places Doughty among the poets of the "egotistical sublime," a phrase made possible for Keats by William Hazlitt's review of *The Excursion*. Hazlitt saw Wordsworth's poem as a version of pastoral: "The *Excursion* may be considered as a philosophical pastoral poem," wrote Hazlitt; instead of offering "a description of natural objects" or "an account of the manners of rural life," Wordsworth "sees all things in his own mind," rejecting "striking subjects of remarkable combinations of events" as "interfering with the workings of his own mind." Hazlitt knew that the remarkable combination of events Wordsworth suppressed were precisely political, and Hazlitt's review ends with his infamous defense of the French Revolution Wordsworth abjured. At the same time, however, Hazlitt recognized that no poet could do anything but "see things in his own mind," and the *TLS* reviewer similarly tempered Treneer's criticism of Doughty by pointing out that it was "no defect in itself" that the poet "insisted on creating a world for himself in his poetry."
     Everything we know about Stevens might lead us to think that he would have acquitted himself in just these terms; for instance, he could have pointed

out (as I have, following Blackmur) that from the start his ideas of order were poised on the edge or were even indistinguishable from disorder. Instead, just after writing what was arguably his finest poem to date ("The Idea of Order"), Stevens rejected those ideas for new formulations—for poems he could have even more readily called "Ideas of Disorder," poems that dramatize more directly the poet's engagement with "troublesome humanity." What would become the first two poems of "Owl's Clover" (1936), "The Old Woman and the Statue" and "Mr. Burnshaw and the Statue," are Stevens's strategic revisions of "The Idea of Order at Key West." The second poem came in October 1935, in immediate response to Stanley Burnshaw; the first appeared the previous summer, even before *Ideas of Order* was published or reviewed.

I have already mentioned how Stevens told Latimer that as he wrote the poems of *Ideas* he never thought it was "a fixed philosophic proposition that every man introduces his own order as part of a general order. These are tentative ideas for the purposes of poetry." That statement epitomizes both the strength of Stevens's position (its skeptical and antidogmatic flexibility) and its weakness (its inability to distinguish dogmatism from a productive political commitment): but it is precisely the strength that kept the weakness from hardening into an unquestioned proposition itself. In "Agenda" (1935) Stevens consequently mocked every idea of order he had ever constructed, equating his poetic work with the statistical extravagances of "Babson's Reports on Business and Investments."

> Whipped creams and the Blue Danube,
> The lin-lan-lone of Babson,
> And yet the damned thing doesn't come right.
>
> Boston should be in the keys
> Painting the saints among palms.
> Charleston should be in New York.
>
> And what a good thing it would be
> If Shasta roared up in Nassau,
> Cooling the sugary air.

Roger Ward Babson believed that any economic fluctuation could be predicted and corrected; and as Stevens's mixed-up litany of place-names suggests, Babson's economic forecasts were predicated on his belief that every business operation, however local, was dependent on not only the nation's but the world's economic fortune. Stevens found such exaggerated ideas of order ridiculous, but because their order is a kind of disorder, the music of these lines is preferable to the final tercet's "College of Heralds" (a repository of genealogical records established by royal charter in 1484), where every-

thing is orderly, nothing changes, and "the well-tuned birds are singing, /
Slowly and sweetly." Similarly, in "Dance of the Macabre Mice" (1935), Stevens satirizes both the turgid order of the statue and the ineffectual disorder
of the mice that dance over its surface; yet again, the mice finally enlist Stevens's sympathy if only because they are capable of change. "I do very much
have a dislike of disorder," said Stevens at the same time that he explained its
necessity.

> This dance has no name. It is a hungry dance.
> We dance it out to the tip of Monsieur's sword,
> Reading the lordly language of the inscription,
> Which is like zithers and tambourines combined:
>
> The Founder of the State. Whoever founded
> A state that was free, in the dead of winter, from mice?

This poem grew from Stevens's work on "The Old Woman and the
Statue," in which the same ideas of disorder are imaged in more complicated
and more culturally specific terms. Several years after it was published, Stevens explained the poem's presuppositions to Simons: "Although this deals
specifically with the status of art in a period of depression, it is, when gen-
eralized, one more confrontation of reality (the depression) and the imagination (art)." While offering a portrait of the troublesome humanity left out
of "The Idea of Order at Key West," "The Old Woman and the Statue"
reemphasizes the earlier poem's insistence that the imagination alone has no
meaning except inasmuch as it interrelates or interacts with those social conditions. The poem opens with an image of marble horses frozen at the brink
of motion: their haunches are "low, / Contorted, staggering from the thrust
against / The earth," their forelegs taut in preparation for "the vivid plunge."
But something more than the will of the sculptor or the very stuff of the
statue is required to give the horses life. Just as the woman's song is mean-
ingless in "The Idea of Order" until it is heard by someone else, so does this
work of art require an audience. "Arranged for phantasy" to complete their
plunge, the horses are instead confronted by a woman—not the solitary singer
of the earlier poem, but a woman such as Stevens might have seen walking
the streets of Key West: "the bitter mind / In a flapping cloak."

> She walked along the paths
> Of the park with chalky brow scratched over black
> And black by thought that could not understand
> Or, if it understood, repressed itself

> Without any pity in a somnolent dream.
> The golden clouds that turned to bronze, the sounds
> Descending, did not touch her eye and left
> Her ear unmoved. She was that tortured one,
> So destitute that nothing but herself
> Remained and nothing of herself except
> A fear too naked for her shadow's shape.

No interaction between the statue and the woman can take place because the woman does not have the economic freedom to think of anything but herself: "What path could lead apart from what she was / And was to be?" Could art alone open that path, the poem asks, could this statue arrange and deepen the chaos of the evening sky? Such ideas of order will not emerge in this scenario because there is no human response. Faced with "the black of what she thought," the "mass of stone collapsed to marble hulk."

In Stevens's terms, the woman's state of mind is partially to blame, since it has become "fixed," a "sovereign shape in a world of shapes." Yet, as in "Dance of the Macabre Mice," the greater fault lies with the nature of the statue—always for Stevens a figure for an art that is itself fixed and unyielding. The final movement of "The Old Woman and the Statue" asks us to imagine what the statue would be like without the woman's gaze: "Without her, evening like a budding yew / Would soon be brilliant." But in contrast to the evening of "The Idea of Order," those brilliant lights would have no human meaning at all. As the image of the yew tree suggests, the evening would flourish in a deadened world. "Untroubled by suffering," the "horses would rise again, / Yet hardly to be seen." Hardly to be seen is to have no relevance or life, a solitary song without a listener. The poem's final lines offer an image of nearly perfect order, but it is an order that will not allow for the presence of suffering or happiness or any troublesome humanity whatsoever.

Stevens began "The Old Woman and the Statue" as part of the larger sequence he had in mind, aware from the start that this conclusion was not satisfactory and would need to be revised by another poem: an art capable of confronting disorder (rather than ignoring it) was what he required. Stanley Burnshaw's review of *Ideas of Order* provided Stevens with the terms for the second poem of "Owl's Clover." "Mr. Burnshaw and the Statue" begins with an extraordinarily vulgar Marxist critique of the statue.

> The thing is dead ... Everything is dead
> Except the future. Always everything

> That is is dead except what ought to be.
> All things destroy themselves or are destroyed.

Since Burnshaw himself never said anything remotely so silly, it is important to see that Stevens uses his name the way he uses "MacCullough" in "Notes toward a Supreme Fiction": it serves as a synecdoche for the galvanized voice of the *New Masses*, whose aesthetic principles Stevens exaggerates only slightly in the opening lines of "Mr. Burnshaw." While we cannot hear the real Burnshaw's voice in the poem that bears his name, we can hear the voice of Michael Gold condemning "the spectacle of Proust, master-masturbator of the bourgeois literature." In Stevens's poem this voice calls for an art plastic enough to become "hot and huge with fact," but the call is as unyielding and programmatic as the statue itself.

"Mr. Burnshaw and the Statue" vacillates between the voice of the vulgar Marxist and a voice addressing the artist's "celestial paramours," whose aesthetic principles are ultimately revealed to be as problematic as the Marxist's. While "Mr. Burnshaw" wants the statue to be inscribed with a declaration of its own self-evident meaning—*"The Mass / Appoints These Marbles Of Itself to Be / Itself"*—the artist figure asks that the light of the paramours, "Astral and Shelleyan," transform the statue with the "rainbow in its glistening serpentines." Such transformation the vulgar Marxist will not allow, but the artist must recognize that the metamorphosis he desires is illusory, since it will have no effect on the real world: the apple "will not be redder" nor "the ploughman in his bed / Be free to sleep there sounder." A way to open a dialogue between the old woman and the statue remains to be found.

The artist figure wants to believe "that Shelley lies / Less in the stars than in their earthy wake," that there will be a "time in which the poets' politics / Will rule in a poets' world." But that wish invokes a stern response from the Stevens who saw the dangers of substituting poetry for politics rather than isolating the specific ways in which poetry and politics interact.

> Yet that will be
> A world impossible for poets, who
> Complain and prophesy, in their complaints,
> And are never of the world in which they live.

This poet's constructed world is one of order and fixity, the statue's world; the world in which the poet actually lives is all disorder and change.

> If ploughman, peacocks, doves alike
> In vast disorder live in the ruins, free,
> The charts destroyed, even disorder may,
> So seen, have an order of its own, a peace
> Not now to be perceived yet order's own.

These lines make explicit the dialectical relationship between order and disorder that is implicit in the earlier poems of order. Stevens could describe "Mr. Burnshaw and the Statue" not as a rejection but as a "justification of leftism" because for him leftism stood for the possibility of change, the ability to recognize (as he would paraphrase his poem) that "life is chaos, notwithstanding its times of serenity." And when "The Idea of Order at Key West" began to sound like a version of pastoral or of the egotistical sublime to Stevens, he wrote the first two poems of "Owl's Clover" in an attempt to accommodate the sublime to the human world of change. "A humanistic sublime is an oxymoron," says Thomas Weiskel in his study of the topic, yet that paradox is precisely what Stevens approaches in "Mr. Burnshaw," however precariously.

To avoid the seductions of the egotistical sublime, "Mr. Burnshaw" does not end simply by asserting that disorder may have an order of its own; Stevens goes on to offer an image of chaos, the wasteland "at the end of the world."

> There buzzards pile their sticks among the bones
> Of buzzards and eat the bellies of the rich,
> Fat with a thousand butters, and the crows
> Sip the wild honey of the poor man's life,
> The blood of his bitter brain.

Despite the carnage here, the buzzards eating the bellies of the rich and the severed head of the sculptor among his horses's heads, the scene is ultimately not apocalyptic—it "moves from waste / To waste, out of the hopeless waste of the past / Into a hopeful waste to come." While we have seen that the astral and Shelleyan lights cast upon the statue had no effect upon the world, the lights cast upon this "immense detritus of a world" make "two immense / Reflections, whirling apart and wide away." And though this light appears astral, it emanates not from the celestial paramours but from a new generation of human voices, "younger bodies" who "rise / And chant the rosepoints of their birth." Chastising the paramours, Stevens says that it is "not enough that you are indifferent": "It is only enough / To live incessantly in change." That admonition applies equally as well to the exaggerated Marxist, who could see only that "Everything is dead," or to the statue itself, which in its stillness happened to be as silly as the Marxist said it was. The song of the paramours is "like porcelain," and Stevens ends "Mr. Burnshaw and the Statue" by inciting the paramours to turn against their own rigidity and dance like mice to the music of disorder.

> Conceive that while you dance the statue falls,
> The heads are severed, topple, tumble, tip
> In the soil and rest. Conceive that marble men
> Serenely selves, transfigured by the selves
> From which they came, make real the attitudes
> Appointed for them and that the pediment
> Bears words that are the speech of marble men.

As the statues are broken, even the Marxist's call for art *"to / Be itself"* is transformed from a naive tenet of socialist realism into the goal of an intricately dialectical process by which art, in all its complexity, engages the world of human speech and makes it "real." The old woman of the previous poem might have seen herself in broken forms, and all poems, Stevens suggests, must in a sense be broken—not ends in themselves but endlessly ambiguous. Stevens would recast these ideas of disorder in "Connoisseur of Chaos" (1938), offering propositions A and B ("A violent order is disorder" and "A great disorder is an order") and concluding that even these ideas of disorder "are not like statuary, posed / For a vista in the Louvre" but "are things chalked / On the sidewalk so that the pensive man may see." The value of disorder is its openness, and for a poet's ethereal politics to have any meaning in a world of ploughmen and peacocks, the propositions must not be carved in stone but chalked on the sidewalk, within view of any old woman or man and soon to be washed away by rain.

In "The Irrational Element in Poetry," written to accompany a reading from "Owl's Clover" in December 1936, Stevens explained that the poet must *resist* "the pressure of the contemporaneous" rather than *escape* it. "There can be no thought of escape," says Stevens. "We are preoccupied with events, even when we do not observe them closely. We have a sense of upheaval. We feel threatened. We look from an uncertain present toward a more uncertain future. One feels the desire to collect oneself against all this in poetry as well as in politics. If politics is nearer to each of us because of the pressure of the contemporaneous, poetry, in its way, is no less so and for the same reason." Having taken on the news of the day in "Owl's Clover," however, Stevens returned in "The Man with the Blue Guitar" (1937) to a poetry that seems even more austerely removed from troublesome humanity than "The Idea of Order at Key West." But just as each poem of "Owl's Clover" throws the previous poem into question, the entire sequence is revised again in the "Blue Guitar." Like the end of "Mr. Burnshaw," the opening lines of the "Blue Guitar" ask if only a realistic art records the contemporaneous. "You have a blue guitar, / You do not play things as they are," says the audience to the musician. The musician replies that he has no choice, since whenever history is represented in a work of art (even in the style we think of as realism) it is necessarily transformed: "Things as they are / Are changed upon the blue guitar." That is less a challenge than a description of what any act of representation does—and the clipped, theoretical lines of "The Man with the Blue Guitar" are no less a product of the historical conditions of the 1930s than the vast cultural wasteland of "Owl's Clover"; they are a different product.

In this context, consider the famous twenty-second poem in the sequence.

> Poetry is the subject of the poem,
> From this the poem issues and
>
> To this returns. Between the two,
> Between issue and return, there is
>
> An absence in reality,
> Things as they are. Or so we say.
>
> But are these separate? Is it
> An absence for the poem, which acquires
>
> Its true appearances there, sun's green,
> Cloud's red, earth feeling, sky that thinks?
>
> From these it takes. Perhaps it gives,
> In the universal intercourse.

That opening line is not an aesthete's credo but a recognition of the limited scope of poetry in a time when great demands were placed on literature. Building on "Mr. Burnshaw and the Statue" (where a poet's politics cannot suffice outside of poetry) and on "The Irrational Element" (where the poet cannot escape the world outside the poem), this passage insists on a dialectical relationship between the "poetry" of the poem and the "reality" to which it refers. As Stevens paraphrased the passage, "imagination has no source except in reality, and ceases to have any value when it departs from reality. . . . There is nothing that exists exclusively by reason of the imagination, or that does not exist in some form in reality. . . . . Imagination gives, but gives in relation." To apply this insight to the poem of which it is a paraphrase is to remember that despite its self-referential and theoretical nature, the "Blue

Guitar" grew from Stevens's engagement with the political and aesthetic questions the Depression threw into high relief. As Stevens explained in "Insurance and Social Change" (1937), an essay that follows the "Blue Guitar" as "The Irrational Element" follows "Owl's Clover": "It helps us to see the actual world to visualize a fantastic world. Thus, when Mr. Wells creates a world of machines, a matter-of-fact truth about the world in which we live becomes clear for all the fiction. When he passes from the international to the interstellar, we hug the purely local."

That way of thinking did not make Stevens any friends at the *New Masses*, but it did at the *Nation*, whose editors awarded the magazine's poetry prize to "The Men That Are Falling" (1936), an elegy for the dead soldiers of the Spanish Civil War. "Of the [over 1,800] poems submitted," said the *Nation*'s editors, "the overwhelming majority were concerned with contemporary social conflicts either at home or abroad." Stevens's poem fit that category, and though it does lean closer to the contemporaneous than many of the poems of the "Blue Guitar," the poem remains elusive. The *Nation*'s editors could still see that "The Men That Are Falling" was a poem of social conflict because it addressed the costs of certainty—lamenting those costs even as it recognized a world of actions where commitments sometimes must be certain.

> God and all angels, this was his desire,
> Whose head lies blurring here, for this he died.
>
> Taste of the blood upon his martyred lips,
> O pensioners, O demagogues and pay-men!
>
> This death was his belief though death is a stone.
> This man loved earth, not heaven, enough to die.
>
> The night wind blows upon the dreamer, bent
> Over words that are life's voluble utterance.

There is, as critics of deconstruction have pointed out, a political danger that may arise from a belief in the absolute ambiguity of discourse. "The Men That Are Falling" reminds us that there is an equally dangerous consequence that may arise from an absolute intolerance of ambiguity: since lives are sacrificed for ideas, it is crucial to understand the limitations and contradictions of those ideas. "To-day the deliberate increase in the chances of death," wrote Auden in lines of "Spain" that he would quickly regret, "The conscious acceptance of guilt in the necessary murder." To Stevens, only demagogues and pay-men could call such a thing necessary. Although he wrote "The Men

That Are Falling" between "Owl's Clover" and the "Blue Guitar," Stevens placed the poem last in *The Man with the Blue Guitar and Other Poems* (which also contained the revised version of "Owl's Clover") as if to suggest what was at stake in all the ideas of ambiguity that preceded it.

Soon after he won the *Nation* award, Stevens was also welcomed at the reconstituted *Partisan Review*, which reappeared in 1937 after a year's hiatus. Stevens's "The Dwarf" was prominently placed in the carefully constructed inaugural issue, and two years later Rahv and Phillips also printed Stevens's "Life on a Battleship." The battleship *Wyoming* was left out of "The Idea of Order at Key West," but here the captain of the ship *Masculine* speaks, explaining how class war might be manipulated into total war. More than any other poem of the 1930s, "Life on a Battleship" expresses Stevens's preference for disorder over any order that is taken for granted as natural and enduring.

> The war between classes is
> A preliminary, a provincial phase,
> Of the war between individuals. In time,
> When earth has become a paradise, it will be
> A paradise full of assassins. Suppose I seize
> The ship, make it my own and, bit by bit,
> Seize yards and docks, machinery and men,
> As others have, and then, unlike the others,
> Instead of building ships, in numbers, build
> A single ship, a cloud on the sea, the largest
> Possible machine, a divinity of steel,
> Of which I am captain. Given what I intend,
> The ship would become the centre of the world.

Published several months before the announcement of the Nazi-Soviet Pact, these lines seconded the *Partisan Review* editors' prescient sense of the conjunctions between fascism and Stalinism; they also reveal how Stevens was aware of certain dangers inherent in his own romance with heroism—which sometimes seems uncomfortably bound to totalitarian desires itself. As much as Stevens longed (in the phrase of Henry Adams that he copied into his commonplace book) for "one man in history to admire," he also recognized how quickly the idea of heroism might become the reality of Stalinism. Adams's remark was culled from an essay by R. P. Blackmur, who pointed out that while Adams longed for the certainty of belief, he was also skeptical of all possible heros: like Montaigne, Adams was for Blackmur a "master of ironic wisdom" who "in reconciling two points of view into one . . . manages to imply the possibility of a third and quite unadjusted point of view"; Adams could never "feel the complexity as reducible into a single energy." To some extent, Blackmur imposes his own ironic wisdom about the dialectical relationship of order and disorder onto Adams: Adams was sometimes seduced by certainty, and so was Stevens—even though he knew better. The specter of the captain of the *Masculine* lurks in some of Stevens's hero poems; there are times at which Stevens will talk about "the centre of the world" and be sincere. But those moments are qualified by Stevens's sense that no conception of what is central or true can last for long without becoming "a paradise full of assassins." Because Stevens understood ambiguity not as an ornament to discourse or an unwanted impediment to action but as an integral aspect of discourse and a sometimes desirable complication of action, there is never any room in his poems for "necessary murder."

Nor is there much room for cultural despair. Although Stevens's ideas of ambiguity developed in dialogue with Burke and Blackmur, they dovetailed easily with the values of the reconstituted *Partisan Review*. Stevens especially admired Philip Rahv (from whom he had learned about Stalinism before he wrote "Life on a Battleship"): when Stevens discussed Henry Church's proposal for a lecture series at Princeton in 1940, he first suggested Rahv "on the relation of the poet to society, or on some aspect of that relation." (Under the influence of Allen Tate, Cleanth Brooks was selected instead—the dogmatic New Critic was not Stevens's choice—but Kenneth Burke would deliver one of the lectures in the following year.) As much as Rahv and Stevens did agree that that relationship was necessarily ambiguous, however, Rahv parted from Stevens in hypostatizing an essential relationship between social disorder and the disorder of modernist texts. Other factions of the American left scorned what they thought of as modernist pessimism, but as Rahv's faith in radicalism waned, his investment in that pessimism grew. So despite the fact that Stevens was welcomed in the *Partisan Review*, his work remained marginalized in a canon of modern literature conceived in either modernist or Marxist terms. Throughout the 1930s, Rahv wanted to assert the political relevance of the modernist masterpieces. To do so even more strenuously in "Twilight of the Thirties" (1939), he borrowed the metaphor that (as I discussed in Chapter 7) Stephen Spender had already borrowed from I. A. Richards, who had borrowed it from Conrad: modern writers "immersed themselves in the 'destructive element,' which has been defined as the awareness of 'a void in the present.' . . . From *René* to *The Waste Land*, what is modern literature if not a vindictive, neurotic, and continually renewed dispute with the modern world?" Stevens had already exposed the shortsightedness of this perspective in "The Comedian as the Letter C" and

"Academic Discourse at Havana." And when he visualized the wasteland at the world's end in "Mr. Burnshaw and the Statue," he was careful not to reify that idea of disorder into an unchanging reality: the scene moves "out of the hopeless waste of the past / Into a hopeful waste to come." Throughout the 1930s, even as he heeded the imperatives of a disordered world, Stevens would continue to insist on the politics of comedy.

12

The Politics of Despair

In a much debated essay on the *Partisan Review*, Frederick Crews remarks that none of the journal's editors "could explain how neo-Marxist political commentary was to be reconciled with 'The Dry Salvages' and highbrow discussions of the modern masters." Ultimately, Rahv and Phillips never could justify their attempts to align modernism and Marxism, but they spent the better part of a decade trying: the value of their effort is not that a happy marriage was achieved but that their effort, even with its moments of blindness, reveals what is at stake in a struggle that has never been comfortably resolved, whether in the pages of the *Partisan Review* or in the annals of the Frankfurt school.

Responding to Lukács's rejection of modern art forms, Theodor Adorno named Lukács's aesthetic ideal of "reflection of objective reality" as a "vulgar-materialist shibboleth," a "mockery of dialectics." To save the work of Schoenberg, Kafka, and Beckett, Adorno maintained that such radically disjunctive art did not retreat from reality but engaged the discontinuities of late capitalism itself: these artists immerse themselves "in the laws of their own forms, laws which are aesthetically rooted in their own social content. It is this alone which gives the work of Joyce, Beckett, and modern composers their power. The voice of the age echoes through their monologues." But in these terms, does the voice of the age echo (the metaphor itself is reductive) through the work of Stravinsky, Stevens, and Woolf? Their art is as "complex and ambiguous" as any modern achievement, but for Adorno, the complexity is not a sign of "the expression of suffering and the pleasure taken in dissonance" that is "inextricably interwoven in authentic works of art in the modern age." While Adorno could save Schoenberg from Lukács's strictures, he himself had no patience for Stravinsky, whose music was not politically engaged because of its moments of "soothing comfort, of the harmonious, of the displacement of horror." Despite Schoenberg's austerely aestheticist disregard for politics, his dissonances revealed to Adorno the political content of his art because they matched Adorno's sense of modern fragmentation. Schoenberg was a doomsayer and therefore politically engaged; Stravinsky was "the yea-sayer of music" and judged accordingly. Lukács recalled that during the First World War, he experienced a "despair over the state of the world"; the present appeared to him as "a condition of total degradation." Even as Adorno uncovered the illusions of Lukács's realism, he inherited the illusions of Lukács's cultural despair.

Similar illusions are bound up in the debates over modernism and Marxism that took place in the *Partisan Review*. Responding to the extraordinarily realist aesthetic of Gold and Hicks, Rahv and Phillips followed the examples of Engels on Balzac or Lenin on Tolstoy: turning to Dostoevsky and Eliot, they wanted to show how these writers' manifest ideologies may be undermined by their writing itself. "Reactionary in its abstract content," said Rahv of *The Possessed*, it is "radical in sensibility and subversive in performance." The slippery word here is *sensibility*. Phillips and Rahv saw that many writers were subversive in performance, but only certain modernists were in touch with that modern sensibility. Responding to the charge that Eliot's poetry "is obscure and pessimistic, and that it expresses private sorrows," Rahv and Phillips maintained in "Criticism" (1935) that the poet's "'restlessness and futility' cannot possibly be private. And the new methods developed by the experimental poets are not mere eccentricities, but the result of the assimilation of urban environments in poetry, reflecting the entire modern sensibility." In a 1935 essay, "Form and Content," Phillips commented again that Eliot's "sensibility has produced a trenchant idiom for the dislocation of bourgeois perspectives amidst a tightening commercial way of life." And again in "The Esthetic of the Founding Fathers" (1938) he asked: "Is not the autumnal sensibility of Eliot a kind of comment on the state of society?" The always canny Virgil Thomson once said, "there is no Modern Spirit" that modern poetry, painting, and music embody. "There are only some modern techniques. If it were otherwise, the market price of music and painting and poetry would not be so disparate as they are." Rahv and Phillips equated a particular kind of technique or style with a particular sensibility, and that sensibility was for them a sign of political engagement. Simply put, this meant that unhappy art was a valuable product; happy art was produced by aesthetes. Responding to Joseph Wood Krutch's "Literature and Utopia" (1934), Rahv insisted unequivocally that the literature of "advanced intellectuals" offers not a "shallow optimism" but "an atmosphere of disillusion."

Krutch's *The Modern Temper* (1929) had been as influential as Eliot's poetry in defining that atmosphere, and when Krutch recanted his pessimism, Rahv was outraged. The title Rahv chose for his response to Krutch's "Literature and Utopia" is particularly revealing: "How the Waste Land Became a Flower Garden." Although he objected to Eliot's fascist sympathies even as he praised Eliot's articulation of the modern sensibility, Rahv attempted to make these discriminations with the very terms forged by Eliot himself. Not simply was Rahv, like Lenin on Tolstoy, trying to isolate the counterideological aspect of Eliot's work; his critical tools were shaped by Eliot's work in the first place—as if Lenin were reading Tolstoy with a Marxist perspective sifted through *What Is Art?* Defending the innovations of Kafka's novels, Rahv conceded that the "intense study by contemporary critics of the relation between tradition and the individual talent" has revealed that a "surplus of originality is more often a sign of weakness than of strength." Criticizing Henry Miller's work for that failing, Rahv maintained that the novelist could not muster "the continual sacrifice of personality that the art of creation requires." These catchphrases from Eliot's essays, almost always uncredited, stud Rahv's and Phillips's essays, coloring their entire effort to reconcile Marxism with modernism. And as the 1930s progressed, the references to Eliot's work increased. At the beginning of the decade, Eliot's work from the 1920s (not the poetry he published during the 1930s) provided the metaphors for the "modern sensibility," a nostalgic sense of lost possibilities; toward the end of the decade, Eliot's metaphors began to speak for a radical movement that found its own hopes equally diminished, a movement disillusioned by the Stalinization of the Russian experiment and by the marginalization of revolutionary politics in the United States. Rahv began his 1938 essay on Stalin's purges ("Trials of the Mind") with an uncredited but easily identifiable epigraph from Eliot's "Gerontion"—"After such knowledge, what forgiveness?" The Eliot who had made his disdain for communism clear could be forced to speak for this predicament: "Our days are ceasing to be. We are beginning to live from hour to hour, awaiting the change of headlines. History has seized time in a brutal embrace. We dread the Apocalypse. . . . Ninety years have passed since the most subversive document of all times, *The Communist Manifesto*, injected its directive images into the nascent consciousness of the proletariat. We were not prepared for defeat." The editors of the *Partisan Review* had become the hollow men.

In the ominously titled "Proletarian Literature: A Political Autopsy" (1939) Rahv equated these dashed ideals of the Russian Revolution with the

American left's failure to develop a truly revolutionary literature: "What we were witnessing was a miniature version of the process which in Russia had resulted in the replacement of the dictatorship of the proletariat by the dictatorship of the Communist Party. Within the brief space of a few years the term 'proletarian literature' was transformed into a euphemism for a Communist Party literature." Rahv was admitting here that much of what the *Partisan Review* had stood for (especially a meeting of modernist literary taste and revolutionary political commitment) had not come to pass. With the autopsy on proletarian literature performed, the only texts still living were the modernists'—especially Eliot's. The marriage between Marxism and modernism had ended in divorce, and the sturdier survivor—the sturdier avant-garde—appeared to be modernism.

As I discussed in Chapter 1, that was the point of Edmund Wilson's "The Politics of Flaubert," in which Wilson took pains to show that the novelist "brought to attention a danger of which Marx was not aware." Rahv went further. In "Twilight of the Thirties" (which appeared a few months after the autopsy) he confessed that a work of art embodying the modernist sensibility was for him "a thousand times more 'progressive'—if that is to be our criterion—was infinitely more disinterested, infinitely more sensitive to the actual conditions of human existence, than the shallow political writing of our latter days." To proclaim Eliot as the true revolutionary in this context is to equate style (and the sensibility for which it appeared to stand) with the whole of politics. While the dislocations of Pound's texts may have some revolutionary force, they stand in constant tension with the manifest ideology of his work, which is, of course, reactionary. In turning to modernism alone to validate his historical pessimism (while ignoring Eliot's manifest politics), Rahv unintentionally makes Virgil Thomson's point clear: the modern sensibility is not something that exists in a historical world of economic and political struggle; it is a collection of techniques, a style. By 1941, when it published "The Dry Salvages," the *Partisan Review* could offer this uncomplicated defense—style was all that mattered: "Mr. Eliot's instinct was right in sending poems to us. . . . For . . . the tide of reaction is running so strongly nowadays that writers like Eliot have 'come to represent again relatively the same threat to official society as they did in the early decades of this century.' It is coming to be something of a revolutionary act simply to print serious creative writing."

At the end of "Twilight of the Thirties," in which Eliot is named directly, Marx becomes the ghostly, unidentified source for a luminous quotation—as Eliot had been in Rahv's "Trials of the Mind." Having validated his own despair as the true sign of political engagement, Rahv offers one hint of optimism: "every metamorphosis, it has been said, 'is partly a swan song and partly a prelude to a great new poem.'" Rahv's new-found faith in modernism is predicated on a rejection of Marxism as deterministic and simple-minded— capable of producing only an undialectical, realist literature. But the line quoted from Marx appears as a sign that Rahv himself knew better than that. In his "Speech at the Anniversary of the *People's Paper*," Marx exposed a politics of despair like Rahv's as itself undialectical and deterministic: its proponents, said Marx, suppress the *ambiguities* that open up the possibility for hope and change.

There is one great fact, characteristic of this our nineteenth century, a fact which no party dares deny. On the one hand, there have started into life industrial and scientific forces, which no epoch of the former human history had ever suspected. On the other hand, there exist symptoms of decay, far surpassing the horrors recorded of the latter times of the Roman empire. In our days everything seems pregnant with its contrary.... All our invention and progress seem to result in endowing material forces with intellectual life, and in stultifying human life into a material force. This antagonism between modern industry and science on the one hand, modern misery and dissolution on the other hand; this antagonism between the productive powers, and the social relations of our epoch is a fact, palpable, overwhelming, and not to be controverted. Some parties may wail over it; others may wish to get rid of modern arts, in order to get rid of modern conflicts. Or they may imagine that so signal a progress in industry wants to be completed by as signal a regress in politics. On our part, we do not mistake the shape of the shrewd spirit that continues to mark all these contradictions.

A more open acknowledgment of these contradictions would have helped the American left out of a self-defeating conception of history as the 1930s came to a close. And, as we saw in chapter 7, it would have helped open the eyes of several generations of American doomsayers from the Civil War to the Great War. Beginning with "Hawkins of Cold Cape," Stevens was always skeptical of apocalyptic rhetoric, and just as "Academic Discourse at Havana" was his response to the wasteland state of mind, the poems of "Owl's Clover" and "The Man with the Blue Guitar" reveal his resistance to an easy equation of cultural despair and political engagement. After reading Stanley Burnshaw's characterization of the Depression as "the murderous world collapse," Stevens responded with his picture of the modern wasteland in "Mr. Burnshaw and the Statue," the second poem of "Owl's Clover." As he later paraphrased this part of the poem, "it is a process of passing from hopeless waste to hopeful waste. This is not pessimism. The world is completely waste, but it is a waste always full of portentous lustres. We live constantly in the commingling of two reflections, that of the past and that of the future, whirling apart and wide away." That gloss makes the poem sound a little more balanced than it truly is. Stevens was sometimes capable of the sort of regressive nostalgia he had admired as a young man in William Jennings Bryan, and "Owl's Clover" at large offers less a balanced accounting of the imperatives of past and future than a struggle to maintain the balance. Simply to take on the task of portraying "troublesome humanity"—of making "poetry out of commonplaces: the day's news"—is to court the possibility of either an easy optimism or a facile despair: the phrase "Great Depression" was coined for good reason. And Stevens himself admitted that writing "Owl's Clover" involved him in a "constant struggle with clichés, both of word and thought." After much vacillation, however, "Owl's Clover" emerges as a new version of "The Comedian as the Letter C": like the earlier poem, "Owl's Clover" points to the virtues of ordinary experience, the life of "medium man," in which historical decline is measured soberly and the possibility of progress is not forgotten in apocalyptic or utopian fantasies. Helen Vendler has remarked that this sequence represents "a ballooning music, a variant of the euphuism of the *Comedian*, soon to be checked by the relatively small-stringed guitar." Even as "The Man with the Blue Guitar" leaves both the news of the day and the high-strung rhetoric of "Owl's Clover" behind, it does not reject the story of "medium man." While examining that story in greater detail, consequently, I will incorporate the "Blue Guitar" into my reading as a commentary on "Owl's Clover," for in fact that is what the later sequence is. "The Man with the Blue Guitar" depends on the poems that precede it, while providing a foundation for many of the poems that follow.

After "Mr. Burnshaw and the Statue" was completed, the remaining three poems of "Owl's Clover"—"The Greenest Continent," "A Duck for Dinner," and "Sombre Figuration"—were written in quick succession, each poem questioning and revising the conclusion of the preceding one. We have seen that in "Mr. Burnshaw" Stevens presented an oversimplified vision of the modern wasteland in order to undermine a seductive fatalism, and he painted an even more reductive picture of Central European decline in "The Greenest Continent." "There was a heaven once," begins the third movement of the poem, forecasting the fifth poem of the "Blue Guitar" ("Poetry / Exceeding music must take the place / Of empty heaven and its hymns"). In the "Blue Guitar," the loss is an occasion not for mourning the past but for building a future; in "The Greenest Continent," the attitude toward the realization that "there was a heaven once" is not so clear. The second movement of "The Greenest Continent" offers an image of the modern fate of Western culture as "a Schloss / Abandoned because of taxes."

It was enough:
It made up for everything, it was all selves
Become rude robes among white candle lights,
Motions of air, robes moving in torrents of air,
And through the torrents a jutting, jagged tower,
A broken wall—and it ceased to exist, became
A Schloss, an empty Schlossbibliothek, the books
For sale in Vienna and Zurich to people in Maine,
Ontario, Canton.

"As a preview of the spiritual decline and fall of the West," Joseph Riddel
has said of this passage, "it is acutely of its time, and powerfully compact"—
"as good as anything Stevens did in 'Owl's Clover.'" That judgment is not
contradicted but confirmed by the fact that when Stevens revised "Owl's Clover" for inclusion in *The Man with the Blue Guitar and Other Poems*, he cut
this passage. Stevens initially juxtaposed the modern wasteland with a time
in the past when "each man / Beheld the truth and knew it to be true," and
that contrast was meant to be undermined by "The Greenest Continent":
Ananke—the black sublime, necessity, the final god, mortality, fate—is
shown to be the governing principle of all ages and cultures, and what seems
to be the particular decay of modern Europe is revealed as one more instance
of Ananke's inescapable power. As he was working on "The Greenest Continent," Stevens was careful not to let Latimer misunderstand his use of the
phrase "complexity of contemporary life": "Have you ever stopped to think
of the extraordinary existence of Milton, in his time and under the circumstances of the world as it was then?" Stevens wanted to resist the illusions of
a uniquely modern sensibility, ironizing his vision of the modern wasteland
with the trans-historical power of Ananke. Yet the vision of modern Europe
as a decayed *Schloss* (as well as that longing for an unsullied golden age)
emerged so vividly that Stevens rightly feared the vision would override the
irony: hence it was deleted—not because the passage was weak but because
it was too strong. The uncut version of "The Greenest Continent" reveals
Stevens's divided mind. While he knows better than to regard the social
upheavals of his time as uniquely terrible, he allows himself to do so, pro-
tected by the poem's ironic framework.

The true subject of "The Greenest Continent," as I mentioned in Chapter
3, was Western imperialism, Mussolini's invasion of Ethiopia. From his
Marxist contemporaries, Stevens had learned to understand imperialism as
the last-ditch effort of a capitalist society in crisis. Fleeing the "heaven" of
the Central European *Schloss*, the angels "come, armed, gloriously to slay /
The black and ruin his sepulchral throne." Just as Stevens attempted to avoid
the seductions of a despair both catastrophic and (paradoxically) self-affirm-

ing as he portrayed the decay of Western culture, he needed to avoid an equally problematic complacency as he portrayed the West's imperialist venture in the Third World—especially since complacency was the American response to Mussolini; Roosevelt issued a hasty proclamation of neutrality even before war against Ethiopia was declared. Since the statue imported from Europe in "The Greenest Continent" belongs "to the cavernous past" and will not stand in Africa (as it would not speak to the old woman in the first poem of "Owl's Clover"), Stevens is able to conclude that the "black will still / Be free to sing, if only a sorrowful song." He could think of this condition as "freedom" because Ananke rules in Africa as in Europe ("The voice / In the jungle is a voice in Fontainebleau"), oppressing all varieties of the human condition. Litz has said that Stevens's "political ambivalence at times may be described as a wavering between a romantic attachment to the past and a blind acceptance of historical necessity": "The Greenest Continent" leans dangerously close to the latter.

I think Stevens came to this conclusion himself, even before he deleted the decaying *Schloss* passage from the poem. Just as "Mr. Burnshaw and the Statue" revises the simpler conclusion of "The Old Woman and the Statue," "A Duck for Dinner" turns against "The Greenest Continent," asking if Ananke, an agent of universal despair, might not be the very means of authoritarian power and not the source of an apparently consolatory freedom. This poem begins with a dialogue between the Marxist "Bulgar," who incites the workers to join "together as one, thinking / Each other's thoughts, thinking a single thought," and a more ethereal voice extolling the individualism of American pioneers, a lost people who were "ends in themselves." The contrast is precisely between an acceptance of historical necessity and a romantic attachment to the past, and neither alternative suffices. The pioneers represent a past moment incompatible with present-day conditions. The workers' apocalypse, extolled by the Bulgar, is a similar illusion, and the Bulgar must admit that his vision of the future is too rich for the present: "But that / Apocalypse was not contrived for parks, / Geranium budgets, pay-roll waterfalls." Both nostalgia and necessity, both "platitude and inspiration are alike / As evils."

That realization left Stevens at an impasse. Without a trustworthy account of past or future, "A Duck for Dinner" nearly capitulates to the wasteland sensibility Stevens had ridiculed in "Mr. Burnshaw and the Statue." In paraphrasing the poem, Stevens explained what the way out of the impasse might entail: "If the future (the hopeful waste about which I was writing the other day [in reference to "Mr. Burnshaw"]) also comes to nothing, sha'n't we be looking round for some one superhuman to put us together again, . . . some one who, if he is to dictate our fates, had better be inhuman, so that we shall know that he is without any of our weaknesses and cannot fail?" Not only Burke and Cowley dreamed of discovering "a man of super-human ability" early in the Depression; as Richard Pells has shown, this cult of leadership gained many converts during the years "when liberals and radicals placed their faith in economic planning boards, specialists in social engineering, government agencies, and official spokesmen for class interests." As the clouds of the Second World War began to form during the final years of the Depression, the editors of the *New Republic* "insisted that democracy could not endure nor could war be won without 'concentrating power in the executive.'" As the *New Republic* helped create Roosevelt's magisterial power, some Americans, Stevens among them, desired something more. "Personally," he told Henry Church, "I feel terribly in need of encountering [a really powerful] character. The other night I sat in my room in the moonlight thinking about the top men in the world today, people like Truman and Bevin, for example. That I suppose is the source of one's desire for a few really well developed individuals. What is terribly lacking from life today is the well developed individual, the master of life, or the man who by his mere appearance convinces you that a mastery of life is possible."

That desire helps to explain Stevens's brief attraction to Mussolini in 1935, but, as we have seen in "Life on a Battleship" (1939), the poet also exposed the delusions lurking in such desires. "A Duck for Dinner" attempts to achieve a middle ground, idealizing the hero while remaining wary of his powers. As he paraphrased the poem, Stevens walked the same tightrope, expressing his desire for someone superhuman to piece the world together, while recognizing that no one must ever be granted the power to dictate our fates—however attractive the idea of such a hero might be. Any dictator will impose his desires on others, just as Ananke leveled the differences between the oppressor and the oppressed. In the terms provided by "A Duck for Dinner," Ananke is not the answer to imperialist oppression but an even more seductive means of preventing us from perceiving that every change "is partly a swan song and partly a prelude to a great new poem."

"It may be the future depends on an orator," Stevens continues in the fourth movement of "A Duck for Dinner," yet the heroic orator is too intolerably human (a measure, paradoxically, of his capacity for inhumanity) to be trusted with the fate of the people at large. The tenth poem of "The Man with the Blue Guitar" is a revised version of this orator's incantation of the future; in contrast to the restrained music of this sequence, the orator's excesses are especially apparent (even more so in this earlier and shorter version of the tenth poem).

> Raise reddest columns. Toll a bell
> And clap the hollows full of tin.

> Throw papers in the streets, the wills
> Of the dead, majestic in their seals.
>
> And the beautiful trombones—behold
> The approach of him whom none believes,
>
> Whom all believe that all believe,
> A pagan in a varnished car.
>
> Subversive poet, this is most rare.
> Forward into tomorrow's past!

The final couplet's ironies expose the illusions of the future that this blustery demagogue would impose on the world: his vision of the future is like a cheap work of art—artificial in the worst sense of the word, a statue that cannot change, a repetition of yesterday's commonplaces masquerading as a world made new. In "A Duck for Dinner" Stevens juxtaposes this false hero with the artist figure he had introduced in "The Old Woman and the Statue" and "Mr. Burnshaw." In those poems the statue could not stand against the changing conditions of the present because it was immobile; but when Stevens returns to the statue in "A Duck for Dinner," he emphasizes not so much the statue itself as the sculptor—not the unchanging artifact but the accommodating process of creation: "The statue is the sculptor not the stone. / In this he carved himself, he carved his age, / He carved the feathery walkers standing by."

In suggesting that the sculptor (not the orator) is the hero flexible enough to embody our present condition and satisfy our yearning for an improved future, Stevens is poised at the point where Philip Rahv chose Eliot as a more potent political force than the American left, the point where Edmund Wilson chose Flaubert over Marx. Yet Stevens realizes that even this heroic artist is precisely too good to be true—and if he were more than a possibility, too dangerous to be true, since he would no doubt become that mountain-minded Hoon, "from whose beard the future springs, elect." Echoing Hoon's aristocratic chant, Stevens reminds us that a "poet's politics" may not suffice outside a poet's world; the heroic artist may too easily confect a private rather than a collective or social vision of the future. Once again, the sculptor must never complete his work, the statue must be broken, for it will suffice only as long as the people to whom it speaks remain "theoretical people, like / Small bees of spring," immune to a "shade of horror" that turns "bees to scorpions blackly-barbed."

In both "A Duck for Dinner" and the "Blue Guitar" neither the orator nor the artist ultimately becomes the hero Stevens so badly desires. (And not until the opening movement of "Notes toward a Supreme Fiction" would Stevens offer a formulation of "major man" that is sustained rather than undermined by its paradoxes: the hero who cannot become the dictator because he is never more than theoretical—and yet a hero who speaks to real rather than theoretical people.) Just as the orator from "A Duck for Dinner" has his counterpart in the tenth poem of the "Blue Guitar," so does the artist-hero figure appear in the fifteenth poem. Here, at the center of the sequence, Stevens borrows the phrase "une somme de destructions" from Christian Zervos's "Conversation with Picasso" (published in the special Picasso number of *Cahiers d'art* in 1935). With the phrase, Stevens addresses the issue Zervos raised in his essay "Fait social et vision cosmique" (also part of the Picasso number), a defense of Picasso against critics who accused him of allegiance to "l'art pur." Zervos concluded rhetorically, "Can we say that [Picasso] has less social conscience because he devotes his attention to the conquest of the unconscious?" This was Stevens's version of that question:

> Is this picture of Picasso's, this "hoard
> Of destructions," a picture of ourselves,
>
> Now, an image of our society?

This was not a rhetorical question for Stevens, despite his constant desire to assert the social relevance of an extravagant art. Picasso painted *Guernica,* his elegy for the town destroyed in the Spanish Civil War, after Stevens completed "The Man with the Blue Guitar," and in 1938 the poet copied these remarks on the painting into his commonplace book, calling them "a just placing of Picasso": "Much of his work—eschewing nature and, therefore, lacking a common denominator between him and the public—remained, except as a matter of abstract designing, unintelligible." When he turned to the artist instead of the orator, the modernist instead of the Marxist, Stevens did not overestimate the power of modern art or take its "destructive element" as a sure sign of its healthy political engagement.

Throughout "A Duck for Dinner" the artist is always in danger of becoming the orator because that common denominator between the artist and the public is never certain. Similarly, in poem XXX of the "Blue Guitar," Stevens seems blithely confident that he will "evolve a man" who will transform the banal suburb of Oxidia into Olympia. But in the following poem Stevens remembers that while "The bubbling sun will bubble up, / Spring sparkle and the cock-bird shriek," the life of "medium man" will remain unaffected by the heroic artist.

> The employer and employee will hear
> And continue their affair. The shriek
> Will rack the thickets. There is no place,

> Here, for the lark fixed in the mind,
> In the museum of the sky.

While the imaginative artist was able to transform Oxidia's unsightly electrical wires ("the cross-piece on a pole / Supporting heavy cables") into the blazing fires of Olympus, these lines assert that such imaginative vision will not affect the lives of the people who erect the poles and cables. At the end of "A Duck for Dinner," even as the artist appears to be the hero who will end the battle between employer and employee—even as he is given a "diamond crown" to replace the dark Ananke's "silent crown"—the people are left asking these questions.

> How shall we face the edge of time? We walk
> In the park. We regret we have no nightingale.
> We must have the throstle on the gramophone.
> Where shall we find more than derisive words?
> When shall lush chorals spiral through our fire
> And daunt that old assassin, heart's desire?

Resisting a nostalgia for what was and a unreal sense of what might be, capitulating to neither fatalism nor necessity, these questions represent the finest eloquence of "Owl's Clover."

In "Sombre Figuration," the final poem of "Owl's Clover," Stevens essays some tentative answers. As the previous poems in the series looked to art, to Ananke, and to the hero for a way to bridge the experiences of disparate individuals and cultures, "Sombre Figuration" postulates the "subman," a sort of collective unconscious that is never articulated with much precision: "a man whom rhapsodies of change, / Of which he is the cause, have never changed / And never will, a subman under all / The rest." Even the "subman" does not provide a satisfactory answer to the questions that end "A Duck for Dinner"—ultimately, no solutions as such will do. As the poems of "Owl's Clover" follow one another, Stevens recapitulates the paradoxes inherent in his earlier ideas of ambiguity: the shadow of certainty looms, and any definitive answers too easily become ways of dismissing the issues that the questions address. Ambiguous as they were, Ananke and the hero quickly became reified, limiting the freedoms they were meant to enable. The "subman" of "Sombre Figuration" is designed to be even more ambiguous and allusive, but its consolations ultimately may not be trusted either. Apparently falling back into the nostalgia of the pioneer passages in "A Duck for Dinner," Stevens eulogizes a time when "The man and the man below were reconciled"; but this complacency is revealed to have been an illusion. Above

these men, "a sprawling portent moves." This sign of the impending apocalypse may be as illusory as the complacency that concealed it.

> It is the form
> Of a generation that does not know itself,
> Still questioning if to crush the soaring stacks,
> The churches, like dalmatics stooped in prayer,
> And the people suddenly evil, waked, accused,
> Destroyed by a vengeful movement of the arms,
> A mass overtaken by the blackest sky,
> Each one as part of the total wrath, obscure
> In slaughter.

For a generation that does not know itself ("If it is the supreme cry of
despair," said Stevens of *The Waste Land*, "it is Eliot's and not his generation's") change appears catastrophic and destruction inevitable—the sprawling portent is the image of that generation itself. But whatever their origins,
such images of the end are undeniably seductive. (And when Stevens cut the
vision of modern Europe as a decayed *Schloss* from "The Greenest Continent" when he revised "Owl's Clover," he also cut this passage from "Sombre
Figuration.") As Stevens goes on to describe this generation's end, he emphasizes that it is a "wished-for ruin"; a product of the subman, it is an "image
of his making," a generation's imagination gone wild. Spinning a fantasy of
the world's destruction, this generation relieves itself of responsibility for the
state of the world (since the source of the destruction is imagined as the
sprawling portent, an inhuman force) along with responsibility for altering
those conditions (since the portent's force is overwhelming and incontrovert-
ible). As Stevens had put it in "The Woman Who Blamed Life on a Spaniard," the "babble of generations magnifies / A mot into a dictum . . . Of inescapable force, itself a fate." And as he would put it in the final poem of the
"Blue Guitar,"

> That generation's dream, aviled
> In the mud, in Monday's dirty light,
>
> That's it, the only dream they knew,
> Time in its final block, not time
>
> To come.

That generation, the generation of the 1930s, could imagine only a catastrophic ending ("Time in its final block") rather than a time to come,
because it had an inadequate sense of its place in history. "The future must

bear within it every past," continues Stevens in "Sombre Figuration," "Not least the pasts destroyed." This vision of a future continuous with the past is not the illusion of "tomorrow's past" (as the tenth poem of the "Blue Guitar" has it), or "the swarm of dreams / Of inaccessible Utopia" (which Stevens exposes in the twenty-sixth poem of that sequence). Instead of a world washed in imagination, the final movement of "Sombre Figuration" offers a return to what Stevens had called "social nature" in "The Comedian as the Letter C"; instead of an end, it offers continuity; instead of the force of a statue, Ananke, a hero, or the subman, it offers Jocundus, the "medium man," the "hum-drum," Crispin grown a little older in suburban shade. "Even imagination has an end," says Stevens, but the everyday life of the "medium man among other medium men" does not. His goal is not to "flourish the great cloak we wear / At night"—just as Crispin shunned "calamitous crape." That is the garb for the "black-blooded scholar" who keeps his world alone; such gestures of finality and isolation—the wished-for ruin—can have no place in the social world of Jocundus.

> A passion to fling the cloak,
> Adorned for a multitude, in a gesture spent
> In the gesture's whim, a passion merely to be
> For the gaudium of being, Jocundus instead
> Of the black-blooded scholar, the man of the cloud, to be
> The medium man among other medium men,
> The cloak to be clipped, the night to be re-designed,
> Its land-breath to be stifled, its color changed,
> Night and the imagination being one.

Echoing the final line of "The Comedian as the Letter C" ("So may the relation of each man be clipped") and forecasting the "shearsman" of the "Blue Guitar," these final lines of "Owl's Clover" reiterate Stevens's long-established interest in the value of limitation and diffidence, the value of what he often called the ordinary, or the normal. Stevens's vision of Crispin at the conclusion of "The Comedian" is as challengingly mundane as his choice of Jocundus over the black-blooded scholar, but only after Stevens had completed his antiapocalyptic poems of the 1930s could he explain precisely what was wrong with Hi Simons's characterization of Crispin's final condition as "fatalism"; this commentary could apply equally as well to the conclusion of "Owl's Clover": "I have been wondering too whether I was quite clear about the difference between fatalism and indifferentism. The last word is not a well-chosen word; the question is whether these two states are distinct enough to be capable of separation. The fatalist relates his experience to a destiny, whether the destiny be the idea of God, the idea of law, or something else. The indifferentist does not relate his experience to anything; he accepts *les valeurs de père de famille*." I think the word *indifferentism* (like the word *normal*) seemed not exactly right to Stevens because it could imply a quietism or a lack of conviction that was alien to him. By "indifferentism," Stevens meant a serious acceptance of one's responsibilities in the world that exists— the humdrum but invaluable life of everyday. As opposed to fatalism, indifferentism depends for its value on an equally stalwart resistance to the attractions of utopia or despair.

In the "Blue Guitar" as in "Owl's Clover," consequently, Stevens dismisses the artist who "held the world upon his nose," certain that all's right with the world to come ("Things as they will be by and by . . . / A fat thumb beats out ai-yi-yi") as well as the black-blooded philosopher who is certain all is wrong with the world he sees ("It is the sea that the north wind makes. / The sea is in the falling snow. / This gloom is the darkness of the sea"). Responding to Krutch, Philip Rahv sang the virtues of "an atmosphere of disillusion" over a "shallow optimism," but Stevens finds the gloom of disillusion equally shallow: it fixes a sea that constantly changes, and that sea ("things as they are") is "a form of ridicule," fighting against utopian or apocalyptic fantasies. Between the bare declarative sentences of poem XXVII ("This gloom is the darkness of the sea") and the nursery rhymes of poem XXV ("ai-yi-yi") stands the poem Stevens published separately as "Inaccessible Utopia": both the poem of excessive despair and the poem of excessive optimism are composed with a "mountainous music"—the language of that mountain-minded Hoon—that imposes human desires on an ambiguous and "shifting scene," fixing things as they are with a certain sense of what will be.

> The swarm of thoughts, the swarm of dreams
> Of inaccessible Utopia.
>
> A mountainous music always seemed
> To be falling and to be passing away.

Ending "Owl's Clover" was necessarily a problem for Stevens, since the sequence fights against endings. Marianne Moore noted that the sequence "embodies the hope that in being frustrated becomes fortitude," and the final line of the final poem ("Night and the imagination being one") seems undeservedly affirmative without another poem to turn against it—the danger of indifferentism is that it could become quietism or fatalism without the fortification of continued frustration. The conclusion of "Owl's Clover" must consequently be seen in dialogue with "The Man with the Blue Guitar." Composing the latter sequence, Stevens avoided all teleologies, placing its poems in the order in which they happened to be written and suggesting that they might easily be rearranged. Between his composition of the two poetic sequences, Stevens wrote "A Postcard from the Volcano," included in the 1936 edition of *Ideas of Order*. One of the finest poems in that volume, "A Postcard" forms a kind of hinge between the two long poems. Antiapocalyptic as these poems may be, Stevens nevertheless realized from his own experience of writing the poems that it is sometimes impossible not to play the fatalist, to succumb to a generation's dream, relating things as they are to a consoling but ineffectual image of religious or political destiny. "A Postcard from the Volcano" offers its readers a few simple words delivered after the apocalypse; but the language survives from a past that is only apparently destroyed, and the historical continuities of the language that forms the poem itself undermine the poem's evocative sense of an ending. Stevens begins by recognizing a new generation's inevitable sense of its distance from its heritage. Yet he speaks with the voice of the dead.

> Children picking up our bones
> Will never know that these were once
> As quick as foxes on the hill;
>
> And that in autumn, when the grapes
> Made sharp air sharper by their smell
> These had a being, breathing frost.

"You ought to understand the pasts destroyed," said Stevens apropos of the conclusion of "Sombre Figuration," but in "A Postcard" he points out that the effect of a past destroyed will linger whether it is understood or not; the children "least will guess that with our bones / We left much more."

> We knew for long the mansion's look
> And what we said of it became
>
> A part of what it is . . . Children,
> Still weaving budded aureoles,
> Will speak our speech and never know.

Marx described this paradox in the famous opening paragraphs of the "Eighteenth Brumaire": "Men make their own history, but they do not make it just as they please; they do not make it under circumstances chosen by themselves, but under circumstances directly found, given and transmitted from the past. The tradition of all the dead generations weighs like a nightmare on the brain of the living." In Stevens's "Postcard" the sky cries out a "literate despair" to the new generation, literate because the children themselves have given it words and the words themselves were spoken by the dead. Like the apocalypse of "Sombre Figuration," this is a "wished-for ruin"; like the image of modern society as a decayed casino in "Academic Discourse at Havana," the children's vision of the past as a shuttered mansion-house is an "infinite incantation of our selves." Stevens does not want to condemn the children for being seduced by such an incantation—he understood how difficult it is to separate "fatalism" from "indifferentism" in a time of social unrest; rather, he hopes the new generation will see that its swan song is also a prelude to a great new poem. "A dirty house in a gutted world" is also a "tatter of shadows peaked to white, / Smeared with the gold of the opulent sun."

In "The Fate of Pleasure," an essay written in response to his *Partisan Review* colleagues' tendency to equate literary pessimism with political engagement, Lionel Trilling articulated a position that Stevens's life and work embody: "it is by no means uncommon for an educated person to base his judgment of politics on a simple affirmation of the principle of pleasure, and to base his judgment of art, and also his judgment of personal existence, on a complex antagonism to that principle." Ironically, such persons end up divorcing art from politics, searching for pleasure in one and vindicating despair in the other. Stevens lived no such double life. As he put it in "Esthétique du Mal," the "greatest poverty" is not only "not to live / In a physical world" but also "to feel that one's desire / Is too difficult to tell from despair."

I have suggested, however, that Stevens did not lead an undivided life: he recognized the social functions that the poet, the politician, or the parent could perform, and he approached each role accordingly. "Separation, simplicity, silent norms of pertinence," counters Edward Said: "this is one depoliticizing strain of considerable force, since it is capitalized on by professions, institutions, discourses and a massively reinforced constituency of specialized fields." Without denying that separate spheres of value are an institutionalized convenience or that aesthetic statements inevitably partake of political values, I would still want to assert that a poem has a different relationship to political action than an essay entitled "Insurance and Social Change." Although I want to argue that the clipped poetry of "The Man with the Blue Guitar" participates in overtly political discourses, I also want to remember that Stevens confronted basic political issues daily in his work at the Hartford. His essay "Insurance and Social Change" followed on the heels of the "Blue Guitar," and like the poetic sequence, the essay is about a generation's dream—utopia. Unlike the poems (and this is the crucial difference), the essay outlines the few basic actions that could be taken in order to realize part of that dream: "If each of us could put his hand on money whenever money was necessary: to repair any damage, to meet any emergency, we should all be willing to stop so far as money goes. To be certain of a regular income, as in the case of social security, is not the same thing as to be able to repair any damage, or to meet any emergency. Obviously, in a world in which insurance had become perfect, the case of social security would be a minor case." To illustrate the difference between a possible "insurance for all" and a utopian "insurance for everything," Stevens asks us to "imagine a world in which insurance had been made perfect."

In such a world we should be certain of an income. Out of the income we should be able, by the payment of a trivial premium, to protect ourselves, our families and our property against everything. The procedure would necessarily be simple: Probably the dropping of a penny each morning in a box at the corner nearest one's place of residence on the way to one's place of employment. Each of us would have a personal or peculiar penny. What is the difference between a personal penny and a social security number? The circle just stated: income, insurance, the thing that happens and income again, would widen and soon become income, insurance, the thing that fails to happen and income again. In other words, not only would all our losses be made good, but all our wishes would come true.

Behind these wishes stands the Social Security Act of 1935. Roosevelt asked Congress for such legislation in January; in June the bill was approved, and on August 15 the president signed it into law. This swift piece of work was part of the second "Hundred Days" of the New Deal, which also saw the completion of the National Labor Relations Act, the Wealth Tax Act, the Public Utilities Holding Company Act, and the Banking Act—legislation that increased the power of labor unions, attempted the most radical redistribution of income in the nation's history, broke apart the great utility empires, and redesigned the Federal Reserve Board as a regulator of the private banking system. Like these other pieces of New Deal legislation, the Social Security Act was perceived by conservatives as the government's intrusion into the private sector; it violated time-honored American values of self-reliance. As Stevens immediately recognized, the Social Security system was modeled on the principles of private insurance. (By financing the system through premiums taken directly from private income, Roosevelt rightly saw that no one would ever be able to justify dismantling Social Security.) And to many members of the insurance community, the Social Security Act appeared to be the government's first step toward nationalizing the insurance business: they feared for the future of their livelihood. To Stevens, however, the act did not appear especially radical: compared with his utopian vision of a world where wishes come true, the scope and effect of Social Security was decidedly limited. This particular aspect of the welfare state was not to be feared but welcomed as a new and probably inevitable aspect of what Stevens called the "insurance era."

The Harvard philosopher Josiah Royce also thought that the twentieth century could be called the "insurance era" and outlined a similar utopian vision in his last book, *War and Insurance* (1914). For Royce, the relationship of the principal, agent, and client was the perfect embodiment of what Charles Sanders Peirce had called the "Community of Interpretation"; it represented "the union of very highly theoretical enterprises with very concrete social applications." In the face of the world war, Royce called for the creation of an international "Community of Insurance" that would prevent all future conflagrations through a fund insuring any nation against the economic debacles that make wars "necessary": "the genuine community of mankind would indeed be begun, not as a merely fantastic hope, but as an institution whereby part of the world's daily business was done."

Although he conceded their attraction, Stevens did not indulge in such dreams precisely because they were based on fantastic hopes. The bulk of "Insurance and Social Change" is taken up with Stevens's summaries of other nations' attempts to nationalize insurance programs: Italy's National Insurance Institute, Germany's Supervision Board of private insurance companies, England's parliamentary committee on obligatory insurance, and, finally, the Soviet Union's Gosstrakh, granted the sole right to operate an insurance business in Soviet territories. This kind of wholesale nationalization of the insurance business did not please Stevens, but he understood its inevitability: "These very inadequate glimpses of the situation in those European countries where social pressure has been most acute and social and political change most marked indicate that, as the social mass seeks to maintain itself, it relies more and more on insurance and treats it as of such significance that the preservation of the insurers becomes a governmental function or a highly important object of governmental solicitude." For Stevens, the problem with such solicitude is that it might mislead its benefactors into thinking that in an insurance era all wishes could come true. Like Trilling, Stevens felt that pleasure was the goal of both his business and his art; but unlike Royce (or the utopian heroes and orators of his own poetry) he could not believe that pleasure was easily legislated. Having confected his vision of a perfectly insured world in order to underscore the benefits of nationalization, he cautions: "We shall never live in a world . . . in which insurance has been made perfect, and where we can buy peace and prosperity as readily and as cheaply as we can buy the morning newspaper."

Given his stringent awareness of these practical limitations of utopian desire, Stevens could assure his colleagues (to whom the legislation of the second Hundred Days appeared catastrophic) that while a governmental "monopoly" on insurance was possible under both fascist and communist systems, it was unlikely in the United States, despite the incarnation of Social Security and unemployment insurance. The New Deal grafted the welfare state onto an unchanged capitalist economy, and, as Stevens recognized, the ultimate question remained one "of making a reasonable profit." Having reflected on the inevitability of nationalization, Stevens could still conclude "Insurance and Social Change" with the quintessential wisdom of American liberalism: "the greater these activities [of the insurance business] are: that is to say, the more they are adapted to the changing needs of changing times (provided they are conducted at a profit) the more certain they are to endure on the existing basis. But this exacts of each of us all that each of us, in his own job, has to give."

This faith in the necessity and the power of individual freedoms always kept Stevens wary of certain visions of socialist collectivity. Like D. S. Savage (whose "Socialism in Extremis" he admired), Stevens felt that the "nominally 'socialist' state" had to "accommodate the values which are based upon a deeply rooted respect for the individual personality." But Stevens's belief in the "individual personality" was not dogmatic; as poems like "The Comedian" and "Owl's Clover" reveal, he was just as skeptical of the powers of the individual personality as he was of the powers of collectivity. Stevens approved of Thomas Mann's *André Gide and the Crisis of Modern Thought* because (as one reviewer put it) Mann explained how in Gide's conception of socialism there need not be a "contradiction between belief in the individual and belief in the communité." Stevens agreed that the "main problem" of his time was "the reconciliation of the inalienable rights of the individual to personal development and the necessity for the diminution of the misery of the masses."

Although he was never willing to dismantle things as they are, Stevens was willing to tinker with them—but always with one skeptical eye cast on a vision of a perfect world. He judged himself fairly when he said that he could not call himself a "revolutionist," even though he did "regret that we have not experimented a little more extensively in public ownership of public utilities." By nature, Stevens did not see change as catastrophe. He approached the problems of social change less as a poetic genius than as an insurance expert grounded in the possible and the permissible; he rejected a "generation's dream" in "The Man with the Blue Guitar," but in "Insurance and Social Change" he worked closely with the same generation's reality. By segregating the practice of his poetry from the practice of his business—whatever their theoretical affinities—Stevens was not indulging in a mystification of separate spheres of value but clearing the space for action. For Stevens, political values became political actions not in dreams of the past's decay or the future's promise but in the small space where individuals make their indispensable mark, the space where there is room, as he put it at the conclusion of "Insurance and Social Change," for what "each of us, in his own job, has to give." That was one lesson John Jay Chapman passed to Stevens from Emerson in the last year of the nineteenth century.

The lesson is of course questionable. Even when Daniel Bell proclaimed the "end of ideology" after the Second World War, he cautiously recognized the value of "some need for utopia, in the sense that men need . . . some vision of their potential, some manner of fusing passion with intelligence." There are times, reading Stevens, when one cannot help but desire in his lifestyle or his values somewhat more of the extravagance that he occasionally allows himself in his verse; the endlessness of his common sense sometimes begins to wear, and one could wish that he succumbed more often to the urgency that talk of utopia, catastrophe, or apocalypse may breed. Still, whenever Stevens does indulge those urges (as in "The Greenest Continent" or "A Duck for Dinner"), we are reminded of the value of his usually measured position. And at the end of the 1930s, Stevens's position was even enviable. When the Second World War began in 1939, even the relatively level-minded Rahv found his dreams shattered, and poets from Auden on the left to Eliot on the right entered a new decade needing to distance themselves from utopian or apocalyptic fantasies. Their retreat from political engagement altogether marked a crucial turn in their careers. Stevens's career is markedly different in its strong continuity from the later 1930s through the end of the war. Not having succumbed to the lure of an unobtainable utopia, he had no need to lament its demise; not having overestimated the powers of poetry, he had no need to exaggerate its limitations. Instead, Stevens was prepared to face a world at war and see it for the catastrophe it was—not as an image of his own shattered dreams. As much as the war devastated him, thinking about it was an act for which he was well prepared.

V

Rethinking War

13

Violence Within, Violence Without

The year 1939 marked the sesquicentennial of the French Revolution, and to writers of a certain generation it seemed as if very little time had passed. Just as post-Romantic poets have repeated Wordsworth's mode of imaginative internalization, so have they appropriated his evaluation of the French Revolution as a way to contain or justify their own retreats from historical events that similarly failed to bolster their political ideals. As the ideals of the early 1930s dissolved in the wake of the Munich accords, the Nazi-Soviet Pact, and finally the commencement of the Second World War, Auden looked back to Wordsworth in "New Year Letter" (1940).

> And weaving a platonic dream
> Round a provisional régime
> That sloganized the Rights of Man,
> A liberal fellow-traveller ran
> With Sans-culotte and Jacobin,
> Nor guessed what circles he was in,
> But ended as the Devil knew
> An earnest Englishman would do,
> Left by Napoleon in the lurch,
> Supporting the Established Church.

With Wordsworth began the Romantic poet's dilemma, the apparently unbridgeable gap between poetry and politics, and for Auden the dilemma had not changed, though the historical events had. Throughout the 1930s he had expected "the Millennium / That theory promised us would come: / It didn't."

A similar rhetoric of recantation and disappointment marks the work of a wide range of writers who made the uneasy transition from the Depression to a war that had seemed vaguely inevitable ever since Woodrow Wilson had forsaken the ideal of a nonremunerative peace at Versailles. After Hitler invaded Poland, T. S. Eliot discontinued the *Criterion*, speaking of a "depression of spirits so different from any other of fifty years as to be a new emotion." Eliot's politics were scarcely compatible with Auden's, but throughout the 1930s both writers had sustained an unworldly faith in the political efficacy of poetry, and the new war exposed the empty center of their ideals. The editors of the *Partisan Review* looked back to the early 1930s as "a moment perhaps never to be recovered in our lifetime, when many intellectuals, enraptured by the mythology of triumphant socialism in Russia, experienced an emotion of historic depth such as Wordsworth's generation must have felt in the first years of the French Revolution." Here Rahv and Phillips quoted from the sixth book of *The Prelude*—"But Europe at that time was thrilled with joy, / France standing on the top of golden hours, / And human nature seeming born again"—and concluded: "Put Russia in place of Wordsworth's France, add America to his Europe, and you can conceive of the buoyant mood that impelled us to seek enlightenment and our share of social responsibility in the sphere of Soviet Communism." Having drawn this parallel between Wordsworth's early euphoria and their own, Rahv and Phillips did not suggest that their outlook during the 1940s would bear any resemblance to Wordsworth's later years. (Auden was more honest in this respect.) When their political ideals disintegrated, they justified their retreat by equating the failure of those particular ideals with the inevitable failure of all ideals.

The *Partisan Review* editors became so divided over the fate of their earlier commitments that they eventually had to confess that the magazine could "have no editorial line on the war." After the Nazi invasion of the Soviet Union in 1941, the socialist cause regained some of the prestige it had lost after the Nazi-Soviet Pact, and Dwight Macdonald eventually left the *Partisan Review*, unwilling to second his colleagues' support of the Allied forces. Throughout the war, Rahv and Phillips led the magazine on its Wordsworthian trajectory, welcoming a wider separation of culture and politics while gazing back to the previous decade as if it really were the glorious moment of 1789. "Some day," said a myopic Clement Greenberg, "it will have to be told how 'anti-Stalinism,' which started out more or less as 'Trotskyism,' turned into art for art's sake, and thereby cleared the way, heroically, for what was to come."

What distinguishes Stevens's career from most of his contemporaries' is that the events of September 1939 did not disrupt his effort to understand the relationship of poetry and politics, forcing him to condemn a decade's achievement. Harold Bloom has remarked that after Stevens completed "The Man with the Blue Guitar" rarely a month passed without a major poem of his being published. That productivity is itself a product of Stevens's interest in the events of the Second World War—which he followed as he had followed the events of the First World War twenty years before. Stevens arranged the poems of *Parts of a World* (1942) largely by the chronology of their initial publication; the volume traces Stevens's turn from the concerns of the Depression to the concerns of war: there is no recantation of untenable ideals, no retreat from political reality as a way of excusing ideals altogether. During that winter of 1940 he explained that he was "at one of those stages at which it is hard to get away from one's thoughts. . . . The desire is to get them down as they come."

This period of intense activity culminated in the great wartime achievements, "Notes toward a Supreme Fiction" and "Esthétique du Mal." Marjorie Perloff has named the former "a kind of antimeditation, fearful and evasive, whose elaborate and daunting rhetoric is designed to convince both poet and reader that, despite the daily headlines and radio bulletins, the real action takes place in the country of metaphor. For, as Stevens puts it in one of his 'Adagia,' 'Reality is a cliché from which we escape by metaphor.'" Stevens sometimes felt that way (especially during the cold war years), but more often he resisted this position—especially during the Second World War. Quoting Stevens, Perloff neglects the following adage (the quintessentially Stevensian caveat)—"Some objects are less susceptible to metaphor than others. The whole world is less susceptible to metaphor than a tea-cup is." This complete text seems to me especially significant. Throughout the First World War, Stevens was excruciatingly aware of his distance from the violence of a soldier's life, and during the Second his distaste for the ease with which some writers aestheticized violence increased. He addressed the issue explicitly in "The Noble Rider and the Sound of Words" (1941): "We are confronting, therefore, a set of events, not only beyond our power to tranquillize them in the mind, beyond our power to reduce them and metamorphose them, but events that stir the emotions to violence, that engage us in what is direct and immediate and real." It would be the burden of "Extracts from the Academy of Fine Ideas" and "Esthetique du Mal" to dramatize the confrontation of poetry and a real world that simultaneously necessitates and resists the metaphors. And in another wartime sequence, "The Pure Good of Theory," Stevens would explain even more directly the dangers of not understanding our

citizenship in the country of metaphor: "to speak of the whole world as metaphor / Is still to stick to the contents of the mind. . . . It is to stick to the
nicer knowledge of / Belief, that what it believes in is not true."

During the war years, Stevens began to use the words *real* and *fact* with
increasing urgency. After the final poem in *Parts of a World*, "Examination
of the Hero in a Time of War," Stevens printed a brief prose statement: "In
the presence of the violent reality of war, consciousness takes the place of the
imagination. And consciousness of an immense war is a consciousness of
fact. . . . The poetry of a work of the imagination constantly illustrates the
fundamental and endless struggle with fact. It goes on everywhere, even in
the periods that we call peace. But in war, the desire to move in the direction
of fact as we want it to be and to move quickly is overwhelming." At the same
time that Stevens made these remarks, Kenneth Burke was explaining in his
essay "War and Cultural Life" why such a movement toward the exigencies
of "fact" should take place during war: a shift from a peacetime to a wartime
economy, from a "commercial-liberal-monetary nexus of motives to a collec-
tive-sacrificial-military nexus of motives," resulted in a "change from an idealistic to a realistic grammar." In part, this change was similar to the one he
described in his account of the First World War in *Counter-Statement*: a
grammar of irony and detachment breaks down in the face of the brutal reality of mass death and destruction, just as in Stevens's "Letters d'un Soldat"
all metaphors for death collapse in the face of the soldier's decaying corpse.
The change from an idealistic to a realistic grammar was also the function of
a shift to wartime modes of production that drastically reduced the inflated
and illusory value of the culture's commodities, whether economic or aesthetic: "War does compel a people to conceive the reality of forces in much
more realistic terms than need prevail under conditions of peace, when the
monetary symbols of wealth can actually assume a greater appearance of reality than the material things that are their backing." Under conditions of war,
in contrast, the disparities between the real and the ideal are not only high-
lighted but politically charged: "The 'idealism' of financial speculation, the
'futurism' of investment, while they still figure in wartime, diverge from the
brute reality of 'logistics,' involving the immediate concern with the relation
between material obstacles and material resources."

Illustrating this point, Burke recalls a writer who some years before had
equated the losses suffered in a massive hurricane with the losses suffered in
a slump in Wall Street securities: "Yet the hurricane had destroyed real physical property, houses, roads, bridges, barns, timber, etc., whereas the market
losses had been purely symbolic, with all the underlying properties in quite
as good material condition the day after the market loss as the day before."
The comparison or metaphor loses much of its force in wartime because peo-

ple are generally more aware of the realities of destruction. Since poems are made of nothing but metaphors, a wartime poetry that attempts to account for the realities of destruction always runs the risk of appearing supercilious. As Burke put it in a 1940 essay on surrealist poetry, "there is, in the violation of syntax, this kind of 'pure' violence"; and though such textual violence "may be the reflex" of the violence of war, "there is a 'radical' distinction between Surrealist and practical violence."

Always careful to underscore his lack of immediate experience of war, Stevens made the same distinction between physical and spiritual or textual violence in "The Noble Rider," written a few months before the attack on Pearl Harbor: "in speaking of the pressure of reality, I am thinking of life in a state of violence, not physically violent, as yet, for us in America, but physically violent for millions of our friends and for still more millions of our enemies and spiritually violent, it may be said, for everyone alive." Although Stevens could describe poetry as "a violence from within that protects us from a violence without," he did not equate these two kinds of violence; he did not believe it was possible to escape reality by metaphor. Sounding much like Burke, Stevens concluded that "when one is trying to think of a whole generation and of a world at war, . . . the plainest statement of what is happening can easily appear to be an affectation." Late in the war, when knowledge of the Holocaust reached the Allies, many writers besides Burke and Stevens would express similar feelings of artistic helplessness; words seemed more necessary and more inadequate than ever before. Stevens copied into his commonplace book this sentence from Janet Flanner's account of the French response to Auschwitz: "These young Maquis intellectuals, disoriented and restless, spurn left-over literature as unreal."

It is a tribute to Stevens's honesty that when confronted by these events he looked back to his remarks on the Depression, commenting: "My own remarks about resisting or evading the pressure of reality mean escapism, if analyzed." There can be no thought of escape, he had said in "The Irrational Element," and in "The Noble Rider" he admits that while the war is not escapable, he would, like most human beings, want to escape it. (Like Burke's remark that he would really rather not be a worker, whatever his political sympathies, this is the kind of admission that is easy to attack out of context.) Whatever his desires, such a retreat is never possible: even the desire to escape, Stevens points out, is itself conditioned by the reality the poet would transcend: "the pressure of reality is . . . the determining factor in the artistic development of an era and, as well, the determining factor in the artistic character of an individual." In making that statement, Stevens was bolstered by an essay of Stephen Spender's that he read in preparing to write "The Noble Rider." Stevens marked this sentence in Spender's "The Creative Imagination

in the World Today" (1940): "Every significant movement in English poetry
could be interpreted as a reaction to the central facts of the political
situation."

That dictum made Stevens look back to Wordsworth for a precedent other
than the one Rahv and Phillips found. In "The Noble Rider" Stevens resists
even his own desire to believe that there ever existed a time when people
could remain unruffled by world-historical events. Surveying the "pressure of
news" in the present day, he concludes that it is not easy to see such pressure
in the past—but not because the pressure was not there: "It is a question of
pressure, and pressure is incalculable and eludes the historian. . . . It seems
possible to say that [Coleridge, Wordsworth, Austin, and Scott] knew of the
events of their day much as we know of the bombings in the interior of China
and not at all as we know of the bombings of London, or, rather, as we should
know of the bombings of Toronto or Montreal." Stevens agrees that the political pressure felt by the Romantic poets was different in degree from the pressure he feels today, but he resists the notion that it was different in kind. That
twist to the argument is crucial for Stevens, since it allows him to argue that
literature that does not bear the scars of its age is, as Spender suggested, nevertheless a reaction to the political situation of the age. It also allows him, at
the end of "The Noble Rider," to quote Wordsworth's apparently apolitical
sonnet, "Composed Upon Westminster Bridge," aware that its vision of London "All bright and glittering in the smokeless air" was not an escape from
political turmoil but was both a product of and an address to the world as
Wordsworth found it in 1802.

As in both "Owl's Clover" and "The Man with the Blue Guitar," Stevens
was wary in "The Noble Rider" of any historical teleology that posited a catastrophic break between past and present. Although he acknowledged that
"one of the peculiarities of the imagination [is] that it is always at the end of
an era," Stevens wanted to resist apocalyptic fantasies—especially in a time
of war. He was suspicious of the idea that "the Napoleonic era was the end
of one era in the history of the imagination," and he would not allow himself
that assertion about the Second World War either. At a time when even Rahv
and Phillips were retreating into aestheticism, Stevens stood on the ground
he had formulated slowly and carefully throughout the 1930s. Avoiding apocalyptic rhetoric had been difficult then, and the war made the rhetoric more
enticing as it made the task of resisting it more necessary: if people were to
conceive of the war as an event that they could manage and ultimately prevent, then it needed to be understood as an event in the ongoing arc of history
and not as the bitter end. "I very much like the idea of something ahead,"
wrote Stevens in 1938, and the poems collected in *Parts of a World*, written
between 1937 and 1942, thematize the value of cultural continuity, which

they embody as a chronological sequence. Contrary to Perloff's sense of this phase of Stevens's career, it is even possible to read the events of the period through the poems of *Parts*. The volume itself supports the dictum Stevens admired in Spender—"Every significant movement in English poetry could be interpreted as a reaction to the central facts of the political situation." Together with "The Noble Rider" and "Notes toward a Supreme Fiction," the poems of *Parts of a World*—unfairly undervalued though that volume generally has been—mark for me the richest point in Stevens's career.

I have already had the occasion to examine several prewar poems from *Parts of a World*, particularly those from the rich "Canonica" sequence (1938), and I will now look at one more poem from that sequence: "The Man on the Dump." Holly Stevens remembers the dump that served as the locus of her father's imagination: "Just beyond the bridge which spanned the Hog [River] on Albany Avenue was a vast stretch of barren land that people used as a dump. It was full of tin cans, old bottles, rags, crates, and miscellaneous junk. It was a mess and an eyesore, but it glittered here and there on days when the sun shone. On this lot a man, seemingly coming from nowhere, built his home. . . . I remember Dad saying that the occupant was a White Russian. We spent hours imagining things about him, and making up stories." One of those stories became "The Man on the Dump," in which Stevens records the man's nationality through the objects he gathers around him: "The cat in the paper-bag, the corset, the box / From Esthonia: the tiger chest, for tea"—all these compose "the janitor's poems / Of every day." As a refugee from a nation whose sovereignty was threatened (Estonia would ultimately fall under Soviet domination after the Nazi-Soviet Pact), the man on the dump embodies a cultural ethos that is preserved no matter how the boundaries of nations are drawn. An image of historical continuity himself, he gathers a culture's refuse around him.

Stevens dubs the Estonian man Cornelius Nepos, a name that might slip past us like Fernandez, Babson, or MacCullough if we do not remember that Nepos was a Roman historian of the first century B.C. What remains of Nepos's work is several lives from *De Viris Illustribus*, but he is best known for the work that has not survived, a massive history of the world. Catullus praised this work as he dedicated his own poems to Nepos; the historian dared "to set forth the whole history of the world in three volumes," said Catullus, hoping that his own poems might survive a century or two. It is Catullus, of course, and not Cornelius Nepos who has survived, but Stevens chose the appropriate name for his man on the dump. Stevens's Nepos is one of the children from "A Postcard from the Volcano" grown up, engaged in the everyday task of building a future from what remains of the past. The task is endless, and much of the work may be lost, but the process of recovery itself is essential: although Nepos's major work is lost to us today, he was during his lifetime an essential transmitter of Greek culture and history into Rome. It is only on that vast and unsorted cultural garbage dump (not an image of a wasteland for Stevens but for the world as it is) that those things we consider beautiful or permanent—the poems of Catullus—have any value. "One grows to hate these things," says Stevens, speaking for his modern-day Estonian Nepos, "except on the dump."

Although not a wasteland, the dump could use a little landscaping. Stevens's dump is an image of a world that in its essentials does not change enough, even with the turning of the seasons. Stevens's catalogues diffuse whatever beauty these individual components of the dump might possess.

> Now, in the time of spring (azaleas, trilliums,
> Myrtle, viburnums, daffodils, blue phlox),
> Between that disgust and this, between the things
> That are on the dump (azaleas and so on)
> And those that will be (azaleas and so on),
> One feels the purifying change. One rejects
> The trash.

That action, rejecting the trash, is the beginning of meaningful change, the building of a future: not everything on the dump is trash. When the man on the dump begins selecting and preserving his world, then the dump itself begins to seem more interesting than ever before: "That's the time / One looks at the elephant-colorings of tires." The important change here is in the quality of the act of looking; the tires themselves have not changed.

By the end of the poem, Stevens moves away from the specific condition of the man on the dump, implying that all human beings or at least all poets share the condition of his poem's protagonist. Here "The Man on the Dump" emerges as a grown up version of "Sunday Morning"—funnier and less hysterical—a description of how we are responsible for our own values. Instead of dancing naked in the summer morn,

> One sits and beats an old tin can, lard pail.
> One beats and beats for that which one believes.
> That's what one wants to get near. Could it after all
> Be merely oneself, as superior as the ear
> To a crow's voice? Did the nightingale torture the ear,
> Pack the heart and scratch the mind? And does the ear
> Solace itself in peevish birds? Is it peace,
> Is it a philosopher's honeymoon, one finds

> On the dump? Is it to sit among mattresses of the dead,
> Bottles, pots, shoes and grass and murmur *aptest eve*:
> Is it to hear the blatter of grackles and say
> *Invisible priest*; is it to eject, to pull
> The day to pieces and cry *stanza my stone?*
> Where was it one first heard of the truth? The the.

When Harold Bloom reads these lines, he cannot help but see them as a diminution of the poet's high-flown mission, just as he reads "Stars at Talapoosa" as a confession of a failure of poetic nerve. To me, "The Man on the Dump" is the finest and most serious characterization of the poet's work that Stevens ever gave us. The series of questions that conclude the poem do not challenge a high Romantic argument but prevent us from overestimating the power of the argument in the first place. Does birdsong solace the ear?—sometimes, but, like the sight of azaleas, only when we make the effort to appreciate what often passes by unnoticed (when we reject the trash). Does one find peace on the dump?—sometimes, but to ask the question in these terms ("philosopher's honeymoon") is to expect more than a dump may offer. Should one ignore the trash, survey the dump and murmur "*aptest eve*," hear the birdsong and find not only peace but the voice of an "*Invisible priest?*" Or should one recognize that these epithets are ridiculously hyperbolic, unsupported by an ugly world that exists only in pieces? None of these propositions are viable on the dump, since both the easy optimism and the equally easy pessimism forsake the work of manufacturing a world that has the value we grant it—by beating an old tin can or by preserving a box from Estonia, a container from the past to hold the valuable objects of the present. Only the poem's final question receives an answer—"The the"—the definite article itself: that is, we heard of the truth only when we began to specify the singularity of truth, preventing us from comprehending the value of our history, however broken it might be. "On the Road Home," the poem that follows "The Man on the Dump" in both "Canonica" and *Parts of a World*, reinforces this sense of "The the."

> It was when I said,
> "There is no such thing as the truth,"
> That the grapes seemed fatter.

In emphasizing the value of cultural continuity, "The Man on the Dump" encapsulates much of the wisdom of "Owl's Clover" and the "Blue Guitar," and it also provides the best indication of the state of mind with which Stevens approached the outbreak of war, the human act that threatens all continuities. In the early autumn of 1939, the Stevens family took a trip to Reading, Pennsylvania. "We are going back to the natal soil," said Stevens, "to correct our spirits." Stevens was not yet deeply involved in his genealogical studies, but the impulse that fueled that research was already with him. The family also visited Virginia on this trip, and while they were there, Hitler finally invaded Poland. Stevens recorded his reaction in a letter to Leonard Van Geyzel, who lived in Ceylon.

When the war broke out I was in Virginia and in a part of it where the influence of the English on both houses and landscape still persists. The influence on the houses, which are as a rule modest affairs, is shown in this fact, that so few of them are really matter-of-fact houses. The people who live in them have some sense of style about living. The influence on the landscape is shown in a resemblance to an 18th Century park. Where I was there was very little of the ordinary fields of other parts of the country, which at this time of year, when all the crops have been gathered except corn, have a definiteness which makes the whole country look like a huge prosperous farm.

As the news of the development of the war comes in, I feel a horror of it: a horror of the fact that such a thing could occur. The country is more or less divided between those who think that we should hold aloof and those who think that, at the very least, we ought to help the British and the French. Our sympathies are strongly with the British and the French, but this time there is an immensely strong feeling about staying out. I hope that this war will not involve you in your far-off home, but even in Ceylon you are bound to feel some of the effects of this unbelievable catastrophe.

This rich letter offers, in a highly compacted form, a personal reaction to the outbreak of the Second World War that may serve as a synecdoche for the nation's divided response. It is clear that Stevens was moved by the "horror" of this "unbelievable catastrophe"; this is not a rhetoric he employed with any frequency or carelessness. While he is aware of his own distance from the horror, Stevens is also ominously suspicious of the ways in which this "total" war will affect everyone. His assessment of the country's response is fair: extreme reaction to the war was split between a collective security faction that encouraged the United States to support the British and a diehard isolationist faction that opposed intervention in any form. The large middle ground generally leaned toward the isolationist position. When the nation was preoccupied with domestic economic concerns in the 1930s, isolationism had dominated foreign policy, and the official stand in the face of both Mussolini and Franco had been one of neutrality (formalized by the Neutrality Acts of 1935 and 1937). American liberals supported neutrality, remembering their disillusion with Wilson's doomed efforts to legislate world peace; the American right also advocated an isolationist position, but an isolationism sometimes distended into a grotesque disregard for human suffering. As the war escalated in 1940, the first peacetime conscription law was enacted. In exchange for military bases throughout the Western Hemisphere, the United States gave Britain fifty destroyers. Responding to these commitments, one faction of the right announced the formation of the America First Committee. Arguing that the United States itself was in no danger of Nazi attack, they saw Roosevelt's movement away from neutrality as a challenge to the traditional shape of American democracy; consequently, the group attracted not only Charles Lindbergh (who became its most prominent spokesman) but a range of anti-Semites, racists, and Nazi sympathizers. This put liberal isolationists in a tight spot. Responding to Dwight Macdonald's refusal to support the Allied cause, Rahv explained that "it is not Roosevelt who now looms up as the potential Fuehrer but the isolationist Lindbergh; and it is not the various interventionist committees but the America First outfit which is today leading the proto-fascist organization in the United States."

Stevens supported neither a radically isolationist nor an interventionist position, and his letter to Van Geyzel registers the contradictions of this troubled middle ground. While Stevens needs to convey his horror at Hitler's aggression, his immediate response to the catastrophe is to emphasize the historical continuities that the catastrophe threatens to explode: like his own man on the dump, Stevens pulls the artifacts of the Virginia landscape into a coherent cultural structure, emphasizing its connections not only with its American past but with its English origins. The danger Stevens courts by emphasizing cultural continuity here is that the real catastrophic rupture of the war might be obscured. But Stevens avoids the opposite danger—naming the catastrophe as the apocalypse that renders all actions irrelevant and terminates the still necessary work of history. As is usually the case with Stevens, a fine line divides complacency from a carefully modulated position allowing for different kinds of political engagement.

Complacency was the response of both the American right and left to the so-called phoney or bore war that lasted until April 1940, when Hitler swiftly conquered Denmark, Norway, Belgium, and the Netherlands. "The second world war is now in its eighth month," wrote Macdonald, "and it seems not yet really to have begun. . . . Who anticipated that, after eight months of it, there would not yet have occurred a single bombing raid by either side on an important city or industrial district, and that the loss of life among pedestrians run down by automobiles in the blacked-out cities would be many times the casualties among the opposing armies on the so-called battle front?" Soon after Macdonald published these remarks, the unimaginable would come to pass: France would capitulate to Nazi forces in just fifteen days, and soon

Churchill would walk through the rubble that was Parliament. Macdonald had needed to trivialize the war's destruction in order to bolster his political objections to American intervention, but faced with these events, American isolationism—whether Macdonald's or Lindbergh's—collapsed as quickly as Paris.

In contrast, Stevens's sense of the war's seriousness returned before the fall of France. During the summer of 1939, before the war began, Stevens wrote "Variations on a Summer Day," a collection of twenty brief and loosely connected images or meditations. When the poem appeared in the *Kenyon Review* the following September, Stevens told Hi Simons that although such poetry had its justifications, it was not the kind of poetry he was now writing. A phrase in a French newspaper had caught his eye ("the primordial importance of spiritual values in time of war"), and Stevens could tell that the war seemed far less "phoney" to the French who were building fortifications along the Maginot Line than it did to most Americans, however docile Hitler appeared: "if one happened to be playing checkers somewhere under the Maginot Line, subject to a call at any moment to do some job that might be one's last job, one would spend a good deal of time thinking in order to make the situation seem reasonable, inevitable and free from question. I suppose that, in the last analysis, my own main objective is to do that kind of thinking." This letter registers an awareness of the economies of wartime mortality that Stevens knew well from the First World War. He himself was not somewhere under the Maginot Line, but he once again found himself obsessed with such experience, reading French newspapers to get closer to it. A few weeks after he wrote to Simons, Stevens told Van Geyzel of his anxiety over "the more or less universal disaster. . . . It must be an odd thing to go to bed at night in Colombo with the sense that some German boat may let loose a half-dozen planes at any time." The phoney war was a war of nerves, a war of waiting, and before the fall of Paris, Stevens felt that anxiety himself; when Hitler's troops crossed the Maginot Line, he did not need to alter his estimation of the danger. "I make no reference in this letter to the war," he wrote to Van Geyzel in May 1940. "It goes without saying that our minds are full of it."

Stevens did refer to the war directly in poems written in response to the events of September 1939. "Martial Cadenza" and "Yellow Afternoon," poems that rehearse the American tension between isolationism and interventionism, were published the following February, when their urgency stood at odds with American frustration at the "bore" war. "Martial Cadenza" expresses a desire for a "world without time." The evening star rises low in the winter sky, returning "as if life came back" and "found us young." Such cyclical repetition is always suspect for the later Stevens: it disguises the more subtle and profound change that takes place within cycles (the difference within similarity), and it diverts our attention from the particularities of the world in which such minute but crucial changes take place. In "Martial Cadenza" that world is at war, yet the star speaks of "armies without / Either trumpets or drums, the commanders mute, the arms / On the ground, fixed fast in a profound defeat." As the poem progresses, Stevens attempts with increasing desperation to ignore that earthly defeat.

> What had this star to do with the world it lit,
> With the blank skies over England, over France
> And above the German camps? It looked apart.

The paradox of these lines is that Stevens cannot maintain the isolationist position without describing the world that the position seeks to ignore. The companion poem, "Yellow Afternoon," makes the paradox more explicit by emphasizing the earthly defeat that "Martial Cadenza" invokes only to transcend. Here we may love "visible and responsive peace" precisely because we are part of "the fatal unity of war." While the speaker of "Martial Cadenza" gazes at the stars, the protagonist of "Yellow Afternoon" is decidedly earthbound.

> Everything comes to him
> From the middle of his field. The odor
> Of earth penetrates more deeply than any word.

Returning to "Martial Cadenza" with this wisdom, the reappearance of the evening star signals not so much a timeless world of peace as the recurrence of world war. If the star "is full / Of the silence before the armies," then the armies must march after the star disappears, as they have marched before.

Stevens could not help thinking back to his poems of the First World War as he wrote these new war poems. His mind was full of this war, as it had been full of the First World War, but the tensions of his desire for engagement were subtly different in a war now perceived as "total," a war in which the division between soldiers and civilians (and men and women) was much less sharply drawn. Robert Graves complained that in comparison with his First World War forebears, the soldier of the new war "has lived a far safer life than the munition-maker whom in World War I he despised as a 'shirker'; he cannot even feel that his rendezvous with death is more certain than that of his Aunt Fanny, the firewatcher." That feeling was more potent in London than in Hartford, of course, but even in the United States the First World War poet's sharply ironic contrast of the trenches and the drawing rooms lost its power; popular anthologies of Second World War poetry edited by Oscar Williams and by Richard Eberhart (both of which included Stevens's work) stressed that "the spectator, the contemplator, the opposer of war have their hours with the enemy no less than uniformed combatants." By the end of the summer of 1940, Stevens concluded that those hours would soon take up everyone's day: "I am afraid that what is going on now may be nothing to what will be going on three or four months from now, and that the situation that will then exist may even involve us all, at least in the sense of occupying our thoughts and feelings to the exclusion of anything except the actual and the necessary." By the end of the year, after Japan signed a treaty of alliance with the Rome–Berlin Axis, Stevens would speak unequivocally of "the great disaster in which we are all involved."

After Pearl Harbor was bombed, Henry Church would report to Stevens from Arizona, "Strangely enough war psychosis seems to be intense out here in the desert." Church may have thought he left such anxieties behind in Paris, but Stevens could have explained to him in particular ways how the public experience of war could become virtually indistinguishable from private suffering. For Stevens, the summer of 1940 saw not only the unsettlingly swift collapse of European democracies, but the death of his brother and mother-in-law. John Bergan Stevens, his only surviving brother, died in July; his mother-in-law was killed in an automobile accident in August. "This sort of thing," he told Church, "and the demnition news . . . makes me feel pretty much as a man must feel in a shelter waiting for bombing to start." Here Stevens does not compare his experience of death, as he might have done during the First World War, with that of a soldier in the trenches; a British civilian's experience of the blitz seemed equally precarious. Near the end of the war, Stevens would remember that "at first, when someone that we had known was lost, there was an extraordinary shock; later, this became something in the ordinary course of events, terrifying but inevitable." The private losses accumulated with the public. Stevens's last remaining sibling, Elizabeth Stevens McFarland, died in February 1943. When Hi Simons died two years later, the eloquence of Stevens's letter to the widow grew from the depths of his own losses—and the sense that these private losses were part of a culture's mourning: "All of us are having a special experience of the loss of friends and relatives to-day, so much so that we shrink from each new one and feel it with an accumulated intensity and feeling of helplessness."

In February 1940, just before this sequence of deaths began, the Stevens family migrated from Hartford to Key West, fearing (as they would again in the winter of 1943) that there would not be enough oil to heat the house. This would be the last trip to Key West; after 1940 the Navy requisitioned the Casa Marina, where the Stevenses stayed, and Key West was no longer a refuge from wartime hardships. Planning the family's trip in 1940, Stevens asked his Florida associate Philip May about "a place that you once took me to that I have never forgotten, and that was the plantation down the river. . . . There were some very attractive woods with jasmine nearby." Stevens was remembering the Kingsley Planation on Fort George Island: like the Virginia countryside, such a place might have helped Stevens place the war within the larger sweep of American culture (in its opulence and its oppressions), but a poem provoked by this trip to Florida, "Asides on the Oboe," suggests that the jasmine islands had already succumbed to the fate that would befall the Casa Marina: "One year, death and war prevented the jasmine scent / And the jasmine islands were bloody martyrdoms."

These lines open the third movement of "Asides," published in December 1940. The prologue to the poem proclaims that "The prologues are over," that the "final belief / Must be in a fiction," and the first movement surveys the fictions that no longer suffice, proposing the hero as the new object of belief. As ever, Stevens's hero is a tissue of contradiction, human and inhuman, real and unreal—"The impossible possible philosophers' man." The second movement characterizes the accomplishment of this "central man."

> He is the transparence of the place in which
> He is and in his poems we find peace.
> He sets this peddler's pie and cries in summer,
> The glass man, cold and numbered, dewily cries,
> "Thou art not August unless I make thee so."

That makes the hero's task sound easy, a fait accompli, as if the punning speech of the poet were enough to make the summer of 1940 what it is (August) and what it is not (august). But the terms of the poet-hero's cry belie their inadequacy; he "dewily cries," recalling the bitter parody of such cries in "The Man on the Dump": "dew dresses, stones and chains of dew, heads / Of the floweriest flowers dewed with the dewiest dew. / One grows to hate these things except on the dump." And except on the dump, one would grow to hate the central man's dewy cries and find no peace within his poems. Beginning with the destruction of the jasmine islands, the poem's last movement places the poet in a time of war that resists his cries and by resisting them makes the cries more meaningful.

> One year, death and war prevented the jasmine scent
> And the jasmine islands were bloody martyrdoms.
> How was it then with the central man? Did we
> Find peace? We found the sum of men. We found,

> If we found the central evil, the central good.
> We buried the fallen without jasmine crowns.
> There was nothing he did not suffer, no; nor we.

In an important reading of *Parts of a World*, David Bromwich notices that the war helped to humanize Stevens's conception of the hero. Throughout the 1920s and 1930s, Stevens used the word *generation* only with irony or contempt, suspicious as he was of an Eliotic rhetoric of idealized suffering. Stevens did not belong to the "mobs of men" he surveyed in "Sailing After Lunch," and he did not share the "generation's dream" of destruction in the "Blue Guitar." But in a time of total war, the soldier more adequately embodied for Stevens the anxieties and the desires of the people at large, whatever their class. In "Asides on the Oboe" the poet cannot make the jasmine return—despite his dewy boast, he cannot even it make it seem "as if the jasmine ever returned." What he can do is confront the death and war that has overtaken the islands and chant for soldiers "buried in their blood." That chanting allows both the poet and his auditors to participate in the suffering and to develop the most useful wartime fiction: "that we were wholly one." By the time Stevens came to write "Dutch Graves in Bucks County" (1943), he could see his own future in "These violent marchers of the present," who "in arcs / Of a chaos composed in more than order, / March toward a generation's centre." Throughout the first half of this poem, the "Angry men and furious machines" of the modern warfare seem distant and alien to the ghosts of Stevens's ancestors until we realize that there are "other soldiers, other people" who wander "creeping under the barb of night."

> But these are not those rusted armies.
> There are the lewdest and the lustiest,
> The hullaballoo of health and have,
> The much too many disinherited
> In a storm of torn-up testaments.

Once Stevens is able to see a generation's plight in the soldier's plight, including even himself in the struggle, then the gap between the past and the present is narrowed; and the ghosts who at the opening of the poem "are crusts that lie / In the shrivellings of your time and place" now "behold in blindness / That a new glory of new men assembles."

"Asides on the Oboe" was written when Stevens returned to Hartford from Key West in 1940, part of an outburst of poetic activity that coincided with the Nazi invasions of western Europe. "Man and Bottle" and "Of Modern Poetry," published in May as "Two Theoretic Poems," were also products of this period. The latter poem appears to have grown, in part, from some remarks of Stephen Spender's that Stevens had copied into his commonplace book in 1938: "Now the poet is someone who devotes his life to exactly such a process of self-revelation as drama attempts to produce in characters: his poems are speeches from the drama of the time in which he is living." In "Of Modern Poetry" Stevens makes a similar demand of the poet, except that during the world war his comparison of poetry and theater had an additional political resonance that Spender's could not. Once, Stevens begins, the mind did not have to search for its satisfactions: "the scene was set; it repeated what / Was in the script."

> Then the theatre was changed
> To something else. Its past was a souvenir.
> It has to be living, to learn the speech of the place.
> It has to face the men of the time and to meet
> The women of the time. It has to think about war
> And it has to find what will suffice. It has
> To construct a new stage.

This stage is a theater of war, and though the actor who treads the boards must think of war, his speech "may / Be of a man skating, a woman dancing, a woman / Combing," images of the ordinary or the humdrum, as Stevens put it at the end of "Owl's Clover." Thinking back to those lines when he wrote a memorandum to help Henry Church define the nature of the poetry chair he wanted to endow at Harvard, Stevens said, "It is the aspects of the world and of men and women that have been added to them by poetry. These aspects are difficult to recognize and to measure." The syntax here is even more subtle than in the poem, but it would appear that Stevens means that poetry does not give us the world and its inhabitants as such but gives us their "aspects"—and gives those aspects to the very men and women whose aspects they are. In the memorandum, Stevens quotes a line from his own "Asides on the Oboe" to illustrate this point ("Thou art not August unless I make thee so") but the ironic qualification provided by the poem's context is lost. "Of Modern Poetry" and its companion poem, "Man and Bottle," similarly make the poet's power appear rather more grand and essential than Stevens usually allows—he probably called them "theoretic" poems because he realized they were programmatic, lacking his typical qualifications. Despite the subtle discriminations of internal and external violence Stevens would make in "The Noble Rider," he dares to propose in "Man and Bottle" that "The poem lashes more fiercely than the wind."

> It has to content the reason concerning war,
> It has to persuade that war is part of itself,
> A manner of thinking, a mode
> Of destroying, as the mind destroys.

These lines repeat the act of internalization with which Stevens had concluded his first sequence of First World War poems: "War has no haunt except the heart." Stevens had immediately questioned that line during the war, just as the actual violence of the Second World War made him uncomfortable with "Man and Bottle." War, as many readers have noticed, is one of the unifying conceits of *Parts of a World*, and in that conceit the war between nations is sometimes conflated with the war between the mind and the sky. In his own wartime achievement, *A Grammar of Motives* (1945), Burke explored some of the dangers of making war such a "constitutive anecdote": "For if we took war as an anecdote, then in obeying the genius of this anecdote and shaping an idiom accordingly, we should be proclaiming war as the essence of human relations." "Man and Bottle" seems to do that. Burke's thoughts on the difficulty of using war as a constitutive anecdote in the first place suggest how other poems in *Parts of a World* diffuse the dilemma: "modern war ('total war') itself is so complex, that we could hardly use it as our representative anecdote until we had selected some moment within war to serve in turn as representative of war." If the governing or gathering metaphor of *Parts of a World* is war in general, then the force of the volume's title must be measured against the total war and the totalitarian governments that waged it. One of Dwight Macdonald's arguments against American intervention was that it would not be possible for the United States to enter the war without totalizing its economy: remembering the suppression of American radicals that began during the First World War, he feared that as the nation mobilized for war no political space would be left for dissent. Appropriately, Stevens's "Life on a Battleship" stood beside Macdonald's "War and the Intellectuals" in the 1939 *Partisan Review*, and when this poem appeared in *Parts of a World* (Stevens did reprint the poem here but not in his collected volume) it underscored the political force of the volume's Jamesian brief for something like a pluralistic universe. While the totalitarian captain proclaims that "the part / Is the equal of the whole," a contrary voice insists that the sum of those individual parts can never quite constitute the singular totality which the captain has in mind. In "Landscape with Boat," published immediately after the two theoretic poems of 1940, Stevens responds to a voice that, like the captain's, insists on "A truth beyond all truths"—and he responds to his own "theoretic" dogmatism as well:

> He never supposed
> That he might be truth, himself, or part of it,
> That the things that he rejected might be part
> And the irregular turquoise, part, the perceptible blue
> Grown denser, part, the eye so touched, so played
> Upon by clouds, the ear so magnified
> By thunder, parts, and all these things together,
> Parts, and more things, parts.

Here the words *part* or *parts* not only are opposed to the totality but also are divided against themselves, repeated so often that they diffuse the very sense of a whole to which a part belongs. In contrast, the commanding lines of "Man and Bottle" ("It has to persuade that war is part of itself") sound almost like the totalizing voice of the battleship's captain. As I have had several occasions to point out, Stevens's politics often appear divided on precisely this fulcrum: wanting to preserve the integrity of every part of the world, he nevertheless fears the anarchic energy those parts set free.

The chronological sequence of poems I have examined so far ("Variations on a Summer Day," "Yellow Afternoon," "Martial Cadenza," "Man and Bottle," "Of Modern Poetry," "Landscape with Boat," "Asides on the Oboe") were placed in *Parts of a World* in the order in which they were published, leading up to the long poem "Extracts from Addresses to the Academy of Fine Ideas." As "Landscape with Boat" counters the totalizing impulses of the theoretic poems, "Extracts" opposes their willful internalization of war (just as Stevens's second sequence of First World War poems responded to the first—"No introspective chaos"). What happens, Stevens asked in "Extracts," when the soul is faced with a world at "total war," a world where every locality is alien and from which there can be no retreat? If "Man and Bottle" shows an easy victory for the mind in the war between mind and sky, "Extracts" places that war in the context of total war, forcing the mind to measure the real cost of its desire to proclaim that "war is part of itself."

Stevens said that "Extracts from Addresses to the Academy of Fine Ideas" (completed by November 1940) grew in part from his dismay over "the Lightness with which ideas are asserted, held, abandoned," and the fifth movement of the sequence offers a parable in which "ideas are men" who kill one another in their effort to impose ideas on the world: "In the end, these philosophic assassins pull / Revolvers and shoot each other." This triumph is achieved at great cost, since the assassin who remains alive may now sing only to himself, encased in his single idea, his "systematic thinking." The poem's following movement reveals this triumph to have been illusory after all: echoing his own theoretic pronouncement in "Man and Bottle," Stevens says that every philosophic assassin, whether victorious or defeated, was "Sure that the ultimate poem was the mind, / Or of the mind." For Stevens, we begin to take ideas seriously when we see their limitations and do not use them to treat lightly the world outside the mind. Around this war of ideas, waged by philosophic assassins, is a war in which assassins point weapons that are anything but metaphors.

"Extracts" is about the need to distinguish between the poems of war and the physical reality of war, but it is also about the difficulty of maintaining that distinction. The sequence begins by offering a common-sense opposition between the real and the artificial, between the "blood-rose living in its smell" and the "false roses" made of paper. That duality is immediately complicated by a wiser voice insisting, "Messieurs, / It is an artificial world." We know the living rose because we have inscribed it in "so many written words; the sky / Is blue, clear, cloudy, high, dark, wide and round." Where, asks the voice, may we find ourselves in a land beyond the mind? It appears that the whole world is something from which we have always already escaped by metaphor. But it is here that Stevens unfolds the crucial difference between the reality of a teacup (or a rose) and the reality of total war. The first part of "Extracts" ends with the confident assertion that "The false and true are one," and the second section explodes that easy wisdom with the threat of a reality far more aggressive than a rose. Although the blood-rose may be nothing but words, what poem can contain the blood of ten thousand violent deaths?

> Let the Secretary for Porcelain observe
> That evil made magic, as in catastrophe,
> If neatly glazed, becomes the same as the fruit
> Of an emperor, the egg-plant of a prince.
> The good is evil's last invention. Thus
> The maker of catastrophe invents the eye
> And through the eye equates ten thousand deaths
> With a single well-tempered apricot, or, say,
> An egg-plant of good air.

The voice that had explicated the comfortably artificial world is dubbed the Secretary for Porcelain, and while his equation of the true and false roses seemed harmless enough, this aestheticization of total war is immediately repugnant. *Catastrophe* is once again not a word Stevens uses lightly; his secretary becomes complicit in the disaster (a "maker of catastrophe") by so blithely asserting that mass death may be encompassed and neutralized by metaphor. In a short verse paragraph, the terms of "Extracts" have been altered completely, and we are ripped from the world as poem to a world where a poem that is not itself evil—or at best irrelevant—seems impossible to forge.

The remaining movements of the sequence search for a way out of this impasse, and it is not easily found. We have already seen how sections V and VI uncover the pretensions of the "philosophic assassins." Sections III and IV are more helpful. Here Stevens postulates a world where all people are priests who collect their thoughts into one single thought to impose upon the world. These priests are not so different from the assassins or the secretary; like them, the priests trivialize their own doctrine because they trivialize the world—"they are preaching in a land / To be described." That distinction is crucial for the poem's ultimate recuperation of the power of poetry. In part IV the poet wakes in winter and wonders about the condition of the water in the lake. In order to describe rather than preach to this world, he needs to understand "that difference between the and an"—the difference that is the task of any man on the dump: by understanding that he lives not in "the empty place" (a place whose character is already determined, a place to be preached about) but in "an empty place" (a particular place that may be described) he opens up the possibility for changing that place. The Secretary for Porcelain helps to preserve the evil of mass death by aestheticizing it. This less ambitious poet breaks the well-wrought urn by looking at the world and describing its nearly insignificant modalities.

> If,
> When he looked, the water ran up the air or grew white
> Against the edge of ice, the abstraction would
> Be broken and winter would be broken and done.

That act would break the spell of the preachers and the secretaries. Yet this poet cannot muster the effort alone. The "If" that begins this passage is potent, and Stevens is stern: he will not tell us if there is any possibility for change in this winter world of ten thousand deaths. To Stevens in the summer of 1940, it seemed that this winter would endure for some time.

Stevens had suggested to the Secretary for Porcelain that only good or natural death would put an end to evil or mass death. That was the hope of the final stanza of "Sunday Morning," which offers its Keatsian tableau as an antidote to the desperate longing of the fellowship of men that perish. "Be tranquil in your wounds," said Stevens to the ten thousand dead in "Extracts," and though that line had sounded genuinely humane in contrast to the secretary, by the end of the poem it smacks of preaching. The final movement of "Extracts" asks: How indeed may anyone lie tranquil in death?

How may any death be natural or good in total war? If the earth itself is evil, how may anyone rest easily in their wounds? In such a world, of what possible use could the words of a poet be?

> We live in a camp . . . Stanzas of final peace
> Lie in the heart's residuum . . . Amen.
> But would it be amen, in choirs, if once
> In total war we died and after death
> Returned, unable to die again, fated
> To endure thereafter every mortal wound,
> Beyond a second death, as evil's end?
> It is only that we are able to die, to escape
> The wounds. Yet to lie buried in evil earth,
> If evil never ends, is to return
> To evil after death, unable to die
> Again and fated to endure beyond
> Any mortal end. The chants of final peace
> Lie in the heart's residuum.
>
>   How can
> We chant if we live in evil and afterward
> Lie harshly buried there?

In "Asides on the Oboe" the poet unifies the living by "chanting for those buried in their blood." Here even that chant seems defeated by an earth infected by the blood of the dead. In "Extracts" Stevens attempts to answer this most difficult question, but he begins again with an "If" on whose resolution any answer depends.

> If earth dissolves
> Its evil after death, it dissolves it while
> We live. Thence come the final chants, the chants
> Of the brooder seeking the acutest end
> Of speech: to pierce the heart's residuum
> And there to find music for a single line,
> Equal to memory, one line in which
> The vital music formulates the words.

If the heart's residuum can be pierced, if that vital chant could be uttered, if that chant did not seem useless in the face of evil, then the chant would sound something like this—the final two lines of "Extracts from Addresses to the Academy of Fine Ideas" are set apart like an Imagist poem:

> Behold the men in helmets borne on steel,
> Discolored, how they are going to defeat.

Behold is as noble and questing a word for Stevens as it was for Wordsworth, yet what Stevens asks us to behold is a world described as plainly as his poem can manage: for the soldier, this is defeat and nothing more; the poet's task is just to say so. The diffidence of these lines, concluding the extravagant sequence, is difficult to underestimate. And I think Stevens would have liked them to be plainer still. It was soon after writing "Extracts" that he explained in "The Noble Rider" that "when one is trying to think of a whole generation and of a world at war, . . . the plainest statement of what is happening can easily appear to be an affectation."

That careful diffidence had marked Stevens's work from the very beginning of his career, and, just as he was nervous about making emphatic statements about the relationship of poetry and politics in the 1930s, he was wary of issuing programmatic statements on the relationship of poetry and war. Although Stevens ended *Parts of a World* with a brief prose statement on poetry and war, he was unwilling to repeat the performance for Oscar Williams's anthology of war poetry. "A prose commentary on War and Poetry is out of the question," he told Williams; and to Allen Tate he confessed, "I have nothing to say about the war." Tate had wanted to print such a commentary in the *Sewanee Review*, but after receiving Stevens's response he was chastened: "I feel exactly as you do about writing a prose statement on poetry and war. But Williams will be able to get out an anthology of such statements simply because many people can't resist blowing off on any subject matter whatever." Stevens feared the Secretary for Porcelain a poet can so easily become in tossing off such statements, especially at a time when Archibald MacLeish was condemning many American writers as "irresponsibles" for not making explicit their commitments to the war effort. Stevens saw a different kind of irresponsibility in placing such pressure on poetry, and like Yeats during the First World War, he found himself in the difficult position of writing at length about the virtues of keeping silent. Like Yeats as well, however, there was another part of Stevens that did not want to stay quiet at all. *Parts of a World* does not end with "Extracts" but with a poem called "Examination of the Hero in a Time of War": Stevens had already had much to say about heroes, and he would have much more to say about soldiers than the two lines he allowed himself at the end of "Extracts from Addresses to the Academy of Fine Ideas."

14

It Must Be Masculine

"There must be mercy in Asia": It seems likely that in "Montrachet-le-Jardin," published a month after Japan bombed Pearl Harbor, Stevens addressed the nation he now thought of as an enemy. But "Montrachet" is more profoundly marked by a wartime consciousness of an enemy in its call for the poet to speak simply "of good in the voice of men." Just a few years earlier, in "Idiom of the Hero," a disdainful Stevens had pronounced that "The great men will not be blended" with the weak; now the simple act of speaking humanly of human things is to "equate the root-man and the super-man, / The root-man swarming, tortured by his mass, / he super-man friseured, possessing and possessed." As we have seen, the war allowed Stevens to feel that a generation's will is a healthy thing, and these lines reveal him attempting to smooth the class-bound tensions that once marked his work.

Not only for Stevens but for the nation, Pearl Harbor facilitated a feeling of unprecedented cultural unity. The presence of a common enemy relieved much of the pressure from the class conflicts of the 1930s; labor unions volunteered no-strike pledges for the duration of the war. The United States could now conceive of itself as a nation more sinned against than sinning, and any remaining isolationist patriotism was quickly converted to the Allied cause: to think of "America First" was now synonymous with an interventionist position. In part, these new-found feelings of American solidarity were economically based. An economy mobilized for military production took the "mobs of men" off city streets as the programs of the New Deal could not. Less than a year after Pearl Harbor, the average income for a family in Hartford was more than double what it had been in 1938, and part of it was diverted back to the government in war bonds. In retrospect, it is nevertheless clear that even the combined force of common enemies and rising prosperity did not generate an ideologically unified nation without the help of government propaganda. War bonds themselves were designed to manufacture a collective response to the war; as the Secretary of the Treasury admitted, the government decided "to use *bonds* to sell the *war*, rather than *vice versa*." One nameless observer of wartime America remarked, "Europe has been occupied, Russia and China invaded, Britain bombed; only the United States among the great powers was 'fighting this war on imagination alone.'"

After Pearl Harbor, the soldier as hero—or, more potently, the common man as soldier as hero—became a primary historical locus around which American consensus could be imagined. As John Morton Blum explains in his social history of the Second World War, "the GI as athlete, farm hand, mechanic, soda jerk, college student, and organization man—the GI as the ordinary American boy—gave the American people exactly the symbol with which they could easily identify. . . . The selectivity of war reporting sharpened lines already drawn in life. GI's were for the most part ordinary Americans, products of the culture they represented and seemed to reinforce." Whether published in the *Life* or in the *New Yorker*, profiles of soldiers "displayed the hero as a man like other men, not least the man who wanted to admire someone whose place and ways might have been his own, had chance so ruled."

Stevens had been that man at least since 1915, but by the 1940s the nature of his identification with soldiers had changed. During the First World War, Stevens was entranced yet terrified by a soldier's lot; as much as he was drawn to the idea of the soldier's life, he imagined the soldier as a man who carries a bag of severed heads on his back, and "The Death of a Soldier" was an event for which he had no language at all. During the Second World War, Stevens could admire soldiers with less guilt and anxiety; when Samuel French Morse was about to enter the army in 1943, this was the older Stevens's advice: "The lot of a soldier is one of the great experiences, and I hope that you are happy to be having it: a chance to step out of the life that is more or less nothing much, and to look over the whole thing and to think about it as part of it." That sentence almost sounds as though it could have been culled from an early letter by Eugène Lemercier—a sentence that during the First World War, Stevens would have punctured with a flat description of a soldier's corpse. In the later years of the Second World War, Stevens's idealization of the soldier only increased.

Considering the differences between the two world wars in "War and Cultural Life," Burke saw throughout American culture a movement from the tendency to ironize war to the need to idealize it. If the new conditions of total war narrowed the gap between soldiers and civilians, then civilians needed to admire the soldiers in whom they more readily saw themselves: "War, when fought under conditions of totality, obviously requires . . . such identification between the leaders and the led as attains its natural fulfilment in a swing back from debunking to heroism (that is, from an attitude of individualist rejection to one of group identification)." During the Second World War, Stevens could write the poems of "heroism" or "group identification" that he could not muster during the First. "The common man is the common hero," begins the fifth section of "Examination of the Hero in a Time of War," a line that might be interpreted as Stevens's rejection of the merely common hero until we read the second line: "The common hero is the hero." The following section explains that in a time of war, the hero must be devised in "a civiler manner" than before.

> Unless we believe in the hero, what is there
> To believe? Incisive what, the fellow
> Of what good. Devise. Make him of mud,
> For every day.

In the "Examination" Stevens now allows that the great men and the common men are blended in the hero as soldier; "the hero is his nation, / In him made one." While "Idiom of the Hero" had insisted that the great men will "not be blended," the "Examination" is explicit in insisting that a "thousand crystals' chiming voices" are "blended, / In hymns, through iridescent changes, / Of the apprehending of the hero."

Even as class difference is elided in this humanization of the hero, however, the hero's superior stature is now measured more sharply on the axis of gender. In a stanza Stevens deleted from the "Examination" he is equally explicit in insisting that when "an immense drum rolls through a clamor of people," then "the women with eyes like opals vanish." Only then are men free to "look inwardly" and locate the hero, bearing "virile grace before their fellows." In the penultimate stanza of the "Examination," that inward turn embraces everything—"Man-sun, man-moon, man-earth, man-ocean"— until the hero arrives "at the man-man as he wanted." Typically, Stevens cannot allow so extravagant a fiction to stand for long, and the final stanza begins by reminding us that this hero is a thing confected: "Each false thing ends." That turn against the hero complicates but does not dissipate the gendered terms of its confection. And while those terms operate throughout Stevens's poetry at large, the stridency of those terms increases in the poems of the Second World War, especially in the later heroic poems collected in *Transport to Summer* (1947). While Stevens could not identify completely with the "fellowship / Of men that perish" in 1915, he could see himself more comfortably in the common-man-as-soldier-as-hero of 1943. In that year, when he wrote "The Figure of the Youth as Virile Poet," Stevens would characterize the historical continuities embodied in and thematized by so many poems of this period in patriarchal terms: "The centuries have a way of being male." Examining the gender-inflected terms of Stevens's definition of the soldier-hero is not just an exercise in exposing Stevens's sexism (since his sexism will surprise no one). What is more interesting is to see how those terms break down. Although Stevens banishes the feminine, it returns to haunt him, underwriting the ground from which he speaks.

In his 1945 anthology of war poetry, Richard Eberhart compared Stevens's "Esthétique du Mal" with Marianne Moore's "In Distrust of Merits," another response to the Second World War: "If Stevens had left Hartford for a battlefield, he might have done worse, and it is idle to speculate whether he would have done better. . . . The meaning has dictated the sincerity, as it did to Marianne Moore when she abandoned her complacencies of the peignoir to write 'In Distrust of Merits.' . . . The bloodshed of which she writes has caused her to break through the decorative surface of her verse to the different kind of utterance in this poem." If war has, in Eberhart's terms, caused Moore to break away from decorative or feminine verse to a poetry of masculine or sincere statement, where does that leave the poet who in "Sunday Morning" wrote of "complacencies of the peignoir" in the first place? Stevens did not leave Hartford for the battlefield, and he remains dressed in the decorative luxury of "Sunday Morning"; but because he is a male poet, he somehow understands bloodshed without abandoning those complacencies. As a female poet, Moore must leave the feminine space defined by a male poet before she is qualified to write "the different kind of utterance."

Stevens himself was less sure of his qualifications than Eberhart. Examining "Sunday Morning" in the light of Stevens's fascination with soldiers, we saw how deeply his ambivalence ran: seduced and repulsed by the fellowship of men that perish, he cast his uneasy lot with the complacencies of the peignoir. Like Moore, Stevens was accused (often by himself) of writing a poetry that was merely decorative, especially when his work was compared with Williams's idealization of brute "experience." The very act of writing poems had always seemed feminine to Stevens. His struggle, as we saw him explain to his wife early on, was to make himself a "man-poet": "Those who say poetry is now the peculiar province of women say so because ideas about poetry are effeminate. Homer, Dante, Shakespeare, Milton, Keats, Browning, much of Tennyson—they are your man-poets." To combat his suspicions that his habits were indeed "lady-like," Stevens needed to redefine his status as a poet and the status of his poetry as masculine. In his personal life, as all his biographers have demonstrated, this effort involved the literal naming and silencing of his wife. A similar desire to suppress feminine energies (or to characterize the feminine as something that, in contrast to his own role as man-poet, is defined by its very lack of energy) is evident throughout much of the poetry. When the man on the dump rejects a world of "dewy" beauty, it is clear that such a rejection bolsters manhood on the dump: "how many women have covered themselves / With dew, dew dresses, stones and chains of dew." When the "central man" offers his "dewy" cry in "Asides on the Oboe," he is not yet the man-poet Stevens idealizes: the cry is not masculine enough until the central man encounters death and war in the jasmine islands. "What should we be without the sexual myth?" asks Stevens in the late poem "Men Made Out of Words," and the answer is "castratos of moon-mash."

There are moments when Stevens seems intent on exposing the oppressions of the sexual myth, however. In "Life on a Battleship" we have seen how he underscores the patriarchal values of the Stalinist left: "The rape of the bourgeoisie accomplished, the men / Returned on board *The Masculine*," begins the poem, and the ship's captain goes on to explain that "the true masculine" consists not in the name of his ship but in his totalizing power over all things. Yet in both the *Partisan Review* and the first edition of *Parts of a World*, "Life on a Battleship" is paired with "The Woman That Had More Babies than That," in which Stevens diminishes the power of childbirth as nothing but mere repetition: "The merely revolving wheel / Returns and returns, along the dry, salt shore." "There is a mother whose children need more than that," and what they need is the "central man" who helps them hear the whole sound of the sea and not just the dull (feminine) repetition of the waves along the shore. The men remain haunted by the "maternal voice," but the mother's power persists only in her role as handmaiden; true creativity consists not in childbirth but in the masculine rage to order. Stevens attempts to sustain this reduction of feminine power in "Illustrations of the Poetic as a Sense" (1939). In the opening poem of this sequence, "The Common Life," the sexual myth has collapsed—"The men have no shadows" and a woman "is not a woman for a man." The final poem of the sequence, "Of Hartford in a Purple Light," explains what is lacking in this common life: "light masculine, / Working, with big hands, on the town, / Arranged its heroic attitudes." The phallic power of the organizing central man gives shape to the chaos of feminine repetition, and the common life itself grows hard: "When male light fell on the naked back / Of the town, the river, the railroads were clear. / Now, every muscle slops away."

In "Mrs. Alfred Uruguay," collected in *Parts of a World* along with these poems, the central man's phallic power is asserted even more directly over a comically diminished feminine force. The poem juxtaposes two poetic questers, the Mrs. of the title and the male "figure of capable imagination," the former walking beside her donkey and the latter speeding past on horseback. The female quester is a reductionist ("I have said no / To everything") who is responsible for the commonness of the world: "she could never differently be, / Her no and no made yes impossible." The male quester is, in contrast, the vehicle of sexual and hierarchical difference that makes the common world inhabitable. Like Browning's Childe Roland, he rides across a land of "martyrs' bones," but unlike those predecessors (or Childe Roland) he is immortal, an eternally virile youth. And though he is "a lover with phosphorescent hair," his conception of the world is immaculate, untouched by feminine desire. He "passed her there on a horse all will"

> And, capable, created in his mind,
> Eventual victor, out of the martyrs' bones,
> The ultimate elegance: the imagined land.

"Mrs. Alfred Uruguay" is the most bluntly masculine poem collected in *Parts*: unlike the other poems from the volume that I have examined, it was written after the war began, and the poem's especially violent diminution of feminine power is its mark of a wartime consciousness. During the 1940s Stevens struggled harder than ever before to ensure his credentials among the man-poets, the central men, the men of capable imagination—the fellowship of men that do not perish. The factors that made Stevens write a series of defensively programmatic poems about the masculine power of the hero are not only personal but cultural as well.

I have already suggested that the terms in which Stevens articulates heroism undergo a shift in emphasis from class to gender, a shift that was evident in what Burke would have called the grammar of American culture at large. In a discussion of wartime Hollywood cinema, Michael Renov suggests that "in the context of American social life during the World War II years, it was sexual difference rather than class conflict that constituted the crucial problematic to which countless cultural artifacts and public utterances were addressed." At the same time that it relieved pressure from class conflicts, the war increased pressure on gender conflicts by offering women a way to alter their position in American culture. Sandra Gilbert has documented the ways in which the First World War allowed women to enter traditionally masculine professions; while women's cultural power increased, so did hostility to women. But during the Second World War, women not only took on masculine roles in civilian life but for the first time served as regular members of the armed forces. The feminist historian Susan Hartman explains that "two elements were new to women's military service in the 1940s: they were utilized in nearly every activity short of combat, and they achieved permanent, regular status in the military establishment." In addition, "because the nation mobilized for war required the active support of every member, the media continuously made women aware of their importance, not alone as mothers, wives and homemakers, but also as workers, citizens, and even as soldiers."

Women did enter traditionally masculine realms of American culture, but, at the same time, their entrance challenged established constructions of masculinity, ironically forcing a more stringent reinforcement of gender differences. Discussing Stevens's sexual anxieties during the First World War, I introduced Nancy Huston's "Samson Complex" as a way to explain the power of masculine camaraderie: "Contact with women is perceived as debilitating, enervating and ultimately destructive of virility, whereas battles can apparently indefinitely regenerate the strength of males." Unlike the First World War, the Second World War made it more difficult for male soldiers to avoid contact with women. If women were now involved in those battles, then the independence and apparently essential virility of men needed to be asserted more strenuously and more insidiously—more insidiously because during the Second World War, given the sheer scope and complexity of the military effort, many men had as little direct experience of warfare as most women. Consequently, at the same time that women entered the masculine domain of war, they were made to understand how their apparently essential femininity nevertheless prevented them from harnessing masculine power. While war broke down traditionally gendered patterns of behavior, it limited new patterns of behavior with more extreme expressions of women's inferiority. Women entering the armed forces or the workplace were reminded that their services were required "for the duration," that they should be careful to preserve their femininity, that their first duty was to the family to which they would return as wives and mothers at the war's conclusion. A wartime advertisement for lipstick (titled "War, Women and Lipstick") placed this text beside a photograph of a female pilot stepping from a cockpit: "It's a reflection of the free democratic way of life that you have succeeded in keeping your femininity—even though you are doing man's work! . . . No lipstick—ours or anyone else's—will win the war. But it symbolizes one of the reasons why we are fighting . . . the precious right of women to be feminine and lovely—under any circumstances."

Encouraged by the possibility of new employment opportunities in military and civilian life, over 25,000 young women left college between 1940 and 1944. Stevens's daughter, Holly, was one of them. She recalls that in November 1942, she "left Vassar College during her sophomore year, where she had felt no purpose after Pearl Harbor and the entrance of the United States into World War II." Holly Stevens's dissatisfaction with her father's plans for her life had been growing over the previous year. After a tense summer at home, she sent her father a letter stating that the next time he said "Don't argue with me," she certainly would: "This letter, in a nutshell, demands independence and freedom from criticism, but with a more understanding attitude on your parts my independence will not be so demanding, and I will become the critic of my own freedom." Stevens might have received this letter whether he had had a daughter or a son, but gender played a role in this generational conflict: Stevens was confronted with a woman whose life he could not script and whose voice he could not silence. He wrote to a member of the faculty at Vassar, asking her to arrange for some right-minded young woman to make friends with Holly and convince her to stay at school. That subterfuge failed, and Stevens's final plea to his daughter went unheeded. When he wrote this sentence to Robert Frost in the autumn of 1942, Stevens was talking about a public world at war and a private war with his daughter: "How nice it would be to sit in the garden and imagine that we were living in a world in which everything was as it ought to be."

During the summer of 1942, Stevens began to work strenuously on the mountain of genealogical research that took the place of his poems: that research facilitated his effort to restore the values which the war (in general) and his daughter (in particular) had challenged. Stevens's mother had joined the Daughters of the American Revolution and his brother the Pennsylvania Society of Sons of the Revolution, tracing their heritage through female lines. Stevens was proud of this heritage, and he particularly admired two female ancestors, Clothilde Zeller and Kitty Conover, who performed heroic acts during Indian raids and in the War of Independence. Despite these connections to his past, however, Stevens became obsessed with uncovering a direct male line of descent. This work was stymied by uncooperative women. Stevens doubted his genealogist's research because of some "very lurid background" she uncovered in his ancestry. The woman named as Stevens's great-great-great-great-great-great-grandmother apparently caused an argument between her husband and another man, whom she later married after leaving her husband. On the basis of this information, Stevens rejected the genealogist's research: "all of the Stevenses that I have ever known have been perfectly straightlaced about women."

This desire for a purely patriarchal descent stood behind the aesthetic values Stevens outlined in "The Figure of the Youth as Virile Poet," which he prepared for the Entretiens de Pontigny Conference at Mount Holyoke in August 1943. Throughout his life, Stevens often described the source or ground of poetry in feminine terms, implying that the detached masculine poet requires the stability of "feminine" reality. In "The Figure of the Youth" he tends to say the opposite—yet even as he articulates an explicitly patriarchal conception of literary history in this essay, Stevens's idea of masculinity tends to unravel, reincorporating the idea of femininity he has rejected. When we look back to a particular moment in the past, Stevens explains, the figure of the youth as virile poet represents the age to us: "This younger figure is the intelligence that endures. It is the imagination of the son still bearing the antique imagination of the father. . . . It is the spirit out of its own self, not out of some surrounding myth, delineating with accurate speech the complications of which it is composed." It is crucial for Stevens (as it would be for Harold Bloom) that this virile poet appear to bear no debts to the past even as he carries its burden; Stevens disapproves of *The Elizabethan World Picture* because Tillyard maintains that "the 'thoughts' of Shakespeare or Raleigh or Spenser were in fact only contemporary commonplaces"; to seem derivative for Stevens is to be feminized, to lose the essential virility that defines the true poet. Like the soldiers of Stevens's "Examination," the virile poet must reject women altogether—his credo is, "No longer do I believe that there is a mystic muse, sister of the Minotaur." The virile poet must cleave close to the real world, rejecting untethered flights of the imagination. Stevens is explicit in cautioning that the poet loses his "masculine nature" if he "dwells apart in his imagination." And by losing his masculine nature, the poet forsakes his power as "the master of our lives."

The demarcations of gender difference that Stevens enforces are typical: a masculine poet is original, aware of his fathers but not bound to them, and he is a realist, in touch with the brute facts of "experience"; the feminine poet is derivative and prone to flights of fancy. The demarcations are far from stable or consistent, however. For both Burke and Stevens, we have seen, the war increased the power of the sheer otherness of "facts" or the "real"; as Stevens explained in the prose statement that follows the "Examination" in *Parts of a World*, the war's large-scale destruction of human achievement made people feel that "everything moves in the direction of reality" or "in the direction of fact." But in making a no-nonsense engagement with reality a requirement for masculinity in "The Figure of the Youth," Stevens put himself in the uneasy position of needing to reject half his achievement as a poet; in the prose statement he points out that the poet's job is not only to come to terms with "fact" but (having no choice to do otherwise) to resist it, to "come back to what we wanted fact to be, not to what it was, not to what it has too often remained." Throughout the 1930s, he had similarly been at pains to demonstrate how a fictive and fanciful art was as deeply engaged with his culture as the art we call realistic; but now, in poems like "Oak Leaves are Hands," he diminishes the merely fanciful as feminine: the ineffectual

Lady Lowzen merely "Skims the real for its unreal." The problem with this equation of the feminine with the fanciful or figurative is that all language, even the language of realism as opposed to the language of fable, is figurative. In that sense, if Stevens insists on the equation, he must reject not only half of his achievement but the whole of poetry.

On the one hand, these paradoxes will ultimately prevent Stevens from insisting that it must be masculine without insisting simultaneously that it must be feminine. On the other hand, the paradox should not obscure my observation that as the war unsettled Stevens's conceptions of sexual difference, he felt compelled to reassert those differences more schematically than ever before. The same values that shape his hypothetical virile poet shape his ongoing examination of the hero in a time of war. *Parts of a World* ended with the "Examination" itself, and Stevens's next volume, *Transport to Summer*, contains numerous poems that idealize the soldier as the necessary master of our lives. Stevens's soldier is not the soldier as he or she actually existed in the Second World War, since most soldiers never experienced combat and since some of the soldiers were women. The soldier of "Gigantomachia" (1943) is the hero Stevens and his culture required to repair this disruption of the Samson Complex. His is the "body that could never be wounded, / The life that never would end."

> Each man himself became a giant,
> Tipped out with largeness, bearing the heavy
> And the high, receiving out of others,
> As from an inhuman elevation
> And origin, an inhuman person,
> A mask, a spirit, an accoutrement.
> For soldiers, the new moon stretches twenty feet.

The Stevensian hero is always nothing but human and yet somehow more than human; nothing but a human form and yet formless. Or to put it in more precise terms of gender, he is a man and yet not a man. Measured against the categories with which Stevens himself measures the virile poet or the central man, the problem with this hero is that he is in danger of being feminized. If he receives his being out of others, he is derivative; if he is inhuman and substanceless, he lacks contact with the real world of experience; if he is a fictive thing, a fancy, he is not masculine. "The hero who emerges from Stevens's poems of the forties," says Milton Bates, "is . . . a creature of contradictions. He is a man and more than a man, physical and ideal, a doer of ordinary deeds and a prophet who can make his prophecies come true." Part of the tension that motivates Stevens's desire to maintain these contradictions is sexual. The hero must be masculine, and yet if he is to be "more than man" he becomes feminized.

Stevens's larger and more complicated hero poems of the 1940s, "Chocorua to its Neighbor" and "Repetitions of a Young Captain," invite this feminization and yet resist it, incorporating the feminine into an even more precarious sense of what it means to say "it must be masculine." In "Repetitions of a Young Captain" Stevens begins by literalizing the "theater of war" metaphor: as in "Of Modern Poetry" the outbreak of war has caused a change of scenery, and as they sit in the theater of war, men and women have lost a clear sense of what is "real."

> It had been real. It was not now. The rip
> Of the wind and the glittering were real now,
> In the spectacle of a new reality.

The men and women cannot make sense of this new reality because they cannot experience it directly; it is as if they are watching newsreels in this theater, and only through the soldiers' direct experience of war will they be able to comprehend this "new reality." By going to war, the soldiers become "major men," each one "being larger than he was" and yet himself.

Yet the experience of the major men is not available to everyone in the theater. Some members of the audience will remain encased in the illusions of the stage, and others will, through the heroic soldier, come to know the actual theater of war.

> And if it be theatre for theatre,
> The powdered personals against the giants' rage,
> Blue and its deep inversions in the moon
>
> Against gold whipped reddened in big-shadowed black,
> Her vague "Secrete me from reality,"
> His "That reality secrete itself,"
>
> The choice is made. Green is the orator
> Of our passionate height. He wears a tufted green,
> And tosses green for those for whom green speaks.

Predictably, it is the women who resist a confrontation with this new reality, the men who want to force the confrontation. Women remain encased in the private world of "powdered personals"; men engage the public world of violence and rage. Yet as the first line of this passage implies, the governing metaphor of the poem challenges this distinction. If we are exchanging "theatre for theatre," then the apparently new reality of the war may be no more or less "real" than the world on the stage. And though men are differentiated from women because of their innate ability to experience directly a world that women resist, this experience may be no less fanciful than the female spectators' experience.

In "Chocorua to its Neighbor" Stevens similarly courts what he must think of as a feminization of experience even as he tries to make it masculine. "Gigantomachia" ends with a hero so enlarged that he is almost completely inhuman, but "Chocorua" insists on the paradoxical nature of the hero's status as simltaneously human and inhuman. In the nineteenth stanza, Stevens comes as close as he ever would to a resolving this tension, and with this humble characterization of what makes "acutest speech," the lines describe Stevens's own eloquence at its best.

> To say more than human things with human voice,
> That cannot be; to say human things with more
> Than human voice, that, also, cannot be;
> To speak humanly from the height or from the depth
> Of human things, that is acutest speech.

Throughout most of "Chocorua" this goal lies just out of reach. And when the tension between the human and the inhuman increases, the sexual nature of the tension becomes more pronounced. The poem is spoken by the mountain Chocorua, and the mountain speaks only to the man who climbs its back, the hero who is also a soldier. Our mission, we learn in the first stanza, is "To perceive men without reference to their form." Measured in their own terms, soldiers are all form, physical bodies and nothing more.

> The armies are forms in number, as cities are.
> The armies are cities in movement. But a war
> Between cities is a gesticulation of forms,
> A swarming of number over number, not
> One foot approaching, one uplifted arm.

Properly conceived, the soldier as hero will shape this chaos. He is the "self of selves: / To think of him destroyed the body's form"; the substance of the hero's body seems "Both substance and non-substance, luminous flesh / Or shapely fire"; his body is a perfectly masculine shape, yet he is "more than muscular shoulders, arms and chest, / Blue's last transparence." Stevens asserts that his hero is "not man yet he was nothing else"; yet if he is transparent, substanceless, ethereal, the something else he is must be, in Stevens's use of the terms, feminine. This threat of feminization is in turn

combated by a more strenuous assertion of the Samson Complex. The hero
may be conceived as nothing but masculine because he rests, as the mountain
puts it, "Upon my top"—he is "Cloud casual, metaphysical metaphor, / But
resting on me." Bonded to the mountain, the hero is also intimate with all
soldiers. The mountain-mounting hero himself tells us that "the simplest soldier's cry" is part of "what I am. . . . Of what I am, / The cry is part." And
when the hero momentarily doubts his ability to hold the misery of all men
within himself, the mountain assures us that this lapse does not threaten his
phallic power: "In spite of this, the gigantic bulk of him / Grew strong, as if
doubt never touched his heart."

After speaking these lines, the mountain wonders about the origin of this
inflationary force. Where "had his body birth," he asks, and the answer has
nothing to do with women; as in "The Woman That Had More Babies than
That," the power of childbirth is usurped in a vision of male bonding: "He
rose because men wanted him to be," a central man "beyond / Their form,
beyond their life, yet of themselves, / Excluding by his largeness their
defaults." Larger than all other men and undeflatable, the hero is the "collective being" of all men, as big as they could wish to be. The captain, the
cardinal, the scholar, and even the mother are able to see their better selves
in the hero, but the hero is the mother of us all—inside him are "Gigantic
embryos of populations." Having thwarted the danger of an etherealized femininity, the hero now appropriates the power of childbirth. At the end of the
poem, the soldiers who had been nothing but physical forms cohere in the
man who is both their father and their mother.

> Integration for integration, the great arms
> Of the armies, the solid men, make big the fable.
> This is their captain and philosopher,
> He that is fortelleze, though he be
> Hard to perceive and harder still to touch.

Stevens's strategy here is similar to that of Stephen Dedalus in *Ulysses*. Appropriating the image of childbirth to dignify the ethereal act of artistic creation
("I have an unborn child in my brain"), Stephen then uses this bolstered
conception of creativity to diminish the mere physicality of childbirth: "In
woman's womb word is made flesh but in the spirit of the maker all flesh that
passes becomes the word that shall not pass away."

Unlike Joyce, Stevens is explicit in casting his maker in the role of soldier,
and in doing so he depends on a long tradition of metaphorical equations
between the pain of childbirth and the injuries of war. When Agamemnon is
wounded, Homer compares his anguish "to the throes / a writhing woman

suffers in hard labor." The old saying goes "How long will men make war?—as long as women have children," but Nancy Huston speculates that it might be rewritten as "men make war *because* women have children": "given that women are 'marked' by their capacity for having children (whatever efforts may be made to minimize or even to eradicate the importance of that fact), men have been compelled to find a similarly distinctive trait for themselves, something that could ratify, as it were, their masculinity. And the trait they have chosen to emphasize is that of physical strength, even if this has meant depriving women of *their* physical strength, and sometimes going so far as to mutilate them, in order that in one area at least male supremacy could remain irrefutable." In these terms, the Stevensian soldier-hero offers men a power equal to that of childbirth—and we have seen that Stevens goes so far as to recast childbearing as a masculine power.

This appropriation underscores the paradox of Stevens's association of feminity with figurative language. Working from feminist appropriations of Lacan, Margaret Homans maintains in her cannily titled *Bearing the Word* that "the very structure of childbearing, in which something becomes real that did not exist before—or that existed only as a word, a theory, or a 'conception'—is a structure of literalization, by which the relatively figurative becomes the relatively literal." For Stevens to assert that women are essentially detached from reality, that their experience of the world is thin, he must associate men's brute experience of reality with childbearing: to be a man, he must become a woman. This, as Susan Schweik points out, is the paradox of a critic like Randall Jarrell saying that Moore's "In Distrust of Merits" is not sufficiently in touch with lived experience: he means that the poem is insufficiently masculine, and he means to criticize the poem for its femininity; but in another sense, he must criticize the poem for being insufficiently feminine—for indulging in fanciful language rather than "bearing" the weight of reality. In both "The Figure of the Youth as Virile Poet" and "Repetitions of a Young Captain," Stevens characterizes the power to experience the world directly and profoundly as one of the marks of masculinity; and yet in poem after poem about such confrontations with the real, images of childbearing are used to characterize the intensity of this "masculine" experience. In "Holiday in Reality," for instance, the sheer groundedness of the real is represented as inherently feminine ("Spring is umbilical or else it is not spring"), even though the heroic man asserts that "these are real only if I make them so." And in "The Pure Good of Theory," where Stevens takes pains to explain the danger of speaking "of the whole world as metaphor" and sticking "to the contents of the mind," he condemns the ungrounded existence of "Man, that is not born of woman but of air." In "Repetitions of a Young Captain" women cannot "bear" anything because the power of childbearing, of giving life, had been usurped by the power of war, of taking life away. In the wartime context of "Esthétique du Mal," when Stevens seeks comfort in a vision of the mother as the "softest woman," the man is nevertheless the mother of his own self, just as the hero gestates the embryos of all men in "Chocorua": he holds "the child of a mother fierce / In his body."

Stevens is able to outline firmer distinctions between masculinity and femininity in "The Figure of the Youth," but as soon as those distinctions are established in the hero poems, they break down, and it becomes impossible for him to say that it must be masculine without saying that it must be feminine as well. Similarly, Huston points out that once the symbolic equivalence between war and childbirth is established, it is not possible to determine whether the metaphor is employed to give men a kind of suffering as powerful and spectacular as childbirth or whether it is employed to confer on women and childbearing the social prestige of the battlefield: "Although childbirth indisputably has biological precedence over war, neither phenomenon can be said to have symbolic precedence, and therefore only the *interaction* between the two can be the object of analysis." That interaction can never be stabilized for long. Because the values of masculinity and femininity are defined in a particular cultural moment, their very contingency ensures that the values will immediately impinge on one another—or even, as in Stevens's hero poems, reverse themselves. During the cultural moment of the Second World War, Stevens was witnessing a real increase in the power of women, and, like many other voices at the time, he responded by creating a world where masculinity and femininity were constructed in such a way that the threat of women's power was contained. But just as feminine power in the military could not be emphasized without simultaneously diminishing that force (as in the lipstick ad), so could Stevens not extol masculine power without diminishing it in turn.

Perhaps it is not paradoxical, then, that the poems of the 1940s in which Stevens does try to create a generous discursive space for women end up creating the position only to diminish it. We have seen a rehearsal of this strategy in "The Woman That Had More Babies than That," where the mother is not banished from the poem but allowed to reenter it as a servant or muse to the central man. But the primary exhibition must be one of Stevens's greater poems of the Second World War, "Esthétique du Mal" (1944). To do this complicated sequence justice, I need to expand the categories of my analysis. "Esthétique du Mal" more than any other poem of the 1940s reveals how the consideration of gender is inseparable from the full range of issues that troubled Stevens throughout the war: pain, evil, catastrophe, and the precarious place of poetry in a world infected by those conditions.

15

The Heart of the Debacle

Soon after "Esthétique du Mal" was published in 1944, its seventh canto ("How red the rose that is the soldier's wound") became a standard selection in anthologies of war poetry. The canto depends on several familiar conventions of war poetry, but it also condenses some of the characteristics we have seen throughout Stevens's own soldier-hero poems of the 1940s—the hero's ability to unify the suffering of all individual men and the need to assert that the suffering of war may ultimately be assuaged by the ongoing continuities of normal life. In its final lines, the canto both offers an image of male bonding and delineates a wartime role for women.

> The shadows of his fellows ring him round
> In the high night, the summer breathes for them
> Its fragrance, a heavy somnolence, and for him,
> For the soldier of time, it breathes a summer sleep,
>
> In which his wound is good because life was.
> No part of him was ever part of death.
> A woman smoothes her forehead with her hand
> And the soldier of time lies calm beneath that stroke.

Once again, these are lines Stevens would not have written during the First World War (nothing could be farther from the stern reticence of "The Death of a Soldier"), and Helen Vendler has been highly critical of the canto's sentimentality, suggesting that "Stevens has averted his mind from the visual scene and has fixed it not on experience but on pious value. It is a betrayal of Stevens' most ambitious aesthetic to name death a summer sleep, to call a wound a rose, to palliate finality by a stroking hand, and to blur the tragic outline by a spell of Parnassian language." As if the terms of this critique were not strong enough, one could add that by making that stroking hand a woman's, Stevens has invited women into the masculine ring of fellows simply to facilitate male bonding; the woman cast as mother or nurse is paradoxically forced to underwrite death and destruction. That sexual dynamic may account for the fact that while the poem seems so reprehensible to Vendler, it seemed one of Stevens's greatest achievements to anthologists of war poetry. Paul Fussell has pointed out that the "wound-rose" is a time-honored image in European war poetry. And the palliating force of grieving woman is equally conventional; Wilfrid Owen's "Anthem for Doomed Youth" ends by resolving that "the pallor of girls' brows shall be their pall."

In either case, it is misleading to read this canto (as it was anthologized) in isolation from the whole of "Esthétique du Mal." One impetus for the sequence was John Crowe Ransom's "Artists, Soldiers, Positivists," published in the *Kenyon Review* in 1944. "What particularly interested me," Stevens wrote Ransom, "was the letter from one of your correspondents about the relation between poetry and what he called pain. Whatever he may mean, it might be interesting to try to do an esthétique du mal." The poem of that title was completed six weeks after Stevens read this letter.

What *are* we after in poetry? Or, more exactly, what are we attempting to rout? The commandos of contemporary literature are having little to do with Eliot and even poets of charming distemper like Wallace Stevens (for whom we all developed considerable passion). Not necessarily a poetry of time and place, either. The question of poetry as in life (and in the Army) is one of survival, simply. . . . Men like Karl Shapiro (his "Anxiety," in *Chimera* recently, is notable), John Berryman, Delmore Schwartz transcend the aesthetic of poetry—thank God! I find the poetry in *Kenyon Review* lamentable in many ways because it is cut off from pain. It is intellectual and it is fine, but it never reveals muscle and nerve. It does not really matter whether poetry of men in war, or suffering the impact of communiqués, has a large or small "frame of reference." It must, I feel, promise survival for all who are worth retrieving—it must communicate a lot of existence; an overwhelming desire to go on. . . .

I'm waiting for an American poem of the forties called "The Quip at the Heart of the Debacle."

Here highly compressed are all the worries that plagued Stevens as he attempted to address war in poetry: that he lacked the requisite experience of war, that his poetry of war itself lacked "muscle," that poetry itself was irrelevant in a time of war, incapable of penetrating to the heart of the debacle. Ransom's comment on the letter made war's challenge to poetry even clearer:

"The time scarcely comes when there is enough of dedicated public service to fight the evil in the world, and improve the lot of citizens; when is there time for art?"

While Ransom wanted to dismiss this challenge (it "turned many first-rate literary men into commandos"), preserving poetry's place above politics, Stevens wanted to write "The Quip at the Heart of the Debacle." The opening canto of "Esthétique du Mal" dramatizes the confrontation between poetry and war in a scene describing a young man in Naples reading paragraphs on the sublime while Vesuvius towers above him, groaning and trembling. As Eleanor Cook has noted, the scene is not so historically displaced as it might seem. Vesuvius had erupted in March 1944, reburying Pompeii in a foot of ash; the volcano was for many other people besides Stevens a figure for the apocalyptic threat of the Second World War: "When Stevens wrote the poem, then, Naples had just passed into Allied hands and Vesuvius had just repeated the geological phenomenon known to ancients and moderns alike. The place and time seem made to order for a war poem about the aesthetics of pain, as desired by Ransom's correspondent. More than one observer of Vesuvius in eruption compared the sight and sound to the guns of war. Quite apart from war, volcanoes are places of terror, where warlike language sounds appropriate." As Cook proceeds to point out, volcanoes are conceived traditionally not only as places of sublime terror, the mouth of hell, but as a figure for poetic voice. For Stevens, however, this conjunction of poetry and catastrophe is not natural or given, and though his young man does send postcards from the volcano, he possesses no language adequate to the disaster. Not only is a quip from the heart of this debacle difficult to write, but the debacle itself seems to have no heart that the quip could penetrate or communicate.

> He could describe
> The terror of the sound because the sound
> Was ancient. He tried to remember the phrases: pain
> Audible at noon, pain torturing itself,
> Pain killing pain on the very point of pain.
> The volcano trembled in another ether,
> As the body trembles at the end of life.
>
> It was almost time for lunch. Pain is human.
> There were roses in the cool café. His book
> Made sure of the most correct catastrophe.

These lines not only reiterate the complaint of Ransom's soldier against war poetry; they proleptically assert Vendler's critique of "Esthetique du

Mal" itself. As the young man reviews poetic conventions and looks at the roses in the café, one could imagine him writing a line like "How red the rose that is the soldier's wound." This young man has read his book on the sublime too well, and for him the reality of catastrophe can be nothing more than a topos, conventions that are "correct" but seem historically irrelevant. As we have seen over and over again, that is always the reason for Stevens's discomfort with apocalyptic rhetoric—it obscures the real urgency or danger of historical change and relieves us of responsibility for acting in the face of danger: "It was almost time for lunch." Given this critique of the merely correct but emotionally and historically lifeless metaphor, one has to wonder if the line "How red the rose that is the soldier's wound" (a line strikingly unlike most of Stevens's poetry in the baldness of its conceit) is not meant as an example of an inadequate wartime rhetoric.

I do not mean to suggest that "Esthétique du Mal" provides a framework so stable that the wound–rose lyric must be read as an ironic utterance, that anthologists were simply duped in reading the lyric as a sincere utterance, or that the irony negates the poem's marginalization of femininity. My point, more simply, is that Stevens has made the poem wary of its own rhetoric. At the same time that he wants to come to terms with catastrophe and suffering, he doubts those terms. Rather than the successful embodiment of its title, "Esthétique du Mal" is more properly a poem about the sheer difficulty of formulating a coherent aesthetic of evil. (Recognizing this about the poem, Stevens advised Ransom that he was "thinking of aesthetics as the equivalent of aperçus, which seems to have been the original meaning.") While the poem does not reject the responsibility of representing pain, and while it laments the fact that we are unable to grasp the truly catastrophic pain of war, it does not assert that representing or grasping such pain is easy. "How has the human spirit ever survived the terrific literature with which it has had to contend," asks Stevens in the "Adagia." "Esthétique du Mal" shows how the weight of all previous literature, each "past apocalypse" (an oxymoron from "Extracts"), prevents us not only from writing about pain but from knowing the pain of disaster when we experience it.

After the second canto, Stevens dismisses the too well-read young poet from the poem. Several of the remaining cantos ask why we have no language that does justice to a world that might legitimately be called "evil." "The fault lies with an over-human god," suggests canto three. "If only he would not pity us so much." The problem here is what Nietzsche called anthropomorphic error: having displaced our desire for consolation onto a force independent of the self, the consolation becomes nothing more than "self-pity's kin," and it belittles our pain. Instead of an independent force that might ideally distinguish between catastrophes and nuisances, the over-human god

"Weaken[s] our fate" by relieving "us of woe both great / And small." The eighth canto suggests that we might have been better off with the Old Testament god of retribution rather than the god of nineteenth-century therapeutic Protestantism. "The death of Satan was a tragedy / For the imagination" because it deprived human beings of an inhuman sense of evil—illusory as that sense might have been—an independent force against which human catastrophes might be judged and rendered meaningful. For Stevens, we have been left with a world in which either nothing is evil or all things are evil. Our desire, as the final canto has it, is too difficult to tell from our despair. When we are faced with the monumental catastrophe of the Second World War, we consequently have no words for it, and even if we try to honor the catastrophe by casting the war in our grandest metaphors of apocalypse and despair, the metaphors nevertheless trivialize the reality. The problem, as Walter Benjamin put it just before the war, is that we have become so alienated from ourselves that we can experience our "own destruction as an aesthetic pleasure of the first order."

The eleventh canto of "Esthétique du Mal" reinforces that point by offering slightly too well-wrought scenes of wartime destruction.

> The paratroopers fall and as they fall
> They mow the lawn. A vessel sinks in waves
> Of people, as big bell-billows from its bell
> Bell-bellow in the village steeple. Violets,
> Great tufts, spring up from buried houses
> Of poor, dishonest people, for whom the steeple,
> Long since, rang out farewell, farewell, farewell.

This is the work of what Stevens called in "Extracts" the Secretary for Porcelain, and it is dismissed accordingly as "a well-made scene." The famous couplet that follows the scene ("Natives of poverty, children of malheur, / The gaiety of language is our seigneur") turns sour in this context: the gaiety of language is indeed what Stevens seeks throughout "Esthétique du Mal," but in canto nine the gaiety is offered at the expense of suffering, and its art is not a cure for suffering but is complicit in the disease.

"A man in his own secret meditation," said Yeats in "Nineteen Hundred and Nineteen," "Is lost amid the labyrinth that he has made / In art or politics." Like "Esthétique," Yeats's poem asks why art that seemed an answer to violence may engender violent acts, and, like "Nineteen Hundred and Nineteen," Stevens's poem asks this question of the "art" of both poets and politicians. While canto nine gives us the labyrinth of art, canto fourteen displays the labyrinth of politics, beginning with a quotation from Victor

Serge's "The Revolution at Dead-End" (published in Dwight Macdonald's *Politics* in June 1944).

> Victor Serge said, "I followed his argument
> With the blank uneasiness which one might feel
> In the presence of a logical lunatic."
> He said it of Konstantinov. Revolution
> Is the affair of logical lunatics.

Serge, a member of the Left Opposition to the Leninist regime, describes in his memoir a meeting with Konstantinov, who was suffering from paranoid delusions. Serge's conclusion is not that "Revolution / Is the affair of logical lunatics" but that there was an accidental yet profound truth in Konstantinov's ravings: "in what he said there was the germ of a basic idea, and it was not the idea of a madman: 'We did not fight the revolution for this.'" Stevens twists Serge's point into a condemnation of political labyrinths in general, but the condemnation is no less severe than his rejection of artistic labyrinths, and both critiques depend on the same values. While the maker of well-made scenes recalls the Secretary for Porcelain, Stevens's Konstantinov recalls the "philosophic assassin" from "Extracts," the man of the "single thought."

> He would not be aware of the lake.
> He would be the lunatic of one idea
> In a world of ideas, who would have all the people
> Live, work, suffer and die in that idea
> In a world of ideas.

Harold Bloom suggests that these lines are "too political" in the context of "Esthétique du Mal," but they are so only in the sense that the well-made scenes of destruction in canto eleven are "too poetic."

Stevens's point is not to reject poetic and political labyrinths outright, but to scrutinize them and come to understand what aspects of the world they reveal and what aspects they disguise. Despite Stevens's sense of the inadequacy of any aesthetics of evil, he emphasizes that our job is to learn to live with inadequacy. Hypostatized into a force independent from human desires, neither art, politics, Satan, nor God will help manage human suffering. "Esthétique du Mal" pushes us to accept the proposition Stevens copied into his commonplace book from an essay by William Troy: "the human will, taken either in the individual or in society as a whole, is the principle of evil." Canto four suggests that only the "sentimentalist" thinks otherwise: in contrast to the sentimentalist who looks to art, politics, or divinity either for consolation or for the locus of evil, the "genius of misfortune" knows that "He is / That evil, that evil in the self." Stevens is being very stern here, but he is not playing the nihilist. "You are fascinated by evil," he once told Delmore Schwartz. "I cannot see that this fascination has anything on the fascination by good." Canto five counters both the sentimentalist and the genius of misfortune with the "true sympathizers" who allow us to "forego / Lament" by reminding us of the simple, everyday acts of affection that take place "Within what we permit, / Within the actual."

> Be near me, come closer, touch my hand, phrases
> Compounded of dear relation, spoken twice,
> Once by the lips, once by the services
> Of central sense, these minutiae mean more
> Than clouds, benevolences, distant heads.

In emphasizing the power of these "minutiae," Stevens returns to the place he had discovered in both "The Comedian as the Letter C" and "Owl's Clover"—the place of the humdrum, the ordinary, the place of "medium" rather than "major man." In reading "Owl's Clover" and the "Blue Guitar," I suggested that Stevens was circling around the paradox of a humanistic sublime. In "Esthétique du Mal" Stevens is even more direct in his rejection of these Longinian terms (he noted this quotation from Longinus in I. A. Richards's *Coleridge on Imagination*): "The little fire we kindle for ourselves keeps clear and steady, yet we do not therefore regard it with more amazement than the fires of Heaven, which are often darkened, or think it more wonderful than the craters of Etna in eruption." Stevens insists that in the shadow of Vesuvius or the shadow of war, that is exactly what we must do.

When Stevens says in canto eight that the death of Satan was a tragedy for the imagination, he does not mean to suggest that the cure lies in a recovery of Satan or in an acceptance of the imagination's demise. He is adamant that "we require / Another chant" to replace what we have lost, a chant that grows out of the minutiae for which we have a language. The tenth canto offers a new chant, a new fiction, that recalls the elegy of canto seven by casting women in the role of the healing mother. I have already suggested that Stevens himself found that elegy inadequate, but these lines suggest that he did not find it useless. However much "Esthétique du Mal" might ironize Stevens's vision of femininity, the vision persists.

> He had studied the nostalgias. In these
> He sought the most grossly maternal, the creature
> Who most fecundly assuaged him, the softest

Woman with a vague moustache and not the mauve
Maman. His anima liked its animal
And liked it unsubjugated, so that home
Was a return to birth, a being born
Again in the savagest severity,
Desiring fiercely, the child of a mother fierce
In his body, fiercer in his mind, merciless
To accomplish the truth in his intelligence.
It is true there were other mothers, singular
In form, lovers of heaven and earth, she-wolves
And forest tigresses and women mixed
With the sea. These were fantastic. There were homes
Like things submerged with their englutted sounds,
That were never wholly still. The softest woman,
Because she is as she was, reality,
The gross, the fecund, proved him against the touch
Of impersonal pain. Reality explained.
It was the last nostalgia: that he
Should understand. That he might suffer or that
He might die was the innocence of living, if life
Itself was innocent. To say that it was
Disentangled him from sleek ensolacings.

Read from a Lacanian perspective, all the anxiety about language in "Esthétique du Mal" could be linked with this nostalgia for the mother: language
itself, the law of the father, is what intervenes between mother and child, yet
it is only through symbolic language—through representation, figuration,
metaphor—that the child can hope to recover a substitute for the mother. In
these lines (in contrast to "The Figure of the Youth"), Stevens does figure
the mother as "reality" itself, a "return to birth"; yet at the same time, as I
have mentioned, that figure is appropriated to enhance masculine power
("the child of a mother fierce / In *his* body"). And if language itself is ruled
by the father, then the figuration of the mother cannot return us to birth but
instead reinforces a masculine symbolic order. Stevens seems to understand
some of the futility of his desire by insisting that it is a "nostalgia"; life may
not be innocent, but he nevertheless needs "To say that it was."

In more culturally specific terms, Stevens's invocation of the mother as a
force that underwrites and cures the masculine pain of war may be seen as
another wartime convention; in Richard Eberhart's "Brotherhood of Men"
(1949) the soldier under attack is preserved by a vision of his "mother in the
midst of terror: 'Persevere. Persevere. Persevere. Persevere.'" This convention
was also questioned during the Second World War. In Virginia Woolf's
Between the Acts (1941), Lucy Swithin wonders about the phrase "knock on
wood": "what's the origin of that? Touch wood . . . Antaeus, didn't he touch

earth?" The warrior Antaeus is saved from death when he touches wood—
the goddess embodied in the earth revives him—and he dies only when
crushed, suspended in midair. Woolf's novel is about patriarchy's appropriation of women in war; she wants to resist this fetishization of woman as healing mother or nurse who cures the suffering of war and underwrites the
advancement of patriarchal culture itself. Stevens is offering just that role to
women in "Esthétique du Mal," and the healing mother will return again
and again in his later poetry, most prominently in "The Auroras of Autumn."
But notice just how he figures the mother in "Esthétique du Mal." Although
there are "other mothers," Stevens does not desire the overpowering "she-
wolves / And forest tigresses"; neither does he desire the weakling "mauve /
Maman." He chooses "the softest / Woman with a vague moustache," an
image that grants the mother a suggestion of masculine power—just the right
amount and not too much. Discussing Lacan's and Kristeva's writings on the
maternal, Kaja Silverman points out that desire for the mother must be recognized as "profoundly ambivalent": "the image of the infant held within the
environment or sphere of the mother's voice" may be "an emblem of infantile
plenitude and bliss," or it may be "an emblem of impotence and entrapment."
Stevens will work hard to figure the mother as the former, but in a later poem
("Madam La Fleurie") the softest woman with a vague moustache realizes
the extent of her phallic power and becomes the she-wolf: "His grief is that
his mother should feed on him, himself and what he saw, / In that distant
chamber, a bearded queen, wicked in her dead light." Just as his fiction of the
soldier-hero becomes feminized against Stevens's will, so does his fiction of
the mother partake of the masculine power Stevens would like to reserve for
the hero: once again, Stevens cannot employ these conceptions of masculinity
and femininity without their impinging on each other. In "Esthétique du
Mal" the hand that strokes the forehead, letting dead soldiers lie peacefully,
is also the hand that pulls the trigger.

Perhaps it is for this reason that, as charged with desire as the fiction of
the mother may be in canto ten, the fiction is dispelled in canto eleven along
with the other "well-made scenes": "Life is a bitter aspic," Stevens admits.
"We are not / At the centre of a diamond," and the soldier-hero is not
Antaeus, eternally revivified by the maternal ground. The stronger fiction of
"Esthétique du Mal" is that of canto five, that of the true sympathizers. With
its famous opening lines, the poem's final canto returns to the value of life's
minutiae: "The greatest poverty is not to live / In a physical world."

> And out of what one sees and hears and out
> Of what one feels, who could have thought to make
> So many selves, so many sensuous worlds,
> As if the air, the mid-day air, was swarming

>With the metaphysical changes that occur,
>Merely in living as and where we live.

In these concluding lines Stevens finds the language that escaped the
young poet in the shadow of Vesuvius. The whole force of the poem is to
neutralize the apocalyptic threat of war, embodied in the volcano, and while
the poem begins (in Longinian terms) not even with our awe at the fires of
heaven but with our failure to feel that awe, the poem ends with our awe at
the little fire we kindle for ourselves. Cook quotes a passage from the *Critique
of Judgement* to emphasize the traditional association of war with the sublime,
but she does not notice how the terms of the association are gendered: Kant
says that war "has something sublime about it, and gives nations that carry it
on in such a manner a stamp of mind only the more sublime the more numerous the dangers to which they are exposed, and which they are able to meet
with fortitude." A prolonged peace, he continues, encourages "a debasing
self-interest, cowardice, and effeminacy, and tends to degrade the character
of a nation." In "Esthétique du Mal" Stevens finally chooses the "effeminacy" of peace over the nobility of war. Yet the conclusion of the poem
remains ambivalent—ambivalent in both sexual terms and in terms of the
poem's relation to the Second World War. Stevens declined to end "Esthétique du Mal" with the question mark that the syntax demands, but his desire
for affirmation does not disguise his doubt that war's apocalyptic threat can
be neutralized simply by forsaking the sublime for the minutiae, the humdrum, the merely human. How can that be so if the human will, as Stevens
insisted earlier in the poem, is as fully capable of evil as it is of true sympathy?
In 1944, remarks Charles Berger, "merely by living as and where we live, we
fill the skies with engines of destruction." Stevens emphasized that the fiction
of the mother was one of many "nostalgias," and I think he wants us to
understand that we should be suspicious of the poem's final affirmation as
well—not in order to strand us with no effective story to tell ourselves about
evil but because we ought to be suspicious of all our nostalgias even as we are
soothed by them. While the air is "swarming / With the metaphysical
changes" at the end of "Esthétique du Mal," only a few pages away "Dutch
Graves in Bucks County" reminds us that "Angry men and furious
machines / Swarm from the little blue of the horizon."

To emphasize that Stevens's fictions of the hero or of the mother are indeed
fictions, contingent on the vagaries of cultural and linguistic duplicities, will
complicate the terms of Stevens's sexism but will not neutralize their implications. Given Stevens's position in American patriarchal culture, those terms
should be expected; what is nevertheless distressing about some of his Second
World War hero poems is the particular vehemence with which he inflates

masculine power and marginalizes feminine power. "Mrs. Alfred Uruguay" and "Repetitions of a Young Captain" are far less generous poems than "Esthétique du Mal." Helen Vendler points out that in "Mrs. Alfred Uruguay" the virile poet's "easy victory includes no redemption of the lady, who is simply annihilated"; in other poems, "when Stevens moves freely and confidently back and forth among his intuitions, we sense a respect for all versions of experience: the claims of logic and the claims of metaphor, the vitality of observation and the vitality of fantasy, the pressure of accuracy and the resisting pressure of longing." That fundamental generosity forced Stevens, at his best moments, to see the absurdity of his most inflated heroic figures. In "Contrary Theses (II)" (1942) he grows tired of "the bombastic intimations of winter / And the martyrs à la mode," longing for what he calls "the abstract." A letter written to José Rodríguez Feo helps clarify Stevens's meaning: "The long and short of it is that we have to fix abstract objectives and then to conceal the abstract figures in actual appearance. A hero won't do, but we like him much better when he doesn't look it and, of course, it is only when he doesn't look it that we can believe in him." The figure of the hero won't do for Stevens because it is not abstract—because as soon as he represents his ideal in his culture's language, the idea begins to look a bit absurd, a martyr à la mode.

Published in *Parts of a World*, "Contrary Theses (II)" looks forward to the long poem that came between that volume and *Transport to Summer*, the poem that is Stevens's greatest achievement: "Notes toward a Supreme Fiction," written in just ninety days in the spring of 1942 and published as a small book by the Cummington Press that autumn. Properly the conclusion to *Parts*, "Notes" came to rest in the collected poems at the end of *Transport*. But Stevens placed the poem in that position with care. The penultimate poem of *Transport to Summer* serves as a hinge between all the hero poems preceding it and the poem that begins by demanding "It Must Be Abstract." "The Pastor Caballero" (1946) might have been titled "The Dismissal of the Hero in a Time of Peace": a hat with a sweeping brim transforms the common man into the hero figure "meant to bear / Its poisoned laurels in this poisoned wood"; but once the poisoned wood is cured, the heroic figure looks out of place, and the hat that had metamorphosed into a helmet looks much better as a simple hat.

> The formidable helmet is nothing now.
> These two go well together, the sinuous brim
> And the green flauntings of the hours of peace.

These lines were published after the war was over. Written just as the United States was entering the war, "Notes toward a Supreme Fiction" shows Stevens in the act of preserving a place for minutiae in a time that demands the sublime. In that effort, the poem builds on "Owl's Clover" and "The Comedian as the Letter C." Fat Jocundus and Crispin are nothing but masculine, but we do not feel quite so oppressed by them as we do by the virile poets of the 1940s: Jocundus and Crispin are exemplars of ordinary experience—the insignificant, the domestic. And like "The Comedian," "Notes toward a Supreme Fiction" is an extravagant poem about the value of being humdrum.

16

It Must Be Humdrum

To many readers, the coda to "Notes toward a Supreme Fiction" has seemed uncharacteristically explicit following the ambiguous undulations of the sequence at large. Helen Vendler calls the coda "something of an anticlimax," and Harold Bloom finds it "deliberate" and "overtly personal." But Stevens himself thought this final address to the soldier was central to the entire poem. In correspondence with Katharine Frazier of the Cummington Press, he suggested that she print "on the back outside cover of the book a border consisting of a line or two of the poem beginning 'Soldier, there is a war' etc: enough to state the idea." For Stevens, the "idea" of a poem is never as rich or complicated as the poem in its full texture and design, but he wanted readers who picked up the first edition of "Notes toward a Supreme Fiction" in the autumn of 1942 to approach the poem through these lines:

> Soldier, there is a war between the mind
> And sky, between thought and day and night. It is
> For that the poet is always in the sun,
>
> Patches the moon together in his room
> To his Virgilian cadences, up down,
> Up down. It is a war that never ends.
>
> Yet it depends on yours. The two are one.
> They are a plural, a right and left, a pair,
> Two parallels that meet if only in

>The meeting of their shadows or that meet
>In a book in a barrack, a letter from Malay.

These lines turn not only on "Notes" but on many years devoted to the shadowy relationship of poetry and politics: the two are one, but only in the sense that they remain distinct from each other, meeting not so much in the theory of what constitutes the domain of poetic or political discourse, but in specific historical moments: a book in a barrack, a letter from Malay. When a phantom composed of the "genius of poets in old lands" appeared to Whitman in "As I Ponder'd in Silence," charging that "the theme of War, the fortune of battles, / The making of perfect soldiers" is the only subject fit for "ever-enduring bards," Whitman responded that his book also sang of a war, "and a longer and greater one than any." Stevens also wants to emphasize the importance of his poetic war, but not at the expense of the war that soldiers fight; unlike Whitman, he was demure in the face of the phantom. Speaking in the coda to "Notes" is the same voice that offered this opinion in a 1939 *Partisan Review*: "The question respecting the responsibility of writers in war is a very theoretical question respecting an extremely practical state of affairs. A war is a military state of affairs, not a literary one. Conceding that the propagandists don't agree, does it matter that they don't agree? The role of the writer in war remains the fundamental role of the writer intensified and concentrated." This statement does not represent an aesthete's credo but testifies to years of worry given to formulating an unexaggerated account of the social function of poetry.

The "idea" of "Notes toward a Supreme Fiction" is the role of the writer in a time of war, which is tantamount to saying, in the terms of Stevens's statement, that the poem is about a writer's purpose at any time—even a time of peace. There is a tension here, and the sequence acknowledges the imperatives of both positions. At the conclusion of "Extracts from Addresses to the Academy of Fine Ideas," Stevens would allow himself only the most circumscribed comment on the soldier, recognizing how a poet's words might seem either trivial or pretentious in contrast to the enormity of wartime loss; but, of course, Stevens went on to write many poems about the enormity of soldiers themselves. Similarly, having concluded *Parts of a World* with a statement on the relation of poetry and war, he later not only refused to make such statements but chastized poets who did so. And having directed his publisher to focus the reader's experience of "Notes" through the final canto's address to the soldier, Stevens was uncertain once the book appeared. Wondering if he had capitulated to the public taste for war poetry, he called "the lines on the back" the "only thing that I have ever felt any doubt about." More than the address to the soldier as such, it is this tension between explic-

itness and reticence—between the need to acknowledge the special imperatives of a war and the desire to return to the humdrum world of peace—that
marks "Notes" as the product of the world as Stevens found it in 1942. Stevens never thought he had completed the sequence; he entertained plans to
expand it to "at least double its present length." And if he felt that the idea
of the sequence could be apprehended through the soldier poem, he did not
think of that canto as a resting place. In this sense, readers of Stevens who
have reservations about the coda to "Notes" are right; but neither the discomfort nor the coda itself may be dismissed.

Examining the place of Stevens's poetry in the 1930s, I pointed out that
the challenge poets felt during that decade was not new; the political conditions of the decade only made more explicit a challenge Stevens had felt (in
the most matter-of-fact ways) ever since he left Harvard and found a job.
During the Second World War, new conditions made the challenge seem
urgent in new ways. As soon as the war began, the question was raised—
Where are the war poets?—but in 1939 the question did not bear the same
cultural authority that it had in 1914. Stevens was recognizing a common
opinion when he noted this remark from an essay on the duty of a writer in
wartime: "Art is individual and the artist, therefore, is an individualist and no
demands can be made on him from the outside." Statements such as this were
common because extraordinary demands were being placed on writers. During the 1930s, the pressure for poetry to make its political allegiances explicit
had generally come from the left, but during the war it tended to come from
the conservative establishment, reinforced by the wartime ideological consensus of American culture: these were the voices Stevens named "propagandists" in his remark in the *Partisan Review*.

First as Librarian of Congress and later as chief of the wartime Office of
Facts and Figures (a vehicle for government propaganda), Archibald Mac-
Leish was swiftly becoming the most prominent voice of America's literary
conscience. Future generations, said MacLeish in "The Irresponsibles"
(1940), "will note that certain young novelists and poets . . . gave up their
lives as writers and enlisted in the hopeless armies to fight brutality with force.
But of those who truly faced this danger not with their bodies but with their
minds, . . . they will record the names of very few." MacLeish makes the
comparison of soldier and poet that Stevens offers in the coda to "Notes,"
but unlike Stevens, he does not wax elegiac or even generous in the face of
the soldier's bitter end: poets, not soldiers, fight the true battle for democracy,
and it ought to be the poet's duty not only to support the Allied cause but to
make its ideals a reality. Even when Stevens came close to granting poetry
such power, he rarely allowed it to trivialize the function of discourses more
directly linked to action. MacLeish was a parody of Whitman for his time,

and Stevens is reported to have turned "purple with rage" at the mention of MacLeish's name.

Responding to MacLeish and to Van Wyck Brooks (who was offering similarly sweeping condemnations of contemporary writers), Dwight Macdonald wrote in the *Partisan Review* that these critics were themselves becoming mouthpieces "for totalitarian cultural values": "It is an attempt to impose on the writer *from outside* certain socio-political values, and to provide a rationalization for damning his work *esthetically* if it fails to conform to these *social values*." Macdonald was not indulging in hyperbole. Brooks had suggested that communities organize committees to collect objects made in Germany and destroy them in public bonfires. In the same month that France fell to the Nazis, the Supreme Court upheld the right of a Pennsylvania school system to expel students who refused to salute the flag; the following month, Roosevelt signed the Smith Act, requiring 3,500,000 aliens to be fingerprinted and stipulating legal penalties for any spoken or written word that provoked "insubordination, disloyalty, mutiny, or refusal of duty by any member of the military or naval forces."

Such violent expressions of nationalism gained enormous prestige during the war, and Stevens sometimes succumbed to their pressure—despite his usual contempt for MacLeish. This was the period when Stevens and his wife became fascinated with genealogy, and their concern with private history led to an equally passionate interest in their American heritage. "It is a curious thing that virtue should show itself in the love of one's country," Stevens told Barbara Church, "but it does." Although he protested that it was "not a question of nationalism," Stevens advised José Rodríguez Feo that work published in his Cuban magazine ought to be "expressing the genius of your country." By 1940 Stevens was not alone in searching out a "usable past" for himself (Van Wyck Brooks's phrase itself became popular once again), and neither was he unique in idealizing American soldiers or remarking that the United States should not enter the war without a commitment to dominate the postwar world. Even some Europeans agreed with the latter sentiment. "We may and should deplore Mr. Brooks's bludgeoning attacks on modern writers," said René Wellek in 1942, but ". . . Mr. Brooks gives voice to a genuine need of our time: a return to the sources of the American national tradition which fortunately is also the hope of all humanity."

Stevens was not undivided, however, and it is this division which makes "Notes toward a Supreme Fiction" a far richer poem than Stevens's wartime odes to soldiers. In addition to the Stevens who wrote the soldier poems, there is once again the Stevens who declined to offer statements on war poetry, the Stevens who for many years had scorned the kind of ideological coercion Brooks and MacLeish now championed: these two tendencies in Stevens had been at war ever since William Jennings Bryan had led the Populist charge in 1900. If the former Stevens becomes all too apparent in "Repetitions of a Young Captain," the latter Stevens dominates "Notes toward a Supreme Fiction," the poem in which he makes good on the promise offered in "Contrary Theses (II)," rejecting "the bombastic intimations" and "the martyrs à la mode" for (I choose this word carefully) the generosity of the "abstract." Neither was this Stevens alone in demanding in 1942 that "It Must Be Abstract"; the phrase had a strong political charge. For writers and painters who opposed MacLeish during the war, modernist extravagance regained its authority, and the intricacies of a text like *Ulysses* or a painting by Picasso began to seem less elitist than generous—a common language rather than a private one, an internationalist art rather than an art of nationalist or regionalist allegiance.

The insistence (by Stevens or by Jackson Pollock) that it must be abstract was not a retreat from the political content of the social realism of the 1930s; it was a rebellion against the coercive demand for ideological explicitness, and it was an assertion of internationalist values. The Abstract Expressionists' "globalist" aesthetic coincided with Wendell Willkie's wartime crusade for "one world." Willkie began his career as a Wilsonian Democrat, moved to the opposite party when Democrats distanced themselves from that progressive tradition, and was ultimately rejected by fellow Republicans for his internationalist views. After losing to Roosevelt in the presidential election of 1940, Willkie set out on a 31,000 mile trip to the Soviet Union, China, and the Middle East. *One World* (1943), his chronicle of the journey, was an idealistic plea for international cooperation: Willkie praised the Soviet Union as a "vital new society," excoriated the last-gasp imperialism of the British Empire, criticized Roosevelt's unwillingness to come to terms with American racism, condemned the League of Nations as an excuse for perpetuating the European colonial system, and championed the United Nations as the means to avoid the nationalist conflicts that had led to both world wars. The painters Adolph Gottlieb and Mark Rothko offered the aesthetic counterpart to this credo when they titled their 1943 Abstract Expressionist manifesto "Globalism," condemning "narrow political isolationism" and calling for art that made sense of "the present world upheaval" in a language transcending the barriers of nationality and class—the language of abstraction.

It is necessary to remember that wartime internationalism eventually became a kind of cold war "nationalist internationalism" in which Abstract Expressionism was implicated: in worlds artistic and military, a vision of the international community was to be sustained (as Wellek's remark suggests) only by the force of American dominance. Serge Guilbaud makes this point forcefully in his account of the politics of Abstract Expressionism, but he also maintains that during the war, an aesthetic of abstraction initially arose as a healthy kind of "political apoliticalism": it "provided a way for avant-garde artists to preserve their sense of social 'commitment' (so important to artists of the Depression generation) while eschewing the art of propaganda and illustration." Scorned throughout the 1930s for being disengaged from historical reality, abstract art now seemed like a viable political alternative as the right appropriated the left's commitment to social realism. Even during the 1930s, the most intelligent theorists of abstraction—like Meyer Schapiro, in "The Nature of Abstract Art" in the short-lived *Marxist Quarterly* in 1937— saw that the distinction between realism and abstraction was in the first place built on a naive conception of representation. Schapiro pointed out that an utterly "realistic" art (directly engaged with historical reality) and an utterly "pure" art (divorced from historical reality) were equally impossible: "All renderings of objects, no matter how exact they seem, even photographic, proceed from values, methods and viewpoints which somehow shape the image and often determine its contents. . . . There is no 'pure' art, unconditioned by experience; all fantasy and formal construction . . . are shaped by experience and by non-aesthetic concerns." To say "it must be abstract" is to assert that "it cannot possibly be otherwise than abstract" and that "it cannot possibly leave the historical world behind."

Stevens would have agreed with all these corollaries to his first "note." The painter Robert Motherwell recognized as much when he quoted from "The Poems of Our Climate" in his essay "Painters' Objects" (1944). Stevens's poem bolstered his assertion that while "painting plainly has always been a species of abstraction," and while wartime abstract painting was "a protest against naturalistic descriptiveness," a purely abstract painting, divorced from the historical world, would be undesirable—even if it were possible.

> Say even that this complete simplicity
> Stripped one of all one's torments, concealed
> The evilly compounded, vital I
> And made it fresh in a world of white,
> A world of clear water, brilliant-edged,
> Still one would want more, one would need more,
> More than a world of white and snowy scents.

The first movement of "Notes toward a Supreme Fiction," headed "It Must Be Abstract," begins with a desire for a reduction to "complete simplicity" or what Stevens now calls the "first idea." What do you mean by abstract? asked Hi Simons after the poem was published. "The abstract does not exist," answered Stevens, "but . . . the fictive abstract is as immanent in the mind of the poet, as the idea of God is immanent in the mind of the theologian. The poem is a struggle with the inaccessibility of the abstract." If the supreme fiction is abstract, in other words, it is unrepresentable; yet in order to be talked about, it must assume a representable shape. That paradox had dogged Stevens throughout the poems of "Owl's Clover," as he tried again and again to locate some force that could bridge the gap separating classes, nations, and races. Could that ideal common denominator be art? asks Stevens in "Mr. Burnshaw and the Statue"; no, art does not speak to all people in all places and of all classes equally well. "A Duck for Dinner" offers the idea of the hero, but heroes can become monsters as soon as they are more than abstract—as soon, that is, as we begin to paint or sing or talk about them. Finally, "Somber Figuration" proposes the possibility of the "subman," a shared unconscious, and because this entity is more chimerical, more universal because more indefinite, it may suffice—but not for long. We have seen that in writing "Owl's Clover" (each poem revising the one before) Stevens learned just how much hinged on the imperative that "it must be abstract"— and learned how difficult an imperative it is to obey.

"I have no idea of the form that a supreme fiction would take," said Stevens to Henry Church, the bewildered dedicatee of the poem. "The NOTES start out with the idea that it would not take any form: that it would be abstract." Ideally, the supreme fiction must bear no shape, since any particular shape (the soldier as hero, for example) depends on particular cultural values in which some people may see themselves but in which others may not. In "Notes toward a Supreme Fiction" Stevens was able to find a way to explain (as he could not in "Owl's Clover") that the impossibility of sustaining the imperative "it must be abstract" is not a failure to be overcome but a dialectic to be embraced: the inhibiting struggle of "Owl's Clover" became the productive tension of "Notes," when Stevens saw that the phrase "it must change" is in a way synonymous with "it must be abstract." "Notes toward a Supreme Fiction" does not offer art, Ananke, a hero, or a subman as a globalist idea; instead, it offers necessarily quizzical lines like these, part of the first canto's injunction for the "ephebe" to "become an ignorant man again" and see the sun in its first idea.

> Phoebus is dead, ephebe. But Phoebus was
> A name for something that never could be named.
> There was a project for the sun and is.
>
> There is a project for the sun. The sun
> Must bear no name, gold flourisher, but be
> In the difficulty of what it is to be.

The sun must bear no name, the abstract must not be imaged, yet to speak of the sun is necessarily to name it—gold flourisher—even as we reject previous mythologies of the sun. To "be / In the difficulty of what it is to be" is not only the project of the sun but the mission of the thinker of the supreme fiction: whatever our ultimate value may be, we must constantly rethink it, replacing one representation with another. Stevens suggests in "The Poems of Our Climate" that after the reduction to "complete simplicity" we would want more than that. In the opening of "Notes" he suggests that we have no choice but to feel that desire; we push ourselves toward the complete simplicity of abstraction and in doing so we push ourselves back to the complicated multiplicity of representation. In the third poem of the sequence, Stevens calls this a dialectical movement from "that ever-early candor to its late plural." And in canto VI, when he insists that "It must be visible or invisible, / Invisible or visible or both," he is describing the paradox he faces in attempting to share in language what must (but cannot) remain unrepresented. The danger for Stevens is to become content with any single representation. If the purely abstract as such is never available to us, then the continual effort to remake the supreme fiction is the only way we can approach the condition of abstraction, retaining the fiction's availability to all people in all places and times, international or global rather than national or regional. The job of the ephebe is consequently not simply to dispense with all previous ideas of the sun but to build new ideas, new sets of value, all the while recognizing their contingency, their status as humanly constructed metaphors.

This task of continual remaking is not poetic in the narrow sense of the word. Because Stevens addresses the ephebe in canto V as the typical poet in the typical garret—"you, ephebe, look from your attic window, / Your mansard with a rented piano. You lie / In silence upon your bed"—we tend to overlook the full resonance of the word *ephebe:* in ancient Athens the ephebe was a young man who spent two years on garrison duty, guarding the city of which he was preparing to become a full-fledged citizen. Throughout "Notes" the ephebe's mission is poetic inasmuch as it is civic. The address to the soldier in the coda is an address to the ephebe, and even in canto V the ephebe is a poet who works nights in the garrison. He contends not only with a violence within ("You writhe and press / A bitter utterance from your writhing") but with a violence without; as a modern day ephebe, he is a firewatcher, surveying the rooftops of the blacked-out city: "You look / Across the roofs as sigil and as ward / And in your centre mark them and are cowed . . ." Stevens wrote these lines during the height of the blitz (3000 Londoners were killed on May 10, 1942, alone), but he represented the

aggression in pointedly antihuman and internationalist terms, emphasizing
(as he told Leonard Van Geyzel in Ceylon) that the inhuman "catastrophe"
was inescapable throughout the world: the lion, "Master by foot and jaws and
by the mane, / Most supple challenger," overpowers the desert, while the
elephant "Breaches the darkness of Ceylon with blares." Although the
ephebe is intimidated by this violence, Stevens concludes that this young poet
will one day master the challenge of a violence within—and that this young
soldier will one day tame the animalistic aggression of the violence without.

> These are the heroic children whom time breeds
> Against the first idea—to lash the lion,
> Caparison elephants, teach bears to juggle.

The ephebe has much to learn before he can shoulder these full responsibilities of citizenship (only in the coda do soldier and poet finally stand side
by side, different but necessary to each other), and the rest of "Notes" is the
ephebe's education. Here in canto V his heroism is only a measure of his
potential, and the purpose of the remaining cantos of "It Must Be Abstract"
is to confect an idea of heroism that will allow the potential to be realized.
Two qualifications persist: the ephebe must build that idea for himself, and
the idea must remain abstract. In pointed contrast to the other poems of the
Second World War, Stevens is adamant in "Notes toward a Supreme Fiction"
that the hero not be imagined as a soldier or as anything else, that the hero's
power remain a possibility rather than a necessity. It is "not to be realized,"
insists the opening line of canto VI.

Stevens once speculated that a fourth movement of "Notes" would
demand that "It Must Be Human," but canto VI begins the task of building
the abstraction by examining not the idea of the human but the idea of the
weather. "I turn to the weather because that is not inaccessible and is not
abstract," said Stevens of this canto; but just as the nameless sun could exist
only by being named, the weather is already abstracted in the sense that it is
characterized in terms provided by the paintings of Frans Hals. (Stevens's
point here is similar to Schapiro's: what we call realism is abstract in the sense
that it depends on prior representations.) Stevens nevertheless goes on to juxtapose the weather as such with the abstracted idea of the weather ("the giant
of the weather"), but the opposition is not simply between the real and the
unreal; a new idea of the weather is replacing an older one.

> The weather and the giant of the weather,
> Say the weather, the mere weather, the mere air:
> An abstraction blooded, as a man by thought.

As Helen Vendler has noticed, the human enters the poem here "only as an illustration" of this complex relation between the weather and its "giant." That suggests that the ensuing discussion of the idea of the human is as mediated or contingent as the discussion of the weather has been. Having constructed a gigantic or heroic idea of something as ethereal but undeniably present as weather, Stevens approaches the even more elusive but even more present idea of what it means to be a citizen of humanity—the role the ephebe must assume. "It feels good as it is without the giant," begins canto VII, but the final three cantos of "It Must Be Abstract" insist on the necessity of the process of realizing (more than the realization of) the abstract idea or "giant" of humanity. Stevens will want to remember how pleasant the everyday world seems without this giant, because here again the danger is to become content with any single idea—to allow the giant to become our master rather than the vehicle of our mastery over the wild beasts threatening our peace. Yet he also wants to remember, as he pointed out in the juxtaposition of the weather with its idea or giant, that this opposition is more complicated than it seems. We never live without some idea of what it means to be human, and in this sense to say that it feels good "without the giant" is to deceive ourselves. When we feel that way, we have simply become so used to one idea of what it means to be human that we think of our humanity as natural rather than manufactured; we deny our responsibility for the terms of our humanity.

Canto VIII begins by interrogating the method of constructing this giant or "major man" out of "the MacCullough," the sample human being who will be our model.

> Can we compose a castle-fortress-home,
> Even with the help of Viollet-le-Duc,
> And set the MacCullough there as major man?

Because Viollet-le-Duc is usually dismissed as the poetaster of architects, the answer to this question is commonly assumed to be no. B. J. Leggett has shown on the contrary that in Henri Focillon's *Life of Forms in Art*, the source from which Stevens learned about this nineteenth-century restorer of medieval buildings, Focillon praises Viollet-le-Duc for his understanding that "even the largest cathedrals are always at human scale. But the relation of that scale to such enormous dimensions impresses us immediately both with the sense of our own measure—the measure of nature itself—and with the sense of a dizzy immensity that exceeds nature at every point." The help of Viollet-le-Duc is precisely what Stevens or his ephebe requires in constructing an idea of human potential that is both immense, transcending the merely human, and yet nothing but human. Still, Viollet-le-Duc may help construct the dwelling place of "major man" (the home that is in wartime not only a castle but a fortress), but the construction of the giant who lives there remains more difficult: how does the MacCullough become the major man without becoming a giant unrelated in size to our humanity? This MacCullough is "the" MacCullough in the sense that Yeats writes of "the" O'Rahilly (marking that particular O'Rahilly the head of his clan); and though "the Mac-Cullough is MacCullough" (though "the" person remains "a" person), it "does not follow that major man is man." Here Stevens is especially wary of the oppressive side of heroism that he elides in the more explicit soldier poems: as he puts it in "Contrary Theses (II)," he does not want the "bombastic intimations" of the inhuman master, but he desires something more than what the ordinarily human world may offer—something that will differentiate human beings at their best from the wild beasts we can too easily become.

Stevens said that MacCullough was "any name, any man," and in the sense that he is the brother of Crispin and Fat Jocundus, those champions of the humdrum, he is. Stevens did not pick the name casually, however, for as Bloom points out, "MacCullough was the name of a hardheaded clan, producing eminent political economists, geologists, and even the American Secretary of the Treasury when Stevens was a student at Harvard." MacCullough is a grown-up ephebe: a responsible citizen, a poet only in the limited sense in which Crispin, having returned to "social nature," might be said to be a poet. An exchange of letters Stevens had with Henry Church helps clarify MacCullough's place in the poem. After Church read "Notes," he sent Stevens one of Nietzsche's aphorisms, suggesting it as a possible gloss on the poem: "Why might not the world *which concerns us*—be a fiction?" Stevens dismissed this remark as "the commonplace idea that the world exists only in the mind," adding that while that sense of the word *fiction* is present in "Notes," the poem pushes for a more communal and active sense of the word: "We are confronted by a choice of ideas: the idea of God and the idea of man. The purpose of the NOTES is to suggest the possibility of a third idea: the idea of a fictive being, or state, or thing as the object of belief by way of making up for that element of humanism which is its chief defect." Once again Stevens approaches the paradox of the abstract: he wants something more than merely human, something unrepresentable and universal, yet something that remains merely human in the finest sense—ordinary, humdrum, a state or place where all human beings might feel at home. Church was confused, for he could think of humanism as concerning something humdrum only in the worst sense; to him, humanism conjured up "invariably the picture of some supreme court justice . . . who has taken his 'retraite,' gone to the country to translate Horace or Pindar." Church was still confused, for

Stevens told him that such an idea of humanism was exactly what he had in mind: "Your 'Supreme Court Justice' is the MacCullough of the NOTES." Stevens thought more of the daily lives of Court justices and Treasury Secretaries than Church did, but the project of "Notes" remains the difficult task of discerning the heroic potential in a life of dull routine, of constructing a heroic idea of the human being who (as Stevens will put it in the crucial ninth canto of "It Must Give Pleasure") is not "the exceptional monster" but "he that of repetition is most master."

Canto VIII concludes with an attempted apotheosis of the MacCullough into a "leaner being" of "greater aptitude and apprehension"; but even though the canto's syntax renders the transformation triply contingent ("If . . . might . . . As if"), the following canto dismisses this "romantic intoning": "apotheosis is not / The origin of the major man." And neither is "reason's click-clack" the source. Stevens is pushing toward what he will ultimately call "sensible ecstasy," a way of living with human limitation that does not disguise the ordinary with a hyperbolic grandeur or an equally exaggerated sense of loss; MacCullough is not the exaggeratedly masculine hero of "Repetitions of a Young Captain." This figure is infinitely elusive, and the final cantos of "It Must Be Abstract" defer his proper realization over and over again. "Give him / No names. Dismiss him from your images," insists canto IX, emphasizing again that this ideal hero must exist only as an abstraction, a potential. But just as the effort to allow the sun to remain nameless involved the naming of the sun, and just as the effort to isolate the weather as such depended on prior representations of the weather, it is ultimately impossible not to violate these commands. Canto X attempts to sidestep the injunction against naming or representing the abstraction by discussing the nature of its heroic potential.

> The major abstraction is the idea of man
> And major man is its exponent, abler
> In the abstract than in his singular,
>
> More fecund as principle than particle,
> Happy fecundity, flor-abundant force,
> In being more than an exception, part,
>
> Though an heroic part, of the commonal.
> The major abstraction is the commonal,
> The inanimate, difficult visage.

These lines do not solve the problems proposed by the previous three cantos: we still do not know if MacCullough may become the major man who may stand for the major abstraction, and we still have not found a substitute for the romantic intonings of apotheosis. The lines do tell us that this idea of man is abstract in the sense that it is plural rather than singular, standing for the many rather than for the individual, for the principle rather than the example, for the rule rather than the exception. And, more important, the lines emphasize that this major abstraction, though heroic or more than human, is not only part of the "commonal"—"The major abstraction *is* the commonal." And still the question remains: What could possibly represent this "difficult visage"? Stevens seems to be pushing toward a condition that could be embodied only by a Wittgensteinian silence or Dante's multifoliate rose. Yet the canto demands "Who is it?"—who will bear this image, if only for a moment, of everything that everyone holds dear? The question must be answered, yet the stricture to "dismiss him from your images" stands firm, and the question only breeds more questions: Who does not survey the multitudes of humanity, "these separate figures one by one, / And yet see only one"? Who is it? Just when it seems that the canto could not possibly answer the question, Stevens capitulates, violating the strictures against naming, and wrenches the canto from the theory of abstraction to the practice of social realism. Expecting something like the multifoliate rose or an image by Mark Rothko or Barnett Newman, we meet instead the man on the dump.

> Cloudless the morning. It is he. The man
> In that old coat, those sagging pantaloons,
>
> It is of him, ephebe, to make, to confect
> The final elegance, not to console
> Nor sanctify, but plainly to propound.

Thinking back to the beginning of "Notes," with the first canto's instant contradiction of the call for abstraction ("The sun / Must bear no name, gold flourisher"), this image of the supreme fiction should come as no surprise; yet the lines are among the most surprising in all of Stevens's poetry. If we are prepared for the paradox that it is not possible to discuss the supreme fiction without ignoring the poem's opening admonition, we are not prepared after all the talk of giants and heros for the particular image Stevens selects in the inevitable descent into representation. The Chaplinesque tramp, the image of humanity at its most humdrum, seems impossibly distant from the heroic figure who "in a million diamonds sums us up." But that disjunction is precisely Stevens's point: "The long and short of it is that we have to fix abstract objectives and then to conceal the abstract figures in actual appearance. A hero won't do, but we like him much better when he doesn't look it." No response to the question "Who is it?" is fully adequate, but if the major abstraction is to encompass the full range of the "commonal," then the poem cannot strain to inhuman heights but must hug the ordinary human world, propounding it plainly. The man in the coat and sagging pantaloons is far more likeable than any of Stevens's more bombastic wartime heros, and while not everyone may see him- or herself in this figure (no single representation could be truly universal), it is designed to evoke our common sympathies. It is an image of the "lingua franca" Stevens will invoke in the ninth canto of "It Must Change": the common tongue, the "peculiar potency of the general."

The climax of "It Must Be Abstract" demonstrates, as Schapiro pointed out in another context, that the political impulse behind the abstract canvas is not necessarily so different from what we call social realism. Stevens chooses an image evoking a conventional idea of the historically engaged aesthetic because he wants to emphasize that the abstraction is not a retreat from the "commonal" or from the everyday historical world. Unlike MacLeish, who insists on that realist aesthetic (not recognizing the conventionality of its terms) and presents its images as universally valuable, Stevens immediately recognizes the inadequacy of his man in the sagging pantaloons. Once unveiled, the image is immediately dismissed from the poem—along with any talk of giants, heros, or major men—never to reappear. The man in the old coat and sagging pantaloons must go the way of Ananke and the subman, since the only way to approach the fulfillment of the desire for a universal abstraction is to keep the desire unfulfilled—to keep the question "Who is it?" difficult to answer, and, having offered an answer, insist that "It Must Change."

The second canto of that division of "Notes" is Stevens's response to "propagandists" like MacLeish. "No politician can command the imagination," said Stevens in "The Noble Rider," "directing it to do this or that. Stalin might grind his teeth the whole of a Russian winter and yet all the poets in the Soviets might remain silent the following spring." When Stevens wrote these lines, Dwight Macdonald was accusing the American government of Stalinism. The president was Roosevelt; the director of his Office of Facts and Figures was the poet whose most famous lines ordained that "a poem should not mean / But be."

> The President ordains the bee to be
> Immortal. The President ordains. But does
> The body lift its heavy wing, take up,
>
> Again, an inexhaustible being, rise
> Over the loftiest antagonist
> To drone the green phrases of its juvenal?

Such a being may describe its juvenility, its youth, its changeability, but it may not sing the lines of Juvenal, poet of the Roman state—at least it cannot be ordained to do so; as "Notes" demonstrates at large, the task of becoming a civic poet is never so simple. These lines suggest that we could paraphrase "it must change" as "it cannot possibly do otherwise than change," but the following canto shows what would happen if the propagandist could have his way. If we could answer the question "Who is it?" definitively, if we were able to set up the MacCullough as major man, accepting his unalterable image as the commonal itself, then the man on the dump would become the statue of General Du Puy, immobile, funereal, still, a martyr à la mode—

> a permanence, so rigid
> That it made the General a bit absurd,
>
> Changed his true flesh to an inhuman bronze.
> There never had been, never could be, such
> A man.

Since there is nothing human here, there is nothing heroic; since there is nothing ordinary, there is nothing extraordinary. The statue is the product of the apotheosis Stevens rejected, and like "Esthétique du Mal," "Notes toward a Supreme Fiction" insists that whatever sublimity the world contains will be found in the near, the ordinary, the commonal, the humdrum—and less in the humdrum as such than in our unending effort to discern our finest values in the world Stevens sometimes liked to call "normal": "the chief problems of any artist, as of any man, are the problems of the normal."

In "The American Scholar" Emerson liked to call it the common, the familiar, the low, the suburban.

I ask not for the great, the remote, the romantic; what is doing in Italy or Arabia; what is Greek art, or Provençal minstrelsy; I embrace the common, I explore and sit at the feet of the familiar, the low. Give me insight into to-day, and you may have the antique and future worlds. What would we really know the meaning of? The meal in the firkin; the milk in the pan; the ballad in the street; the news of the boat; the glance of the eye; the form and the gait of the body;—show me the ultimate reason of these matters; show me the sublime presence in the highest spiritual cause lurking, as always it does lurk, in these suburbs and extremities of nature.

As Stevens's thoughts about the American sublime suggest, this sense of wonder in the humdrum is not something Emerson or Stevens could take for granted; paradoxically, sitting at the feet of the familiar requires more effort than rising to the heights of the extraordinary. In his ongoing investigation of ordinary experience, Stanley Cavell asks (apropos of Emerson and Wittgenstein) why the detailing of our everyday world "is something we have to be *made* to do, why it is hard to do." If the idea of "Notes toward a Supreme Fiction" concerns the recovery of ordinary experience (or, more specifically, poetry's role in that act of recovery during a time of war), then why is the poem so defiantly extraordinary? Why is it that when Stevens remarked that the normal is the chief problem of the artist, he also said that in order to solve that problem, the artist needs "everything that the imagination has to give"? And isn't poetry as such—or at least what Stevens called the "essential gaudiness" of poetry—inimical to the normal or the ordinary? Stevens has no ready answer for these questions, but he comes armed with paradoxes. To approach the "potency of the general" in the ninth canto of "It Must Change," he must employ "a peculiar speech," the "lingua franca" compounded with "the imagination's Latin." On another occasion, he remarked that the normal could not exist without the abnormal: "With me, how to write of the normal in a normal way is a problem which I have long since given up trying to solve, because I never feel that I am in the area of poetry until I am a little off the normal. The worst part of this aberration is that I am convinced that it is not an aberration."

The paradox Stevens describes here is what Cavell tries to encapsulate in the phrase "in quest of the ordinary": "the ordinary is always the subject of a quest and the object of an inquest." Following Emerson, Cavell wants to show that there is in philosophy a deep wish to complicate and escape the ordinary world (he thinks of this desire as skepticism), a wish that is paradoxically a necessary part of the effort to recover that world: the wonder of the meal in the firkin or the man in the sagging pantaloons is not apprehensible until we have become estranged from it first; the sublimity of the humdrum is an achievement—an achieving—and only through the complexities of poems like "The Comedian" and "Notes" will the ephebe achieve a "social nature" in which such poetry is no longer necessary. Only by voyaging to the fantastic "land of the lemon trees" do the mariners of the twenty-ninth canto of "An Ordinary Evening in New Haven" realize the wonder of the common world, which they never really abandoned: "We are back once more in the land of the elm trees, / But folded over, turned round." Discussing the theory of abstraction, Stevens described the same dialectic: abstraction leads the artist to "pick up a certain amount of the metaphysical vision of the day," but "the physical never seems newer than when it is emerging from the metaphysical"; "the momentum toward abstraction" provokes "the counter-effect of a greatly increased feeling for things that one sees and touches." Offered as a description of abstract painting, these sentences even more persuasively characterize the effect of the emergence of the plain MacCullough from the intricate evasions of "It Must Be Abstract." Cavell says that "the self-defeat of skepticism is precisely the point of it," and I think we could best appreciate the power of Stevens's finest work by thinking of its point as the self-defeat of poetry. In saying so, I do not mean to diminish in any way that poetry's power, its verbal delights, its fabulous confections, and its visionary ecstasies—any of the things we expect of a great romantic poet: "The poet represents the mind in the act of defending us against itself," said Stevens; "An art may be of value purely through preventing a society from becoming too assertively, too hopelessly, itself," said Kenneth Burke.

It is a measure of how difficult it is to discern Stevens in quest of the ordinary that the most powerful readers of "Notes" have pushed the poem to the extremities that are the means of the inquest and not the ends of the quest: on the one hand, the Promethean and solipsistic vision of Hoon, and on the other, the inhuman poverty of the Snow Man. Faced with the rejection of apotheosis near the end of "It Must Be Abstract," or with the parallel rejection of the Hoon-like Canon Aspirin near the end of "It Must Give Pleasure," Harold Bloom fights to "clear the Canon Aspirin's good and visionary name" and show that apotheosis is indeed the origin of major man; the qualifications of apotheosis Bloom finds tedious rather than functional: "the reader (any reader) may grow weary of a prophecy that cannot stop deconstructing itself." In contrast, Helen Vendler comes closer to a middle-ground reading of "Notes" when she says that the "most convincing affirmations" in the poem "are those made minimally and depreciatingly"; yet she pushes this reading as close to the reductiveness of the Snow Man as Bloom pushes his to the visionary solipsism of Hoon, and while Bloom finds the Canon Aspirin cantos genuinely apocalyptic, Vendler sees here "the most desperate moment in the whole poem," a moment that "ends in disgust."

There are moments of disgust in "Notes," and there are moments of visionary prophecy. But these moments must be abandoned for what Cavell calls "the willing repetition of days," common experieɪ ce dignified by neither exaltation nor disgust. The task is not easy. The f st canto of "It Must Change" rejects seasonal change as mere repetition: " ɪhe distaste we feel for this withered scene / Is that it has not changed enough. It remains, / It is a repetition." In "Sunday Morning" the vicissitudes of seasonal change made "the willow shiver in the sun"—they made the minutiae of the ordinary world precious, and that was almost consolation enough. Such consolation will ultimately suffice in "Notes" as well, but it must be achieved. In canto VI Stevens expresses his disgust at birdsong, which is nothing but repetition even as it echoes the "bethou, bethou, bethou me" of Shelley's west wind. A minstrel "lacking minstrelsy," the repetitive sparrow does not seem so different from the statue of General Du Puy: "the sparrow is a bird / Of stone, that never changes."

The problem here is not with birdsong as such but with the ear deaf to the song's modulations, the mind that feels an unchanging emotion (disgust, distaste) at a world that changes only in a decidedly uncataclysmic way. In "Sunday Morning" the woman is content with birdsong, but after the birds disperse she feels the "need of some imperishable bliss." Recalling "Sunday Morning," the lover of canto VII "sighs as for accessible bliss," rejecting the "need of any paradise." A desire for bliss merely accessible is somewhat easier to quench, but no sooner is the order filled than the desire "for another accessible bliss" arises. So even if something as earthly and inconsequential as birdsong gives pleasure for only a moment, it would not suffice again. Stevens's humdrum world is not Marvell's garden, where pleasures enact their accessibility. To become reconciled with the ordinary is the quest of "Notes," but the reconciliation does not begin until the phrase "accessible bliss" is revised once more: the eighth canto of "It Must Give Pleasure" proposes "expressible bliss," the new adjective implying that we are responsible for making our pleasures—the world cannot be relied upon to make its pleasures continually accessible. As Stevens put it in the slightly more "theoretic" poem called "Poem With Rhythms" (1941), the mind must turn "to its own figurations," wearing them "*as in the powerful mirror of my wish and will.*"

Yet the opening canto of "It Must Give Pleasure" stands farther from the achievement of "expressible bliss" than any other moment in the poem. Here the desire to belong to a community, the many joined as one, is ridiculed as "common" rather than extolled as the "commonal," as it was at the conclusion of "It Must Be Abstract": to "wear the mane of a multitude" and "to feel the heart / That is the common" is dismissed as "a facile exercise." These lines compose Stevens's most unsympathetic inquest into the limitations of the ordinary experience in "Notes": being customary, even the act of human singing remains static and consequently gives no pleasure—poetry itself has become mere birdsong. What appears to be true pleasure may be found in the extraordinary sensual experience of a glass of Meursault accompanying a dish of lobster Bombay with mango chutney. That is the ambrosial diet of the Canon Aspirin, the uncommon individualist who dominates cantos V through VII. In contrast to his own extravagance, the Canon observes the "sensible ecstasy" of his sister and her two daughters. That phrase, as I have intimated, is crucial, for the simple "poverty" of this small community should not seem lacking in ecstasy beside the Canon: it is the Canon who cannot see the wonder in this family's "pauvred color" and "simple names"—they are to him birdsong, ultimately more mundanely sensible than sensibly ecstatic. As his sister is known for sensible ecstasy, the decidedly masculine Canon ought to be known for "canonical aspiration"—an aspiring so ardent that it becomes merely canonical, like the act of singing exact jubilas, poetry by rote. After humming a fugue of praise to his sister's properly diminished condition, the Canon "came to sleep / And normal things had yawned themselves away." Normal things, above which the Canon must aspire, do not yawn themselves away; the Hoon-like Canon banishes them from the world in which he walked and was: "he was the ascending wings he saw / And moved on them in orbits' outer stars / Descending to the children's bed." When he draws close to earth, the normal world resists his aspirations, forcing him to choose not between his extravagance and the children's ordinariness but *of* them— a choice not to "exclude" the ordinary from the ecstatic but to "include" each in the other. As the oxymoron "sensible ecstasy" suggests, however, that choice was one the Canon's sister had learned to make long before the Canon descended to her ordinary world.

Stevens once defined poetry as "a present perfecting, a satisfaction in the irremediable poverty of life," but I think the struggle of "Notes" is rather to see that this poverty of the ordinary world is remediable. In an early commentary on the poem, Bloom suggested that the choice to "include" the ordinary with the ecstatic at the end of canto VI is "Wordsworthian rather than Blakean, for it insists that the context of fact or nature can be harmonized with the more exuberant context of the poet's apocalyptic desires. The problem in such a harmonization is to cultivate the highly anti-apocalyptic virtue of patience." Stevens had cultivated that virtue for years, but neither the Canon nor Bloom (who ultimately reads the Canon as the high Romantic or Blakean poet whose apocalyptic vision Stevens must not only accept but surpass) is patient enough. The Canon's choice is finally exclusionary, and he recalls the animals that master the landscape with bestial violence, the president who ordains the shape of his world from his self-enclosed capitol, and the lawyers who admire the statue of General Du Puy.

> He imposes orders as he thinks of them,
> As the fox and snake do. It is a brave affair.
> Next he builds capitols and in their corridors,
>
> Whiter than wax, sonorous, fame as it is,
> He establishes statues of reasonable men.

This canto moves on to insist that our orders, our fictions, must be "discovered" rather than "imposed," that our approach to the world (as Hazlitt would suggest) must be disinterested rather than uninterested or interested. The Canon's sister had already achieved that open relationship with her world, and though her "sensible ecstasy" would seem to be what Stevens desires after exposing the Canon's excess, he must exaggerate that excess further before he may see the ordinary world as truly remediable.

Canto VIII begins with the poet's own question ("What am I to believe?"), startlingly flat after the fables of the previous cantos. As usual, the question breeds more questions: If the poet can imagine an angel falling from heaven, an angel willingly forsaking its "golden destiny" and becoming content instead with the very action of his flight, then should not the poet who imagines the angel be no "less satisfied"? Here finally is "expressible bliss," a happiness the self has made rather than accepted, and made from nothing but itself: "I have not but I am and as I am, I am." Bloom reads that line as the Canon's vindication, a confirmation of the Promethean and apocalyptic power; Vendler reads it as a confession of weakness bordering on self-disgust. To me, the line seems poised between these two readings: if the self is everything, it is in danger of becoming nothing, Hoon turned to snow. Bloom needs to choose because he sees the fable of the angel's flight as the point "upon which the whole of *Notes* comes to rest." Canto VIII is indeed the poem's greatest moment of visionary ardor, but the poem rests more steadily (which is to say, paradoxically, more tenuously) on the low point that follows: the neglected but crucial ninth canto, which limps back to the values of sensible ecstasy, community, and the man on the dump. In the return to Crispin's "social nature," the visionary "I" becomes the communal "we"—and "we" can finally hear the beauty of birdsong as "I" alone could not.

> Whistle, forced bugler,
> That bugles for the mate, nearby the nest,
> Cock bugler, whistle and bugle and stop just short,
>
> Red robin, stop in your preludes, practicing
> Mere repetitions. These things at least comprise
> An occupation, an exercise, a work,
>
> A thing final in itself and, therefore, good:
> One of the vast repetitions final in
> Themselves and, therefore, good, the going round
>
> And round and round, the merely going round,
> Until merely going round is a final good,
> The way wine comes at a table in a wood.
>
> And we enjoy like men, the way a leaf
> Above the table spins its constant spin,
> So that we look at it with pleasure, look

> At it spinning its eccentric measure. Perhaps,
> The man-hero is not the exceptional monster,
> But he that of repetition is most master.

Recalling "The Pleasures of Merely Circulating," the "going round / And round and round, the merely going round" might seem in these lines to have "changed to something infinitely more laborious, a treadmill rather than a merry-go-round." The earlier poem does describe a random disorder, innocuous as a child's game. This canto of "Notes" is far less carefree, but instead of the tediousness of middle age, it reveals the sources of the hard-won pleasures of an ordinary life—a life in which the exigencies of surety bonds and poems make equal claims; it offers the achievement of what Cavell calls "the willing repetition of days." Stevens would say of "An Ordinary Evening in New Haven": "here my interest is to try to get as close to the ordinary, the commonplace and the ugly as it is possible for a poet to get. It is not a question of grim reality but of plain reality." Similarly, Stevens's acceptance of repetition in "Notes" is not a descent to grimness; its "serious reflection is composed" (as he would put it in canto XVII of "An Ordinary Evening") "Neither of comic nor tragic but of commonplace." As Eleanor Cook suggests, we must understand in Stevens's use of the word *commonplace* a sense not only of the usual or normal but of the shared or communal. At the conclusion of "Notes," the menu is not Mersault and lobster Bombay but wine at a simple table in the wood; the pleasures of the meal are not, like the Canon's feast, enjoyed by one but by a community: "we look at it with pleasure," says Stevens, using the word *pleasure* in the body of the poem for the first time. The words *joy, bliss, desire,* and *ecstasy* have come and gone, but this pleasure lingers. As part of the "commonal," "we" can now take pleasure in the simplest things—"the way a leaf / Above the table spins its constant spin." And in coming finally to see that the sublime presence does exist in the familiar and the low, we realize that the hero we set out to find was within us all along—not as giant, grotesque, or exceptional monster, but as we are.

In the final canto of "It Must Give Pleasure," the leaf spinning above the communal table becomes the earth itself, its motion nothing but repetition, but repetition now perceived as a continual rebirth rather than routine. "Civil, madam, I am" (not "I have not but I am") says the disembodied voice, addressing an earth now seen as "familiar yet an aberration." This voice is not located in an individual character like the Canon or MacCullough, but as it names the earth the "fat girl," the voice does seem to emanate from a community of men. The terms of Stevens's humanism remain masculine ("we enjoy like men"), and like "Esthétique du Mal," "Notes" casts women in a supporting role; but in "Notes" Stevens seems aware of how experience resists these terms. The poem begins with an injunction against naming, and it ends with a bold act of naming the earth "fat girl." In between, the poem has been at pains to show that we cannot do otherwise than name our world, accepting responsibility for the values that those names impose. While the voice of the final canto says that he must name the earth "flatly, waste no words, / Check your evasions," there is also the recognition that the earth will overthrow his definition as it goes round and round. The repetition here is more uncanny than tedious or palliating, and the quest for stable ground becomes an inquest of the foundation: the name "fat girl" will not stick.

> Even so when I think of you as strong or tired,
>
> Bent over work, anxious, content, alone,
> You remain the more than natural figure. You
> Become the soft-footed phantom, the irrational
>
> Distortion, however fragrant, however dear.

These lines are, in part, a rebuke not only to propagandists like MacLeish but to subtler propagandists like Wallace Stevens—the poet of the wartime hero poems. They are a rebuke to the exceptional monster who may lurk somewhere in even the most generous design for the most ordinary world.

If these final cantos of "Notes toward a Supreme Fiction" seem distant from the historical world that provoked them, the poem's coda restores us to that reality. And the world in the spring of 1942 was far from ordinary. "How gladly with proper words the soldier dies," Stevens concludes, making a desperate attempt to normalize the violence without. Stevens wants desperately to write a poem of peace, not war, and if we are right to approach "Notes" through its war-poem coda, we should leave it through its prologue, a love poem. "And for what, except for you, do I feel love?" begins the poem, leaving the addressee unidentified. It is important to Stevens that this "you" remain ambiguous, a place for possibilities. It could be anything we hold close to ourselves, anything that we might lose: "For a moment in the central of our being, / The vivid transparence that you bring is peace."

Peace: Stevens had concluded "Extracts" with the hope that even though the dead "lie buried in evil earth," the "chants of final peace / Lie in the heart's residuum." And in "The Pastor Caballero" (the poem he chose to precede "Notes" in *Transport*), he dismissed the hero, cutting his "formidable helmet" down to the human size of an everyday hat: "These two go well together, the sinuous brim / And the green flauntings of the hours of peace."

Those hours were achieved when the Second World War ended on September 2, 1945, but at what cost? The Holocaust was a matter of public record in the United States by 1943; and two years later, the total war found its end in the atomic bomb. A cure of this "evil earth" seemed unlikely, and the chants of peace did not come easily to Stevens. Between V-E Day and V-J Day, he already sensed that the transition to peacetime was not to be taken for granted; he speculated that a time of ordinary happiness "among elm trees and farms" was "all over for the present, and for the next generation or two. There is an impression of profound disturbance and of bewilderment as to the outcome, and of intense doubt as to the purposes of the disturbance."

When "Notes toward a Supreme Fiction" was first published by the Cummington Press in 1942, it was designed to be received as a poem of war in a time of war; chosen as the capstone to *Transport to Summer* in 1947, a volume of poetry that already contained the riches of other long poems ("Esthétique du Mal" and "Credences of Summer"), "Notes" was designed to be received as a poem of peace in a time of peace—but a peace still troubled, infected by the debacle of the previous decade: the work's "idea" is altered by its place in history. Like *Parts of a World*, *Transport to Summer* is organized largely chronologically—except that the poem written first is placed last: "Notes" is both the ground and the goal of these poems, the basis of an inquest and the object of the quest. *Transport* in all its senses (but especially military and spiritual) is Stevens's word for this motion; *Summer* is his word for peace. The season does not come naturally, and if it comes at all, following war's extravagant losses, its ordinariness may too easily seem an unwelcome repetition. While "The Pastor Caballero" does prepare us for the dismissal of the hero in a time of peace in "Notes" (MacCullough glimpsed and gone), the shape of *Transport* complicates the transition. Stevens's goal in placing "Notes" at the end of the volume was to make the poem's rehabilitation of the ordinary seem a real possibility after the time of war that other poems recorded. But the enduring success of that recovery is not to be trusted.

In "More Poems for Liadoff," a sequence first published in 1946, Stevens enacts the struggle to put the disaster of the Second World War behind him. Beginning the twelve-poem sequence, "A Woman Sings a Song for a Soldier Come Home" is not optimistic: "the man dies that does not fall. / He walks and dies." The survivors of the war remain infected by its horror. Recalling "Extracts," "Burghers of Petty Death" explains that these ghostly living dead remain victims of the "total" death of total war, not the natural death of peace, which seems petty in comparison: "But there is a total death, / A devastation, a death of great height / And depth, covering all surfaces." Even in peacetime, no chants of peace are possible; only burghers of petty death would be so easily soothed. What is desired here (as Stevens puts it in "Mountains Covered with Cats") is "War's miracle begetting that of peace," but the natural act of "begetting" will not take place naturally.

"Extraordinary References," the penultimate poem in the sequence, suggests a way out of this impasse. Instead of searching the past for a golden age of peace, Stevens takes comfort in the past's disasters. The poem grew from Stevens's postwar visit to the Tulpehocken region of Pennsylvania (described in the essay "About One of Marianne Moore's Poems") and also from the years of genealogical research (the names and incidents are taken from Stevens's ancestry, though he mixes several lines of descent into a single narrative). A mother tells her child about her ancestry: *"Your great-grandfather was an Indian fighter."* The tale is not simply nostalgic or self-congratulatory. Stevens's interest in his past was sometimes both those things, but the interest was also framed, made meaningful, by a commitment to the present: his genealogical investigations coincided, especially after the wartime deaths of his brother and sister, with an equally passionate devotion to his nieces and nephews. Similarly, in "Extraordinary References," the tale of the great-grandfather is told for the benefit of the present, not as a past moment simply yearned for. The placid landscape of the Tulpehocken "refers" to this past—this "barbed, barbarous rising"—and "has peace."

> These earlier dissipations of the blood
>
> And brain, as the extraordinary references
> Of ordinary people, places, things,
> Compose us in a kind of eulogy.
>
> *My Jacomyntje! This first spring after the war*
> *In which your father died, still breathes for him*
> *And breathes again for us a fragile breath.*

The land recovered from previous wars, and Stevens's hope is that the land will recover once again. The "extraordinary" will give way to the "ordinary," and the simple acts of daily life will help to reinforce a fragile peacetime world built on a history of atrocity: the woman of "Extraordinary References" is the Canon Aspirin's sister, and simply by tying "the hair-ribbons of the child" she "has peace." Stevens chooses this phrase ("has peace") carefully, repeating it twice: peace is not to be earned or chosen or longed for. Its origins are mysterious; it is to be had. As in "Esthétique du Mal," Stevens survives in the shadow of the volcano by focusing on little things. In "Attempt to Discover Life," the final poem of "More Poems for Liadoff," a waitress heaps up flowers on a table in "the magnificence of a volcano." A "cadaverous person," one of the living dead from "A Woman Sings a Song for a Soldier Come

Home," enters the restaurant, and "Among fomentations of black bloom and of white bloom. / The cadaverous persons were dispelled."

"Credences of Summer" follows the poems for Liadoff in *Transport*, and as Charles Berger has suggested, it "celebrates the first full summer since the end of the war." It also celebrates the fecund Pennsylvania landscape of "Extraordinary References," but in "Credences" the celebration is wary and tentative: "We should not be surprised that its portrait of a peaceful summer day is shadowed from the beginning by a dark countersong, nor that Stevens becomes the latest poet to discover the significance of *et in Arcadia ego*." One problem with the Oley valley is that its plentiful fecundity has become "A land too ripe for enigmas"; its peace is an "arrested peace"—"the barren-ness / Of the fertile thing that can attain no more." This is a world that must change, and if the need for change is not attended to, a soldier may be the one thing "easily born" from the barrenness.

> The bristling soldier, weather-foxed, who looms
> In the sunshine is a filial form and one
> Of the land's children, easily born.

While in "More Poems for Liadoff" Stevens tried to neutralize the soldier's lingering threat, depending on a war-torn landscape to heal itself, he suggests in "Credences of Summer" that the same landscape generates the soldier, and just as "naturally." There is no war for this soldier to fight, but the implied threat is that his presence will generate one in turn.

From "Credences" we turn in *Transport* to "The Pastor Caballero" and finally to "Notes": the same threat lingers in the "hours of peace" Stevens cherishes in both these poems. The past assures Stevens that the wounds inflicted by the Second World War will heal, and it reminds him that the wounds will be inflicted once again. Published in *Transport to Summer* after the war was over, "Notes" does not seem to be the same wartime sequence it was designed to be in 1942 (just as Abstract Expressionist paintings would eventually not seem part of a struggle over nationalist propaganda). But after Stevens achieves the willing repetition of days that is his peace, after the final cantos extol the ordinary beauties of a bird's song and a summer night, the coda to "Notes toward a Supreme Fiction" reminds us that there is a war that never ends; it suggests that those beauties, however arduously achieved, might lull us into an arrested peace or might allow us to forget. This is something of which Stevens himself sometimes needed to be reminded during the final postwar years of his life. And if the coda to "Notes toward a Supreme Fiction" remains at odds with poems immediately preceding it, that is because, in a necessary way, it is.

VI

The Affluent Mundo

17

The Ultimate Politician

By the time *Transport to Summer* appeared in 1947, Ezra Pound had been incarcerated at the Disciplinary Training Center near Pisa, transported to the United States and arraigned on charges of treason, declared mentally unfit for trial, and remanded to St. Elizabeths Hospital in Washington, D.C. Before the court ruled on Pound's sanity, his supporters mobilized to secure his release, or at least to avert the possibility of his execution. In November 1945 Charles Norman (Pound's future biographer) asked Stevens to join Cummings, Williams, F. O. Matthiessen, Conrad Aiken, and other writers in offering a statement. Stevens declined to make any public remarks, but in correspondence with Norman he responded as the lawyer he was, marking careful discriminations in a case clouded with ambiguities: "There are a number of things that could well be said in his defense. . . . One such possibility is that the acts of propagandists should not entail the same consequences as the acts of a spy or informer because no one attaches really serious importance to propaganda." What may or may not constitute propaganda, Stevens recognized from his own experience, is difficult to say; and the point when propaganda becomes an act with real consequences is equally difficult to isolate, especially when the alleged propaganda takes the form of Pound's particular kind of ranting: "I don't believe that the law of treason should apply to chatter on the radio when it is recognizably chatter." Stevens would not commit himself to an opinion on Pound's guilt or innocence without more complete information on the relationship of his words and his actions. On the one hand, he remained wary of a condemnation fueled by the cheapened patriotism of postwar élan; on the other hand, he was equally suspicious of any special pleading for a so-called poetic genius: "I repeat that the question of his distinction seems to me to be completely irrelevant. If his poetry is in point, then so are Tokyo Rose's singing and wise-cracking."

In July 1948 the *Pisan Cantos* were published, and the following February they were awarded the first annual Bollingen Prize for poetry by the Library of Congress. This would be the only Bollingen Prize awarded under the auspices of the Library of Congress; given the controversy Pound's work aroused, the government decided that poetry was too politically volatile for the Library to handle, and responsibility for the prize was remanded to an institution better equipped to deflect the attention: Yale University. Selecting the *Pisan Cantos* for the award, the Fellows in American Letters of the Library of Congress (Aiken, Auden, Louise Bogan, Eliot, Lowell, Allen Tate, and Robert Penn Warren, among others) knew they were asking for trouble, and they defended their choice in advance: "To permit other considerations than that of poetic achievement to sway the decision would destroy the significance of the award and would in principle deny the validity of that objective perception of value on which civilized society must rest." Stevens had earlier maintained that Pound's poetic distinction was irrelevant to questions concerning his political actions; using what Stevens might have called the Tokyo Rose defense, the fellows maintained that Pound's political actions were irrelevant to the judgment of his poetic distinction.

Their subsequent statements defending the prize marked the ultimate attenuation of the New Criticism into a vehicle for cold war quietism and retreat. A criticism that had been shaped by Burke, Empson, and Blackmur as a participant in a dialogue among varieties of politically minded criticism in the 1930s had settled into the apolitical formalism for which New Criticism is most often remembered today. Faced with a text so extraordinarily blatant in its autobiographical and historical resonances as the *Pisan Cantos*, the fallacies intentional and affective could be maintained only by a blinded will. If such critical perspectives were to retain their power, and if future political controversies were not to infect the judgment of literary merit, then a text more suitable than Pound's was required. When the judges convened the following year under the auspices of Yale University, the second Bollingen Prize was awarded to Wallace Stevens.

I think that three different versions of Stevens must compete for our attention when we look back to this moment in 1950: first, the poet who wrote "Owl's Clover" and "Notes toward a Supreme Fiction" in the late 1930s and early 1940s; second, the poet whose postwar work of the late 1940s was collected in *The Auroras of Autumn* (1950); and third, the poet whose entire corpus could be appropriated in the 1950s by the principles of the later New Criticism. The third Stevens received the Bollingen Prize, and he is closer to the second Stevens than to the first. One of my goals throughout this book has been to bring the first Stevens—the poet engaged by the world around him—into sharper focus: to show how Stevens's interest in poetic ambiguity or his concern with the limitations of the social function of poetry is part of a carefully modulated effort to assert the historicity of poetry and the political power of poets. Along the way, I have tried to answer those readers who see Stevens's aesthetic as one of retreat or mere aestheticism. There are moments when Stevens was such a poet (particularly in the late 1940s and early 1950s—my second Stevens), but the times when he was not were as much the result of the contradictions of his sensibility as of the complexities of the world in which he lived: Stevens's major achievements coincide with the major historical events of his lifetime—the Great Depression and the two world wars.

Stevens tended to remain silent when his responsibility as a citizen of this historical world did not demand his attention; in its strengths and its weaknesses, writing poetry was a civic act for Stevens. During the years from 1900 to 1914 and from 1923 to 1934, Stevens's life was dominated by struggles less historical than personal (though in being primarily economic, the struggles were not isolated or uncommon). During the years following the Second World War, the struggles took place more within a world Stevens had created (in both economic and aesthetic terms) than with historical forces outside his self-contained existence. "The House was Quiet and the World was Calm" (1946) was a kind of poem that Stevens may have wished for at many junctures in his career, but he could not write the poem until he was able to convince himself that nothing more than the act of reading or writing poetry could quiet the house and calm the world. Even in his later years, Stevens did not feel that way all the time; almost as often as he said otherwise, Stevens also said, "we have to live in the world as it is—that is to say: face it, not back away from it." But Stevens was now willing to settle for a narrow version of what the world "as it is" might be, and his endless summer of peace was often sustained only by the sensual pleasures his income afforded him and the aesthetic pleasures his accumulated capital of poetry could sustain. In the same week that the bombs were dropped on Hiroshima and Nagasaki, Stevens could make this comment in a letter to Allen Tate, who he knew would agree: "Sitting there [in the garden], with a little of Kraft's Limburger Spread and a glass or two of a really decent wine, with not a voice in the universe and with those big, fat pigeons moving round, keeping an eye on me and doing queer things to keep me awake, all of these things make The New Republic and its contents (most of the time) of no account."

> The house was quiet and the world was calm.
> The reader became the book; and summer night
>
> Was like the conscious being of the book.
> The house was quiet and the world was calm.

This last phase of Stevens's career was not exactly a retreat from political exigency but part of a more widespread movement among American intellectuals and artists away from the kinds of political engagement that had marked the Depression and war years. We saw a turn toward aestheticism at the end of the 1930s in even so stalwart a custodian of American culture as Philip Rahv; at the end of the war, Dwight Macdonald—who had broken with Rahv over what he saw as his colleague's capitulation to ideological despair—capitulated as well. Looking back to the crisis of 1939, he now conceded that Rahv had been right: "The only historically real alternatives in 1939 were to back Hitler's armies, to back the Allies' armies, or to do nothing. But none of these alternatives promised any great benefit for mankind, and the one that finally triumphed has led simply to the replacing of the Nazi threat by the Communist threat, with the whole ghastly newsreel flickering through once more in a second showing." Macdonald concluded: "This is one reason I am less interested in politics than I used to be." Daniel Bell would name this feeling with the phrase "the end of ideology," pointing to a shared sense that political ideals were exhausted, a feeling that an interest in politics (especially on the part of artists and writers) was useless.

Just as there is a difference between the New Criticism of 1935 and that of 1950, so is there a difference between the Abstract Expressionism of 1945 and of 1960. What began as a "political apoliticism" degenerated into a more simply detached apoliticism: forged in the face of the nationalist demands placed on art by Brooks and MacLeish, the political edge of an antipropagandist aesthetic fell away when the demands fell away, leaving an aesthetic that could even be enlisted as propaganda in a cold war battle for American cultural dominance.

Similarly, Stevens's use of the slogan "it must be abstract" has a different emphasis in 1952 than in 1942. The aesthetic it names was achieved under the stress of the Second World War, but when the stress slackened, the aesthetic was strong enough to perpetuate itself on its own terms. The phrase "Poetry is the subject of the poem" from "The Man with the Blue Guitar" (1937) may seem similar to the phrase "One poem proves another and the whole" from "A Primitive like an Orb" (1948), but unlike the second, the first was made in dialogue with historical conditions, conceiving poetry's relationship to those conditions differently; it is not part of an attempt to build a world from poetry but to build poetry a place in the world. As Stevens admitted in "Two or Three Ideas" (1951), "how easy it is suddenly to believe in the poem as one has never believed in it before" now that "at this very moment nothing but good seems to be returning." In his later years, when Stevens began to offer other temptingly totalizing phrases ("the theory / Of poetry is the theory of life" or "Life consists / Of propositions about life" or "It is a world of words to the end of it"), it became possible for readers to shape his entire career into a misleadingly coherent whole, focusing all his work through the lens of the poetry of 1947 to 1954 instead of reading different phases of his career as different achievements, parts of a historical dialogue in which the interlocutors continually changed. For later New Critics and for some post-structuralists, the only Stevens was the Stevens who won the Bollingen Prize.

By examining the history of Stevens's career, I have tried to complicate any sharp distinction between a Stevens who existed apart from political or economic concerns before 1935 and an apparently more socially minded Stevens who emerged in *Ideas of Order*. In contrast, the most important distinction to be recognized in Stevens's career is between the poetry of 1938 to 1945 (*Parts of a World*, "Notes toward a Supreme Fiction," and much of *Transport to Summer*) and the postwar poetry collected in *The Auroras of Autumn*. Even this distinction is far from sharp (since, as we will see, Stevens worked to correct his postwar faith in poetry in the final short poems of his career). But in contrast to the long poems of *Auroras*, the poetry produced during the period of the Second World War seems to me the richest in Stevens's career because it was the product of the conjunction of poetic maturity, economic stability, and historical crisis. It is especially difficult to sustain the always illusory division between a public and a private life when reading the work from this phase of Stevens's career. If an awareness of any of the factors that influenced this body of poetry is neglected, the poetry suffers.

"Notes toward a Supreme Fiction" is the watershed in Stevens's career. Visible at once in this poem is the Stevens who wrote a statement on war poetry and the Stevens who scorned the writing of such statements. After "Notes," these impulses tend to split apart, reinforcing a stronger division between public and private realms. The gap is not so wide as it was in the year 1900, when the editorial "Political Interests" and "Ballade of the Pink Parasol" marked the poles of Stevens's divided sensibility, but the width of the gap may be judged by laying "Esthetique du Mal" (1944) beside "Description Without Place" (1945). We have already seen how the former poem is rent by struggles political, historical, and sexual; the task of the poem is to learn to live in the shadow of the volcano, since there is no other place to dwell. While "Description Without Place" is not by any means immune to these struggles, its manifest effort is to suppress rather than negotiate them.

Stevens began working on "Description" in the spring of 1945, having been asked to give the Phi Beta Kappa poem at Harvard's commencement that June. In April, he wrote to Henry Church of the poem's progress and expressed his concern for Barbara Church's parents, who were still living in France, perhaps near "the area of the fighting." Places weighed heavy on Stevens's mind. "People in Germany must be in an incredible predicament," he continued, thinking of the atrocities in which Hitler's government had implicated its citizens, "in which even correctness is incorrect." Stevens then described his poem and the occasion at which he would read it: "It seems to me to be an interesting idea: that is to say, the idea that we live in the description of a place and not in the place itself, and in every vital sense we do. This ought to be a good subject for such an occasion." The occasion was what would turn out to be the final wartime graduation of conscriptable young men; the place was France or Germany or Cambridge or Hartford. Bloom notes that the poem began as a pendant to "Notes," growing from that poem's declaration "that we live in a place / That is not our own and, much more, not ourselves." But those lines describe not the visionary power of our descriptions but the resisting power of places. Stevens rejected the Nietzschean aphorism that Church offered as a gloss on "Notes" ("Why might not the world *which concerns us*—be a fiction?") as "the commonplace idea that the world exists only in the mind." In "Description" he is happier to embrace that idea, evoking Nietzsche as its exemplar.

> Nietzsche in Basel studied the deep pool
> Of these discolorations, mastering
>
> The moving and the moving of their forms
> In the much-mottled motion of blank time.
>
> His revery was the deepness of the pool,
> The very pool, his thoughts the colored forms,
>
> The eccentric souvenirs of human shapes,
> Wrapped in their seeming, crowd on curious crowd,
>
> In a kind of total affluence.

In contrast to Nietzsche, who is the master of his place, Stevens describes Lenin, who is mastered by it. Seated on a bench beside the same body of water, Lenin does not transform the floating swans into "eccentric souvenirs of human shapes"; he "disturbed / The swans. He was not the man for swans. / The slouch of his body and his look were not / In suavest keeping"—refusing to participate in "a kind of total affluence."

In "Esthétique du Mal" all descriptions are only more or less powerful in the place of the volcano (Stevens's figure for wartime violence and destruction); in contrast, "Description Without Place" is a resolutely Paterian poem in which a metaphor's power to shape experience is championed with little sense of how a place like wartime Germany might resist even the most powerful descriptions of it. Missing in these lines is that diffidence—up to this time central to Stevens's poetic vision—that led Stevens to stress the limitations of poetry's power to transform a stubbornly material world.

> There might be, too, a change immenser than
> A poet's metaphors in which being would
>
> Come true, a point in the fire of music where
> Dazzle yields to a clarity and we observe,
>
> And observing is completing and we are content,
> In a world that shrinks to an immediate whole,
>
> That we do not need to understand, complete
> Without secret arrangements of it in the mind.

These lines amount to a powerful wish, an overpowering desire for a world turned right, and, given their moment in Stevens's life and times, it is a wish that could not only elicit the understanding but evoke the sympathies of people who shared that moment. Who would not wish for a change immenser than a poet's metaphors that could dissipate "the death of a soldier" and the "more than human commonplace of blood"? Stevens mentions those realities before his paean to the power of metaphor, and they do not reappear in the poem. "Description is revelation," Stevens goes on to say, and as description supersedes place, "the theory of description matters most." "Notes" had demanded that it must change, but the poem did not present change as something simple or easy or natural. In "Asides on the Oboe" (1940) the poet's cry—"Thou art not August unless I make thee so"—is challenged by the untransformable reality of "war and death"; in "Holiday in Reality" (1944) a similar boast—"These are real only if I make them so"—rests uncontested. In "Description Without Place," Stevens's portrait of Nietzsche sounds suspiciously like the self-portrait of the poet in the garden, blurring the pages of the *New Republic* with a glass or two of really decent wine: a kind of total affluence. Three years after writing "Description Without Place" Stevens cast himself as the Nietzsche of his own poem in a letter responding to Barbara Church's description of Munich: "If there is any place in Germany which I could have thought of describing as blue and white, it would have been Hanover, which no-one over here seems to know anything about and which I know nothing about but which, nevertheless, is one of the places that I go to when I want to go anywhere and sit in the park without really getting up."
Bloom admires "Description" more than I do, but I think he is right to

say that it is "more prophetic of Stevens's last phase than anything in *Notes* or in the rest of *Transport to Summer*." Stevens concludes in "Description" that it "is a world of words to the end of it," and in the last decade of his life he produced many poems to bolster the dictum. Stevens's hero poems of the 1930s and 1940s are problematic in several ways, and Stevens came close to resolving their problems in "Notes," where the desire for a collective being is balanced against the danger of realizing the wish. But when Stevens dismissed the hero altogether after 1945, the poems lost an important tension, and the idea of the language of poetry was forced to bear much of the weight previously laid on the idea of the hero.

In defending the cultural relevance of poetry, Stevens had for many years refused himself the easy consolation of assuming its mythically political power, struggling instead with the particular ways in which that power might be claimed. Writing his memorandum concerning Church's proposed poetry chair at Princeton in 1940, Stevens was characteristically humble: "This memorandum makes it look as if I were trying to bring about a *seelensfriede durch dichtung*. Of course, I have no such fanatical idea; I merely think that poetry has to be taken seriously." But in "Sketch of the Ultimate Politician" (1947) he sounds as "fanatical" as (though far more eloquent than) Archibald MacLeish: a "freedom of the soul through poetry" is just what Stevens desires.

> He is the final builder of the total building,
> The final dreamer of the total dream,
> Or will be. Building and dream are one.
>
> There is a total building and there is
> A total dream. There are words of this,
> Words, in a storm, that beat around the shapes.

To some sensibilities, these lines will seem like a victory for Stevens: he has taken on the full measure of Whitman's boast. Seductive as they are, the lines achieve their power by forsaking what I called (appropriating Cavell's characterization of philosophy) the necessary defeat of poetry through poetry. Without that struggle, Stevens's lifelong interest in the "normal" or "commonplace" began in his later years to take on the narrower resonances of those words; his lifelong diffidence in the face of political action became a lack of sympathy for political action. Examining Stevens's early years, I located the roots of the diffidence in Emerson, and in Emerson as well as Stevens, a healthy doubting of the self's capability for action sometimes becomes, in self-defense, a denial of the public will. The tension was part of Stevens's intellectual heritage.

When the *Yale Literary Magazine* asked Stevens to comment on the "major problem" facing writers in 1946, Stevens offered a prose version of his "Sketch of the Ultimate Politician," describing the urgent necessity of maintaining individual freedom ("poetry") in the face of any totalitarian system ("politics").

> The role of the poet may be fixed by contrasting it to that of the politician. The poet absorbs the general life: the public life. The politician is absorbed by it. The poet is individual. . . . He must remain individual. As individual he must remain free. The politician expects everyone to be absorbed as he himself is absorbed. This expectation is part of the sabotage of the individual. The second phase of the poet's problem, then, is to maintain his freedom, the only condition in which he can hope to produce significant poetry.
>
> If people are to become dependent on poetry for any of the fundamental satisfactions, poetry must have an increasing intellectual scope and power. This is a time for the highest poetry.

This is vintage cold war rhetoric. Stevens had always been suspicious of political systems that encroached on individual freedoms, but the rejection of politics as inherently repressive (along with the embracing of poetry as inherently free) is a luxury Stevens could not have afforded in the 1930s. In the late 1940s and early 1950s, Stevens moved closer to the attenuated liberal position epitomized by Arthur Schlesinger's *The Vital Center: The Politics of Freedom* (1949): "the essential strength of democracy as against totalitarianism lies in its startling insight into the value of the individual." From the perspective of cold war liberalism, even the New Deal began to look suspiciously like an infringement of individual liberties. Confessional poetry, emphasizing a poetics of personal experience, found a willing audience—the same audience that supported the vogue for existentialism: anxiety was championed as the natural product of the choices an individual had to make in a free society. Congress approved the Truman Doctrine (to contain the threat of totalitarian communism) in 1947 and ratified the Marshall Plan (to encourage the economic growth of foreign democracies) the following year. By 1950 the Senate was calling for a worldwide "Marshall Plan of ideas," and throughout the decade, the State Department subsidized the exhibition of Abstract Expressionist canvases in Europe. Jackson Pollock's splattered canvases became the badge of American individualism, and one rationale for the exhibitions sounded much like Stevens describing the poet as the ultimate politician: "Artistic freedom, experimentalism and diversity are products of democracy, and fundamentally opposed to authoritarianism"; they are "the most convincing proof of the strength of democracy. In the troubled world of today, the artist's absolute freedom of thought, his uncontrolled expression of ideas and emotions, and his disinterested pursuit of perfection, are more needed than ever in our history."

With his ultimate politician in place, Stevens approached the election of 1946 with disdain, dismissing politics proper as "a rather tiring game for the superficial," a game that has nothing "to do with the Government of ourselves." The United States did not choose a new president in 1946, but the election did produce the first Republican Congress since the Hoover administration: in the Twelfth Congressional District of California, veteran Democratic representative H. Jerry Voorhis was unseated by a young Republican named Richard Nixon; in Wisconsin, incumbent Democratic senator Robert M. La Follette, Jr. (whose father had led the Progressive Party in Stevens's youth) lost to Joseph McCarthy. In February 1950, McCarthy delivered the infamous speech "Communists in the State Department." The month before, Alger Hiss was convicted on charges of espionage. "Mr. Chambers and Mr. Hiss all give me a prolonged pain in the neck," commented Stevens. "I wish I could forget all about them when I am taking my walk in the park in the mornings by sitting down and having a little talk with the ducks, but I am sure that the ducks are Russian spies."

Stevens's apparent boredom with all things political enabled him to dismiss the trials, though he admitted "an occasional thought" about Andrei Vyshinsky, who proclaimed in *The Law of the Soviet State* that there "can be no place for freedom of speech, press, and so on for the foes of socialism." The force of Stevens's idealization of American freedoms, enforced through poetry, depends on a contrast with such evidence of Soviet oppression. But like certain politicians, Stevens was willing to limit freedom in the service of freedom, paradoxically echoing the Vyshinsky whom the ultimate politician scorned: Soviets were "taking advantage of [the freedoms of speech and thought] here and . . . limiting them at home. The total freedom that now endangers us has never existed before, notwithstanding Voltaire, and so on. We might need a police state before long to protect ourselves against Communism." That wish had of course already come true in several ways. When William Carlos Williams was chosen as Consultant in Poetry at the Library of Congress in 1952, his appointment was delayed by a drawn-out investigation by the Civil Service Commission and the FBI. It appeared that Williams had published poems in the *New Masses* and the *Partisan Review* during the 1930s. Early the following year, Williams received the Bollingen Prize— shared with the unimpeachable Archibald MacLeish—along with the news that his "loyalty investigation" and his appointment as Consultant were canceled. "Now," speculated a recent winner of the prize, "if something has been discovered and if [Williams's] record is not clear, one wonders what effect this may have on the Bollingen Prize which is already involved on Pound's account." In 1955, Stevens's own record seemed clean enough for

Henry Kissinger to invite him to an "International Seminar" at Harvard University.

Whatever Stevens's dreams, poetry was not doing much to ensure the individual freedom of poets, playwrights, and actors. When Stevens wrote that the poet's greatest task is to maintain his freedom through poetry, he had settled into his fluent mundo, forgetting that throughout his career he could not even begin to write poetry until he had achieved economic freedom: "Sunday Morning" and "The Idea of Order at Key West" were each produced by a decade of poetic silence and economic striving. "Unlike most writers in the romantic tradition," notes Lentricchia, "[Stevens] knew that feelings of power and freedom in imagination were precisely the sorts of effects produced by a capitalist economic context in those (writers and intellectuals) who hate capitalist economic contexts; he seemed to know that aesthetic purity was economically encased; that imaginative power was good, to be sure, but that economic power was a more basic good." By 1950 Stevens could forget this wisdom—and perhaps one goal in acquiring such knowledge is to reach the point where one is able to forget it. That Stevens worked at the Hartford almost until the day he died, long past the age of mandatory retirement, suggests that part of him did not forget.

In its complexity, "Notes toward a Supreme Fiction" left the door open to this oversimplification of Stevens's previously subtler understanding of the relationship of poetry and politics. There is an aphorism often brought to bear on "Notes": "The final belief is to believe in a fiction, which you know to be a fiction, there being nothing else. The exquisite truth is to know that it is a fiction and that you believe in it willingly." There is less of this Arnoldian mission in "Notes" than the aphorism implies, but its Jamesian aspect was crucial for Stevens: he needed to recognize his beliefs as constructions at the same time that he recognized their efficacy—the actual power of the phrase "as if." But there was a problem with the "philosophy of 'as if'" (as Hans Vaihinger dubbed it) that Stevens was unwilling to recognize. He once recalled how a student at Trinity College in Hartford argued with him about "Notes": "I said that I thought that we had reached a point at which we could no longer really believe in anything unless we recognized that it was a fiction. The student said that that was an impossibility, that there was no such thing as believing in something that one knew was not true. It is obvious, however, that we are doing that all the time." Before Stevens had this conversation walking home one winter afternoon in 1942, he had already rejected a more authoritative voice than the student's. Stevens read *The Future of an Illusion* while preparing "The Noble Rider and the Sound of Words." Midway through the essay, Freud rejects the consolation of Vaihinger's philosophy of "as if," maintaining that the theory of fictionality collapses in practice.

This [philosophy] asserts that our thought-activity includes a great number of hypotheses whose groundlessness and even absurdity we fully realize. They are called "fictions," but for a variety of practical reasons we have to behave "as if" we believed in these fictions. This is the case with religious doctrines because of their incomparable importance for the maintenance of human society. . . . But I think the demand made by the "As if" argument is one that only a philosopher could put forward. A man whose thinking is not influenced by the artifices of philosophy will never be able to accept it; in such a man's view, the admission that something is absurd or contrary to reason leaves no more to be said. It cannot be expected of him that precisely in treating his most important interests he shall forgo the guarantees he requires for all his ordinary activities [*gewöhnlichen Tätigkeiten*].

Stevens ultimately had to ignore the imperatives of "ordinary activities" in order to sustain his philosophy of "as if." The problem with the philosophy is that when the belief leads to action, to result, it matters little whether the foundation of the action is a self-conscious fiction or a reified truth: the distinction is nullified in practice. In order to maintain the idea that a self-consciousness about the fictionality of belief makes a difference, consequently, Stevens had to segregate matters of practice from the theory of the fiction. In "Notes" Stevens is willing—despite his statement to the student—to let the fiction unravel, returning to ordinary activity. But in "Description Without Place" he asserts that the "theory of description matters most" in order to bracket the threat of particular descriptions and places: it then becomes easy for him to assume that a change in language will effect greater changes, since a world to which language refers has dropped out of the equation: "as if" collapses simply and easily into "is."

"The Auroras of Autumn" (1948) is a late and beautiful instance of Stevens's lifelong meditation on apocalypse; but unlike "The Comedian" or "Owl's Clover," it depends on the power of "as if" to neutralize the catastrophic threat. Confronted by the terrifying lights in the sky in which "the serpent lives," Stevens wonders if by the powers of imagination we could find "a time of innocence" in which

>   these lights are not a spell of light,
> A saying out of a cloud, but innocence.
> An innocence of the earth and no false sign
>
> Or symbol of malice. That we partake thereof,
> Lie down like children in this holiness,
> As if, awake, we lay in the quiet of sleep,
>
> As if the innocent mother sang in the dark
> Of the room and on an accordion, half-heard,
> Created the time and place in which we breathed . . .

As if, as if, stresses Stevens, unwilling to say that his interpretation of the unnaturally lighted sky as a sign of innocence is any more inevitable than its interpretation as a sign of chaos. We have seen throughout Stevens's career that the danger Stevens courts with his skepticism of apocalyptic rhetoric is that the actual threat of catastrophe or the dire need for change might be ignored. In "Auroras" Stevens dismantles that threat as if it were just one more of the mind's illusions, easily replaced by another. If the internalization is successful, it depends on a faith in the power of "as if," sustained only by willed ignorance of the threat; in Helen Vendler's phrase, there is an "affirmation beneath the hypothesis." Stevens has become the Canon Aspirin. And like the Canon's, his affirmation will fall away, leaving uneasy questions: "Shall we be found hanging in the trees next spring?"

Despite such questions, Stevens would repeat the affirmation of "Auroras" in poem after poem. In "Puella Parvula" (1949) "great Africa [is] devoured / And Gibraltar is dissolved," but over all these disasters "the mighty imagination triumphs." In even more historically specific terms, Stevens asks in "Imago" (1950),

> Who can pick up the weight of Britain,
> Who can move the German load
> Or say to the French here is France again?

The answer is a kind of Marshall Plan of the mind: "Imago. Imago. Imago." These lines suggest that "The Auroras of Autumn" might be more historically specific than it seems. If, as Charles Berger proposes, the auroras are Stevens's figure for the atomic bomb, then the ease with which the threat is undone is even more discomfiting. ("I cannot say that there is any way to adapt myself to the idea that I am living in the Atomic Age," said Stevens, "and I think it a lot of nonsense to try to adapt oneself to such a thing.") But in contrast to Stevens's earlier poems of apocalypse, "The Auroras of Autumn" seems to me less involved with the crises of its time; instead, "Auroras" (or even the apparently more engaged "Imago") is more involved with earlier poems—its easy undoing of the threat of catastrophe is made possible by Stevens's reliance on earlier undoings, which were themselves responses to the potential catastrophes of world war and economic depression. A. Walton Litz has made this important point about Stevens's later poetry: "The long poems of Stevens's final years do not derive their extraordinary consistency from an argument which builds toward a conclusion, but from the integrity of a presiding mind which rehearses again and again the premises and possibilities of an achieved vision." This statement describes not only Stevens's poetic development but his relationship to the world outside the poems.

One conclusion to draw from this observation might be that although a poem like "An Ordinary Evening in New Haven" appears to have a more "open" form than the symmetrically designed "Notes toward a Supreme Fiction," that apparent openness is sustained only because "An Ordinary Evening" rehearses the achieved vision of "Notes." (In a study of the politics of Pound's and Eliot's "open poems," Cairns Craig has proposed that an open poem paradoxically requires the achieved vision of an articulated tradition in order to be understood.) Stevens published two versions of "An Ordinary Evening in New Haven," the full thirty-one-canto version in *The Auroras of Autumn* and an eleven-canto version, which he read for the Connecticut Academy of Arts and Sciences in 1949 and later included in his Faber and Faber *Selected Poems*. The shorter version (which Stevens culled from the longer) ends with the canto numbered XXIX in the full sequence.

> When the mariners came to the land of the lemon trees,
> At last, in that blond atmosphere, bronzed hard,
> They said, "We are back once more in the land of the elm trees,
>
> But folded over, turned round." It was the same,
> Except for the adjectives, an alteration
> Of words that was a change of nature, more
>
> Than the difference that clouds make over a town.
> The countrymen were changed and each constant thing.
> Their dark-colored words had redescribed the citrons.

As I suggested in my reading of "Notes," these lines offer a parable of Stevens's quest for the ordinary: only by voyaging to an extraordinary world does he come to appreciate the commonplace world around him, recognizing that he never really left it. Because the dialectic of ordinary and extraordinary is bound up with the contrary demands of war and peace, that voyage seems a thing of consequence in "Notes"; in "An Ordinary Evening," the consequences of the voyage are less apparent because the poem rehearses the dialectic of "Notes," refining it, but forgoing its historical weight. In the terms of "Description Without Place," "An Ordinary Evening" provides the "theory of the description" rather than the description itself; as in "The Auroras of Autumn," an "alteration / Of words" transforms the world without encountering much resistance. And since canto XXIX appears to settle on the recovery of the ordinary world, Stevens ends the full version of his "endlessly elaborating poem" with a more "open" canto, suggesting that, at least in theory, the transformations will never cease.

> It is not the premise that reality
> Is a solid. It may be a shade that traverses
> A dust, a force that traverses a shade.

Unlike the coda to "Notes toward a Supreme Fiction," these final lines do not make us stop short, reconsidering the pleasures of an endlessly revolving world. Like "An Ordinary Evening," "Notes" could have been endlessly elaborated; but its demand for continual change was balanced by an ominous awareness of the forces resisting that demand—forces that had real consequences whether they were "solid" or not.

Frank Lentricchia has suggested that Stevens's late long poems, despite their distance from lived experience, are not an escape from the exigencies of capitalism but their apotheosis:

To write a long poem . . . without plot or historical subject or philosophical system, is to write the epic of bourgeois interiority, wherein the life of the spirit is hard to distinguish from the special sort of desire stimulated in the time and place of first-world consumer capitalism: when the life of the spirit is subjected to endless need for the new which alone can break us out of the grooves of boredom. . . . Capitalism and poetry are not opposites but symbiotic complements, the basis in Stevens of an integrated life, a unified sensibility quite unlike anything dreamt of in the utopian imagination.

Since Stevens's poetry never stands apart from capitalism, the particular nature of that relationship should be interrogated. While Stevens did not lead a double life as insurance executive and poet, his life was not undivided: that is, while it was inevitable and natural that bonds and poems claimed his attention, it was not natural that their discourses operated in exactly the same way; the practical differences between bonds and poems kept a single life from becoming double. And, to borrow Lentricchia's phrase, the other point at which poetry and capitalism became the indistinguishable components of Stevens's "integrated life" or "unified sensibility" was when Stevens wrote "Sea Surface Full of Clouds," a sequence that resembles his late long poems in its infinite deferral of experience and its uneasy aura of having been written as if by rote, a filling in of blanks. Inasmuch as these poems may (like any poems) reveal the confluence of poetry and capitalism, it is an unhappy confluence, not a healthy one, and far from utopian. Both "Sea Surface Full of Clouds" and "An Ordinary Evening in New Haven" offer their readers an exquisite experience of poetry, but for Stevens it was a poetry of impasse. John Crowe Ransom said this about the former poem (and might have said it of the latter as well): "the poem has no moral, political, religious, or sociological value." That might seem a virtue to the kinds of readers who awarded Stevens the Bollingen Prize in 1950, but to Stevens at his best, it was a limitation.

It was not a limitation with which Stevens was content to live—or to die. In the very last years of his career, Stevens gave up long meditative poems like "An Ordinary Evening" for short stark poems like "The Course of a Par-

ticular"—poems gathered in "The Rock" section of the *Collected Poems* or
left uncollected at Stevens's death. Those short poems are the fitting conclusion to the career of a poet who always worked to overcome or at least
acknowledge his limitations. Jerome McGann suggests that the "greatest
moments of artistic success" in a Romantic poetry of internalization and
retreat "are almost always associated with loss, failure, and defeat—in particular the losses which strike most closely to the Ideals (and Ideologies) cher-
ished by the poets in their work." While the "grand illusion of Romantic
ideology is that one may escape such a world through imagination and
poetry," the "great truth of Romantic *work* is that there is no escape." Stevens's final short poems are a product of his acknowledgment of this imperative—he could not go on writing endlessly elaborating poems until the end.
These poems embody Stevens's final attempt to know the world, and they
offer his most chilling condemnations of his failure to do so. The power of
these final poems—in comparison not only with Stevens's career but with
Romantic poetry at large—is often said to be astonishing, and it seems to me
appropriate that McGann makes his argument by manipulating the vocabulary of the later Yeats and Stevens: "there is no place of refuge, not in desire,
not in the mind, not in imagination. Man is in love and loves what vanishes,
and this includes—finally, tragically—even his necessary angels."

18

A New Knowledge of Reality

The first instance of Stevens's luminous final style came even before he had written "The Auroras of Autumn" or "An Ordinary Evening in New Haven." In March 1947 he inscribed his editor's copy of *Transport to Summer* with these words: "The Only Copy of TRANSPORT TO SUMMER together with *First Warmth*, 1947." The poem began:

> I wonder, have I lived a skeleton's life,
> As a questioner about reality,
>
> A countryman of all the bones in the world?

The poet who had recently completed "Description Without Place" asks this difficult question of himself, and the question demands an austerity of language that surpasses even the spareness of "The Snow Man" or "The Poems of Our Climate." Sometime before his death, Stevens would revise "First Warmth" in "As You Leave the Room," in which the terms of his self-interrogation become even more severe: "I wonder, have I lived a skeleton's life, / As a disbeliever in reality . . . ?" Stevens had raised this question even before the long poems of *The Auroras of Autumn* were written, but he would postpone a full confrontation with its implications until the final years of his life. The chill of late poems like "The Course of a Particular" and "A Clear Day and No Memories" comes from the poet's wish that the poems he had self-consciously constructed as his greatest achievements—the long poems of *Auroras*—might have been different. These short poems are the final utterance of an old man wishing he might have asked different questions. In "Questions Are Remarks" the old questioner of reality looks at his grandson Peter, who says, "Mother, what is that." "His question is complete," Stevens comments. "He does not say, 'Mother, my mother, who are you,' / The way the drowsy, infant, old men do."

That question is central to the best of Stevens's later long poems, "The Auroras of Autumn" and "The Owl in the Sarcophagus." But as Stevens himself explained, the inspiration behind these attempts at a major achievement was also bound up with literary ambition: "at my age a poet starts to write a long poem chiefly because he persuades himself that it is necessary to have a long poem among his works." Stevens's long poems were (as Poe said that they must be) successions of shorter poems; but over time, a sequence of poems became easier (and paradoxically less ambitious) for Stevens to write: endlessly elaborating a poetic donnée allowed Stevens the luxury of avoiding the question he first asked in "First Warmth"; it allowed him to sustain a hovering poetic vision that occluded the possibility of interrogating the vision's principles. That skepticism, as we have seen over and over again, had been essential to the development of Stevens's poetry from the start, and the later sequences—especially the lesser ones like "Things of August"—suffer from its absence. Stevens knew that was so. When he completed "An Ordinary Evening" in the summer of 1949, he paused before moving on to write "Things of August," the final long poem to be included in *The Auroras of Autumn*: "I thought before starting on another long poem with which to build up that book I should try to write a number of shorter things for people to whom I have made promises. As a matter of fact, a short poem is more difficult to write than a long one because a long poem acquires an impetus of its own. With each short poem one is making a fresh start and is experiencing a new subject." To experience a new subject was, for Stevens, to break down the self-enclosed world of the long poems—to reestablish a dialogue with the world outside that had been central to his work until "Notes toward a Supreme Fiction" built the foundation for a world so large that Stevens could sometimes exist exclusively within its boundaries. The act of writing short poems at the end of his career was for Stevens a return to the ordinary world he valued most of all.

The return was not easy for him. The short poems he wrote after "An Ordinary Evening" (published as "A Half Dozen Small Pieces" late in 1949) did not please him completely—they could not appear on what Stevens thought of as the ideal page of poetry: "At least what one ought to find [on that page] is normal life, insight into the commonplace, reconciliation with every-day reality." Rather than push himself to establish that contact with the ordinary world, however, Stevens returned to the easier task of a long meditative poem. Beginning "Things of August," he confessed again: "It is much easier to make progress on a single long poem, in which one goes ahead pretty much as one talks, as one thing leads to another." Stevens had been writing as he talked—prodigiously so—since the war had ended. But after *The Auroras of Autumn* was published, Stevens almost collapsed into the third silence of his career. "The Rock" and a handful of inconsequential lyrics appeared in 1950. And after the powerful short poems "The Course of a Particular" and "Final Soliloquy of the Interior Paramour" appeared in the spring of 1951, Stevens would have very little to say until "To an Old Philosopher in Rome" appeared at the end of 1952. When he remastered the rigor of the short poem—a rigor that demanded that Stevens become a more harassing taskmaster, a more interested questioner of his life and work—then the final three years of his life saw the production of some of his most astonishing poems. The only long poem of these years, "The Sail of Ulysses," Stevens considered a failure because it was nothing more than a self-generating elaboration of ideas.

At the same time that Stevens was explaining the difficulty of writing short poems, he was extolling (in both his essays and his correspondence with younger poets) the supreme virtue of poetry's contact with the ordinary world of daily lives. Most eloquent was his comment on the poetry of John Crowe Ransom.

> One turns with something like ferocity toward a land that one loves, to which one is really and essentially native, to demand that it surrender, reveal, that in itself which one loves. This is a vital affair, not an affair of the heart (as it may be in one's first poems), but an affair of the whole being (as in one's last poems), a fundamental affair of life, or, rather, an affair of fundamental life; so that one's cry of O Jerusalem becomes little by little a cry to something a little nearer and nearer until at last one cries out to a living name, a living place, a living thing, and in crying out confesses openly all the bitter secretions of experience. This is why trivial things often touch us intensely. It is why the sight of an old berry patch, a new growth in the woods in the spring, the particular things on display at a farmers' market, as, for example, the trays of poor apples, the few boxes of black-eyed peas, the bags of dried corn, have an emotional power over us that for a moment is more than we can control.

This is a variation on a tune Stevens had sung throughout his life. In the poems of *Harmonium*, Stevens had worked to avoid the seductions of apocalyptic transcendence, preserving a "diminished" Romanticism's protection of little things. In the 1930s, he resisted for similar reasons the utopian or apocalyptic seductions of a "generation's dream." And during the Second World War, he worked harder than ever to preserve the peacetime imperatives of ordinary life. But during the 1950s, Stevens's comfortable call for the evi-

dence of the ordinary in poetry was not so easily matched by the presence of
such evidence in his own poems. This is not simply ironic; behind statements
such as the one on Ransom lurks an insecurity, a painful recognition that
Stevens was no longer able to perform the task he admired most of all.

Stevens could joke about the thinness of his own experience at this stage
of his life ("The Stevenses shrink from everything. This means that we are
tired of staying at home and at the same time do not have a thought of going
away"), and simultaneously he could reprimand younger poets for the same
failing. This letter to Peter Lee, a young Korean poet, sounds like Stevens
talking to himself: "I had the pleasure of reading your poems this morning.
They do not penetrate very far into the tough material of this world. . . . Isn't
it the function of every poet, instead of repeating what has been said before,
however skillfully he may be able to do that, to take his station in the midst
of the circumstances in which people actually live and to endeavor to give
them, as well as himself, the poetry that they need in those very circumstances?" Over and over again, Stevens sent similar warnings to José Rodríguez Feo; he composed the poem "The Novel" about what he saw as Feo's
propensity to live in books, and he sent to Feo this sentence from Henry
James's notebooks (particularly precious to Stevens) in order to help the
young poet out of his impasse: "To live *in* the world of creation—to get into
it and stay in it—to frequent it and haunt it—to *think* intensely and fruitfully—to woo combinations and inspirations into being by a depth and continuity of attention and meditation—this is the only thing." The editors of
Stevens's correspondence with Feo conclude that it is "ironic that an older,
increasingly reticent Stevens felt it his place to persuade José to leave his
world of books and live all he could while he could—no less ironic, at any
rate, than Lambert Strether's similar insistence to *his* young friend." That is
to simplify the multiple ironies of both Stevens's career and *The Ambassadors*;
in both cases, the irony is not an easy duality, a question of either/or. Like
James's Strether, Stevens was looking back on what now seemed to him a
skeleton's life. But like Strether's advice to Bilham, Stevens's advice to Feo
or Lee was not offered in the spirit of knowing better; it was offered, with
generosity and with pain veiled by pride, in the spirit of knowing worse.

There is no bleaker instance of that pain than "Seventy Years Later," the
opening movement of "The Rock." "It is an illusion that we were ever alive,"
Stevens begins, not only acknowledging the emptiness of the present but
denying the past whatever fullness it once seemed to have.

> Even our shadows, their shadows, no longer remain.
> The lives these lived in the mind are at an end.
> They never were . . . The sounds of the guitar

> Were not and are not. Absurd. The words spoken
> Were not and are not. It is not to be believed.
> The meeting at noon at the edge of the field seems like
>
> An invention, an embrace between one desperate clod
> And another . . .

These stubbornly metonymic lines are part of a short poem that Stevens did not have the strength to write. For if these lines are distinguished even among Stevens's last poems for their bleakness, the lines that follow them are distinguished by the wondrous ease with which the bleaknes⸢ is dispelled. Reverting to the idiom of "Sketch of the Ultimate Politician" and "Description Without Place," Stevens explains in the second movement of "The Rock" ("The Poem as Icon") that "the poem makes meanings of the rock" so that "its barrenness becomes a thousand things / And so exists no more."

Because of its faith in the power of language to disperse even the most stubbornly painful meaning, "The Rock" is perfectly suited to deconstructive analysis. As J. Hillis Miller has said, "the poem annihilates the rock, takes the place of it, and replaces it with its own self-sufficient fiction—the leaves, blossom, and fruit that come to cover the high rock. At that point its barrenness has become a thousand things and so exists no more." While a reader may want "to find in the poem a personal voice and a personal drama, the voice and drama of Stevens himself n old age," the poem undermines any such grounded meaning. I think Miller offers a fair characterization of "The Rock," but to me that characterization helps explain why a poem that begins so powerfully dwindles into a paean to the power of poetry that by 1950 Stevens could literally write with his eyes closed. Stevens himself needed to undermine the ground of his personal drama, and he was not strong enough to let the opening lines of "The Rock" stand alone—as he would let similar lines stand in "The Course of a Particular" and "A Clear Day and No Memories." In part, Stevens was constricted in writing "The Rock" by the pattern of long poems established by "Notes," "Credences of Summer," "The Auroras of Autumn": the long poem of winter was required to complete the cycle.

Stevens almost immediately rewrote the opening lines of "The Rock" as the short poem they should have been in "The Course of a Particular," which was published beside "Final Soliloquy of the Interior Paramour" early in 1951. He began the latter poem thinking it too was going to become part of a larger effort: while he "had originally intended to write a long poem on the subject of the present poem," he had "not particularly felt like going on with it." Since "Final Soliloquy" extends the speculations of the latter movements of "The Rock" ("The world imagined is the ultimate good"), it seems especially significant that Stevens abandoned these consolations for the bleak challenge of "The Course of a Particular." While the fiction of the leaves possesses a healing power in "The Rock," the cry of the leaves now "cures" nothing; more pointedly, it "concerns" no one at all.

> Today the leaves cry, hanging on branches swept by wind,
> Yet the nothingness of winter becomes a little less.
> It is still full of icy shades and shapen snow.
>
> The leaves cry . . . One holds off and merely hears the cry.
> It is a busy cry, concerning someone else.
> And though one says that one is part of everything,
>
> There is a conflict, there is a resistance involved;
> And being part is an exertion that declines:
> One feels the life of that which gives life as it is.
>
> The leaves cry. It is not a cry of divine attention,
> Nor the smoke-drift of puffed-out heroes, nor human cry.
> It is the cry of leaves that do not transcend themselves,
>
> In the absence of fantasia, without meaning more
> Than they are in the final finding of the ear, in the thing
> Itself, until, at last, the cry concerns no one at all.

This poem is the first completely successful product of Stevens's effort to throw off his endless elaborations and write poems that are not (in a phrase he used to chastise his own work) "unbelievably irrelevant to our actual world." The word *particular* recalls a passage in "The Relations between Poetry and Painting" (1951): recognizing that poets like Baudelaire believed in "a universal poetry that is reflected in everything," Stevens confesses that he "is better satisfied by particulars." Similarly, the word *cry* recalls Stevens's preference for "a cry to something a little nearer" in his comment on John Crowe Ransom. In "The Course of a Particular" Stevens rejects his own attempts to construct a totalizing "universal poetry" and cleaves so close to the particulars of the world that he is not even able to sustain the fiction that little things touch him. Rejecting not only the "cry of divine attention" ("O Jerusalem") and the cry of "puffed-out heros" (once so potent for Stevens), he rejects the "human cry" as well, a denial of the pathetic fallacy that makes even "The Snow Man" seem comfortably whimsical in comparison. While in the aborted long poem "Final Soliloquy" Stevens tried to insist again that "We feel the obscurity of an order, a whole," he rejects any such wholeness in "The Course of a Particular"—especially a wholeness manufactured by poetry; he refuses to gloss over the "conflict" and the "resistance" involved in "say[ing] that one is part of everything."

With this achievement behind him, Stevens was willing to admit in 1952 that "the French say long poems are only written by people who cannot write short ones. I think they are right. So that I do not even have in mind writing a long poem." The group "Eight Poems," which Stevens published later that year, including "To an Old Philosopher in Rome," are among the most austerely beautiful of his career. Stevens's lifelong fascination with Santayana, the subject of "To an Old Philosopher," has been well documented. But as I suggested in Chapter 2, the complicated nature of Stevens's identification with Santayana has not always been adequately described. Even when he knew Santayana at Harvard, Stevens felt compelled to check the influence of the philosopher's aristocratic way of life on him with the more engaged perspective of John Jay Chapman. And when Stevens reconsidered Santayana in "Imagination as Value" (1948) he was as wary as ever, despite his continuing fascination with Santayana's peculiarly specialized life-style. Stevens's brief portrait of Santayana grew from Edmund Wilson's 1946 essay "Santayana at the Convent of the Blue Nuns," in which Wilson comments that the philosopher was "interested in his own thought as a personal, self-contained system, and in his life as a work of art," and concludes: "he reposes in his shabby chaise longue like a monad in the universal mind." Like Wilson, Stevens was both intrigued and repulsed by the philosopher who claimed that he had as much knowledge of the Second World War as he did of the Battle of Cannae. In "Imagination as Value" he invokes Santayana as an exemplar of the "improbable sort of thing" that happens when someone chooses to live in the world according to "aesthetic value."

To use a single illustration: it may be assumed that the life of Professor Santayana is a life in which the function of the imagination has had a function similar to its function in any deliberate work of art or letters. We have only to think of this present phase of it, in which, in his old age, he dwells in the head of the world, in the company of devoted women, in their convent, and in the company of familiar saints, whose presence does so much to make any convent an appropriate refuge for a generous and human philosopher. To repeat, there can be lives in which the value of the imagination is the same as its value in arts and letters.

As he was in 1900, Santayana was to Stevens in 1948 a person who lived in the confined space of poems—a secretary for porcelain. In the terms with which "Imagination as Value" concludes, Santayana was not for Stevens someone who could use the imagination for its most important purpose: the recovery of the ordinary from the extraordinary.

Wilson's account of Santayana's "life as a work of art" was not the only impetus for Stevens's poem. In his discussion of "agency" in *A Grammar of*

Motives (1945), Kennenth Burke offers a sequence of chapters on Berkeley, Hume, Leibniz, Kant, Hegel, Marx, Santayana—and Wallace Stevens. The poet was naturally flattered to be considered the culmination of so august a lineage (he returned the compliment in "Effects of Analogy," grouping Burke with La Fontaine and Spenser)—especially a lineage that stressed his potential affinities with figures so disparate as Santayana and Marx. Typically, Burke's thinking was more craftily dialectical than Wilson's, and he argued that a focus on the power of human agency may lead to both the engagement of Marx and the retreat of Santayana; for Burke, each representative figure is haunted by the ghost of the other, and Stevens's work seemed haunted by both. Santayana's philosophy did nevertheless represent an extraordinarily attenuated extreme for Burke, and like Stevens he was intrigued with the philosopher's perverse desire to limit his experience so severely that his very existence became questionable: Santayana's "ultimate delight is in the contemplation of essence, which in the last analysis is a *benign* contemplation of death"; his was finally "a long life of euthanasia." In "To an Old Philosopher in Rome" Stevens similarly presents Santayana poised eternally on the cusp of death—not so much because he is dying but, as Burke suggests, because his very way of living in the world is to simulate death: a skeleton's life. And, as in "Imagination as Value," Stevens emphasizes that this is a life Santayana has "chosen."

> It is a kind of total grandeur at the end,
> With every visible thing enlarged and yet
> No more than a bed, a chair and moving nuns,
> The immensest theatre, the pillared porch,
> The book and candle in your ambered room,
>
> Total grandeur of a total edifice,
> Chosen by an inquisitor of structures
> For himself. He stops upon this threshold,
> As if the design of all his words takes form
> And frame from thinking and is realized.

In a provocative reading of these final stanzas of the poem, Charles Berger points out that "no disabling return of the merely ordinary is allowed to undo the philosopher's achieved position. Santayana belongs to that class of purer and narrower consciousnesses created by Stevens for the purpose of measuring his own nature against a hypothetical ideal." Santayana's life, so narrow and so pure, represents a negative ideal for Stevens. The word *total*, used three times in these stanzas, is a measure of Stevens's distance from Santayana. Only recently Stevens had felt himself trapped in his own "total" world, a poetry in which all things were "realized." But after the long poems of his fluent mundo were written, Stevens had no desire to maintain that state of completion or wholeness: "I have no wish to arrive at a conclusion," he wrote in a late letter resisting an oversystematized account of his poetry. In contrast to his own final attempts to grasp an ordinary world, Stevens presents Santayana as Burke did—"as one who is the end of a line; his concern is with culminations." Yet "To an Old Philosopher" remains poignant rather than judgmental (more like Burke's discussion of Santayana than Wilson's) because rather than rejecting the old philosopher's vision outright, Stevens exposes its seductions as well as its limitations. Stevens tells us something about himself in "To an Old Philosopher in Rome," but the poem reveals not so much the poet Stevens wanted to be as the poet he feared he could too easily become. In distancing himself from Santayana, Stevens was also distancing himself from the author of "A Primitive like an Orb."

In asserting that "To an Old Philosopher in Rome" does not offer Stevens's ideal, consequently, I do not mean to suggest that Stevens does not respect the life Santayana was financially and emotionally equipped to choose. But Santayana's life was, as Stevens had known for fifty years, one he could never hope to emulate. To conceive of the world as fully realized in thought or poetry was to deny the randomness of ordinary experience; it was to deny the fact that unlike Santayana, Stevens did not devote himself exclusively to the life of the mind but worked for a living until he died. In his late essay "The Whole Man: Perspectives, Horizons" (1954) Stevens contrasted the aesthetic "specialist" with the "all-round man" who is able to meet his "day to day" problems in a world that may have more to do with business than poetry. Like his Santayana, Stevens's "specialist" constructs the "final harmony" of things rather than participating in the daily process of their becoming: "If these venerable men, by reducing themselves to skin and bones and by meditation prolonged year after year, could perceive final harmony in what all the world would concede to be final form, they would be supreme in life's most magnificent adventure. But they would still be specialists." Once again, Stevens will not denigrate the chosen life of the old philosopher, but he recognizes the cost of such a life as well as its almost certain failure: much hangs on the "If" with which this sentence begins.

In contrast to the Santayana poem (and in particular contrast to Stevens's own totalizing poems like "A Primitive like an Orb"), most of the later short poems present a world anything but realized, complete, or final—a broken world that does not take form from "the design of all his words." While the end is desirable for Santayana, it is the ultimate horror in "Madame La Fleurie": "Weight him down, O side-stars, with the great weightings of the end. / Seal him there." In "A Quiet Normal Life" Stevens is adamant that his "place" (though similar to Santayana's—"Here in his house and in his room, / In his chair") is decidedly "not / In anything that he constructed." And in "July Mountain" Stevens emphasizes even more emphatically that unlike the aristocratic Santayana, most of us live in a world that is neither single nor final and nothing like "a page of poetry."

> We live in a constellation
> Of patches and of pitches,
> Not in a single world,
> In things said well in music,
> On the piano, and in speech,
> As in a page of poetry—
> Thinkers without final thoughts
> In an always incipient cosmos,
> The way, when we climb a mountain,
> Vermont throws itself together.

For Stevens, Santayana had no thoughts that were not "final." Stevens himself, in contrast, wants to embrace a world that is never realized but always "incipient." Placed beside "To an Old Philosopher," "July Mountain" reveals what is missing in a life that is complete.

In *A Grammar of Motives* Burke brings to Stevens's work the terms he developed in "War, Response, and Contradiction" (1933), which I first discussed in Chapter 1: Stevens's ideas of philosophy and reason "seem equated with the vocational (with office hours)," while his ideas of poetry and imagination "seem equated with the vacational (after hours)." But as we would expect, Burke wants to show how this opposition is phoney: he points out that Stevens ultimately asks poetry to elucidate the predicaments of everyday. Stevens, in turn, admired Burke for making that point. In "Effects of Analogy" he quotes Burke's condemnation of narrow-minded, aestheticizing New Critics who "confine logic to science, rhetoric to propaganda or advertising, and thus leave for poetic a few spontaneous sensations not much higher in the intellectual scale than the twitchings of a decerebrated frog." In his final years, Stevens was as adamant as ever about his desire to write poetry rather than propaganda or advertising, but he did not want poetry to be excluded from the "vocational" world in which those discourses are usually thought to operate. "The close approach to reality has always been the supreme difficulty of any art," he told Barbara Church in 1952: "the communication of actuality . . . has been not only impossible, but has never appeared to be worth while because it loses identity as the event passes. Nothing in the world is deader than yesterday's political (or realistic) poetry. Nevertheless the desire to combine the two things, poetry and reality, is a constant desire."

In "The Plain Sense of Things" Stevens tries to place the power of poetry not in opposition to ordinary experience but in the service of its recovery. But because Stevens does not want his poems of "reality" to be what he considered "merely" topical, the poem tend to take the form of allegories or parables about this act of recovery. Like "The Course of a Particular," "The Plain Sense of Things" begins where the consoling fiction of "The Rock" ends. The leaves disguising the barrenness of our world have fallen; the effort to exist within the realized structures of the mind has ended—a "fantastic effort has failed" and the "great structure has become a minor house." When Stevens mounted his most successful recovery of ordinary experience in "Notes toward a Supreme Fiction" he was careful to point out (like Stanley Cavell) that the quest for the ordinary took place through the extraordinary and not in spite of it. Stevens emphasizes this point again in the last two stanzas of "The Plain Sense of Things." First, he states the matter directly: "the absence of the imagination had / Itself to be imagined"—it would have taken less effort to dwell inside the fiction of "The Rock." And finally, he illustrates this dictum with a parable equating the return of ordinary experience with a rat's low vantage point on the world; viewed from the higher perspective that human beings usually occupy, the surface of the water would be clouded by mirror images.

> The great pond,
> The plain sense of it, without reflections, leaves,
> Mud, water like dirty glass, expressing silence
>
> Of a sort, silence of a rat come out to see,
> The great pond and its waste of the lilies, all this
> Had to be imagined as an inevitable knowledge,
> Required, as a necessity requires.

This act of recovering the ordinary world is not in itself inevitable or necessary—nothing can force us to be like a rat when we have the power to be an old philosopher: we must make the act necessary through the power of perceiving. As Stevens explains in "Local Objects," the everyday world becomes precious when we develop for it a "fresh name."

In "Lebensweisheitspielerei" we are richly rewarded for this effort. Dispelling the heroic presence of "The proud and the strong," we are left with "the unaccomplished, / The finally human."

> Each person completely touches us
> With what he is and as he is,
> In the stale grandeur of annihilation.

Comforting as this reward for the task of reduction and denial may be, however, Stevens will reject it as he had rejected the ideal of hero and the ideal
of the poem that he briefly allowed to take the hero's place. Placed beside
"The Course of a Particular," even "Lebensweisheitspielerei," "Local
Objects," and "The Plain Sense of Things" seem optimistic. Rejecting the
world of poetry as a place to dwell, these poems make the world of ordinary
experience seem hospitable. As "First Warmth" initially demonstrated, Stevens knew better than that—or worse. The most powerful poems of his final
phase not only enforce a rejection of imaginative wholeness but offer almost
no consolation for the rejection.

What Stevens must imagine as a necessity in "The Plain Sense of Things"
becomes something even more bleak and more plain in "The River of Rivers
in Connecticut." Once again in contrast to "To an Old Philosopher," Stevens
pulls back from the edge of death in this poem. He does not move beyond
the river Styx but remains resolutely beside a river "this side of Stygia."

> On its banks,

> No shadow walks. The river is fateful,
> Like the last one. But there is no ferryman.
> He could not bend against its propelling force.

> It is not to be seen beneath the appearances
> That tell of it. The steeple at Farmington
> Stands glistening and Haddam shines and sways.

This earthly river reflects the ordinary world around it, the local towns of
Connecticut. But in contrast even to the Styx, it is empty: no one walks along
its banks; there is no ferryman to take us across. As Helen Vendler notes in
one of her finest readings, this poem rejects Stevens's usual shoreline figure
of imaginative power; it "will not invoke the imagination or the poet's duty
to imagine well, as though imagining were an ethical or practical act." This
river of rivers could not be bent by Charon, ferryman of the Styx, and it could
not be mastered by any human force either. "We live in the tradition which
is the true mythology of the region," said Stevens in "Connecticut Composed" (written for the Voice of America's "This Is America" series in 1955).
To him, the "gray, bleached and derelict" landscape of his adopted state mirrored a "strength of character" derived from "necessity." Focusing stubbornly on that landscape, "The River of Rivers in Connecticut" does not offer
the consolation of enhanced human feeling that is our reward in "Lebensweisheitspielerei"; it even makes the afterworld seem more fully populated, a
friendlier place than earth. And yet Stevens chooses to remain on this side of

the Styx, having looked beyond. He concedes that the life he leads may be a skeleton's life, less than human, but he chooses that life over any mythology of death.

To say that is to beg the contested question of Stevens's deathbed conversion to Catholicism. It would seem that Stevens's attitudes toward his own end were not unconflicted, and even if the conversion did not take place, the famous poem "Of Mere Being" does speak (in contrast to "The River of Rivers") of Stevens's longing for a world utterly foreign to ordinary experience, a world "without human meaning, / Without human feeling." Although they are less opulent than "Of Mere Being," "The River of Rivers in Connecticut," along with "A Mythology Reflects its Region" and "A Clear Day and No Memories," are for me the more powerful poems because they entertain Stevens's conjecture that he might live every day in a world without human feeling; they do not dodge the questions Stevens asked in "First Warmth" and had to ask again in "As You Leave the Room": they are the fitting conclusion to the story I have told about Stevens's career. Throughout his life, Stevens's best poems arose from his engagement with the world around him. When the engagement was not possible, he fell silent. After the Second World War, silence was no longer possible, but neither was engagement, and he wrote some poems that lack his usual vigor. But at the very end, Stevens was able to write a few poems that accepted silence instead of spinning a web to disguise it. In the quiet and luminous "A Clear Day and No Memories" Stevens turns away from everything once dear to him—the soldiers of two world wars, the dead he spent years mapping in genealogical charts, and the living whom he felt he loved too little.

> No soldiers in the scenery,
> No thoughts of people now dead,
> As they were fifty years ago:
> Young and living in a live air,
> Young and walking in the sunshine,
> Bending in blue dresses to touch something—
> Today the mind is not part of the weather.
>
> Today the air is clear of everything.
> It has no knowledge except of nothingness
> And it flows over us without meanings,
> As if none of us had ever been here before
> And are not now: in this shallow spectacle,
> This invisible activity, this sense.

These lines empty out the accumulation of a lifetime, even the existence of the poet's self. Yet "A Clear Day and No Memories" appeared a few months after Stevens said plainly in his essay on Connecticut: "It is a question of coming home to the American self in the sort of place in which it was formed." Two years before, Stevens had returned to Cambridge—one of the places in which he was formed—to see an exhibition at the Fogg Museum. On that day he did have memories, and he recalled the museum as a place whose only real public consisted of "young persons of honorable intentions." When Stevens was a student at Harvard in the year 1900, he visited the Fogg Museum to hear a speech by John Jay Chapman. Fired by Chapman's words, he wrote his editorial calling for all young persons to become "readily acquainted with political conditions." Looking back fifty years later, Stevens knew the haphazard fate of honorable intentions. In a poem that relinquishes the memories of soldiers in the scenery and the thoughts of people now dead, Stevens commemorates a life spent honoring the plain sense of things.

Notes

Unless noted otherwise, Stevens's poems (identified by title in the text) are quoted from the *Collected Poems* (New York: Knopf, 1955) and the revised edition of *Opus Posthumous*, ed. Milton Bates (New York: Knopf, 1989). In referring to Stevens's published works, the following abbreviations are employed.

L   *The Letters of Wallace Stevens*, ed. Holly Stevens (New York: Knopf, 1966)

NA   *The Necessary Angel* (New York: Knopf, 1951)

OP   *Opus Posthumous*, ed. Milton Bates (New York: Knopf, 1989)

SP   *Souvenirs and Prophecies: The Young Wallace Stevens*, ed. Holly Stevens (New York: Knopf, 1977)

SPBS   *Sur Plusieurs Beaux Sujects: Wallace Stevens' Commonplace Book*, ed. Milton Bates (Stanford: Stanford University Press, 1989)

In referring to previously unpublished writings or to books from Stevens's personal library, the locations of the manuscripts or books are noted with the following abbreviations.

Chicago   Special Collections, Joseph Regenstein Library, University of Chicago

Harvard   Houghton Library, Harvard University

Maryland   University of Maryland Library, College Park

Massachusetts   Special Collections, University of Massachusetts at Amherst Library

Princeton   Princeton University Library

When no location is specified, the materials are part of the Wallace Stevens Collection
in the Henry E. Huntington Library.

I The First Silence

p. 3   "Where is the"   SP 66. On this poem's place in Stevens's development, see
          Robert Buttel, *Wallace Stevens: The Making of Harmonium* (Princeton,
          1967), 37–38.

p. 4   "of becoming"   Stevens, "Political Interests," *Harvard Advocate* 69 (24
          March 1900): 17.
          "See the blind"   SP 58, 62.
          "Sonnets have their"   L 42.

p. 5   "Won't you have"   Stevens, "Four Characters," *Harvard Advocate* 69 (16
          June 1900): 120.
          "always been intensely"   L 413.
          "the mind of"   W. B. Yeats, *Letters to the New Island,* ed. George Bornstein
          and Hugh Witemeyer (New York, 1989), 102.

p. 6   "Instead of the"   W. H. Auden, *The English Auden,* ed. Edward Mendelson
          (New York, 1977), 366.
          "two or three"   Walt Whitman, *Prose Works,* ed. Floyd Stovall, 2 vols. (New
          York, 1964), 2:368.
          "This is [Pound's]   Hugh Kenner, *The Pound Era* (Berkeley, 1971), 377.
          "reciprocal kinship"   Michel Foucault, *The Order of Things* (New York,
          1970), 89.

p. 7   "into two different"   Stéphane Mallarmé, *Selected Prose Poems, Essays, and
          Letters,* trans. Bradford Cook (Baltimore, 1956), 42; Mikhail Bakhtin,
          The Dialogic Imagination, trans. Michael Holquist and Caryl Emerson
          (Austin, 1981), 286.
          "Dennis Breen with"   James Joyce, *Ulysses,* ed. Hans Walter Gabler (New
          York, 1986), 198, 210.

p. 8   "only two alternative"   Edmund Wilson, *Axel's Castle: A Study of the Imagi-
          native Literature of 1870–1930* (New York, 1931), 287.
          "insistence that the"   Edmund Wilson, *The Triple Thinkers* (New York,
          1948), 263.
          "a country where"   Wilson, *Axel's Castle,* 293.
          "figured for decades"   Wilson, *Triple Thinkers,* 72, 74, 82–83.

p. 9   "Whenever you find"   Kenneth Burke, *A Rhetoric of Motives* (Berkeley,
          1969), 28.
          "Several doctrines"   Kenneth Burke, *Counter-Statement* (Berkeley, 1968),
          viii–ix, 90, 91, 105.
          "represents the mind"   OP 199; L 641.

p. 10 "Does antimilitarism"   Kenneth Burke, "War, Response, and Contradic-
          tion," in *The Philosophy of Literary Form,* 2d ed. (Baton Rouge, 1967),
          234–57.

p. 11   *"double consciousness"*   Ralph Waldo Emerson, *Complete Works,* Centenary
Edition, 12 vols. (Boston, 1903), 6:47; 11:217. On Emerson's politics,
see Cornel West, *The American Evasion of Philosophy: A Genealogy of
Pragmatism* (Madison, 1989), 9–41. On Stevens's relation to Emerson
more generally, see Harold Bloom, *Wallace Stevens: The Poems of Our
Climate* (Ithaca, 1977).

p. 12   *"His products are"*   Emerson, *Complete Works,* 7:11; 11:300. Stevens owned
the edition of Emerson published by Houghton Mifflin in 1896 to
1898; to avoid confusion, all references are made to the Centenary
Edition.
   "a war is"   OP 310.

p. 13   *"A week of"*   SPBS 41.

p. 14   *"Come, said the"*   SP 29–30.
   "reality–imagination"   L 792.

p. 15   *"There is one"*   Stevens's speech was published in "Gold Medals Awarded
on 'Alumni Night,'" *Reading Eagle,* 23 December 1986, 5.
   "Our young folks"   SP 71; L 18. On Stevens and his father, see Milton Bates,
Wallace Stevens: A Mythology of Self (Berkeley, 1985), 1–48; George
Lensing, *Wallace Stevens: A Poet's Growth* (Baton Rouge, 1986), 3–22;
and Joan Richardson, *Wallace Stevens: A Biography,* 2 vols. (New York,
1986, 1988), 1:35–56.

p. 16   *"Do not be."*   L 16, 39. On the professionalization of law, see Burton J.
Bledstein, *The Culture of Professionalism* (New York, 1976), 184–
91.
   "Study electricity"   F. Scott Fitzgerald, *The Great Gatsby* (New York, 1953),
174.

p. 17   *"The mere prospect"*   L 63.
   "practical life"   L 32.
   "like Keats"   Stevens wrote this in Arnold's *Essays in Criticism, Second Series*
(London, 1898), 111.
   "low rank among"   W. D. Howells, *Literature and Life* (New York, 1902), 6,
34.
   "Decadence in art"   "Professionalism in Art," *Times Literary Supplement,* 31
January 1918, 49–50; T. S. Eliot, "Professionalism, Or . . . ," *Egoist* 5
(April 1918): 61. See Louis Menand, *Discovering Modernism: T. S. Eliot
and His Context* (New York, 1987), 97–132.

p. 18   *"I must try"*   L 34.
   "Matthew Arnold was"   Herbert Paul, *Matthew Arnold* (New York, 1903),
176.
   "completely satisfied"   L 32, 27, 94, 150.
   "Pre-Raphaelite"   Van Wyck Brooks, *An Autobiography* (New York, 1965),
105.
   "one had to"   SP 37.
   "anyone a little"   Unsigned review of *Interpretations of Poetry and Religion,*

by George Santayana, *Harvard Advocate* 69 (24 March 1900): 32. Samuel French Morse quotes part of this review in *Wallace Stevens: Poetry
as Life* (New York, 1970), 54–55.

p. 19 "*religious doctrines*" George Santayana, *Interpretations of Poetry and Religion* (New York, 1927), v.

"*art for art's*" L 24.

"*[Chapman] believes that*" Unsigned review of *Practical Agitation*, by John
Jay Chapman, *Harvard Advocate* 69 (10 May 1900): 80.

p. 20 "*Almost every*" John Jay Chapman, *Practical Agitation* (New York, 1900),
55–56.

"*the other pole*" Richard B. Hovey, *John Jay Chapman—AnAmerican Mind*
(New York, 1959), 91.

"*no writer of*" Edmund Wilson, "John Jay Chapman," *New Republic* 59 (22
May 1929): 33.

"*Emerson made*" M. A. DeWolfe Howe, *John Jay Chapman and His Letters*
(Boston, 1937), 150.

p. 21 "*when in power*" Emerson, *Complete Works*, 3:210, 205.

"*if a soul*" John Jay Chapman, *Emerson and Other Essays* (New York,
1899), 106, 5.

"*It is hard*" Chapman, *Practical Agitation*, 34, 83, 84, 97, 51.

p. 22 "*the first step*" L 431.

"*We must leave*" SP 179.

"*use the drama*" "Propaganda by the Play," *Nation* 1 (13 April 1907): 254–
55. On Robins's *Votes for Women*, see Elaine Showalter, *A Literature of
Their Own* (Princeton, 1977), 220–22.

p. 23 "*I am in*" SP 179. For Hartman on "The Snow Man," see "The Poet's
Politics," in *Beyond Formalism* (New Haven, 1970), 247–57.

p. 24 "*In the street-life*" Horatio Alger, *Ragged Dick and Struggling Upward*, ed.
Carl Bode (New York, 1985), 125.

"*All New York*" L 38.

"*There was no*" T. J. Jackson Lears, *No Place of Grace: Antimodernism
and the Transformation of American Culture, 1880–1920* (New York,
1981), 48.

p. 25 "*the roads are*" SP 111, 81, 142.

"*mere length of*" SP 97.

"*His voice trembled*" "Full Penalty for All," *New York Tribune*, 30 June
1901, 4.

p. 26 "*The enormous*" Stevens, "Notes on Drawing and Engraving." See also
Alan Trachtenberg, *The Incorporation of America* (New York, 1982),
123–26.

"*the whole thing*" SP 78–79.

"*We talked about*" L 52.

p. 27 "*Well, I'm home*" L 67.

"*was an extremely*" L 317, 105, 85.

p. 28 "*I need badly*" SPBS 71.

"dull as dull" SP 90, 89.

p. 29 "You shall not" Bryan's speech is reprinted in American Populism, ed.
George McKenna (New York, 1974), 131–39.

"the leaders of" Eugene Roseboom and Alfred Eckes, The History of Presidential Elections (New York, 1979), 122.

"Saw Bryan the" SP 88.

p. 30 "They want the" "Bryan Ignores the Free Silver Issue," New York Tribune,
17 October 1900, 2.

"a very mongrel" F. O. Matthiessen, The James Family: Including Selections
from the Writings of Henry James, Sr., William, Henry and Alice James
(New York, 1948), 623, 626.

"England's rule in" Theodore Roosevelt, The Strenuous Life (London,
1902), 18; see Larzer Ziff, The American 1890s (New York, 1966), 219–
22.

"the assassin of" "The March of Events," The World's Work 2 (October
1901): 1239.

p. 31 "it is often" Richard Hofstadter, The Age of Reform: From Bryan to F.D.R.
(New York, 1955), 19. For a contrary view, see Norman Pollack, The
Populist Response to Industrial America (Cambridge, Mass., 1962).

"Once ... he had" H. L. Mencken, "'The Monkey Trial': A Reporter's
Account," in D-days at Dayton: Reflections on the Scopes Trial, ed. Jerry
Tompkins (Baton Rouge, 1965), 48.

p. 32 "any large number" T. S. Eliot, After Strange Gods (New Y rk, 1934), 20.

"Italians have as" L 290; OP 310.

"Now we have" Phillip Rahv, "10 Propositions and 8 Err. ." Partisan
Review 8 (November–December 1941): 499.

p. 33 "James" and "Nietzsche" David Bromwich, "Stevens and the Idea of the
Hero," Raritan 7 (Summer 1987): 1–27.

"someone talented" Auden made this comment in his foreward to the third
edition of The Orators (London, 1966), 7.

"suggests Authority" T. S. Eliot, "Commentary," Criterion 4 (April 1926):
222.

"bouffe-proclamation" Matthiessen, James Family, 625. On Mussolini's
attraction to James, see Frank Lentricchia, "On the Ideologies of Poetic
Modernism, 1890–1913," in Reconstruction American Literary History,
ed. Sacvan Bercovitch (Cambridge, Mass., 1986), 220–49.

p. 34 "James is a" West, American Evasion of Philosophy, 60.

"Art for art's" SP 185; trans. in Richardson, WallaceStevens, 1:272.

p. 35 "The poet is" NA 115–16.

p. 36 "This is not" Unidentified newspaper clipping included in letter from Stevens to Elsie Stevens, 20 August 1911; part of this letter appears in the
published correspondence (L 171–72).

"What have I" SP 196.

p. 37 "I have no" OP 200.

"I am far" L 170.

II   Thinking About War

p. 41   *"Well a book"*   William Carlos Williams, *Imaginations,* ed. Webster Schott (New York, 1970), 15.

p. 42   *"I wish that"*   L 86.

"But my flag"   SP 29. On "diminished" romanticism, see James Richardson, *Thomas Hardy: The Poetry of Necessity* (Chicago, 1977), and James Longenbach, "Ezra Pound and the Vicissitudes of Post-Romantic Ambition," *Southern Review* 24 (Summer 1988): 481–501.

p. 43   *"vast and broad"*   L 30, 110.

"a furnished country"   Henry James, *Picture and Text* (New York, 1893), 5.

p. 44   *"I am often"*   Ezra Pound, *Gaudier-Brzeska* (New York, 1970), 94.

"no longer deals"   T. E. Hulme, *Further Speculations,* ed. Sam Hynes (Minneapolis, 1962), 72.

"The pressure of"   OP 229.

p. 45   *"Disciples of Art"*   Burke, *Counter-Statement,* 65.

p. 46   *"if anyone could"*   "Chicago Poets and Poetry," *Minaret* 1 (February 1916): 26.

"the earth of"   William James, *Pragmatism and the Meaning of Truth* (Cambridge, Mass., 1978), 62.

p. 47   *"If we could"*   Donald Evans, *Sonnets from the Patagonian* (New York, 1918), [ii]; see Glen MacLeod, *Wallace Stevens and Company* (Ann Arbor, 1983), 3–17.

p. 48   *"One cannot think"*   Walter Pach, "Universality in Art," *Modern School* 5 (February 1918): 46–55.

"With Jean Le Roy"   Walter Pach, "Jean Le Roy," *Modern School* 5 (October 1918): 296.

p. 49   *"there is such"*   *The Papers of Woodrow Wilson,* ed. Arthur S. Link, 61 vols. (Princeton, 1966–), 33:149.

"The Mexican mess"   Stevens to Elsie Stevens, 23 June 1916.

"Toronto is full"   Stevens to Elsie Stevens, 15 October 1916.

p. 50   *"I want to"*   L 209.

"I am completely"   L 212.

"The lake was"   Stevens to Elsie Stevens, 31 May 1919.

"Never as long"   Catharine Stevens's journals are held in the Wallace Stevens Collection at the Huntington Library.

p. 51   *"the twentieth century's"*   Lears, *No Place of Grace,* 160.

"had been written"   Robert McAlmon, *Being Geniuses Together,* rev. ed. (San Francisco, 1984), 6.

p. 52   *"Poetry and Manhood"*   L 26. See Frank Lentricchia, *Ariel and the Police: Michel Foucault, William James, Wallace Stevens* (Madison, 1988), 136–76. See also Ann Douglas, *The Feminization of American Culture* (New York, 1977).

"outlast art"   Bliss Carman and Richard Hovey, *Songs from Vagabondia* (Boston, 1894), 3, 36.

"*The trenches are*" L 117.

p. 54 "*When shall I*" L 151; see Richardson, *Wallace Stevens*, 1:428.

p. 55 "*the very idea*" Richard Poirier, *The Renewal of Literature: Emersonian Reflections* (New York, 1987), 210.

p. 56 "*Who indeed knows*" Judith Shklar, *Ordinary Vices* (Cambridge, Mass., 1984), 17.

p. 57 "*I wonder whether*" L 289.

"*Yesterday a terrific*" Eugène Lemercier, *A Soldier of France to His Mother*, trans. Theodore Stanton (Chicago, 1917), 71–72. Stevens recommended this translation to Harriet Monroe.

p. 58 "*You do not*" Ibid., 22, 6, 42–43.

"*out of tune*" Ibid., 25, 67, 25, 163.

p. 59 "*Never before has*" Ibid., 16, 25.

p. 60 "*a firm hope*" Ibid., 68, 109. See Margaret Peterson, "*Harmonium* and William James," *Southern Review* 7 (Summer 1971): 658–82, and David M. La Guardia, *Advance on Chaos: The Sanctifying Imagination of Wallace Stevens* (Hanover, N.H., 1983).

p. 61 "*unreal enough at*" L 464; see Lensing, *Wallace Stevens*, 113.

"*a war with*" *Papers of Woodrow Wilson*, 31:423; 33:149; 41:527.

"*That's a sad*" Stevens to Elsie Stevens, 23 June 1916.

p. 62 "*blind and deaf*" John Maynard Keynes, *The Economic Consequences of the Peace* (New York, 1920): 41.

"*From time to*" Lemercier, *Soldier of France*, 163.

"*War is a realist*" *The Journals and Miscellaneous Notebooks of Ralph Waldo Emerson*, ed. William Gillman, 16 vols. (Cambridge, Mass., 1960), 15: 299.

p. 63 "*a small minority*" SPBS 77–79.

"*all values ultimately*" Ezra Pound, *Selected Letters*, ed. D. D. Paige (New York, 1971), 181; see also 48.

"*is not to*" Marianne Moore, "Reinforcements," *Egoist* 5 (June–July 1918): 83.

p. 64 "*the death of*" Lemercier, *Soldier of France*, 146.

p. 65 "*To-day I have*" L 139–40.

p. 66 "*Death will no*" Sigmund Freud, *Character and Culture*, ed. Philip Rieff (New York, 1963), 124.

"*much of the*" See Douglas, *Feminization of American Culture*, 225.

"*what a ghastly*" NA 76.

"*After all*" L 174, 206.

p. 67 "*Everyone's individual*" *The Letters of T. S. Eliot, Volume I: 1898–1922*, ed. Valerie Eliot (New York, 1988), 214.

"*Applied for voluntary*" *Harvard College Class of 1901 War Records* (Norwood, Mass., 1920), 111–12.

p. 68 "*has been ill*" Stevens to Elsie Stevens, 11 August 1914; part of this letter appears in the published correspondence (L 182).

"*If her horny*" See Richard Ellmann, "Wallace Stevens' Ice Cream," in

Aspects of American Poetry, ed. Richard Ludwig (Columbus, 1962), 203–22.

p. 69 *"emergence of the"* Bloom, *Wallace Stevens,* 48, 50.

p. 71 *"how harmonious death"* Lemercier, *Soldier of France,* 146. On death in "Extracts," see Charles Berger, *Forms of Farewell: The Late Poetry of Wallace Stevens* (Madison, 1985), 84–85.

"nature is" Lemercier, *Soldier of France,* 104, 92–93.

p. 72 *"Sunday Morning" and "Phases"* See Buttel, *Wallace Stevens,* 230–41.

p. 74 *"Contact with women"* Nancy Huston, "The Matrix of War: Mothers and Heros," in *The Female Body in Western Culture,* ed. Susan Suleiman (Cambridge, Mass., 1986), 121. This is an interpretive crux in "Sunday Morning" that Frank Lentricchia, Sandra Gilbert, and Susan Gubar have debated without appreciating fully its historicity (Lentricchia, *Ariel and the Police,* 136–95; Gilbert and Gubar, "The Man on the Dump versus the United Dames of America; or, What Does Frank Lentricchia Want?" *Critical Inquiry* 14 [Winter 1988]: 386–406).

"the great common" *The Selected Correspondence of Kenneth Burke and Malcolm Cowley,* ed. Paul Jay (New York, 1988), 50, 99, 42.

p. 76 *"the wild ducks"* Lemercier, *Soldier of France,* 155–56.

"why a man" L 193.

"Come to Jesus" William Carlos Williams, *Paterson* (New York, 1963), 173. Williams refers to Billy Sunday's 1913 visit to Paterson, New Jersey.

"A sunny Easter" "The Storm," *New York Tribune,* 4 April 1915, 10.

"avoided the subject" L 349.

p. 77 *"somewhat aloof"* A. Walton Litz, *Introspective Voyager: The Poetic Development of Wallace Stevens* (New York, 1972), 51; Bates, *Wallace Stevens,* 111–14.

"tendency to consider" L 133, 136. Stevens paraphrases Paul Elmer More's "Lafcadio Hearn," *Shelburne Essays, Second Series* (Boston, 1905), 46–72.

p. 78 *"the literary historicity"* Lentricchia, *Ariel and the Police,* 160.

"is not situated" Eleanor Cook, *Poetry, Word-Play, and Word-War in Wallace Stevens* (Princeton, 1988), 105. On the final stanza, see Helen Vendler, *On Extended Wings: Wallace Stevens' Longer Poems* (Cambridge, Mass., 1969), 48–49.

p. 80 *"why should we"* *A Critical Edition of Yeats's A Vision (1925),* ed. George Mills Harper and Walter Kelly Hood (London, 1978), xvi.

"Unreal, give back" The manuscript of "To the One of Fictive Music" is reproduced in Louis Martz, "Manuscripts of Wallace Stevens," *Yale University Library Gazette* 54 (October 1979): 53.

p. 81 *"there is such"* Robert Frost, *Selected Prose,* ed. Hyde Cox and E. C. Lathem (New York, 1959), 115.

p. 82 *"the mind in"* OP 199.

"no picture of" Emerson, *Complete Works,* 6:19.

"Does the artist" Hartman, *Beyond Formalism,* xi.

p. 83 "there was little" Stevens, "Hawkins of Cold Cape," *Harvard Advocate* 69 (10 March 1900): 9.

p. 84 "You've no idea" Stevens to Elsie Stevens, 4 May 1909.

p. 85 "the morass of" Barrett Wendell, *The Privileged Class* (New York, 1908), 114; Thomas Watson, *The People's Campaign Book 1892* (Washington, D.C., 1892), 220. See Frederic Jaher, *Doubters and Dissenters: Cataclysmic Thought in America, 1885–1918* (New York, 1964).

"But a day" Joyce, *Ulysses,* 523.

"the war was" Christopher Lasch, *The New Radicalism in America, 1889–1963* (New York, 1965), 224.

p. 86 "immense panorama" T. S. Eliot, "Ulysses, Order, and Myth," in *Selected Prose,* ed. Frank Kermode (London, 1975), 177. See Frank Kermode, *The Sense of an Ending* (New York, 1967), and James Longenbach, "Matthew Arnold and the Modern Apocalypse," *PMLA* 104 (1989): 844–55.

"All these writers" Stephen Spender, *The Destructive Element: A Study of Modern Writers and Beliefs* (Boston, 1936), 14.

"sense of desolation" I. A. Richards, "A Background for Contemporary Poetry," *Criterion* 3 (July 1925): 520.

"the Waste Land" Wilson, *Axel's Castle,* 104, 106.

p. 87 "We are apt" T. S. Eliot, *Selected Essays* (New York, 1964), 166.

"And midway" These drafts appear in Brom Weber, *Hart Crane: A Biographical and Critical Study* (New York, 1948), 425.

"If I could" William Carlos Williams, *Collected Poems, Volume I: 1909–1939,* ed. A. Walton Litz and Christopher MacGowan (New York, 1986), 179–85.

p. 88 "To see the gods" OP 260.

p. 89 "It discloses the" Hi Simons, "'The Comedian as the Letter C': Its Sense and Its Significance," in *The Achievement of Wallace Stevens,* ed. Ashley Brown and Robert S. Haller (New York, 1962), 112.

"prodigious reputation" OP 240.

"sustained nightmare" Frank Kermode, *Wallace Stevens* (London, 1967), 45.

"I should guess" Roy Harvey Pearce, *The Continuity of American Poetry* (Princeton, 1961), 424.

p. 90 "Eliot's poem is" Stevens to Alice Henderson, 17 November 1922; "Voicing the Desert of Silence: Stevens' Letters to Alice Corbin Henderson," ed. Alan Filreis, *Wallace Stevens Journal* 12 (Spring 1988): 19.

"but never in" Robert McAlmon to Stevens, undated [Autumn 1922].

p. 93 "if Stevens is" Bloom, *Wallace Stevens,* 82, 70. On the tension between apocalypse and "social nature" in American literature, see Douglas Robinson, *American Apocalypses: The Image of the End of the World in American Literature* (Baltimore, 1985).

p. 94 "old-fashioned" L 836.

p. 95 *"considerably longer"* L 335.

"anthropomorphic error" See Friedrich Nietzsche, *Philosophyand Truth: Selections from Nietzsche's Notebooks of the Early 1870s*, ed. and trans. Daniel Breazeale (Atlantic Highlands, N.J., 1979), 79–97.

p. 98 *"the doctrines of"* Burke, *Counter-Statement*, 89, 104–6.

p. 100 *"It is the kind"* Stanley Burnshaw, "Turmoil in the Middle Ground," *New Masses* 17 (1 October 1935): 42.

"more interesting *to"* Floyd Dell, "Colors of Life," *Liberator* 1 (December 1918): 45–46. See Daniel Aaron, *Writers on the Left* (New York, 1961), 49–50.

"Rodker has been" Stevens to Ferdinand Reyher, 28 October 1921 [Maryland]; Richardson, *Wallace Stevens*, 1:518.

p. 101 *"furthermore and forever"* Reyher to Stevens, 2 December 1921.

"too much has" See Robert Murray, *Red Scare: A Study in National Hysteria, 1919–1920* (Minneapolis, 1955), 261.

"At the moment" L 350, 352.

p. 102 *"The period during"* OP 243.

III   The Second Silence

p. 105 *"the end of"* William Leuchtenberg, *The Perils of Prosperity, 1914–32* (Chicago, 1958), 89.

"I'm as busy" Stevens to William Carlos Williams, 7 September 1927; *Antaeus* 36 (Winter 1980): 146.

"Can you tell" Williams to Stevens, 28 March 1950; Richardson, *Wallace Stevens*, 2:52.

"People suppose" See OP 237–39.

p. 106 *"This society will"* See Edward C. Lunt, *Surety Bonds: Nature, Functions, Underwriting Requirements* (New York, 1922), 3.

"is like being" Peter Brazeau, *Parts of a World: Wallace Stevens Remembered* (New York, 1983), 188.

p. 108 *"nothing has made"* Stevens to R. P. Blackmur, 16 November 1931 [Princeton]; Holly Stevens, "Flux[2]," *Southern Review* 15 (1979): 773–74.

"This is where" Brazeau, *Parts of a World*, 24.

p. 109 *"Poetry and surety"* Lewis Nichols, "Talk with Mr. Stevens," *New York Times Book Review*, 3 October 1954, 3.

"None of the" L 426.

"It gives a" "The Vice President of Shapes," *Time* 66 (15 August 1955): 12.

"As a writer" Stevens to Blackmur, 12 November 1946 [Princeton]; Bates, *Wallace Stevens*, 161.

p. 110 *"Most people avail"* OP 310.

"can't reconcile" L 414, 413.

"horrible double" See Ernst Pawel, *The Nightmare of Reason: A Life of Franz Kafka* (New York, 1985), 190.

p. *111* "cancel order to" See John Tomsich, *A Genteel Endeavor* (Stanford, 1971), 114.

"Does it really" Edmund Wilson, "The Muses Out of Work," *New Republic* 50 (11 May 1927): 320, 321.

"impervious to life" Edmund Wilson, "Wallace Stevens and E. E. Cummings," *New Republic* 38 (19 March 1924): 103.

"Poetry is automatically" John Crowe Ransom, "The Poet and the Critic," *New Republic* 51 (22 June 1927): 125.

p. *112* "which was truly" L 552.

p. *114* "It is very" L 250.

p. *115* "The imagination loses" NA 6.

"Though Valentine" L 245.

p. *116* "should be more" Brazeau, *Parts of a World*, 142.

"say, the next" L 320.

p. *117* "the years of" NA 146.

"Independence to do" Stevens to Henderson, 27 March 1922; "Voicing the Desert of Silence," 17. All further quotations from Stevens's correspondence with Henderson are taken from this letter.

"Our young folks" SP 71.

"Generally speaking" L 263. For details on Stevens's finances, see Brazeau, *Parts of a World*, 231.

p. *118* "I am no longer" Stevens to Elsie Stevens, 18 March 1907; Brazeau, *Parts of a World*, 261.

"Nothing short of" L 261, 269.

"the master of" L 301, 78.

p. *119* "What was most" Dana Goia, "Business and Poetry," *Hudson Review* 36 (1983): 158. Perhaps the most insightful account of Stevens's conflicted attitude toward travel (and toward extravagance in general) may be found in Richard Howard's poem "Even in Paris," in *No Traveller* (New York, 1989), 3–30.

p. *120* "I know the god" McAlmon to Stevens, 2 December 1921; Richardson, *Wallace Stevens*, 1:518–19.

p. *121* "Feeling like aliens" Malcolm Cowley, *Exile's Return* (New York, 1956), 6. See also Richard Fox and Jackson Lears, eds., *The Culture of Consumption* (New York, 1983).

"working at the" L 767, 845.

"I dislike niggling" L 264, 266, 301.

p. *122* This is the: Stevens to Reyher, 13 May 1921 [Maryland].

The list wanders: Stevens to Reyher, 23 November 1920 [Maryland].

p. *123* Stevens wrote back: Stevens to Reyher, 31 January 1921 [Maryland].

"because I have" L 278.

Stevens shot back: Stevens to Reyher, 6 April 1922 [Maryland].

"I bravely steered" McAlmon to Stevens, 20 July 1921.

p. 124 "In a way" Letters of James Joyce, ed. Stuart Gilbert and Richard Ellmann, 3 vols. (New York, 1957, 1966), 1:173.

Stevens was stunned: Stevens to Reyher, 30 June 1921 [Maryland].

"Am here with" McAlmon to Stevens, 28 January 1924.

p. 125 "The baby has" L 245–46.

p. 126 "Since my return" Stevens to Reyher, 2 February 1922; Brazeau, Parts of a World, 97.

"The attorneys in" L 224–25.

p. 127 "I pride myself" Stevens to Reyher, 6 April 1922; Bates, Wallace Stevens, 89.

p. 128 "Saddle bags filled" See OP 209–12.

p. 129 "Les carrièrs réussies" SPBS 21–22.

p. 130 "It is undeniably" Walter Leaf 1852–1927: Some Chapters of Autobiography with a Memoir by Charlotte M. Leaf (London, 1932), 165.

p. 131 "like a lot of" L 295–96.

"Writing again after" L 265.

p. 132 "to think that" Stanley Burnshaw, "Wallace Stevens and the Statue," Sewanee Review 69 (Summer 1961): 360. See also Burnshaw, "Reflections on Wallace Stevens," Wallace Stevens Journal 13 (Fall 1989): 122–26.

IV   Poetry and Social Change

p. 135 "Wallace Stevens is" Edwin Rolfe, "Poetry," Partisan Review 2 (April–May 1935): 33, 34. For a recent reevaluation of Rolfe's poetry, see Cary Nelson, Repression and Recovery: Modern American Poetry and the Politics of Cultural Memory, 1910–1945 (Madison, 1989), 113–14.

"The mood of" William Phillips and Philip Rahv, "Literature in a Political Decade," in New Letters in America, ed. Horace Gregory (New York, 1937), 170–80.

p. 136 "Every profession" A Virgil Thomson Reader (New York, 1981), 88, 102.

"was a great" L 274.

"only a man" Selected Correspondence of Burke and Cowley, 196.

p. 137 "Do you take" OP 307.

"I am not" Selected Correspondence of Burke and Cowley, 202.

"It is only" William Phillips and Philip Rahv, "Private Experience and Public Philosophy," Poetry 48 (May 1936): 102.

"I hope I am" L 286.

p. 138 "as a matter" Stanley Burnshaw, [Response to Edwin Rolfe], Partisan Review 2 (April–May 1935): 49.

"For the later" Alan Wald, The New York Intellectuals: The Rise and Decline of the Anti-Stalinist Left (Chapel Hill, 1987), 74. See also Terry A. Cooney, *The Rise of the New York Intellectuals: Partisan Review and Its Circle* (Madison, 1986); Richard Pells, *Radical Visions and American Dreams: Culture and Social Thought in the Depression Years* (New York, 1973); and Harvey Teres, "Notes Toward the Supreme Soviet: Stevens and Doctrinaire Marxism," *Wallace Stevens Journal* 13 (Fall 1989): 150–67.

"the illusion has" Wallace Phelps [William Phillips] and Philip Rahv, "Problems and Perspectives in Revolutionary Literature," *Partisan Review* 1 (June–July 1934): 3–10.

"a Marxist who" *Writings of Leon Trotsky [1932]*, ed. George Breitman and Sarah Lovell (New York, 1973), 296.

"the American" "What Is Americanism?" *Partisan Review and Anvil* 3 (April 1936): 13; "Sanctions Against Williams," *Partisan Review and Anvil* 3 (May 1936): 30.

p. 139 *"organically related"* *Selected Correspondence of Burke and Cowley*, 198.

"the writer's best" Kenneth Burke, "Revolutionary Symbolism in America," in *American Writers' Congress*, ed. Hary Hart (New York, 1935), 87–94.

"vacillating intellectuals" "To John Dos Passos," *New Masses* 10 (6 March 1934): 8–9.

"The point was" Daniel Aaron, "Thirty Years Later: Memories of the First American Writers' Congress," *American Scholar* 35 (Summer 1966): 506–7. See also Frank Lentricchia, *Criticism and Social Change* (Chicago, 1983), 21–38.

p. 140 *"lead the proletarian"* Granville Hicks, "The Crisis in American Criticism," *New Masses* 8 (February 1933): 3–5.

"We shall resist" "Editorial Statement," *Partisan Review* 1 (February–March 1934): 2.

"sensibility of" Wallace Phelps [William Phillips], "Three Generations," *Partisan Review* 1 (September–October 1934): 53.

"Well, does this" Wallace Phelps [William Phillips] and Philip Rahv, "Criticism," *Partisan Review* 2 (April–May 1935): 16–25.

p. 141 *"extraordinarily stimulating"* L 296, 287, 332.

"been formed to" Kenneth Burke, "The Writers' Congress," *Nation 140 (15 May 1935): 571.*

p. 142 *"afford to drive"* Stanley Burnshaw, "'Middle-Ground' Writers," *New Masses* 15 (30 April 1935): 19–21.

"Acutely conscious" Stanley Burnshaw, "Turmoil in the Middle Ground," *New Masses* 17 (1 October 1935): 41–42.

p. 144 *"On the one"* Stevens to C. L. Daughtry, 24 October 1938.

"gone incredible" L 767.

p. 145 *"I believe in"* L 351.

"The last question" L 291–92.

p. 146 *"Why shouldn't the"* See William Leuchtenberg, *Franklin D. Roosevelt and the New Deal, 1932–1940* (New York, 1963), 190.

p. 147 *"qualified assertions"* See Helen Vendler, "The Qualified Assertions of Wallace Stevens," in *The Act of the Mind,* ed. Roy Harvey Pearce and J. Hillis Miller (Baltimore, 1965), 163–78.

p. 148   *"By associating"*   R. P. Blackmur, *Form and Value in Modern Poetry* (New York, 1957), 190.

"One of the"   Stevens to Blackmur, 16 November 1931 [Princeton]; Holly Stevens, "Flux²," *Southern Review* 15 (1979): 773.

"I hadn't thought"   Blackmur to Stevens, 2 December 1931.

p. 149   *"a system of"*   Kenneth Burke, "Counterblasts on 'Counter-Statement,'" *New Republic* 69 (9 December 1931): 101. Hick's review, "A Defense of Eloquence," appeared on 2 December 1931: 75–76.

"a return to"   Burke, *Counter-Statement,* 91, 118–19.

p. 150   *"Thought is a"*   Blackmur, *Form and Value,* 343, 352–53.

"the greatest of"   Edward Said, "The Horizon of R. P. Blackmur," *Raritan* 6 (Fall 1986): 36, 32, 33.

"changes, and I"   L 289, 293.

p. 151   *"there is nothing"*   Stevens to Ronald Latimer, 1 February 1938 [Chicago].

"I dare say"   L 305.

"If you can't"   Williams to Ezra Pound, 25 March 1935; Paul Mariani, *William Carlos Williams: A New World Naked* (New York, 1981), 375.

"We think of"   OP 222–23.

"excludes, or pretends"   Benedetto Croce, *A Defence of Poetry* (Oxford, 1933), 19, 13–14, 27–28 [Massachusetts]. See A. Walton Litz, "Wallace Stevens' Defense of Poetry: *La poésie pure,* the New Romantic, and the Pressure of Reality," in *Romantic and Modern,* ed. George Bornstein (Pittsburgh, 1977), 111–32.

p. 153   *"progression on certain"*   Marianne Moore to Stevens, 10 March 1936.

p. 154   *"The profane multitude"*   SPBS 39.

"would be intolerable"   OP 214.

p. 155   *"If men have"*   L 348.

"the mind in"   OP 199; SPBS 51.

p. 156   *"delicate and joyous"*   L 267, 266.

"Owing to the"   L 268. See Samuel Farber, *Revolution and Reaction in Cuba, 1933–1960* (Middletown, Conn., 1976).

p. 157   *"The philosopher could"*   SPBS 33.

p. 158   *"Drawing upon two"*   John Hollander, "The Sound of the Music of Music and Sound," in *Wallace Stevens: A Celebration,* ed. Frank Doggett and Robert Buttel (Princeton, 1980), 236.

p. 159   *"Poetry is not"*   OP 189.

p. 160   *"a transcendental poetic"*   Bloom, *Wallace Stevens,* 104.

"what we witness"   Marjorie Levinson, *Wordsworth's Great Period Poems: Four Essays* (New York, 1986), 37.

p. 161   *"merely added the"*   Phillips and Rahv, "Literature in a Political Decade," 172–73.

"not intended to"   L 798.

"a professional fondness"   Ramon Fernandez, "I Came Near Being a Fascist," *Partisan Review* 1 (September–October 1934): 19. See also Fer-

nandez, "Lettre ouverte à André Gide," *Nouvelle revue français* 42 (April 1934): 703–8.

"*the Lightness with*"   L 380, 403.

p. *162*   "*true business*"   R. P. Blackmur, *The Lion and the Honeycomb* (New York, 1955), 161.

"*the seasoned stocks*"   Burke, *Counter-Statement*, 106.

"*Nothing could*"   Barbara Johnson, *A World of Difference* (Baltimore, 1987), 30.

p. *163*   "*in ideological struggle*"   Lentricchia, *Criticism and Social Change*, 34.

"*You know*"   L 300.

"*the social arrangement*"   William Empson, *Some Versions of Pastoral* (New York, 1960), 4, 6.

p. *164*   "*Miss Treneer*"   SPBS 45–47.

"*The* Excursion *may*"   William Hazlitt, *Complete Works*, ed. P. P. Howe, 21 vols. (London, 1930–34), 19:10.

p. *165*   "*a fixed philosophic*"   L 293.

p. *166*   "*I do very*"   L 300.

"*Although this deals*"   L 368.

p. *168*   "*the spectacle of*"   Michael Gold, "Notes of the Month," *New Masses* 6 (September 1930): 5.

p. *169*   "*justification of*"   L 295, 367.

"*A humanistic sublime*"   Thomas Weiskel, *The Romantic Sublime* (Baltimore 1986), 3.

p. *170*   "*the pressure of*"   OP 229–30.

p. *171*   "*imagination has no*"   L 364.

p. *172*   "*It helps us*"   OP 234.

"*Of the* [*over 1,800*]"   *Nation* 143 (24 October 1936): 463.

p. *173*   "*master of ironic*"   R. P. Blackmur, "Henry Adams: Three Late Moments," *Kenyon Review* 2 (Winter 1940): 28, 29. See SPBS 71.

p. *174*   "*on the relation*"   L 383. Marjorie Perloff points out that in a subsequent letter from Stevens to Church (L 384), "the words 'he is a Jew and a Communist. For all that have been excised, so that the sentence reads, 'About Rahv [. . .] he is a man of extraordinary intelligence'" ("Revolving in Crystal: The Supreme Fiction and the Impasse of Modernist Lyric," in *Wallace Stevens: The Poetics of Modernism*, ed. Albert Gelpi [Cambridge, 1985], 63). It should also be pointed out that Church's side of the correspondence reveals that Stevens made this remark more to counter Church's acknowledged prejudices than to express his own.

"*immersed themselves*"   Philip Rahv, "Twilight of the Thirties," *Partisan Review* 6 (Summer 1939): 3–15.

p. *176*   "*could explain how*"   Frederick Crews, *Skeptical Engagements* (New York, 1986), 196.

"*reflection of objective*"   Theodore Adorno, "Reconciliation Under Duress," in *Aesthetics and Politics*, ed. Ronald Taylor (London, 1977), 153, 159, 166, 168.

p. 177   *"soothing comfort"*   Theodore Adorno, *Philosophy of Modern Music*, trans. Anne Mitchell and Wesley Blomster (New York, 1973), 170.

  "despair over the"   Georg Lukács, *The Theory of the Novel*, trans. Anna Bostok (Cambridge, Mass., 1971), 12. See Eugene Lunn, *Marxism and Modernism* (Berkeley, 1982).

  "Reactionary in its"   Philip Rahv, "Dostoevsky and Politics," *Partisan Review* 5 (July 1938): 35.

  "sensibility has"   William Phillips, "Form and Content," *Partisan Review* 2 (January–February 1935): 36; Phillips, "The Esthetic of the Founding Fathers," *Partisan Review* 4 (March 1938): 19.

  "there is no"   *Virgil Thomson Reader*, 91.

  "advanced intellectuals"   Philip Rahv, "How the Waste Land Became a Flower Garden," *Partisan Review* 1 (September–October 1934): 37–42. This exchange between Krutch and Rahv hinged on a phrase on which Stevens would subsequently spin many of the variations in "The Man with the Blue Guitar." Quoting Krutch, Rahv responded: "The artist ostensibly makes existence 'tolerable to those who are compelled to accept Things As They Are.' But the plain fact is . . . that economic conditions compel the masses to revolt against, not to accept, things as they are" (40).

p. 178   *"intense study by"*   Philip Rahv, "The Death of Ivan Ilyich and Joseph K," *Partisan Review* 5 (Summer 1939): 174; Rahv "The Artist as Desperado," *New Republic* 104 (21 April 1942): 558.

  "Our days are"   Philip Rahv, "Trials of the Mind," *Partisan Review* 4 (April 1938): 3.

p. 179   *"What we were"*   Philip Rahv, "Proletarian Literature: A Political Autopsy," *Southern Review* 4 (1939): 620.

  "Mr. Eliot's instinct"   "P.R.'s Literary Principles," *Partisan Review* 8 (November–December 1941): 519.

p. 180   *"There is one"*   *The Marx–Engels Reader*, 2d ed., ed. Robert C. Tucker (New York, 1978), 577–78.

  "it is a process"   L 367, 311.

p. 181   *"constant struggle"*   Stevens to Latimer, 23 March 1936 [Chicago]; Bates, *Wallace Stevens*, 188.

  "a ballooning music"   Vendler, *On Extended Wings*, 80.

p. 182   *"As a preview"*   Joseph Riddel, *Clairvoyant Eye: The Poetry and Poetics of Wallace Stevens* (Baton Rouge, 1965), 128.

  "complexity of"   L 300.

p. 183   *"political ambivalence"*   Litz, *Introspective Voyager*, 220. See also Michael North's reading of "Owl's Clover" in *The Final Sculpture: Public Monuments and Modern Poets* (Ithaca, 1985), 207–19.

  "If the future"   L 371–72.

p. 184   *"when liberals"*   Richard Pells, *The Liberal Mind in a Conservative Age: American Intellectuals in the 1940s and 1950s* (New York, 1985), 13.

  "I feel terribly"   L 518.

"Raise reddest columns"   See L 360.

p. 186   "Can we say"   Christian Zervos, "Fait social et vision cosmique," *Cahiers d'art* 10 (1935): 145; see Glen MacLeod, "Stevens and Surrealism: The Genesis of 'The Man with the Blue Guitar,'" *American Literature* 59 (October 1987): 368.

"a just placing"   SPBS 63.

p. 189   "I have been"   L 354.

p. 190   "embodies the hope"   Marianne Moore, *Complete Prose*, ed. Patricia Willis (New York, 1986), 349.

p. 191   "You ought to"   L 374.

"Men make their"   *Marx-Engels Reader*, 595.

p. 192   "it is by no"   Lionel Trilling, *Beyond Culture* (New York, 1968), 68. It is instructive to recall that Trilling (like Stevens, as we will see in Chapter 17) would allow this careful distinction between the imperatives of art and politics to degenerate into a kind of cold war quietism. See Joseph Frank's seminal essay, "Lionel Trilling and the Conservative Imagination," in *The Widening Gyre* (New Brunswick, N.J., 1963), 253–72.

"Separation, simplicity"   Edward Said, "Opponents, Audiences, Constituencies, and Community," in *The Politics of Interpretation*, ed. W.J.T. Mitchell (Chicago, 1983), 18–19.

p. 193   "If each of"   See OP 233–37. See also Arthur J. Altmeyer, *The Formative Years of Social Security* (Madison, 1966).

p. 194   "the union of"   Josiah Royce, *War and Insurance* (New York, 1914), x, xlv–xlvi. On Royce's work on insurance and community, see Walter Benn Michaels, *The Gold Standard and the Logic of Naturalism* (Berkeley, 1987), 188–94.

p. 195   "nominally 'socialist'"   D. S. Savage, "Socialism in Extremis," *Politics* 2 (January 1945): 18; for Stevens's comments on this essay, see L 486.

"contradiction between"   Enid Starkie, "Books in General," *New Statesman and Nation* 25 (22 May 1943): 639. Stevens makes an uncredited quotation of this review in "The Figure of the Youth as Virile Poet" (NA 64).

p. 196   "end of ideology"   Daniel Bell, *The End of Ideology: On the Exhaustion of Political Ideas in the Fifties*, rev. ed. (New York, 1962), 405.

V   Rethinking War

p. 200   "depression of"   T. S. Eliot, "Last Words," *Criterion* 18 (January 1939) 274.

"a moment perhaps"   William Phillips and Philip Rahv, "In Retrospect: Ten Years of *Partisan Review*," in *The Partisan Reader* (New York, 1946), 682.

"have no editorial"   "A Statement by the Editors," *Partisan Review* 9 (January–February 1942): 2. See S. A. Longstaff, "*Partisan Review* and the Second World War," *Salmagundi* 43 (Winter 1979): 108–29.

"Some day"   Clement Greenberg, *Art and Culture* (Boston, 1961), 230.

p. 201 *"at one of"*   Stevens to Henry Church, 17 April 1940; Richardson, *Wallace Stevens,* 2:170.

"a kind of"   Perloff, "Revolving in Crystal," 42.

"We are confronting"   NA 22.

p. 202 *"In the presence"*   OP 241–42.

"commercial-liberal"   Kenneth Burke, "War and Cultural Life," *American Journal of Sociology* 48 (November 1942): 404–10.

p. 203 *"there is, in"*   Kenneth Burke, "Surrealism," in *New Directions in Prose and Poetry,* ed. James Laughlin (Norfolk, Conn., 1940), 576–77.

"in speaking of"   NA 26–27, 36, 20.

"These young Maquis"   SPBS 85. Stevens quotes from Genêt [Janet Flanner], "Letter from Paris," *New Yorker* (23 February 1946): 50. Paul Fussell explores the relation of the Second World War to an "aesthetics of silence" in *Wartime: Understanding and Behavior in the Second World War* (New York, 1989), 135–37. Stevens heard firsthand accounts of wartime atrocities at the Entretiens de Pontigny Conference at Mount Holyoke in 1943 (see John Peale Bishop, "Entretiens de Pontigny: 1943," *Sewanee Review* 52 [Autumn 1944]: 493–507).

"My own remarks"   NA 30, 22–23.

p. 204 *"Every significant"*   Stephen Spender, "The Creative Imagination in the World Today," in *Folios of New Writing* (London, 1940), 153–54 [Massachusetts]. Stevens also adapted material from Virginia Woolf's "The Leaning Tower," published in the same volume (11–33). On other reading Stevens did while preparing "The Noble Rider," see B. J. Leggett, *Wallace Stevens and Poetic Theory* (Chapel Hill, 1987).

"one of the"   NA 22, 21.

"I very much"   L 333.

p. 205 *"Just beyond"*   Holly Stevens, "Bits of Remembered Time," *Southern Review* 7 (1971): 652.

p. 208 *"We are going"*   Richardson, *Wallace Stevens,* 2:162.

"When the war"   L 342.

p. 209 *"it is not"*   Philip Rahv, "10 Propositions and 8 Errors," *Partisan Review* 8 (November–December 1941): 502; see also Dwight Macdonald and Clement Greenberg, "10 Propositions on the War," *Partisan Review* 8 (July–August 1941): 271–78.

"The second world"   Dwight Macdonald, "Notes on a Strange War," *Partisan Review* 7 (May–June 1940): 170–71.

p. 210 *"the primordial"*   L 346, 353, 356.

p. 211 *"has lived a"*   Robert Graves, *The Common Asphodel: Collected Essays on Poetry* (London, 1949), 310. See also Michael Walzer, "World War II: Why Was This War Different?" in *War and Moral Responsibility,* ed. Marshall Cohen et al. (Princeton, 1974), 85–103.

p. 212 *"the spectator"*   Richard Eberhart, "Preface: Attitudes to War," in *War and the Poet,* ed. Richard Eberhart and Selden Rodman (New York, 1945), xv.

"*I am afraid*" L 365, 381.

"*Strangely enough*" Church to Stevens, 11 February 1942.

"*This sort of*" L 365, 506, 497.

p. 213 "*a place that*" Stevens to Philip May, 31 January 1940 [Harvard].

p. 214 Parts of a World See Bromwich, "Stevens and the Idea of the Hero."

p. 215 "*Now the poet*" SPBS 57.

"*It is the*" L 377.

p. 216 "*constitutive anecdote*" Kenneth Burke, *A Grammar of Motives* (Berkeley, 1969), 328–29.

p. 217 "*the Lightness with*" L 380.

p. 221 "*A prose commentary*" L 479.

"*I feel exactly*" Allen Tate to Stevens, 18 December 1944.

p. 223 "*to use* bonds" John Morton Blum, *V Was for Victory: Politics and American Culture During World War II* (New York, 1976), 17, 16, 64, 54.

"*The lot of*" L 450.

p. 225 "*The centuries*" NA 52.

"*If Stevens had*" Eberhart, "Preface: Attitudes to War," xiii.

"*Those who say*" L 26.

p. 227 "*in the context*" Michael Renov, "From Fetish to Subject: The Containment of Sexual Difference in Hollywood's Wartime Cinema," *Wide Angle* 5 (1982): 17.

p. 228 "*two elements*" Susan Hartman, *The Home Front and Beyond: American Women in the 1940s* (Boston, 1982), 31, 20; see also Sandra Gilbert, "Soldier's Heart: Literary Men, Literary Women, and the Great War," and Susan Gubar, "'This Is My Rifle, This Is My Gun': World War II and the Blitz on Women," in *Behind the Lines: Gender and the Two World Wars*, ed. Margaret Randolph Higonet et al. (New Haven, 1987), 197–226, 227–59.

"*Contact with*" Nancy Huston, "The Matrix of War: Mothers and Heros," in *The Female Body in Western Culture*, ed. Susan Suleiman (Cambridge, Mass., 1986), 120–36.

"*It's a reflection*" See Mary Ann Doane, *The Desire to Desire: The Woman's Film of the 1940s* (Bloomington, 1987), 29.

"*left Vassar*" L 397.

p. 229 "*Don't argue*" Richardson, *Wallace Stevens*, 2:209.

"*How nice*" L 422–23.

"*very lurid*" Stevens to Lila Roney, 11 January 1943; Milton Bates, "To Realize the Past: Wallace Stevens' Genealogical Study," *American Literature* 52 (1981): 612.

p. 230 "*This younger figure*" NA 52–53, 56, 60, 66. Stevens quotes from Raymond Mortimer's review of Tillyard, "The Elizabethan Background," *New Statesman and Nation* 25 (8 May 1943): 310.

"*everything moves*" OP 242.

p. *231* "*The hero who*" Bates, *Wallace Stevens*, 246.

p. *234* "*I have an*" Joyce, *Ulysses*, 171, 320.

p. *235* "*the very structure*" Margaret Homans, *Bearing the Word: Language and Female Experience in Nineteenth-Century Women's Writing* (Chicago, 1986), 26. See also Susan Schweik's excellent essay on Moore, "Writing War Poetry Like a Woman," in *Speaking of Gender*, ed. Elaine Showalter (New York, 1989), 310–32.

p. *237* "*Stevens has averted*" Vendler, *On Extended Wings*, 209.

p. *238* "*wound-rose*" See Paul Fussell, *The Great War and Modern Memory* (New York, 1975), 244.

"*What particularly*" L 468.

"*What are we*" John Crowe Ransom, "Artists, Soldiers, Positivists," *Kenyon Review* 6 (Spring 1944): 276–77.

p. *239* "*When Stevens wrote*" Cook, *Poetry, Word-Play, and Word-War*, 192.

p. *240* "*thinking of*" L 469.

"*How has the*" OP 194.

p. *241* "*own destruction*" Walter Benjamin, *Illuminatins*, ed. Hannah Arendt (New York, 1969), 242.

p. *242* "*in what he*" Victor Serge, "The Revolution at Dead-End," *Politics* 1 (June 1944): 150; see SPBS 79 and D. L. Macdonald, "Wallace Stevens and Victor Serge," *Dalhousie Review* 66 (Spring–Summer 1986): 174–80.

"*the human will*" SPBS 73.

p. *243* "*You are fascinated*" L 693.

"*The little fire*" I. A. Richards, *Coleridge on Imagination* (London, 1934), 24; see Cook, *Poetry, Word-Play, and Word-War*, 211.

p. *244* "*what's the origin*" Virginia Woolf, *Between the Acts* (New York, 1969), 24.

p. *245* "*the image of*" Kaja Silverman, *The Acoustic Mirror: The Female Voice in Psychoanalysis and Cinema* (Bloomington, 1988), 73.

p. *246* "*has something*" Immanuel Kant, *The Critique of Judgement*, trans. James Meredith (Oxford, 1952), 112–13.

"*merely by living*" Berger, *Forms of Farewell*, 31.

p. *247* "*easy victory*" Vendler, *On Extended Wings*, 166–67.

"*The long and*" L 489.

p. *249* "*something of*" Vendler, *On Extended Wings*, 205; Bloom, *Wallace Stevens*, 216.

"*on the back*" L 408.

p. *250* "*The question*" OP 310.

"*the lines on*" L 442.

p. *251* "*at least double*" L 502.

"*Art is individual*" SPBS 75.

"*will note that*" Archibald MacLeish, "The Irresponsibles," *Nation* 150 (18 May 1940): 618.

p. *252* "*purple with rage*" Brazeau, *Parts of a World*, 119. Stevens was at least willing to exploit MacLeish's connections; he suggested that Henry Church might be able to convince Hemingway to lecture at Princeton if he could first interest MacLeish (see L 412).

"It is an"   Dwight Macdonald, "Kulturbolschewismus Is Here," *Partisan Review* 8 (November–December 1941): 446, 450–51. See also Morton Zabel, "The Poet on Capitol Hill," *Partisan Review* 8 (1941): 2–19, 128–45, and the statements collected in "On the 'Brooks–MacLeish' Thesis," *Partisan Review* 8 (January–February 1942): 38–47.

"It is a curious"   L 568, 495.

"We may and"   René Wellek, "Van Wyck Brooks and a National Literature," *American Prefaces* 7 (1942): 306. On the rise of neo-Populist nationalism, see Warren Susman, "The Culture of the Thirties," in *Culture as History* (New York, 1984), 150–83.

p. 253   *"narrow political"*   See Edward Jewell, "'Globalism' Pops into View," *New York Times*, 13 June 1943, sec. 2, p. 9.

p. 254   *"political apoliticalism"*   Serge Guilbaud, *How New York Stole the Idea of Modern Art: Abstract Expressionism, Freedom, and the Cold War*, trans. Arthur Goldhammer (Chicago, 1983), 2.

"All renderings"   Meyer Schapiro, "The Nature of Abstract Art," *Marxist Quarterly* 1 (January–March 1937): 85–86. On the importance of this essay for art historians today, see T. J. Clark, *The Painting of Modern Life* (Princeton, 1984), 3–22. On theories of abstraction generally, see W.J.T. Mitchell, "*Ut Pictura Theoria*: Abstract Painting and the Repression of Language," *Critical Inquiry* 15 (Winter 1989): 348–71; for specific approaches to the issue different from my own, see Charles Altieri, *Painterly Abstraction in Modernist American Poetry* (Cambridge, 1989), and Glen MacLeod, "'Notes toward a Supreme Fiction' and Abstract Art," *Journal of Modern Literature* 16 (Summer 1989): 31–48.

"painting plainly"   Robert Motherwell, "Painters' Objects," *Partisan Review* 11 (Winter 1944): 94–95.

"The abstract does"   L 434.

p. 255   *"I have no"*   L 430.

p. 257   *"I turn to"*   L 434.

p. 258   *"only as an"*   Vendler, *On Extended Wings*, 192.

"even the largest"   Henri Focillon, *The Life of Forms in Art*, trans. Charles Hogan and George Kubler (New Haven, 1942), 24 [Massachusetts]; see Leggett, *Wallace Stevens and Poetic Theory*, 150–51.

p. 259   *"any name"*   L 434; Bloom, *Wallace Stevens*, 189.

"Why might not"   Church to Stevens, 19 April 1943; Stevens to Church, 21 April 1943; see Bates, *Wallace Stevens*, 202–3.

"invariably the"   Church to Stevens, 15 May 1943.

p. 260   *"Your Supreme Court"*   L 448.

p. 261   *"The long and"*   L 489.

p. 262   *"No politician"*   NA 28.

p. 263   *"the chief problems"*   NA 156.

"I ask not"   Emerson, *Complete Works*, 1:111.

p. 264 *"is something we"* Stanley Cavell, "An Emerson Mood," in *The Senses of Walden* (San Francisco, 1981), 144.

"With me, how" L 287.

"in quest of" Stanley Cavell, *In Quest of the Ordinary* (Chicago, 1988), 149.

"pick up a" L 595, 608.

p. 265 *"the self-defeat"* Cavell, *In Quest of the Ordinary*, 138.

"The poet represents" OP 199; Burke, *Counter-Statement*, 105.

"clear the Canon" Bloom, *Wallace Stevens*, 206, 190; Vendler, *On Extended Wings*, 190, 197, 198. Theodore Weiss offers the most incisive discussion of the value of ordinary experience to Stevens in "Wallace Stevens: Lunching with Hoon," in *The Man from Porlock: Engagements 1944–1981* (Princeton, 1982), 58–98.

"the willing repetition" Cavell, *In Quest of the Ordinary*, 178.

p. 267 *"a present perfecting"* OP 193.

"Wordsworthian rather" Harold Bloom, "Notes toward a Supreme Fiction: A Commentary," in *Wallace Stevens*, ed. Marie Borroff (Englewood Cliffs, N.J., 1963), 93.

p. 268 *"upon which the"* Bloom, *Wallace Stevens*, 212.

p. 269 *"changed to something"* Vendler, *On Extended Wings*, 201.

"here my interest" L 636.

p. 271 *"among elm trees"* L 507.

p. 273 *"celebrates the first"* Berger, *Forms of Farewell*, 83.

VI The Affluent Mundo

p. 277 *"There are a"* L 516–17.

p. 278 *"To permit other"* See *A Casebook on Ezra Pound*, ed. William Van O'Connor and Edward Stone (New York, 1959), 45.

p. 279 *"we have to"* L 582, 512.

p. 280 *"The only historically"* Dwight Macdonald, *Memoirs of a Revolutionist* (New York, 1957), 201.

"the end of" In addition to Bell, *End of Ideology*, see Morris Dickstein's chapter on the 1950s in *Gates of Eden* (New York, 1977), 25–50.

"how easy it" OP 262. On the attractiveness of this Stevens to New Criticism and later "theoretical" criticism, see Frank Lentricchia, *After the New Criticism* (Chicago, 1980), 30–35, and Fredric Jameson, "Wallace Stevens," *New Orleans Review* 11 (Spring 1984): 10–19. By slighting the historicity of Stevens's career, however, these accounts tend to represent the Stevens admired by critics of the 1960s as the whole of Stevens.

p. 282 *"the area of"* L 494.

p. 283 *"If there is"* L 605.

p. 284 *"more prophetic"* Bloom, *Wallace Stevens*, 240.

"*This memorandum*" L 377.

p. 285 "*The role of*" OP 311.

"*the essential strength*" Arthur M. Schlesinger, Jr., *The Vital Center: The Politics of Freedom* (Boston, 1949), 248.

"*Artistic freedom*" Lloyd Goodrich, "Art in Democracies," in *The Contemporary Scene: A Symposium* (New York, 1954), 78–79. The symposium was held at the Metropolitan Museum of Art in March 1952.

p. 286 "*a rather tiring*" L 533.

"*Mr. Chambers and*" Stevens to José Rodríguez Feo, 9 January 1949; *Secretaries of the Moon: The Letters of Wallace Stevens and José Rodríguez Feo*, ed. Beverly Coyle and Alan Filreis (Durham, 1986), 160.

"*an occasional thought*" L 619; see Andrei Vyshinsky, *The Law of the Soviet State*, trans. Hugh W. Babb (New York, 1948), 617.

"*taking advantage*" L 620, 768.

p. 287 "*International Seminar*" Stevens declined the invitation for health reasons; Henry Kissinger's letter to Stevens (21 June 1955) and Stevens's response (27 June 1955) are in the Huntington Library.

"*Unlike most writers*" Lentricchia, *Ariel and the Police*, 214.

"*The final belief*" OP 189.

"*I said that*" L 430.

p. 288 "*This [philosophy] asserts*" Sigmund Freud, *The Future of an Illusion*, trans. W. D. Robson-Scott (London, 1928), 44 [Massachusetts]. On Stevens and Vaihinger, see Frank Doggett, *Stevens' Poetry of Thought* (Baltimore, 1966), 98–108.

p. 289 "*affirmation beneath*" Vendler, *On Extended Wings*, 33.

"*I cannot say*" L 839.

"*The long poems*" Litz, *Introspective Voyager*, 287–88.

p. 290 "*open poems*" See Cairns Craig, *Yeats, Eliot, Pound and the Politics of Poetry* (London, 1982).

p. 291 "*To write a*" Lentricchia, *Ariel and the Police*, 204, 228.

"*the poem has*" John Crowe Ransom, *The World's Body* (New York, 1938), 59.

p. 292 "*greatest moments*" Jerome McGann, *The Romantic Ideology* (Chicago, 1983), 132, 131, 145.

p. 293 "*The Only Copy*" OP 323.

p. 294 "*at my age*" L 755, 640.

"*At least what*" L 643, 648.

p. 295 "*One turns with*" OP 248.

p. 296 "*The Stevenses*" L 602, 711.

"*To live in*" L 506; see also SPBS 81 and *Secretaries of the Moon*, 62, 27.

p. 297 "*the poem annihilates*" J. Hillis Miller, *The Linguistic Moment: From Wordsworth to Stevens* (Princeton, 1985), 397, 410. Jerome McGann offers a critique of Miller's conception of "reference" in his introduction to *Historical Studies and Literary Criticism* (Madison, 1985), 3–21.

"*had originally*" L 701–2.

p. 298 *"unbelievably irrelevant"* L 760.

"universal poetry" NA 160.

p. 299 *"the French say"* L 755.

"interested in" Edmund Wilson, "Santayana at the Convent of the Blue Nuns," *New Yorker* 22 (6 April 1946): 67. See Litz, *Introspective Voyager*, 277–82.

"To use a" NA 147–48.

p. 300 *"ultimate delight"* Burke, *Grammar of Motives*, 222–23. Stevens saw some of Burke's remarks on Santayana quoted in Stanley Edgar Hyman, *The Armed Vision* (New York, 1948), 354; see L 598.

"no disabling" Berger, *Forms of Farewell*, 140.

p. 301 *"I have no"* L 710.

"If these venerable" OP 285.

p. 302 *"seem equated"* Burke, *Grammar of Motives*, 224.

"confine logic" NA 110–11. Stevens quotes from Burke's "Criticism for the Next Phase," *Accent* 8 (Winter 1948): 127.

"The close approach" L 760.

p. 304 *"will not invoke"* Helen Vendler, *Wallace Stevens: Words Chosen Out of Desire* (Knoxville, Tenn., 1984), 73.

"We live in" OP 303.

p. 306 *"It is a question"* OP 304.

"young persons" L 804.

Index of Works
by Wallace Stevens

General Index